For Alan
for fifty more —

John Pare Wickman

Atlas of Classical Archaeology

Maps and plans by John Flower

Drawings by Tom Stalker Miller and
John Thompson Associates

Contributors

Roman Britain	A. L. Rivet, Professor of Roman Provincial Studies, University of Keele
The Roman Rhine-Danube Frontier	J. J. Wilkes, Professor of the Archaeology of the Roman Provinces, University of London
Provence	Paul MacKendrick, Lily Ross Taylor Professor of Classics, University of Wisconsin
The Iberian Peninsula	Paul MacKendrick
North Africa	C. R. Whittaker, Fellow of Churchill College, University of Cambridge
Sicily	M. I. Finley, Professor of Ancient History and Master of Darwin College, University of Cambridge
Italy	G. D. B. Jones, Professor of Archaeology, University of Manchester
Illyricum, Moesia and Dacia	J. J. Wilkes
Greece, Macedonia and Aegean Islands	R. M. Cook, Laurence Professor (emeritus) of Classical Archaeology, University of Cambridge
Cyprus	Vassos Karageorghis, Director, Department of Antiquities, Cyprus
The Black Sea	D. M. Pippidi, Professor of Ancient History, University of Bucharest
Asia Minor	M. H. Crawford, Fellow of Christ's College, University of Cambridge
Syria-Palestine	G. W. Bowersock, Professor of Greek and Latin, Harvard University
East of Palmyra	G. W. Bowersock

Edited by M I Finley

Atlas of Classical Archaeology

McGraw-Hill Book Company

New York   St. Louis   San Francisco   Düsseldorf
Mexico   Toronto

Copyright © Rainbird Reference Books Limited 1977

This book was designed and produced by
Rainbird Reference Books Limited
36 Park Street, London WIY 4DE
and published in the United States by
McGraw-Hill Book Company.
1221 Avenue of the Americas, New York, N.Y. 10020

House Editor: Perry Morley
Assistant House Editor: Sally Webb
Designer: Alan Bartram
Indexer: Myra Clark

Library of Congress Cataloging in Publication Data

Main entry under title:
Atlas of classical archaeology

1. Archaeology-Maps. I. Finley, Moses I.
G1046.E15A8 1977   930'.1   76-16761
ISBN 0-07-021025-X

Printed and bound in Italy

Contents

Acknowledgments and Notes on Illustrations

The publishers are indebted to G. Bell & Sons, for the extract from Paul MacKendrick, *Roman France*, 1971

The editor would like to express his grateful thanks to all the contributors and many others who provided or suggested sources of information and illustrations; in particular Professor John Ward-Perkins, the Society of Antiquaries of London, the London University Institute of Classical Studies Library and the Institute of Archaeology Library.

The cartographer would like to thank Ernest Benn Ltd for permission to use material from plans in their current Blue Guides.

The producers are also indebted to all those who are indicated by the following list of illustrations, especially the staffs of the agencies and libraries and individual owners of photographs. Every effort has been made to trace the primary source of illustrations; in one or two cases where it has not been possible, the producers wish to apologize if the acknowledgment proves to be inadequate; in no case is such inadequacy intentional and if any owner of copyright who has remained untraced will communicate with the producers a reasonable fee will be paid and the required acknowledgment made in future editions of the book.

Page 18 J. Allan Cash
Page 23 British Museum
Page 24 Cambridge University Collection: copyright reserved
Page 26 Aerofilms
Page 28 Aerofilms
Page 29 Both photos: Colchester and Essex Museum
Page 30 The Warburg Institute. Photo: Otto Fein
Page 31 National Trust
Page 32 Society of Antiquaries
Page 33 Both photos: National Trust
Page 34 Copyright Walter Scott, Bradford
Page 35 Photo: Derek Phillips, courtesy of York Archaeological Trust
Pahe 38 Archaeological Surveys Ltd
Page 39 Archaeological Surveys Ltd
Page 43 Jean Roubier
Page 44 Deutsche Fotothek, Dresden
Page 47 Both: Museum Carnuntinum. Photos: H. Kral
Page 49 Kunsthistorisches Museum, Vienna
Page 53 Top: Aerofilms. Bottom: Jean Roubier
Page 55 Top: Mansell. Left: Jean Roubier
Page 57 Top: Mansell. Bottom: Jean Roubier
Page 59 J. B. Ward-Perkins and the British School at Rome
Page 60 Jean Roubier
Page 61 Jean Roubier
Page 63 Peter Witte
Page 65 Peter Witte
Page 70 Deutsches Archäologisches Institut, Rome
Page 73 Both photos: J. B. Ward-Perkins and the British School at Rome
Page 74 Fototeca Unione, Rome
Page 75 Deutsches Archäologisches Institut, Rome
Page 76 Fototeca Unione, Rome
Page 77 Left: Deutsches Archäologisches Institut, Rome. Right: Bavaria-Verlag
Page 79 Aerofilms
Page 83 Edwin Smith
Page 84 Top: Fotocielo. Bottom: Deutsches Archäologisches Institut, Rome
Page 87 Top: Soprintendenza alle Antichità, Palermo. Bottom: Hirmer Fotoarchiv München
Page 89 Top: Hirmer Fotoarchiv München. Bottom: Drawing by Tom Stalker Miller after Koldewey and Puchstein, *Die griechihen Tempel in Unteritalien*, plate 143
Page 91 Deutsches Archäologisches Institut, Rome
Page 92 Ashmolean Museum, Oxford
Page 93 Soprintendenza alle Antichità, Palermo
Page 95 Mansell

Page 101 Top: Bavaria-Verlag. Bottom and right: Bildarchiv Foto Marburg
Page 102 Bavaria-Verlag
Page 104 Fototeca Unione, Rome
Page 106 Bildarchiv Foto Marburg
Page 107 Lala Aufsberg, Sonthofen
Page 110 Top: Mansell. Bottom: Deutsches Archäologisches Institut, Rome
Page 111 Fototeca Unione, Rome
Page 112 Top: Drawing by Tom Stalker Miller, after a reconstruction by I. Gismondi
Left and right: Fototeca Unione, Rome
Page 113 Fototeca Unione, Rome
Page 114 Top: Drawing by Tom Stalker Miller after H. Kähler, *Hadrian*, plate 16
Bottom: J. B. Ward-Perkins, and the British School at Rome
Page 115 J. B. Ward-Perkins, and the British School at Rome
Page 117 Mansell
Page 120 Mansell
Page 121 Both photos: Mansell
Page 122 Alinari
Page 124 Edwin Smith
Page 125 Top: Fototeca Unione, Rome Bottom: Mansell
Page 127 Fototeca Unione, Rome
Page 128 Fototeca Unione, Rome
Page 129 Edwin Smith
Page 130 Mansell
Page 134 Alan Bartram
Page 137 Mansell
Page 140 Drawing by Tom Stalker Miller, after F. B. Florescu, *Adamklissi*, plate 13
Page 144 Drawing by Tom Stalker Miller. Drawing and plan, courtesy of Professor A, Cambitoglou
Page 146 Drawing by Tom Stalker Miller, after Alan Sorrell, courtesy Illustrated London News
Page 147 Drawing by Tom Stalker Miller, after BSA LVII fig. 13, courtesy British School at Athens
Page 149 Royal Ontario Museum, Toronto, Canada
Page 151 Agora Excavations, American School of Classical Studies, at Athens
Page 152 Museum of Classical Archaeology, Cambridge
Page 153 Hirmer Fotoarchiv München
Page 155 Lala Aufsberg, Sonthofen
Page 156 Drawing by Tom Stalker Miller, after G. P. Stevens, *Restorations of Classical Buildings*, plate 17, courtesy American School of Classical Studies, at Athens
Page 157 Hirmer Fotoarchiv München
Page 159 Top: H. Wagner, Heidelberg. Right: Hirmer Fotoarchiv München

Note. The names of sites which have their own
entries are set in small capitals when they first
occur in the Introduction or in other entries.

In general preference has been given to the
forms of names most familiar to English-
speaking readers and Latin rather than Greek
spellings have been adopted.

Introduction

'Classical' is a confusing word of many meanings. In this volume it is used in an old, restricted and specific sense, to refer to the world inhabited, or dominated, by the Greeks and Romans in historical times. The chronological limits are rather vague, because neither the beginning nor the end of classical history is marked by a single event. In round numbers, the beginning, in about 1000 BC, followed the collapse of the great Bronze Age civilization in Greece, the so-called Mycenaean civilization; the end, about AD 500, came with the final division of the Roman Empire into separate western and eastern (Byzantine) empires.

During that 1500-year span, the Graeco-Roman world spread over three continents. At its greatest extent, it included all of Europe south of the Rhine-Danube line (as well as Britain and some territory north of the Danube), all of Africa north of the Sahara, and Asia as far east as modern Iraq (with a few outlying communities, even in Afghanistan). Our main map shows this spread.

Today that territory embraces peoples and nations of diverse cultures. It is noteworthy, for example, how much is part of the present 'Arab' world. In antiquity there was also great diversity: the 'classical' label should not mislead on that score. Language is a good test. Although there came a time when the upper class and educated people generally spoke either Latin or Greek or both everywhere, various Celtic, Germanic and Semitic languages remained very much alive, especially among the lower classes. And still other languages, such as Etruscan, were spoken for centuries before becoming extinct.

The time span is as great as that between the end of the Roman Empire and our own day. It is hardly surprising, then, that the classical world saw many changes, in all spheres of human behaviour, though the pace of development was slower than our own. The tempo was also very uneven in different regions, as our chronological table illustrates.

Thus, in the years of the mid-fifth century BC known as the Age of Pericles in ATHENS, when the Parthenon was built and Athens was the most powerful, the richest and culturally the dominant Greek city-state, ROME was scarcely more than a village on the Tiber river, having recently freed itself from Etruscan overlordship and giving no hint of its future role as mistress of Italy and eventually of the classical world. In the same period, North Africa was merely a geographical notion: Egypt was a weak though productive subject of the Persian Empire, CYRENE was an autonomous Greek community, and the regions farther west were dominated by CARTHAGE, a Phoenician settlement in origin. Gaul and Britain were still 'underdeveloped' areas with predominantly Celtic populations living in small settlements and tribal units, who had not acquired the art of writing.

East of the Aegean Sea, in contrast, there were far older civilizations, whose written records stretched back two thousand years or more, who had various contacts with the Greeks but who were not yet part of the classical world (until the conquest by Alexander the Great late in the following century).

A major aspect of the history of the classical world was thus one of acculturation, a phenomenon again marked by great unevenness. Some of the peoples overrun by Greeks or Romans 'disappeared', not genetically of course, but culturally as well as politically. The Thracians, Sicels and Celtiberians, for example, have left hardly any traces at all, apart from references in Greek and Roman writers, various words accepted into the vocabularies of Greek and Latin, an occasional deity or rite incorporated into the religion of the conquerors. The Etruscans disappeared as effectively, though the monuments they left behind reveal that they once enjoyed a material and cultural level that the Sicels, Thracians and Celtiberians had not attained. Still other peoples 'survived', creating with their Greek or Roman elites a mixed culture, once again varied in many ways. The remains of DOUGGA in Tunisia, of JERUSALEM, and of PETRA in Jordan are instances of the manifold possibilities. And, in the end, the most interesting and most important of all the cultural interactions was that between the Greeks and Romans themselves.

Yet, as every traveller notices and as is evident from the illustrations in this book, there was a common core; or rather two, Greek in the eastern regions, Roman in the west. The explanation lies partly in the ecology, partly in the ways in which the Greeks and Romans expanded.

For most of its history the Graeco-Roman world was tied together by the Mediterranean Sea (which includes the Aegean Sea and has direct access to the Black Sea). 'Our sea' (*mare nostrum*), the Romans called it, the great highway over which men and goods moved and ideas were diffused. Navigable rivers were rare, apart from the Po and the French rivers in districts that were not brought into the classical world until a relatively late period; and from the Rhine and Danube on the borders. Land transport, by mule and oxcart, was slow and prohibitively expensive: official Roman figures show that it cost less to transport a shipment of grain from one end of the Mediterranean to the other than to cart it seventy-five miles.

The Mediterranean area constitutes what geographers call a single 'climatic region', characterized by winter rains and long summer droughts, by light soils and dry farming. It is a region of relatively easy habitation and much outdoor living, producing on the coastal plains and large inland plateaus a good supply of cereals, vegetables, grapes and olives, with suitable pasture for sheep, pigs and goats. It is a region for sedentary existence, interrupted only by nomads in the desert borders of Arabia, Syria and North Africa, and by the need to move animals, in Italy for instance, from high summer pasture to low winter grounds.

There were regional variations, of course, in fertility and in resources (availability of metals in particular), but it remains true that a Greek or Roman could travel throughout the Mediterranean region without feeling any serious change in the environment. The great exception was Egypt, incorporated into this world by Alexander's conquest, where everything hinged on the annual flood of the Nile. Irrigation farming was more productive than dry farming and more conducive to a dense population, but it also required a more complex, centrally organized effort.

Then, as the Romans spread their conquest to central and northern Europe and to Britain, another environment was encountered. The climate was different and the soils were heavier, favouring different crops. Where there were no navigable rivers, local self-reliance was essential for existence.

The population of this world is estimated to have been about 60,000,000 at its peak at the beginning of the Christian era. The overwhelming majority were engaged in agriculture, as slaves, peasants, tenants or larger landowners. However, this was a civilization, at least in the Mediterranean region, in which people lived not on their farms but in communities, whether villages, towns or cities (just as today). Classical society, in short, was an urban society. The great villas that grew up in Gaul and Britain under the Roman Empire can thus be seen as one sign of the transition to the medieval world.

For most of the period, cities were small by modern standards. Athens in the age of Pericles had fewer than 100,000 inhabitants, with perhaps another 175,000 or 200,000 living in the harbour town (the Piraeus) and in such villages as Marathon and Eleusis. Yet Athens was the largest Greek city of its day. Under the Roman emperors, a few administrative centres, such as Rome itself, Carthage, Alexandria and ANTIOCH, may have reached, or even exceeded, half a million. They were untypical; POMPEII had only 20,000 when it was destroyed by a volcanic eruption in A D 79. These figures must be borne in mind when we consider the nature and scale of the monumental building that constitutes the chief attraction of these ancient sites today.

This monumental building was almost exclusively public, that is to say, it was sponsored, managed and often financed by the state itself. 'Public splendour, private squalor' – that describes Greek cities. After the destruction of the Mycenaean world, neither the palace nor the royal tomb reappeared among the Greeks until the days of Hellenistic rulers in the east, as in the case of Herod's palace in Jerusalem. Not even the 'tyrants' of AGRIGENTO and SYRACUSE, megalomaniac though they were in their building activity, expressed their wealth, power and munificence in the private sphere. Temples, theatres, fountain houses, council buildings, *stoas* attracted the available wealth and filled the centres of Greek cities. Even large sculptures were normally associated with temples or with such religious precincts as OLYMPIA or DELPHI. (The ancient temple, unlike the modern church, was as much a state affair as any of the other buildings I have enumerated.)

For several centuries the Romans followed the same pattern. They did not even adopt the Etruscan habit of highly decorated and well-stocked tombs. However, as Rome conquered, Roman predilections changed. By the late Republic, and even more in the Empire, elaborate private houses and country villas became increasingly common. Among the earliest and best preserved, curiously enough, were the houses of Italian merchants on the Aegean island of DELOS. The Roman emperors themselves were naturally in the forefront of this development, climaxed by the 7½-acre (3ha) palace Diocletian built in SALONA on the Dalmatian coast after his abdication in A D 305.

The Greeks built their public edifices in stone, normally local stone rather than marble, reserved for the decorative elements. An all-marble temple, such as the Parthenon, was an exception. The Romans made liberal use of stone, too, but they also employed brick extensively, and later concrete. These materials help explain the place of the arch and the dome in Roman architecture, for both are very difficult in stone.

Other differences are still more obvious reflections of basic cultural differences. The most notable are in the field of public entertainment. The Romans did not normally participate themselves, as the Greeks regularly did in athletics, drama and the dance, but were content to watch social outcasts and slaves perform for their amusement, which took on an increasingly sadistic note. Hence there was not only a marked difference between the Greek theatre, as at EPIDAURUS or Syracuse, and the Roman, best exemplified in ORANGE, but the quintessentially Roman structure in this category was the amphitheatre, designed for wild beasts and gladiators. Soon enough after the Roman conquest of Greece, it must be added, the amphitheatre also made its appearance throughout the Greek world.

Notice must be taken of one further difference. Although the Greeks developed the art of fortification to a considerable level, they avoided standing armies and permanent army camps. The Romans, on the other hand, were compelled by their territorial conquests to keep provinces permanently policed as well as to guard frontiers and prepare for further advances. Hence some of the most interesting classical sites today are these Roman encampments and military outposts from Chesters and Housesteads on HADRIAN'S WALL in Britain to CARNUNTUM in Austria and DURA-EUROPUS on the Euphrates river in Syria. Hence, too, the famed Roman road system, primarily a network for military transport.

This fundamental distinction between Greeks and Romans in their political organization and their mode of expansion is what we turn to next. And we begin, perhaps surprisingly, by asking what 'Greek' and 'Roman' mean. 'Greek' is in fact the Latin name; in antiquity (as today) the Greeks were, in their own language, Hellenes. However, where there is now a well-defined land called Hellas, a recognized political and territorial unit (with only marginal problems, as in the case of Cyprus), there was never a classical Hellas in that sense. Then it was a cultural concept, comparable to 'Christendom', a term embracing communities scattered from the eastern end of the Black Sea to Marseilles in France and AMPURIAS in Spain, who shared, and felt themselves to share, a common language, a common culture, common religion, common way of life, distinct from that of other peoples.

Although neither Greek uniformity nor Greek distinctiveness should be exaggerated, they were real enough to warrant the single label. That is evident merely from the

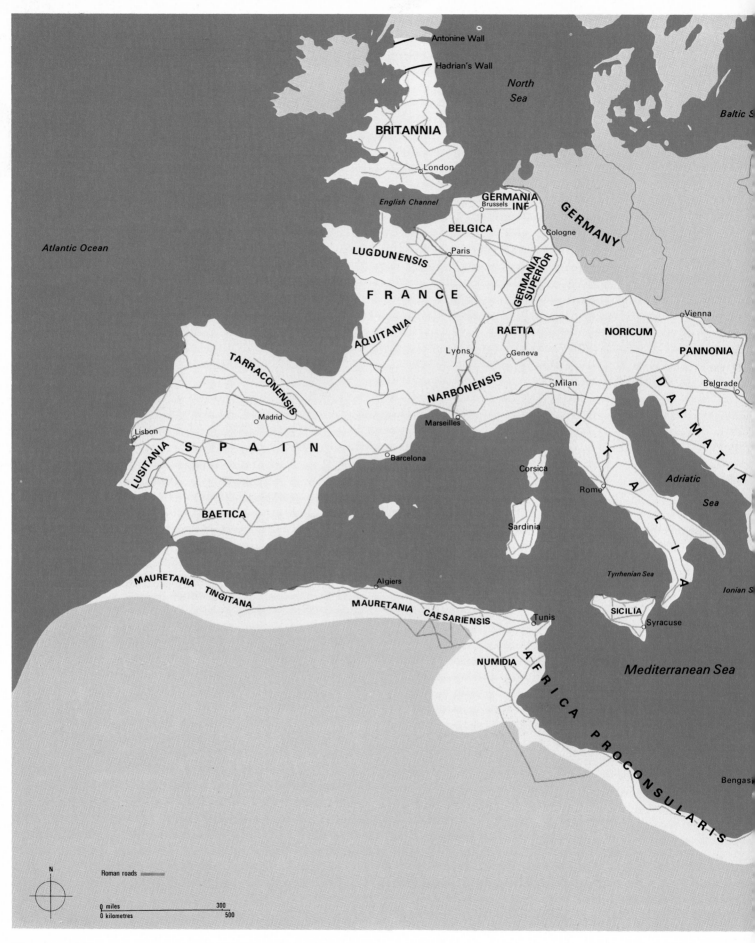

The provinces of the Roman Empire at its greatest extent, AD 117. Cities given with their modern names are included for purposes of geographical reference.

illustrations in the present volume. Wherever an ancient Greek travelled in Hellas, his speech was easily comprehensible, he found a recognizable town square (*agora*) with familiar temples, theatres and other structures, a familiar system of municipal organization, familiar rituals and festivals.

This stability of Greek institutions and culture is all the more remarkable because of the absence of any central political or ecclesiastical authority. In 1000 BC, our approximate starting point, the Greek peninsula was inhabited by small, autonomous communities. From there Greeks migrated during several centuries, in a process called 'colonization' by modern historians in order to differentiate it both from conquest leading to territorial incorporation and from imperialism. Wherever they settled, the migrants founded autonomous communities, *poleis* in their language, conventionally translated as 'city-states'. Although some city-states, such as Athens, SPARTA or Syracuse, succeeded for periods in establishing an overlordship over a group of other city-states, these efforts stopped far short of the creation of larger political units.

Then came the spectacular career of Alexander, the Macedonian king, who in thirteen years conquered all the territory from Greece itself to the Hindu Kush. He died in 323 BC, still on campaign, so that it is impossible to judge his long-range intentions. His successors fought each other for a generation, and when the carnage ended, autocratic monarchies were established in the eastern territories, with a Greek-Macedonian ruling elite dominating and exploiting the native populations. This elite promptly organized 'Greek' cities in which to live, with all the characteristic architecture and institutions, and they even called them *poleis*, though their autonomy was a sham. Historians have adopted the conventional label, *Hellenistic*, for this post-Alexander civilization.

In the Greek peninsula and the Aegean islands, where there was no native non-Greek population, the Macedonians under the Antigonid successors of Alexander found themselves in a continuous, and far from successful, struggle to hold power. More than a century of conflict was finally ended by Roman intervention, followed before the end of the second century BC by a complete Roman take-over. As for the Greeks farther west, outside the sphere of Alexander's conquests, they had already fallen under Roman rule in the previous century.

Conquest is the operative word in Roman history, as it was not in Greek history before Alexander. In 1000 BC central Italy, south of the Po river, was inhabited largely by peoples with a more or less common material culture, who spoke one or another 'Italic' language. Then came two intruders, the Etruscans (according to the prevailing view that they were migrants from Asia Minor) and the Greeks who settled in the south. The Romans were originally just one of the Latin-speaking subdivisions of the larger Italic group, with nothing to set them above the others except perhaps a certain advantage in geographic location on the Tiber river. Yet, once Rome freed herself from Etruscan overlordship in 509 BC, she embarked almost immediately on a series of wars, at first with immediate Latin neighbours then with ever more distant tribes, communities and nations, a series that seems never to have ended and that gives a retrospective air of inexorability to the whole story.

For two centuries Roman expansion was confined to the Italian peninsula, the excuse of a 'just war' in self-defence was maintained, and defeated tribes and communities were converted into 'allies', not subjects; but allies who were required to contribute military manpower to Rome's wars, under Roman command, and who had greater or lesser segments of their agricultural land confiscated for the benefit of Rome, that is to say, largely of the Roman upper classes.

In 264 BC Roman legions marched into Sicily, on a flimsy pretext, initiating the major turning point in Roman imperial history. Two lengthy wars with Carthage, known as the First and Second Punic Wars, followed. By the end of the third century, Rome abandoned her tradition of 'alliances': Sicily became the first province, a possession ruled and heavily taxed by Roman officials directed by the senate and assemblies of Rome.

The taste of imperial profits was sweet. For three hundred years, to the death of the emperor Trajan in AD 117, Rome continued to conquer and add provinces. The process was spasmodic and it lacked a plan or even a clear intent, but it was irresistible. By 117, the empire stretched some 3,000 miles (nearly 5,000km) from east to west and 1,750 (2,800km) from north to south, an area of 1,750,000 square miles (2,600,000km²), approximately half the land area of the United States today.

For most of the long period of expansion Rome retained the machinery of a city-state. Although more and more Roman citizens lived in military colonies and other communities in and outside Italy, voting, office holding and decision making for the entire territory under Roman rule were carried on within the city.

Inevitably there were enormous changes within Roman society, which I cannot examine here. In the final century before Christ, the city-state form of government had become an anachronism, though the republican system survived the growing power of great commanders and the struggles among them with remarkable tenacity. Finally Julius Caesar triumphed in a civil war over Pompey and established one-man rule in 46 BC, which ended with his assassination two years later. Another civil war followed, in which Caesar's great-nephew and adopted son Octavian emerged the victor. His defeat of Antony and Cleopatra in 31 BC at Actium, on the western coast of Greece, followed by his assumption four years later of the name Augustus, marked the beginning of autocratic monarchy. The Roman republican empire was henceforth an empire ruled by an emperor.

The world the Romans had conquered and incorporated was very diversified, according to the different histories of the various regions. The Greek-speaking half ranged from Cyrenaica, Sicily and Greece to the half-Greek, half-Getic cultures of the Danube basin, the half-Greek, half-Iranian cultures of the Crimea, or the Hellenistic states of

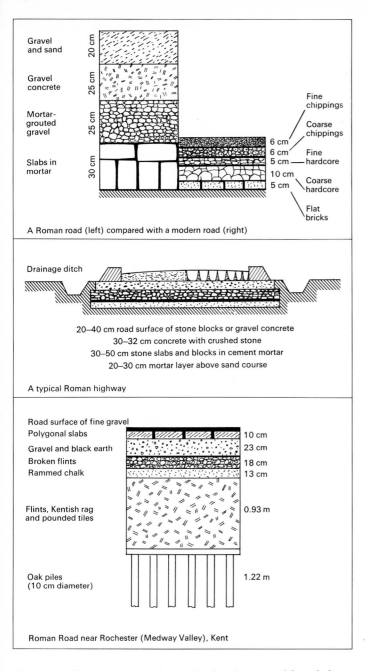

Gravel and sand — 20 cm
Gravel concrete — 25 cm
Mortar-grouted gravel — 25 cm
Slabs in mortar — 30 cm

Fine chippings — 6 cm
Coarse chippings — 6 cm
Fine hardcore — 5 cm
Coarse hardcore — 10 cm
Flat bricks — 5 cm

A Roman road (left) compared with a modern road (right)

Drainage ditch

20–40 cm road surface of stone blocks or gravel concrete
30–32 cm concrete with crushed stone
30–50 cm stone slabs and blocks in cement mortar
20–30 cm mortar layer above sand course

A typical Roman highway

Road surface of fine gravel
Polygonal slabs — 10 cm
Gravel and black earth — 23 cm
Broken flints — 18 cm
Rammed chalk — 13 cm
Flints, Kentish rag and pounded tiles — 0.93 m
Oak piles (10 cm diameter) — 1.22 m

Roman Road near Rochester (Medway Valley), Kent

the east. This was a well-organized urban world and the Romans were content to rule with a minimum of interference, though the spread of the amphitheatre reveals that Roman influences were not negligible.

Italy remained the privileged heartland of the empire. The rest, everything west and north of Italy, Sicily and Cyrenaica, was on the whole underdeveloped and therefore more open to systematic Roman land seizure and migration. Veterans in particular were settled in the west by Roman commanders and emperors, where they acted as agents of 'Romanization'. They were, however, by no means the only migrants from Italy, and as the years crept by, more and more of the local upper classes were also 'Romanized' and acquired Roman citizenship.

The word 'Roman' is therefore shot through with ambiguity: although it always retained the original meaning of a citizen of the city of Rome, it increasingly had the other sense of a man who by culture and citizenship was a 'Roman', regardless of his origin or place of residence. The emperor Trajan was a Spaniard, Septimius Severus a North African, native of LEPTIS MAGNA.

The two most obvious external signs of Romanization were the adoption of the Latin language and the establishment of cities on the Roman model, with the *forum* (the equivalent of the Greek *agora*) as the central square round which the main religious and civic buildings were grouped, and, wherever possible, with a chequerboard street layout quartered by the two arterial roads, called the *cardo* and the *decumanus*.

The Roman government actively fostered city development in the west. Apart from the fact that veterans and other migrants insisted on an urban way of life, cities provided the most efficient machinery for taxation and administration. In the old Greek settlements on the French and Spanish coasts and in former Carthaginian territory in North Africa they found pre-existing cities, of which Leptis Magna is an example. Even there, however, many new ones were needed to receive the tens of thousands of settlers, DJEMILA and TIMGAD in Algeria, for instance. Elsewhere small native communities were converted into proper cities, as at ST ALBANS, or, especially along the Rhine-Danube frontier, cities were created from scratch.

How deeply Romanization penetrated the society of the west is not easy to determine. The surviving literature shows little interest in the culture of peasants, shopkeepers and slaves, and the archaeological remains do not reflect them much more clearly. Latin was the universal language of education, literature and government in the west, but the Punic and Celtic languages were still spoken, pre-Roman religious beliefs and practices survived, and pre-Roman decorative motifs and other art forms, too.

The vast empire which the Romans acquired stretched their resources and their manpower, in a society with a rather static technology and inadequate means of transport. Although provincial revolts were almost non-existent, apart from the complex case of Judaea, signs of social tension, of a growing gulf between the wealthy ruling class of Italy and the provinces and the rest, of a more rigid social stratification and of mounting tax pressures were increasingly visible, even in the so-called 'Golden Age' of the second century A D. What might have developed within the empire if it had existed in isolation is a tempting but impossible question, for the outside world made its presence felt more and more.

The first emperor, Augustus, had stabilized the army at about 300,000 men, and it remained at that figure for nearly two centuries. That was sufficient both for internal policing and for the defence of the frontiers, until the reactivation of the Germanic peoples late in the second century. Not since the days of Caesar and Augustus had they given the Romans any major problems, until the reign of Marcus Aurelius (died in 180), who had to spend much of his time in hard campaigning in Bohemia. From then on, 'barbarian' pressure on the empire was relentless and almost unceasing (as our map of their invasions shows).

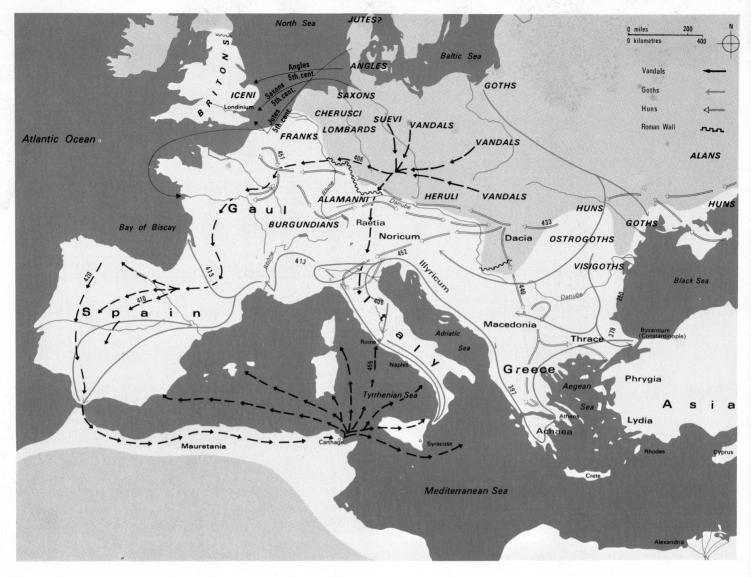

The main movements of the Germanic tribes and Huns into the Roman Empire. A few dates are given

An interplay soon set in between external assaults and internal troubles. In the half-century between 235 and 284 it seemed that the empire could not long survive. That it finally managed to do so is partly attributable to the decision to divide it, in effect if not in name, into eastern and western halves, each under its own emperor. The symbol of that division is the transformation by Constantine (306–337) of the old Greek city on the Bosporus, Byzantium, into a great eastern capital, renamed Constantinople (now ISTANBUL). East-west relations in the following centuries were complicated, confused and often bellicose. In the sixth century, for example, RAVENNA in Italy was part of the eastern (Byzantine) empire, as were Sicily and briefly even North Africa.

It was under Constantine that another profound change was introduced, the establishment of Christianity as the official religion. To state it that bluntly is to overstate it, for more than 150 years were needed before paganism was finally outlawed. Yet from Constantine on, the dominance of Christianity is quickly visible even in the archaeological record, as will be seen in this book.

Nearly every region of the empire is represented in our volume, some much more fully than others. Although the book is designed partly for students and other 'stay-at-home' readers, it is intended at least as much for travellers, and their interests have controlled the selection of the places to be described and illustrated. We have omitted cities and districts, regardless of their importance in antiquity, if, for one reason or another, the visible *classical* remains are scanty and uninteresting (except to specialists). That is why, for example, Mycenae and Thebes in Greece do not appear, or Alexandria in Egypt, Palermo in Sicily, Lyons in France.

The authors of the individual sections are all acknowledged experts. Although they were given a brief of the historical, cultural and archaeological stress of the volume, they were free to present their material as they thought most appropriate. We have neither wished nor sought uniformity. Bibliographies have been appended to each entry, ranging from simpler guidebooks to technical archaeological reports, to help readers pursue their own interests in the classical world further.

The Sites

Roman Britain

Although Britain is an island, the approach to it from the continent of Europe is so easy that in prehistoric times it was repeatedly infiltrated by settlers from the opposite shore. Its pre-Roman Iron Age culture thus had much in common with that of northern Gaul, albeit with insular variations, and it shared with northern Gaul a remoteness from the Mediterranean centres of civilization. The existence of the British Isles had been known to the Greeks since the sixth century B C, but it was not until the expeditions of Julius Caesar in 55 and 54 B C that Roman interest in them was aroused.

Caesar's own experience was limited to the southeast, but the archaeological evidence now available allows us to make some generalizations about the country as a whole. The economy was then a mixed one, in which agriculture and stock raising played almost equal parts, the former predominating in the lowland zone (roughly southeast of a line from the Exe to the Humber), the latter in the highland zone. The chief crops were wheat and barley, cultivated in small 'Celtic' fields; the most important animals were cattle, sheep, and goats. Metalworking was well developed, in iron, bronze and gold, and a high standard of artistry was achieved. Settlements consisted mainly of undefended farmsteads and hamlets in the lowland zone, with enclosed homesteads more common in the highlands; but in both cases they were usually related to hill forts, of which some were permanently occupied, others mere camps of refuge. With the possible exception of the far north, all the inhabitants spoke Celtic, in dialects akin to those of Gaul. Some concentration of political power is already evident in the case of Caesar's chief opponent, Cassivellaunus, and some chieftains were already striking gold coins, but it was in the century between Caesar and Claudius that the main tribal groupings were formed. In this period trade developed, notably with Gaul, and internally the beginnings of a money economy are detectable in the issue not merely of gold and silver but of bronze coins too. The distribution patterns of these tribal coinages correspond closely with the tribal areas of Roman times, as known from other sources.

The occasion for the Roman invasion of A D 43 was the flight to Claudius of Verica, who had been recognized as king of the Atrebates by Rome but had been expelled from his kingdom. Its cause is stated by Suetonius to have been the desire of Claudius for a triumph, supplemented, as Tacitus indicates, by the belief that Britain was rich in gold, silver, and other metals. Four legions, with an appropriate force of auxiliaries, were used in the assault and by A D 47 the country south and east of the Severn and Trent rivers had been overrun. The disarming of the inhabitants of this area

led to a minor revolt, but the defeat and capture of Caratacus in A D 49 encouraged the release of the occupying troops for further conquest. This premature move led to the major revolt of A D 60, led by Boudicca, but after its suppression the advance was resumed; the conquest of Wales, energetically pursued by Frontinus, was completed in A D 78 by Agricola, and by 84 he had carried Roman arms as far north as the Moray Firth, while his fleet circumnavigated Britain.

The occupation of the lowland zone took place in three phases: first, the actual war of conquest; second, the establishment of a tight network of military garrisons, progressively linked by roads; and third, the replacement of these forts by civilian settlements. Evidence for the first phase is naturally slight, but some forty forts relating to the second are now known from structural evidence, and finds of military equipment suggest the existence of as many more. The remains are not impressive, but their implications are important: they show both that detachments were used as often as complete units (there are as many half-size as full-size legionary bases) and that, with very few exceptions, the sites for the cities and towns of Roman Britain (and so also those of medieval and later England) were originally chosen with military rather than commercial considerations in mind.

This applies both to the Roman *coloniae* and to the cities that were founded to be the political and commercial centres of the tribal states that made up the Roman province. The *colonia* at COLCHESTER was founded in A D 49 and its veteran colonists were expected both to provide a reliable reserve and to set an example of Roman life. The *coloniae* at Lincoln (*c.* A D 90) and Gloucester (A D 96–8) similarly occupied the sites of legionary fortresses and stood, significantly, near the edge of what was then the pacified area; and the settlement at YORK, promoted to a *colonia* later, also grew up beside a fortress. Of the 'native' cities, only Verulamium (ST ALBANS) and Canterbury had been laid out in Roman style, with a regular grid of streets, before the Boudiccan revolt, and though both succeeded pre-Roman centres Verulamium certainly, and Canterbury probably, held early garrisons. Of the rest, Exeter and Wroxeter succeeded legionary fortresses, Cirencester, Winchester, Leicester, Carmarthen, and Brough-on-Humber succeeded forts, and forts are suspected at Dorchester, Caistor St Edmund, and Aldborough; only at Caerwent and SILCHESTER is military evidence lacking. The implication is that the tribal cities took over where the military administration stopped, and the statement of Tacitus that the main transfer took place in the Flavian period, especially under Agricola, is supported both

archaeologically and epigraphically.

In the first two centuries Britain was governed by a consular *legatus Augusti pro praetore*, with a *procurator Augusti* in charge of finance, and the existence of a provincial council is known. The local administration of the *coloniae* followed the usual pattern and it is assumed that the same was true of the tribal states, but whereas local senates are well attested we have no evidence for the magistrates who presumably presided over them, as in Gaul. This may be due simply to the rarity of civic inscriptions: most town walls in Britain were built in the late second or early third century, before the barbarian raids, and their foundations do not, as in Gaul, incorporate re-used stones. Britain was divided into two provinces by Severus (Britannia Superior and Inferior, with capitals at LONDON and York respectively) and into four by Diocletian (Britannia Prima and Secunda, Maxima Caesariensis, and Flavia Caesariensis), and a fifth (Valentia) was added by subdivision later. Britain then ranked as a *diocese*, with its *vicarius* at London.

The imposition of a central government, set over a series of local governments in what were expected to evolve into city-states, was the most important result of the Roman conquest. Economically and socially the cities themselves were the most significant innovation, but although they provided political, social, and economic centres, connected by good roads, their effect on the economy was indirect. Although the invaders were quick to develop the mineral resources they did not, apart from the *coloniae*, interfere with agricultural production, but simply taxed it: most of the rural inhabitants continued to farm in the old way. In time, however, the Romanization of the Celtic aristocracy led to the rise of the villas. Of the 620-odd villas known, only a handful originated in the first century, all of them in the southeast, but they became common in the second century and reached their fullest development in the fourth. Almost all of them were working farms as well as country seats and their connection with the much more numerous farms of purely native type is obscure: analogy with other provinces suggests a landlord-tenant relationship, with free tribesmen progressively reduced to dependent *coloni*. This class division seems to have been accentuated in the fourth century, when the Latin-speaking aristocracy of the cities and villas adopted Christianity, while in rural areas pagan temples were maintained, and even built anew, for the Celtic-speaking peasantry.

In the highland zone Romanization did not make so much progress. Agricola's recall was followed by a withdrawal, first to the Clyde-Forth isthmus (leaving the legionary fortress at Inchtuthil unfinished), then to the

Previous page: Hadrian's Wall

Military site
- ⊡ Legionary fortress
- ▪ Fort

Civil site
- ◉ City
- ○ other town

CREONES

CALEDONES

VACOMAGI

TAEZALI

EPIDII

Inchtuthil ⊡

VENICONES

Tava

Antonine Wall

Bodotria

DAMNONII

SELGOVAE

TRIMONTIUM

VOTADINI

NOVANTAE

Tinea

Hadrian's Wall

CORSTOPITUM

Clota

LUGUVALIUM

NOVANTARUM PROM.

Ituna

CATARACTONIUM

MONAVIA INS.

B R I G A N T E S

Ouse

OCELLI PROM.

ISURIUM (Aldborough)

EBURACUM (York)

PARISI

BREMETENNACUM

PETUARIA (Brough)

MONA INS.

DEVA (Chester)

DECEANGLI

CORNOVII

AQUAE ARNEMETIAE (Buxton)

Trisantona

LINDUM (Lincoln)

SEGONTIUM

Deva

ORDOVICES

Witham

GANGANORUM PROM.

VIROCONIUM (Wroxeter)

LETOCETUM

C O R I T A N I

BRANODUNUM

RATAE (Leicester)

DUROBRIVAE

VENTA (Caister)

GARIANNONUM

I C E N I

DEMETAE

Sabrina

DOBUNNI

LACTODORUM

CATUVELLAUNI

TRINOVANTES

OCTAPITARUM PROM.

Isca

GLEVUM (Gloucester)

Walton Castle

MORIDUNUM (Carmarthen)

SILURES

CORINIUM (Cirencester)

VERULAMIUM (St Albans)

CAMULODUNUM (Colchester)

CAESAROMAGUS

ISCA (Caerleon)

VENTA (Caerwent)

OTHONA

AQUAE SULIS (Bath)

BELGAE

Tamesis

LONDINIUM (London)

CANTIACI

REGULBIUM

TANATUS INS.

HERCULIS PROM.

Isca

DUROTRIGES

LINDINIS

ATREBATES

REGNI

CALLEVA (Silchester)

DUROVERNUM (Canterbury)

DUBRIS

VENTA (Winchester)

CLAUSENTUM

LEMANIS

DUMNONII

NOVIOMAGUS (Chichester)

ANDERITA

GESORIACUM (BONONIA) (Boulogne)

ISCA (Exeter)

DURNOVARIA (Dorchester)

VECTIS INS.

ANTIVESTAEUM (BELERIUM) PROM.

DUMNONIUM (OCRINUM) PROM.

N

0 kilometres 150

0 miles 100

Tyne-Solway line, which was subsequently consolidated by HADRIAN'S WALL. Antoninus Pius reoccupied southern Scotland, building the Antonine Wall, with outposts as far as the Tay, but this was abandoned by the end of the second century, and although Severus made expeditions far into Scotland, building a fortress at Carpow, Hadrian's Wall became thereafter the effective frontier of Roman Britain. The manning of this line, however, did not account for all the troops in Britain. The Wall was supported not only by outposts in front of it but also by substantial garrisons in the rear, while in Wales only the Silures and Demetae were effectively civilianized and the country still demanded a strong military presence. In the second century, when our information is fullest, Britain tied down three legions and at least sixty-five units of auxiliaries, more than one tenth of the entire Roman army – which supports the statement of Appian that it was not a profitable province.

In the third century plundering by Germanic pirates led to the erection on the south and east coasts of the forts that were subsequently grouped under the Count of the Saxon Shore, but Britain suffered less than Gaul from barbarian incursions and even after concerted raids in A D 367 Theodosius was able to restore her defences. They were weakened, however, by repeated withdrawals of troops for service elsewhere, and after Honorius had recognized, in A D 410, that it was impossible to maintain full Roman government, the Romano-British cities called in German 'federates' to protect them. Their revolt, probably in A D 442–3, led to the beginning of the Anglo-Saxon domination and the slow disintegration of Roman Britain.

Bonser, W., *A Romano-British Bibliography* (to 1959), Oxford, 1964

Collingwood, R. G., and Richmond, I. A., *The Archaeology of Roman Britain*, 2nd ed., London and New York, 1969

Frere, S. S., *Britannia: A History of Roman Britain*, London and Cambridge, Mass., 1967; 2nd ed. London, 1974

Margary, I. D., *Roman Roads in Britain*, 3rd ed., London and Atlantic Highlands, N.J., 1973

Ordnance Survey Map of Roman Britain, 3rd ed., Chessington, 1956

Ordnance Survey Map of Southern Britain in the Iron Age, Chessington, 1962

Rivet, A. L. F. (ed.), *The Roman Villa in Britain*, London and New York, 1969

Wacher, J. S., *The Towns of Roman Britain*, London, and Berkeley, 1975

Britannia, London. Summary accounts of new discoveries appear annually in this journal.

The Victoria History of the Counties of England (1900 onward, with commentaries of varying quality). Accounts of the Roman remains in each English county are to be found in the relevant volumes.

I London

England

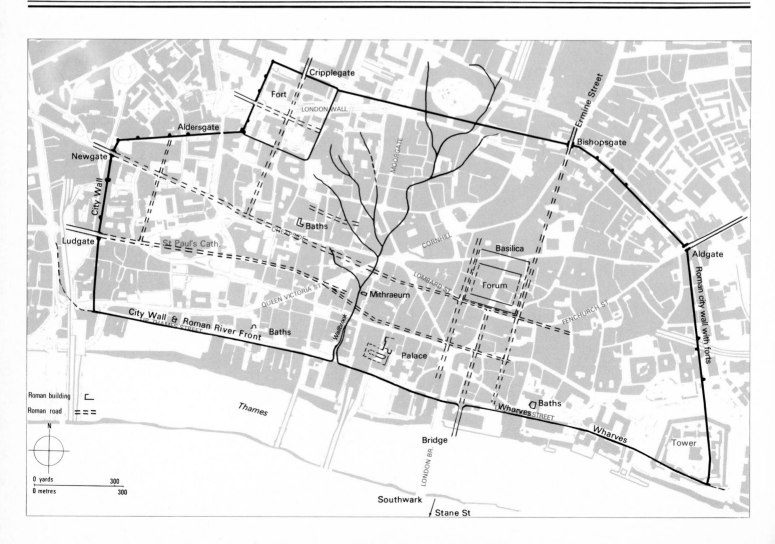

No pre-Roman settlement is known on the site of London (Londinium Augusta) and the town owed its origin to the fact that it offered an ideal port for traffic to and from the Continent, at the lowest point at which the Thames could be bridged. The first stages of its development are obscure and the early fort that might be expected has not yet been found. That it was already a thriving commercial centre by the Boudiccan revolt of AD 60 is attested both by Tacitus and by archaeology; the latter indicates that settlement was then concentrated in the eastern part of the city, while a suburb was already developing south of the river at Southwark. The main reconstruction after the revolt took place in the Flavian period. A monumental *forum*, covering some 8 acres (3.2ha) was built in the Leadenhall area, with a *basilica* up to 490 feet (150m) long. At the same time a large building (interpreted as the governor's palace) was begun on the site of Cannon Street station. This was completed early in the second century, when also a fort, with stone walls more than 4 feet (1.25m) thick enclosing nearly 5 acres (2ha), was built at Cripplegate. The north and west walls of the fort were subsequently incorporated in the city wall, over 8 feet (2.5m) thick and enclosing some 330 acres (134ha), which was built *c.* AD 300 and is now known to have extended along the river front as well as to landward. Whether the external bastions were added in Roman or medieval times is disputed, but present evidence suggests that the western series at least are Roman.

Tacitus states that London was not a *colonia* in AD 60, but the later *forum* indicates municipal status and the name Augusta, conferred in the fourth century, suggests that it ultimately held colonial rank. It is uncertain when it became the provincial capital, but the burial here of Julius Classicianus, procurator in AD 61, points to an early date.

Visible remains are few, partly because many of the houses were always of timber. The city wall is preserved at Tower Hill and on the north and west sides of the fort; the *Mithraeum* excavated on the east bank of the Walbrook in 1953–4 has been reconstructed nearby, and a small bath-house in Lower Thames Street may be seen by appointment. The main public baths have not been located, nor is any theatre, amphitheatre, aqueduct or other large structure known.

Finds are in the London Museum and the British Museum.

The tombstone of Julius Classicianus

Grimes, W. F., *The Excavation of Roman and Medieval London*, London and New York, 1968
Merrifield, R., *The Roman City of London*, London and New York, 1965

---

2   Silchester   **England**

More is known of the plan of Calleva Atrebatum, the tribal city of the Atrebates, than of any other town in Roman Britain. A pre-Roman *oppidum* was established here, probably by Commius, and one of his sons, Eppillus, struck coins with the mint mark CALLEV; but in the time of Verica it was overrun by the Catuvellauni and this partly prompted the Roman invasion. Calleva seems to have been included in the realm of the client-king Cogidubnus and the inner earthwork, enclosing just over 80 acres (32.5ha), is tentatively ascribed to him. After a short time this was obliterated and a larger earthwork enceinte, enclosing 235 acres (95ha) – subsequently reduced to 86ha – was constructed. Some pre-Flavian building is indicated both by anomalies of alignment and by the discovery in the baths of a tile with a Neronian stamp, but it was in Flavian times that the *forum* was built and the regular grid of streets laid out. This was designed to fill the (reduced) outer earthwork, and the fact that many streets were left outside the later defences shows that it was unduly

optimistic. These later defences themselves consisted of an Antonine earthen bank, with stone-built gates, supplemented in the third century AD by a wall, of dressed flint with stone (not tile) levelling courses, cut into it.

The city plan displays some anomalies. The *forum* – built round a court 141 × 131 feet (43 × 40m) with a *basilica* 227 feet (84.5m) long – suggests a military architect, and though it is centrally placed there is no temple associated with it: most of the temples are grouped in an enclosure near the east gate and excavation has shown that the little fourth-century Christian church southeast of the *forum* did not succeed one. Whereas the amphitheatre fits well into the early plan, the public baths are curiously situated. The apparently thin occupation of some *insulae* may reflect the fact that the early excavators did not recognize timber buildings, but there are still surprisingly few houses suitable for occupation by *decuriones*. Estimates of population have varied, but the latest, based partly on the capacity of the public baths, suggests a figure in the second to fourth centuries of about 1,000. No aqueduct is known and some water was certainly obtained from wells; a force pump has also been found.

The only visible monuments are stretches of the town wall, mainly reduced to its core, and the degraded remains of the amphitheatre. The Silchester Collection, including much to illustrate trades, crafts, and domestic appointments, is housed in Reading Museum.

Boon, G. C., *Silchester: the Roman Town of Calleva*, Newton Abbot and North Pomfret, Vt., 1974

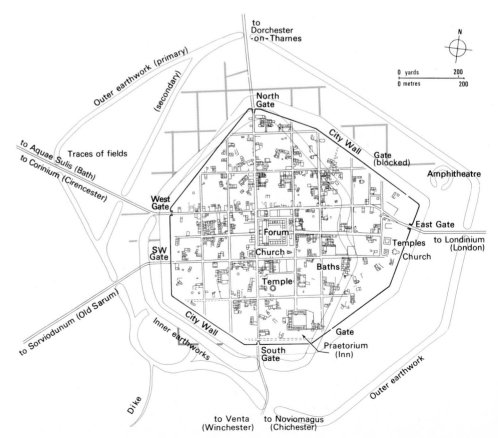

3   St Albans

The Roman city of Verulamium, across the river Ver to the west of St Albans, succeeded a pre-Roman *oppidum*. Tasciovanus minted coins here (inscribed VERLAMIO, usually abbreviated to VER), and even after his son, Cunobelinus, had transferred his capital to Colchester the place remained important. The earliest Roman occupation appears to have been military, but the fort was rapidly succeeded by civil development and Verulamium shares with Canterbury and Colchester the distinction of having been laid out with a regular grid of streets before the Boudiccan revolt of AD 60. Buildings of this period, though of timber, were of refined construction, those in Insula XIV fronted with a colonnade, and suggest that Tacitus may not have been speaking anachronistically when he referred to Verulamium as a *municipium*; the earliest defences, though nor precisely dated, may also belong to this phase.

Recovery after the destruction wrought by the rebels was slow, but the completion of the *basilica* in AD 79 is attested by an inscription (confirming Tacitus' account of the work of Agricola) and a *macellum* was added soon after, followed by at least two temples. Apart from such public buildings, however, timber construction still prevailed and a disastrous fire swept the city *c.* AD 155. This was followed by rebuilding on a much grander scale: two temples were added to the reconstructed *forum*, the theatre was erected (on a site closely related to a temple) and substantial stone-built houses, with mosaic floors and painted walls, became common. Though the first-century defences were now levelled, their limits were commemorated by two monumental arches and the London and Chester gates were built farther out from the city centre. These gates appear to have been sited in relation to the Fosse earthwork, but this was never completed and in the early third century they were finally incorporated in the stone-built city wall, which enclosed an area of some 200 acres (81ha). Little building took place in the third century, but at the beginning of the fourth the theatre was enlarged and many houses were rebuilt. The theatre continued in use until *c.* 390, but it is from Insula XXVII that the best evidence for the later days of the city has been recovered. Here a late-fourth-century house, after several alterations, was succeeded by a large hall and this in turn, after its collapse, was cut through by a wooden water pipe of Roman form. This sequence of events indicates that municipal organization of Roman type must have continued long after AD 429, when St Germanus, visiting the shrine of St Alban, found it still in operation.

The date of Alban's martyrdom has been much disputed but fell more probably in the reign of Severus or Decius than in that of

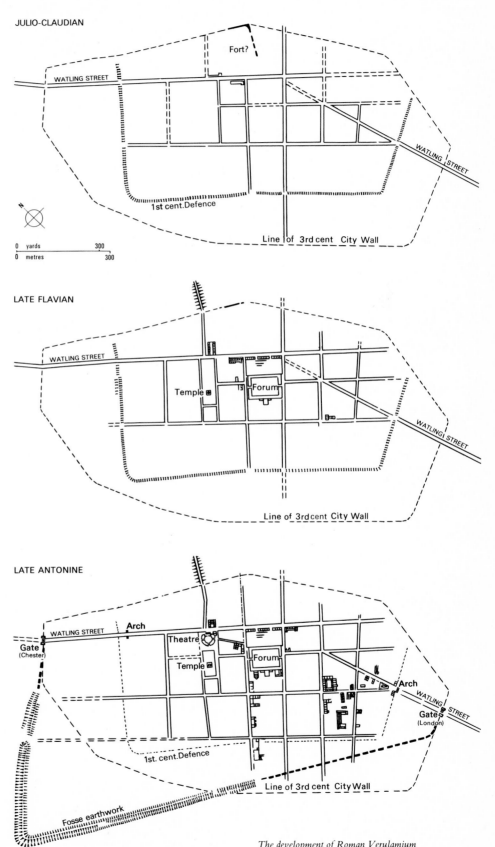

The development of Roman Verulamium

Diocletian, to which the standardized hagio-graphies attribute it. St Alban's Abbey (con-structed largely of re-used Roman brick) stands on the traditional site of his execution; St Michael's Church, overlying the *basilica*, may originally have commemorated the place where he was sentenced.

Portions of the city wall survive and parts of a house are preserved under cover, but the chief extant monument is the theatre. This is of the 'cockpit' or '*théâtre-amphithéâtre*' type common in northern Gaul; in its earlier phase the *cavea* had a diameter of 160 feet (49m), but this was enlarged to 185 feet (56m) later, when also more elaborate stage buildings were erected to bring it more nearly into line with the classical type. The *forum* complex is not visible and the city baths have not yet been located.

Finds from excavations are preserved in the Verulamium Museum, St Albans, which also includes models, and in the British Museum, London.

Right: Verulamium in the fourth century AD

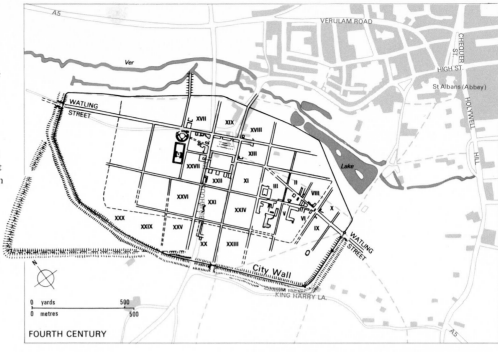

FOURTH CENTURY

Below: Aerial view of the theatre area

Frere, S. S., 'Verulamium, three Roman Cities', in *Antiquity* XXXVIII (1964), pp. 103–12

—, 'Verulamium – then and now', in *Bulletin No. 4 of the Institute of Archaeology*, London, 1964, pp. 61–82

—, *Verulamium Excavations I* (Society of Antiquaries Research Report XXVIII), London, 1972 (Insula XIV)

Kenyon, K. M., 'The Roman Theatre at Verulamium', in *Archaeologia*, London, LXXXIV (1934), pp. 213–61

Lowther, A. W. G., 'Report on Excavations at Verulamium in 1934', in *Antiquaries Journal* XVII (1937), pp. 28–38 (temple)

Richardson, K. M., 'Report on Excavations at Verulamium, Insula XVII, 1938', *Archaeologia*, London, XC (1944), pp. 81–126 (macellum)

Wheeler, R. E. M., and T. V., *Verulamium: a Belgic and two Roman Cities* (Society of Antiquaries Research Report XI), London, 1936

Plan of the central area of Verulamium

4 Colchester

England

Camulodunum – 'the hill of the war-god Camulos' – had been established *c.* AD 5 as the capital of Cunobelinus, *rex Britannorum*, and was the main target of the initial Roman invasion. The Belgic settlement was spread over some 12 square miles (31km²), protected by linear dikes and with a particular concentration in the Sheepen area, and after its occupation by Claudius in AD 43 a legionary fortress was planted in it; the area of this, whose existence had long been inferred from military tombstones, was established in 1972. In AD 49 the Legio XX Valeria was released for service elsewhere by the foundation of a *colonia* of veterans (Colonia Claudia Victricensis Camulodunum). In its original form this occupied the actual site of the fortress, and some of the military buildings continued in use, but the defences were, unwisely, levelled. East of the *colonia*, and slightly downhill from it, there was set up a centre for the imperial cult, first with an altar then with a temple to Claudius (the latter probably begun after his death in AD 54). Nothing remains of the superstructure, but the podium, 79 × 105 feet (24 × 32m), survives beneath the keep of the Norman castle and the area of the precinct, 581 × 351 feet (177 × 107m), has been established. *Colonia* and temple alike suffered severely in the Boudiccan revolt of AD 60, and although the senate house and theatre mentioned by Tacitus have yet to be located, traces of fire in this period are found in all excavations in the city.

The site of Camulodunum, showing pre-Roman dikes, the early Roman legionary fortress and the sacred complex at Gosbeck's Farm

Above: Aerial view of Colchester from the south, showing the line of the colonia defences and the site of the temple of Claudius. Right: Plan of Camulodunum, showing the early legionary fortress, the temple of Claudius and the later city wall

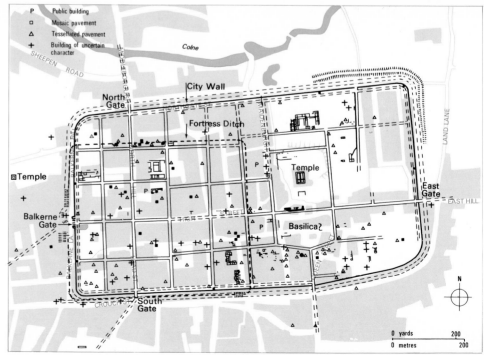

After the revolt, the temple was restored (or completed) and about AD 100 a wall 10 feet (3m) wide was built round its precinct, with a colonnade at least on its south side. The *colonia* was re-established, but recovery was slow and rebuilding on a large scale did not begin until the Flavian period: but in the second century the city grew rapidly in size and splendour, with many substantial houses, piped water, and sewers, though the *forum* and main public buildings have still to be found. The most impressive remains of the city are the walls, though they were much altered in the Middle Ages. The west, or Balkerne, gate was originally erected as a monumental arch, with two carriageways, but about the middle of the second century it

Bronze head of Claudius, found in the Alde river at Rendham, Suffolk, 32 miles (51km) northeast of Colchester, possibly looted from Colchester in the Boudiccan revolt of A D *60*

was incorporated in a town wall, 8 feet 8 inches (2.64m) thick on a base 10 feet (3m) wide, at first free-standing but subsequently reinforced by an earthen rampart behind it. The wall had internal interval towers and some of the semi-circular bastions may be late Roman additions, but are more probably of medieval date.

The walls are enclosed an area of 108 acres (44ha), but there were extensive suburbs outside them, notably on the west, where the sites of six temples are known, and there was an important pottery industry, some of whose kilns produced *terra sigillata*. The most interesting extramural site, however, lies at Gosbeck's Farm, just over 2 miles (3.5km) to the southwest. Here, within a pre-Roman sacred enclosure, there was erected *c.* A D 100 a Romano-Celtic temple and near it a theatre – overall diameter 270 feet (82m) built first in timber, later in stone. Apart from the absence of baths, the complex is similar to many in Gaul and is to be associated not with the *colonia* but rather with the Trinovantes, the tribe in whose territory the *colonia* was set. The geographer Ptolemy indeed attributes Camulodunum to the Trinovantes, but the legal relationship remains obscure.

Though it seems that the seat of provincial government was early transferred to LONDON, Colchester retained its distinction as the first Roman city in Britain and is once referred to in the Antonine Itinerary as simply 'Colonia'. Its final phases are difficult to discover, because of the subsequent removal of most late Roman and early Saxon levels, but such indications as there are suggest that the Roman city did not survive far into the fifth century.

Most of the finds from excavations are housed in the Colchester and Essex Museum.

Crummy, P., *Colchester: Recent Excavations and Research* (Colchester Excavation Committee), 1974

Dunnet, R., *The Trinovantes*, London, 1975

Hawkes, C. F. C. and Hull, M. R., *Camulodunum: Excavations 1930–39* (Society of Antiquaries Research Report XIV), London, 1947

Hull, M. R., *Roman Colchester* (Society of Antiquaries Research Report XX), London, 1958

—, *The Roman Potters' Kilns at Colchester* (Society of Antiquaries Research Report XXI), London, 1963

Chedworth

Chedworth is typical of the notable group of Cotswold villas centred on Corinium (Cirencester), which in Roman times was the city of the Dobunni. The house faces east down a charming valley and its buildings ultimately enclosed two courtyards, with an overall size at least 250×350 feet (76×107m), though only the inner court and the north wing of the outer court have been explored. This final stage was the end product of a long series of additions and alterations, beginning in the early second century with a group of unconnected buildings. Those in what became the south wing were destroyed by fire c. AD 150, but in the subsequent reconstruction they housed the bailiff's office, kitchens, and a latrine. The west wing of the villa was also substantially modified, both in the early third century and later, and in its fourth-century form included a heated dining room and a suite of baths. The latter were a late addition, for the earlier baths occupied the west end of the north wing, where they were ultimately replaced by a *laconicum*, or dry-heat bath, as a supplement or alternative to the damp-heat baths in the west wing. The remainder of the north wing contained a further set of eight rooms, some of them with hypocausts. Water from a nearby spring was fed into a *nymphaeum*, some of whose stones had the Christian *chi-rho* monogram carved on them. The scant remains of a small Romano-Celtic temple survive half a mile (800m) to the southeast of the villa.

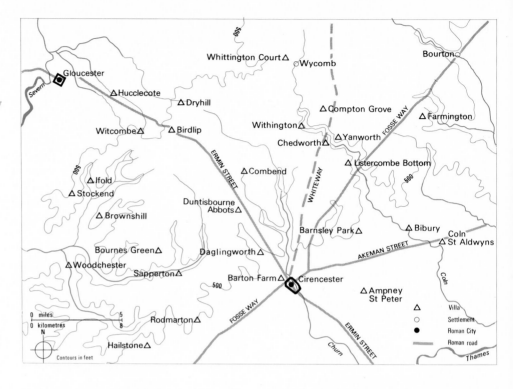

Map showing the location of Chedworth and neighbouring villas

Below: Plan of the Chedworth villa, showing phases of development. Right: Aerial view of the Chedworth villa. The scale of the structures may be gauged by comparison with the modern building in the centre, which includes the curator's house and the museum

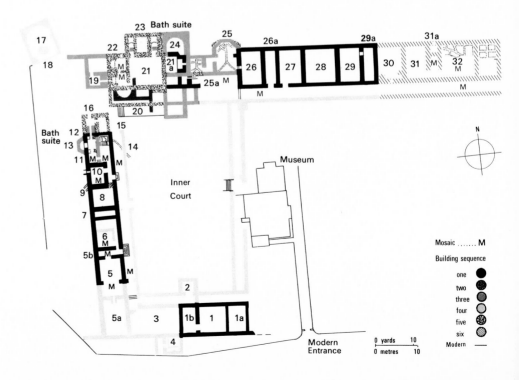

The mosaic pavements (M on the plan) combine the patterned and figured designs typical of the Corinian school of mosaicists. The products of this school represent one of the greatest achievements of Romano-British art and have been found at Cirencester itself, at Barton Farm, Withington, and Woodchester and at six further sites outside the area of the map. Its greatest success was the evolution of a design showing Orpheus charming the beasts, of which the supreme example is the great pavement at Woodchester.

The ultimate fate of the house at Chedworth has not been established, but the neighbouring villa at Withington has been the subject of one of the few attempts by archaeologists to establish continuity of occupation between Roman and medieval times.

The villa is in the care of the National Trust and, along with a site museum, is open to the public.

Finberg, H. P. R., *Roman and Saxon Withington: A Study in Continuity*, Leicester, 1955

Fox, G. E., in *Archaeologia* XLIV (1887), pp. 322–36. The original excavation

Goodburn, R., *The Roman Villa, Chedworth*, London, 1972. General account

Richmond, I. A., in *Trans. Bristol and Gloucestershire Archaeological Society* LXXVIII (1960), pp. 5–23. The establishment of phases

Left: The mosaic pavement of the dining room at
Chedworth
Left, below: A detail (Winter)

Below: The great pavement at Woodchester

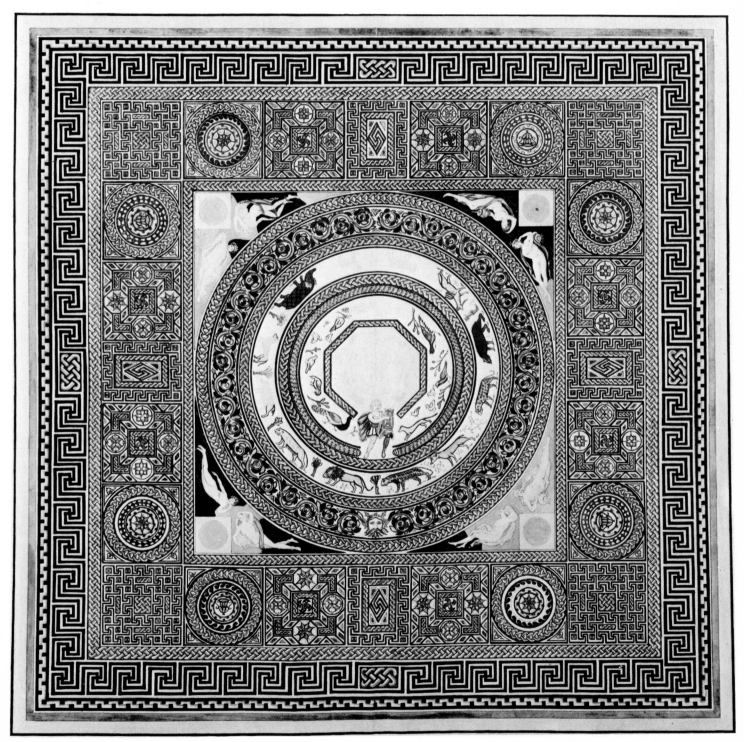

6 York

The multangular tower, York

Eburacum, the ancient name of York, is Celtic, and although no pre-Roman settlement has been identified there it is situated on a morainic ridge which crosses the Vale of York and provided a natural line of communication (subsequently followed by the York–Tadcaster Roman road). The site chosen for the legionary fortress had other attractions for the Roman military engineers: lying in the confluence of the Ouse and the Foss, it was tactically strong, and the fact that both these rivers were then tidal meant that it had access to the sea. The date of the first Roman occupation is disputed – a pre-Flavian auxiliary fort is possible – and the nature of the first base established by Cerialis, whether a full-sized or half-sized fortress or merely a stores base, is also still in doubt. Later in Flavian times, however, almost certainly under Agricola, the

headquarters of Legio IX Hispana were established here in a fortress of normal size, $1,565 \times 1,348$ feet or some 48 acres (477×411m; 19.5ha), with defences of clay and turf, and towers and internal buildings of timber. The rebuilding of this in AD 107–8, with a stone wall 5 feet (1.5m) thick, is attested by an inscription, and on this occasion the Agricolan ditch, 14 feet (4.25m) wide and 4½ feet (1.35m) deep, was filled in and a new ditch, 26 feet (8m) wide and 6 feet (1.8m) deep, was cut 16½ feet (5m) farther out from the rampart. The stone wall was itself rebuilt *c.* 200, on a firmer foundation and with a somewhat greater width. In *c.* 300, under Constantius I, a further substantial remodelling took place: the chief feature of this was the enhancement of the river frontage with a monumental *porta praetoria*, flanked on either side by three pro-

jecting polygonal towers, with large decagonal towers at the south and west corner. Little is known of the internal arrangements of the fortress, but excavations under York Minster have revealed substantial parts of the *principia* and in the southeastern half of the *praetentura* barrack blocks, an internal bath-house and an elaborate system of stone-built sewers have been located.

About AD 120 Legio IX was replaced by Legio VI Victrix; York remained the base of this unit until at least the late fourth century, when it is recorded here in the *Notitia Dignitatum*. The presence of a large body of troops attracted civil settlement, on both banks of the Ouse, and at some time before AD 237 (when the status is given in an inscription) the town was elevated to the rank of *colonia*. On the division of Britain into two

One of the sewers of the legionary fortress; the black and white stick gives the scale in decimetres

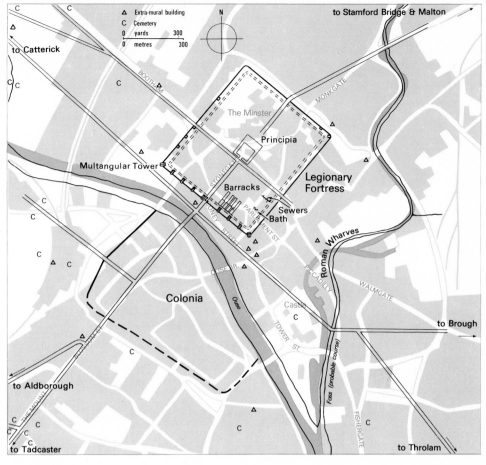

Plan of Eburacum, showing positions of the legionary fortress and the colonia

provinces York became the capital of Britannia Inferior, and it was here, in the (unlocated) palace that Severus died in 211 and here too, in 306, that Constantius I died and Constantine the Great was acclaimed. The precise extent of the *colonia* is not known, but it is assumed that it occupied the area south of the Ouse that was later enclosed in the medieval walls. Of the large population of the place and its importance there is no doubt, and extensive cemeteries have been found along all the roads leading from the fortress and the *colonia*. These have yielded many personal inscriptions and

also testify to numerous religious cults, including those not only of Roman and Celtic deities but also of Serapis and Mithras; and although Christian remains are curiously lacking, a bishop of York was the leading British representative at the Council of Arles in 314.

The main upstanding monuments are the walls of the fortress, especially the multiangular tower at its western corner, but the remains below the minster and the sewers may also be seen. Most of the finds are in the Yorkshire Museum at York.

Addyman, P. V., 'Excavations at York, 1972–3', in *Antiquaries Journal* LIV (1974), pp. 200–31
Butler, R. M. (ed.), *Soldier and Civilian in Roman Yorkshire*, Leicester and Atlantic Highlands, N.J., 1971
Royal Commission on Historical Monuments (England). *Inventory of the City of York I: Eburacum, Roman York*, HMSO, 1962

7   Hadrian's Wall   **England**

Hadrian's Wall is a complex monument, comprising several elements. In order, from the north, these are: a V-shaped ditch, some 30 feet (9m) wide and 13½ feet (4m) deep; a flat berm 20 feet (6m) wide; a stone wall, from 8 to 10 feet (2.4–3m) thick; forts, fortlets and towers related to the wall; a road linking the forts ('the military way'); and the 'vallum',

which is a flat-bottomed ditch, 20 feet (6m) wide and 10 feet (3m) deep flanked on either side by earthen mounds, 20 feet wide and revetted with turf, which are set back 30 feet (9m) from it. Until the nineteenth century it was generally assumed that Hadrian's Wall was simply the 'vallum' (which explains the misleading term) and that the stone wall was

the work of Severus. Subsequent research has established the following sequence.

The withdrawal from Scotland after the recall of Agricola led eventually to the establishment of a *limes* along the Stanegate, the road that linked the Flavian forts at Carlisle and Corbridge. This was accordingly strengthened with forts and fortlets and early in the

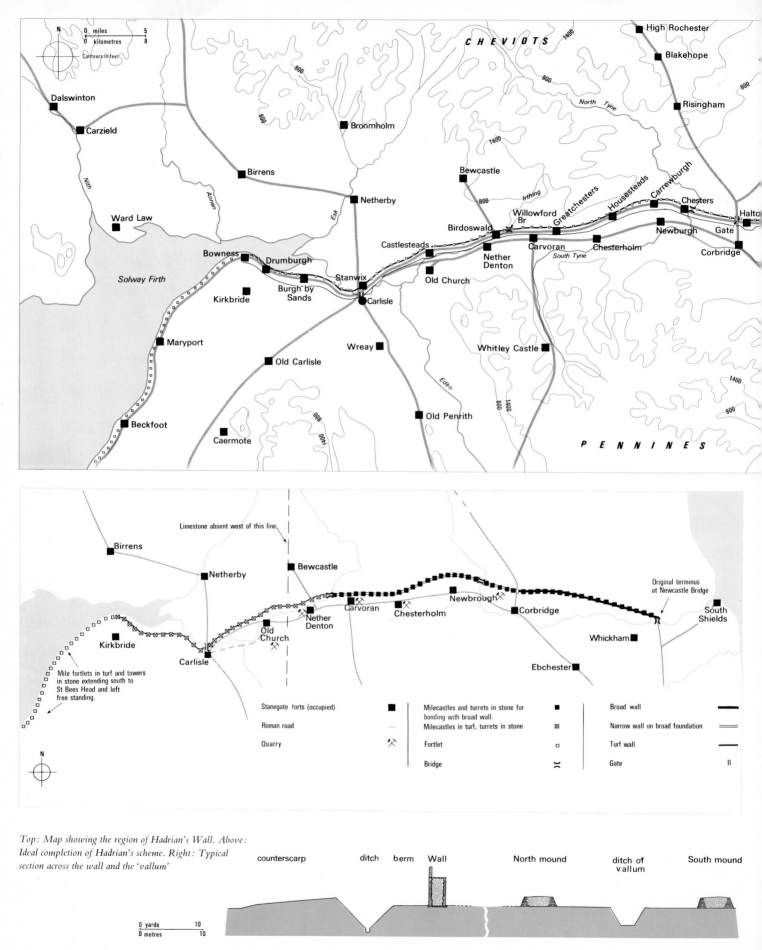

*Top: Map showing the region of Hadrian's Wall. Above:
Ideal completion of Hadrian's scheme. Right: Typical
section across the wall and the 'vallum'*

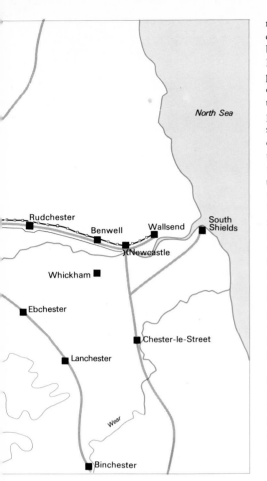

reign of Hadrian, after a frontier war which is commemorated by coins, it was decided to build a continuous wall in front of it, from Newcastle to Bowness. The original scheme provided for a series of fortlets at intervals of one Roman mile (hence 'milecastles'), with two watchtowers ('turrets') between each pair; these were all of stone except in the sector west of the Irthing, where the milecastles were of turf. These milecastles and turrets were to be linked by a wall, which also was to be of stone in the eastern sector, of turf in the west. The width of the stone wall was to be 10 feet (3m) – the 'broad wall' – but while the work was in progress this was reduced to 8 feet (2.4m) – the 'narrow wall'. So from Newcastle to the North Tyne the wall is 'broad', but from the North Tyne to the Irthing it is 'narrow' on a 'broad' foundation, and milecastles and turrets built with wing walls designed for bonding with the 'broad' wall are attached to the 'narrow' wall. In this original scheme the bases of the garrison were to be the forts on the Stanegate which, together with the rampart walk of the wall, provided lateral communication.

Before the work was completed, however, there were further changes of plan. Most of the Stanegate forts were evacuated and new forts were built on the line of the wall itself, and the southern boundary of the military zone was marked off by the 'vallum'; the interlocking of these different phases produced a variety of results. Some forts override the

foundations of milecastles or turrets, and whereas the 'vallum' swerves to avoid forts already built or planned, that at Carrawburgh, which was built late in the series, obliterates it. At some stage after the narrow gauge had been adopted, the wall was extended eastward to Wallsend, where also a fort was built, and some five miles (8km) of turf wall east of the Irthing were replaced by stone wall on a slightly different alignment. At its far western end the wall was supplemented by a series of fortlets and towers down the coast to St Bees Head; no wall was necessary here, nor is there any 'vallum', but recent observation suggests that the military zone was defined by two parallel ditches in front of and behind the fortlets and towers. Finally, although the Wall made a continuous barrier, not all the country north of it was abandoned: at its western end a group of outpost forts were maintained (Birrens, Bewcastle, Netherby, and probably Broomholm), apparently to protect an outlying part of Brigantian territory.

As numerous inscriptions show, the Wall and its forts were built by legionaries, and it is even possible to distinguish the work of each legion, but it was manned by units of auxiliaries, some 10,000 men in all. The proportion of cavalry in the garrison and the siting of the forts in relation to the wall, usually with three gates opening to the north of it, show that it was intended as a springboard rather than a passive defence. Its main purpose, however, seems to have been to secure frontier control.

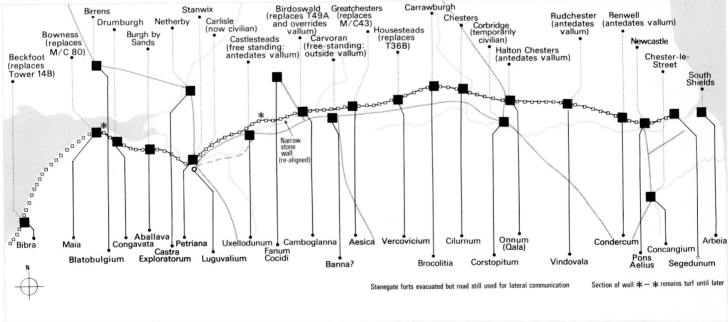

Above: Actual completion of Hadrian's frontier. Right: Ideal sections of the stone and turf walls restored to their original height

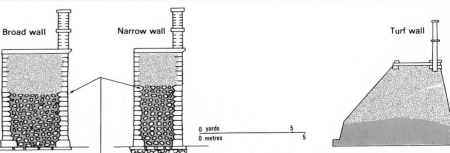

When the Antonine Wall was built in AD 140 some of the forts still remained in use, but Hadrian's Wall itself was put out of commission by removing the gates of the milecastles and by building causeways across the 'vallum'. Some fifteen years later, however, this process had to be reversed, and it was then that the remainder of the turf wall was converted to stone, at an 'intermediate' gauge of 9 feet (2.74m). The history of both walls in the second half of the second century is much disputed, but a major reconstruction took place under Severus, when, too, the 'military way' (which at places runs on the north mound of the 'vallum') was built, and a system of outpost forts now covered the eastern as well as the western sector. Further reconstructions were carried out by Constantius (c. AD 300) and, after the great barbarian raids of 367, by Theodosius. The *Notitia Dignitatum* lists garrisons for the forts *per lineam valli*, but how far this reflects the situation before or after the reduction of forces in Britain caused by the revolt of Maximus in AD 383–8 is debatable.

As elsewhere, all the forts attracted considerable civilian settlement, especially in the third century, and substantial towns grew up outside them, notably at Chesters, Housesteads and, south of the Wall, at Chesterholm. This site (Vindolanda) had been occupied by a large Stanegate fort, and it is from this that the celebrated writing tablets have been recovered. The fort was abandoned when Hadrian's Wall was first built, but in Antonine times it was replaced by a smaller fort and it is this, as subsequently modified, that is now visible.

Long stretches of the Wall have been conserved, together with several milecastles and turrets, and the forts at Chesters and Housesteads. Other structures of particular interest are the temple and 'vallum' crossing at Benwell, the bridge abutments at Chesters and Willowford, the *Mithraeum* and Coventina's Well at Carrawburgh, and the fort at Birdoswald, with a stretch of turf wall to the west of it; to the south of the Wall the fort and town at Corbridge, and the fort and civil settlement at Chesterholm, are especially notable. Besides site museums at Corbridge, Chesters, Chesterholm and Housesteads, and a lapidarium at Lanercost Priory, the main collections are in the Museum of Antiquities at Newcastle University and the Museum and Art Gallery, Carlisle; the former includes scale models of the Wall and its associated structures.

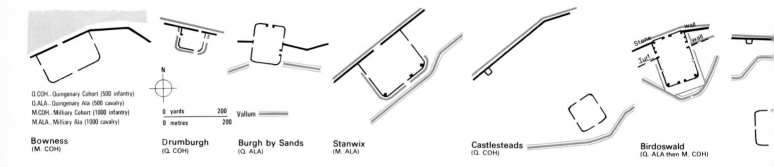

Q.COH.. Quingenary Cohort (500 infantry)
Q.ALA.. Quingenary Ala (500 cavalry)
M.COH.. Milliary Cohort (1000 infantry)
M.ALA.. Milliary Ala (1000 cavalry)

0 yards 200
0 metres 200   Vallum ====

Bowness (M. COH)   **Drumburgh** (Q. COH)   **Burgh by Sands** (Q. ALA)   **Stanwix** (M. ALA)   **Castlesteads** (Q. COH)   **Birdoswald** (Q. ALA then M. COH)

Above: Outline plan of the forts per lineam valli, *showing their relationship to the wall and the 'vallum' and the types of unit for which they were designed. The plan of the fort at Newcastle is unknown*

Below: Vercovicius (Housesteads), looking northeast. Hadrian's Wall runs from A to B, with its foundation continuing just inside the north wall of the fort and its further course obscured by trees; the foundations of Turret 36b, abandoned when the fort was built, are at C. At the bottom of the picture are the buildings of the civil settlements and the museum, marked D.

Birley, E., *Research on Hadrian's Wall*, Kendal, 1961
Collingwood, B. J., *Handbook to the Roman Wall*, 12th
ed., rev. I. A. Richmond, Hindson and A. Reid,
Newcastle, 1966 (13th ed. forthcoming)
Ordnance Survey Map of Hadrian's Wall (2 inches to
1 mile), 2nd ed., Southampton, 1972

In addition to *Britannia*, important papers will be
found in the journals *Archaeologia Aeliana*, Newcastle-
upon-Tyne, and *Transactions of the Cumberland and
Westmorland Antiquarian and Archaeological Society*,
Carlisle.

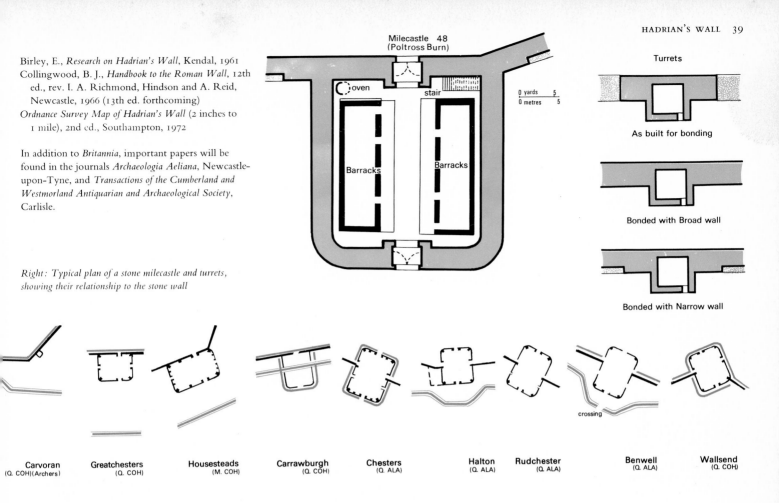

*Right: Typical plan of a stone milecastle and turrets,
showing their relationship to the stone wall*

Milecastle 48
(Poltross Burn)

oven

stair

Barracks   Barracks

0 yards   5
0 metres   5

Turrets

As built for bonding

Bonded with Broad wall

Bonded with Narrow wall

Carvoran	Greatchesters	Housesteads	Carrawburgh	Chesters	Halton	Rudchester	Benwell	Wallsend
(Q. COH)(Archers)	(Q. COH)	(M. COH)	(Q. COH)	(Q. ALA)	(Q. ALA)	(Q. ALA)	(Q. ALA)	(Q. COH)

*Vindolanda (Chesterholm), looking west. The later fort (A), with its headquarters building and gates conserved, is in the
foreground. Beyond it are the bath house (B) and the buildings of the civil settlement (C). The castle-like structure (D)
is a modern replica of elements of Hadrian's Wall. The excavations in the earlier fort, which produced the writing tablets,
took place between this replica and the later fort*

The Roman Rhine-Danube Frontier

Bounded on the west by the Atlantic, on the south by the desert, and confined on the east by a combination of desert and the Parthians, the Roman Empire had its major land frontier in the north across Europe from the North Sea to the Black Sea. The extension of Roman power northward to the Rhine and the Danube was the military achievement of Augustus' principate. In the west the organization of Gallia Transalpina in 121 BC as a Roman province north of the Alps was followed by Caesar's advance across Gaul to the sea on the north and west, and to the river Rhine in the northeast. In the east the proconsuls of the Republic in Macedonia advanced northward along the Vardar-Morava corridor in the first century BC to reach the Danube around Belgrade and northeast toward the Danube delta and the Black Sea.

The Roman advance to the Rhine and Danube

After his victory at Actium in 31 BC Augustus began to plan large-scale campaigns of conquest in central Europe. In 15 BC his stepsons Tiberius and Drusus cooperated to open up the Alps and together overran Raetia as far as the Danube; at about the same time the client kingdom of Noricum was annexed in order to safeguard the northeastern approaches to Italy. In 12–9 BC two great series of campaigns saw Roman armies cross the Rhine under Drusus and overrun territory as far as the Elbe, while under Tiberius operations mounted from northeast Italy secured the land route across Illyricum to Macedonia, Thrace, and Asia Minor, and established the new command of Illyricum as far as the middle Danube. Between 9 BC and AD 6 Roman armies operated beyond the Rhine and Danube on more than one occasion and contemporaries

confidently envisaged further advances beyond the Elbe and even the Carpathians, accompanied also by the conquest of the Dacians in Transylvania, who were then less of a threat than they had been at the time of Caesar under Burebista, or were to become again under Decebalus in the late first century.

In AD 6, however, when Tiberius was on the point of eliminating the power of Maroboduus, king of the German Marcomanni in what is now Bohemia, all Illyricum between Italy and Macedonia rebelled and the army had to be recalled to bases in the interior in order to re-establish control in Illyricum. That had barely been achieved when in AD 9, at a place somewhere in Germany between the Rhine and the Elbe, the Roman general P. Quinctilius Varus was ambushed and his army of three legions destroyed by the Germans under the Cheruscian prince Arminius, who had once served as an allied officer in the Roman army. As a consequence of these two setbacks the Roman legions and auxiliaries remained in bases along the west bank of the Rhine and south of the Danube within Illyricum. At first they were regarded as armies of conquest and occupation awaiting the command to resume the momentum of conquest and annexation. Certainly it was a very long time before they were thought of as a defensive screen to protect the provinces of the Empire from invasion.

From a survey by the historian Tacitus (*Annals*, iv, 5), combined with other evidence, the following deployment of legions on the Rhine and Danube in the aftermath of the Illyrian rebellion and the Varus disaster in Germany may be deduced:

GERMANIA INFERIOR
I Germanica (Cologne)
xx (Cologne)
vv Alaudae (Vetera)
xxi Rapax (Vetera)

GERMANIA SUPERIOR
xiv Gemina (Mainz)
xvi Gallica (Mainz)
ii Augusta (Strasbourg)
xiii Gemina (Vindonissa)

ILLYRICUM
(divided into Pannonia and Dalmatia about AD 9)

PANNONIA
viii Augusta (Poetovio)
ix Hispana (?Siscia)
xv Apollinaris (Carnuntum)

DALMATIA
vii (Tilurium)
xi (Burnum)

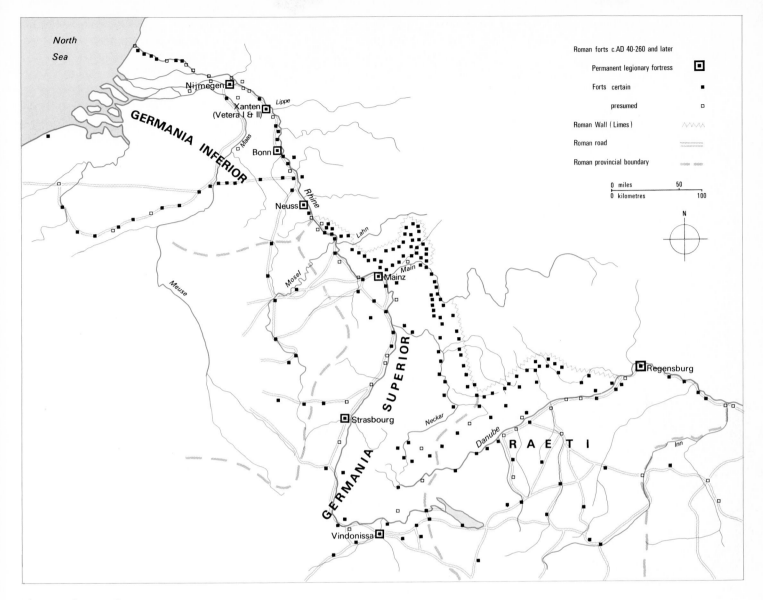

The Roman frontier in Germany

MOESIA
(organized as a province along the lower
Danube some time between 9 BC and AD 6)
IV Scythica (?)
V Macedonica (Oescus)

From about the same time the smaller for-
mations of auxiliary cavalry *alae* and infantry
cohortes began to be stationed in camps along
the Rhine in the intervals between the legionary bases. By the middle of the first century AD
the legions, although individually very mobile,
were being established at permanent bases.
From the time of Claudius these bases began to
be built in stone instead of timber. For much
of the first century eight legions with their
auxilia were based on the Rhine, while a
smaller number, varying from four to seven,
were dispersed along the much longer Danube
in Pannonia, Dalmatia, and Moesia; a deployment still reflecting the mixture of ambitious
conquest and anxious defence that was the
legacy of Augustus' wars.

In the last years of the first century the
Roman position on the Danube was seriously
threatened by the revival of the Dacian kingdom under Decebalus. After a major war under
Domitian, during which there were at least
two Roman disasters involving the loss of
whole legions, the strength of the Danubian
army was increased to more than twelve
legions with their *auxilia*, until in two campaigns (AD 101–2 and 105) Trajan defeated
Decebalus and made Dacia a Roman province.

By the reign of Hadrian, when the deployment of legions began to resume once more a
semi-permanent character, the preponderance
of force remained on the Danube:

GERMANIA INFERIOR
XXX Ulpia Victrix (Vetera)
I Minervia (Bonn)

GERMANIA SUPERIOR
XXII Primigenia (Mainz)
VIII Augusta (Strasbourg)

PANNONIA SUPERIOR
X Gemina (Vienna)
XIV Gemina Martia Victrix (Carnuntum)
I Adiutrix (Brigetio)

PANNONIA INFERIOR
II Adiutrix (Aquincum)

MOESIA SUPERIOR
IV Flavia Felix (Singidunum)
VII Claudia (Viminacium)

MOESIA INFERIOR
I Italica (Novae)
V Macedonica (Durostorum)
XI Claudia (Troesmis)

DACIA
XIII Gemina (Apulum)

Later in the second century the upper
Danube was strengthened by the stationing of
two legions raised during the reign of Marcus

Aurelius, III Italica at Regensburg in Raetia and II Italica at Lauriacum in Noricum.

From the end of Augustus' reign until final collapse at the end of the fourth century, the Roman frontier in Lower Germany remained on the Rhine. It is likely that the Roman fleet based at Cologne (*classis Germanica*) played an important role through control of the river. In Upper Germany south of the Taunus the line of the river ceased to be the frontier after the Flavian period. The re-entrant of territory between the upper courses of the Rhine and Danube began to be annexed in 74, when a road was built from the legionary fortress at Strasbourg to Rottweil and the Danube. A few years later Domitian's war against the Chatti resulted in the occupation of the Taunus hills and the Wetterau. Farther south, land between the Rhine and the Neckar was rapidly annexed about the same time. The military posts along the Taunus were linked by watchtowers and forts were added along the same line. At about the same time, troops in Raetia were moved forward north of the Jura ridge. When this move had been completed the limit of Roman territory in Upper Germany and Raetia, where it did not follow the river Main or the Neckar,

was marked by a wooden palisade which is generally assigned to the reign of Hadrian.

The evolution of the artificial Roman frontier in Germany between the late first and the early third century may be summarized as in the table below.

While the auxiliary units were moved forward to occupy forts along the *limes*, leaving the legions isolated in the rear at their bases Mainz and Strasbourg, all the newly annexed land was organized into autonomous *civitates* right up to the line of the frontier.

In the middle of the third century large-scale invasions in the reign of Gallienus brought about the total collapse of the *limes*, resulting in the abandonment of all Roman territory beyond the Rhine and Danube, to be matched a decade or so later under Aurelian with the evacuation of Dacia because of pressure from the Goths on the lower Danube. It is perhaps a misapprehension to assume that, in the years before such disasters actually happened, the Romans ever looked on their army along and beyond the Rhine as a contrived defence for the Empire where barriers, rivers, watchtowers, small fortlets, auxiliary forts, and

legionary bases all combined in a system to ward off enemy attack on a large scale. When a genuine system of defence was required, as it obviously was after these disasters, it was necessary to organize defence in depth. Forts along the length of the Rhine and Danube were strengthened with massive walls, protected by narrow gates and projecting bastions, while at the same time the number of observation posts was greatly increased.

Yet such expensive installations were intended not so much to frustrate large-scale invasions but rather to ensure that military personnel had somewhere secure to retreat when an invader appeared in overwhelming force. Then, if there was an opportunity, there could be retaliation on a piecemeal scale, although usually not before the enemy had managed to penetrate to the rich cities and rural areas of the interior. Because of this, many towns far from the frontier built new defences and impregnable citadels to ensure their own safety in the same fashion.

In this sense the system of the late Empire may be regarded as a more practical, if pessimistic, system to deal with the threat of invasion. The system as a whole lasted until the end of the fourth century. In 406 large numbers of Franks, Vandals, Alamanni, Suebi, Alani, and the like crossed the Rhine and entered the Empire, never to return to their homelands outside.

Germany	Raetia
1. Road through forests with timber watchtowers behind	Road through forests with timber watchtowers before
2. Timber palisade added in front of road	Timber palisade added in front of towers and road
3. Timber watchtowers rebuilt in stone	Timber watchtowers rebuilt in stone
4. Ditch in front and mound behind added between palisade and road	Palisade replaced by stone wall

Baatz, D., *Der Römische Limes*, 2nd ed., Berlin, 1975
Bogaers, J. E. and Rüger, C. B. (ed.), *Der Niedergermanische Limes*, Cologne 1974
Mócsy, András, *Pannonia and Upper Moesia*, London, 1974
Schönberger, H., *Journal of Roman Studies*, LIX, London, 1969, pp. 144–97

I — Trier

Germany

From its foundation under Augustus to its destruction by Franks in the early fifth century, Augusta Treverorum (Trier or Trèves) was the leading political and economic centre of northeast Gaul. In the first century AD it was already the residence of the imperial finance officer (*procurator*) responsible for the provinces of Belgic Gaul and the Two Germanies. In the third century it became an imperial residence, at first of the separatist Gallic emperor Postumus, but later of Maximian, Constantius I, and their successors until the late fourth century. It was also the seat of the Gallic praetorian prefecture, and its bishop enjoyed a correspondingly high status.

The site lies in hilly country at an important crossing of the river Moselle (ancient Mosella). Perhaps selected as the site for a military post, the town became established under Augustus,

from which time appears to date the earliest nucleus of *insulae* within the later street grid. It became the Colonia Augusta Treverorum under Claudius, when the first stone bridge was built, a short distance downstream from the later bridge whose Roman piers still survive. Cemeteries from the first century attest a Romanized and Latin-speaking population but with native traditions in their material possessions.

Little large-scale public building was undertaken before the end of the first century. In contrast, the second century was a period of great prosperity, reflected by a number of major private and public buildings within the city. A *forum* some 1,300 × 500 feet (400 × 150m) incorporating a sunken portico (*crypto-porticus*), the new bridge across the Moselle on stone piers, an amphitheatre with a capacity of

20,000 sunk into the slope of the Petrisberg, a huge complex of public baths (known now as the Barbarathermen from the nearby church), an aqueduct more than 7 miles (12km) long in the Ruwer valley, and a great sacred precinct in Altbachtal enclosing more than 50 shrines packed closely together were all constructed, or at least had their beginnings, in this period.

The most impressive surviving monuments of the Roman city belong to the time when Trier was an imperial residence. The imposing north gate of the city, the Porta Nigra, was only part of a circuit of defences built probably in the middle of the third century (although some scholars date it a century later). A second block of monumental baths (Kaiserthermen) built in the late third or early fourth century occupied an area in the city as large as the *forum*, and was substantially rebuilt in the later

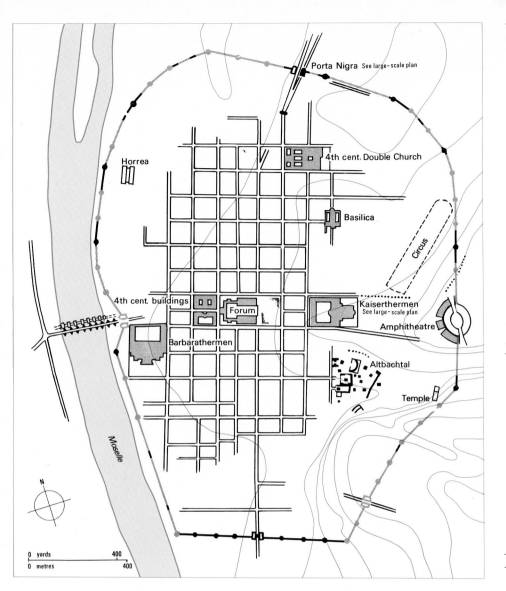

Horrea

Porta Nigra See large-scale plan

4th cent. Double Church

Basilica

Circus

4th cent. buildings

Forum

Kaiserthermen
See large-scale plan

Amphitheatre

Barbarathermen

Altbachtal

Temple

Moselle

N

| 0 yards | 400 |
| 0 metres | 400 |

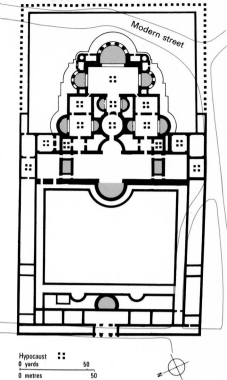

Modern street

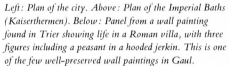

Hypocaust

| 0 yards | 50 |
| 0 metres | 50 |

N

Left: Plan of the city. Above: Plan of the Imperial Baths (Kaiserthermen). Below: Panel from a wall painting found in Trier showing life in a Roman villa, with three figures including a peasant in a hooded jerkin. This is one of the few well-preserved wall paintings in Gaul.

fourth century. The great hall known as the Basilica, probably an imperial audience chamber (*auditorium*) of the early fourth century, survives (now refurbished after extensive war damage) as a wing of the eighteenth-century Elector's Palace. Measuring 220 feet (67m) long, 90 feet (27.5m) wide and 99 feet (30m) high, it is one of the most impressive buildings to survive from antiquity. Within the modern

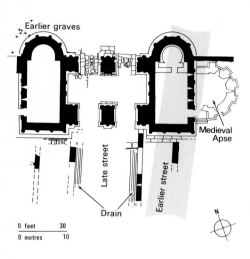

The Roman north gate (Porta Nigra) of Trier – above: plan; right; the north side

cathedral and the adjoining Liebfrauenkirche are the remains of a great Roman double church, comparable with Constantinian churches at Rome (St John Lateran), Bethlehem, and Jerusalem.

Finds are in the Landesmuseum, Trier.

Ternes, C. M., 'Die römerzeitliche Civitas Trevirorum im Bild der Nachkriegsforschung, I Von der Gründung bis zum Ende des dritten Jahrhunderts', in *Aufstieg und Niedergang der römischen Welt*, ed. H. Temporini, II, 4, Berlin and New York, 1975, pp. 320–424

Wightman, Edith Mary, *Roman Trier and the Treveri*, London 1970

2   Xanten   Germany

The site of Xanten is less remarkable for the visible traces of its Roman past than for its situation on the lower Rhine and its importance in the Roman occupation of the Rhineland during the first century AD. Before AD 9 it was the base of Legio XVIII, on the evidence of the tombstone of Caelius, who perished in the Varus disaster of that year. Next it was occupied by two legions, V Alaudae and XXI

Rapax, until *c.* 46 when XXI was replaced by the newly raised XV Primigenia. In AD 70 the legionary fortress together with its civil settlement (*canabae*) was destroyed by the Batavian rebel Julius Civilis.

This fortress, named Vetera, lay on the glacial hill Furstenberg near Birten, about 1¼ miles (2km) from the Rhine and opposite the mouth of the Lippe river. At first built in

timber, it began to be rebuilt in stone under Claudius. An earlier timber fortress of Tiberius, approx. 2,650 × 1,900 feet (800 × 580m) or 111 acres (45ha) was eventually replaced by the Neronian stone fortress of approx. 3,000 × 2,070 feet (915 × 630m) or 138 acres (56ha), with a stone wall, four gates and double ditches. The headquarters (*principia*), residences for the two legionary commanders (*praetoria*), and some

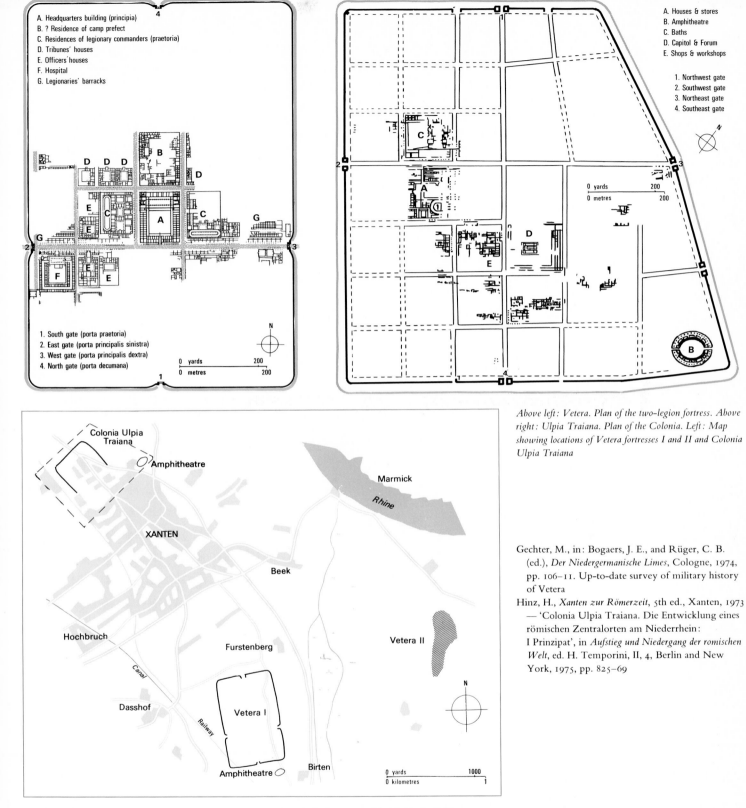

A. Headquarters building (principia)
B. ? Residence of camp prefect
C. Residences of legionary commanders (praetoria)
D. Tribunes' houses
E. Officers' houses
F. Hospital
G. Legionaries' barracks

1. South gate (porta praetoria)
2. East gate (porta principalis sinistra)
3. West gate (porta principalis dextra)
4. North gate (porta decumana)

0 yards 200
0 metres 200

A. Houses & stores
B. Amphitheatre
C. Baths
D. Capitol & Forum
E. Shops & workshops

1. Northwest gate
2. Southwest gate
3. Northeast gate
4. Southeast gate

0 yards 200
0 metres 200

Colonia Ulpia Traiana
Amphitheatre
Marmick
Rhine
XANTEN
Beek
Hochbruch
Furstenberg
Canal
Railway
Dasshof
Vetera I
Vetera II
Amphitheatre
Birten

0 yards 1000
0 kilometres 1

Above left: Vetera. Plan of the two-legion fortress. Above right: Ulpia Traiana. Plan of the Colonia. Left: Map showing locations of Vetera fortresses I and II and Colonia Ulpia Traiana

Gechter, M., in: Bogaers, J. E., and Rüger, C. B. (ed.), *Der Niedergermanische Limes*, Cologne, 1974, pp. 106–11. Up-to-date survey of military history of Vetera

Hinz, H., *Xanten zur Römerzeit*, 5th ed., Xanten, 1973 — 'Colonia Ulpia Traiana. Die Entwicklung eines römischen Zentralorten am Niederrhein: I Prinzipat', in *Aufstieg und Niedergang der romischen Welt*, ed. H. Temporini, II, 4, Berlin and New York, 1975, pp. 825–69

officers' residences have been excavated.

After 98, but probably before 105, Colonia Ulpia Traiana was established on a site alongside the river a few miles to the north; it now lies on the northern edge of the medieval and modern town. A stone wall enclosed an area of 205 acres (83ha) in which four gates were placed symmetrically. The interior was divided into *insulae* by a regular but not altogether symmetrical street grid. Major buildings, wholly or partly excavated, include an amphitheatre, a temple near the northeast gate, a *Capitolium* (insula vi), baths (ii), and a palace complex (v). Shops and workshops occupied another *insula* (vii) close to the centre. The city flourished until the end of the fourth century.

Finds are in the Xanten museum, private collections, and the Landesmuseum, Bonn.

3 Carnuntum

Carnuntum was a Roman legionary fortress and civil town on the Danube east of Vienna between Petronell and Deutsch-Altenburg. Originally part of Noricum, it was probably incorporated in Pannonia around A D 14 when the Legio XV Apollinaris was moved there from Emona (Ljubljana). The legionary fortress was reconstructed during the years following, at first in timber and later in stone (from *c. 73*). Except for a stay in the East from 62 to 71 the legion remained at Carnuntum until about 114 when it was replaced by Legio XIV Gemina Martia Victrix. From the division of Illyricum under Augustus it was the provincial capital of Pannonia (later Pannonia Superior).

The remains of the fortress have been eroded by the river on the north, although systematic excavations between 1877 and 1911 have recovered one of the most complete plans available for a legionary base. An irregular quadrilateral, roughly 1,640 × 1,310 feet (500 × 400m), was surrounded by a stone wall and double ditch, in which three of the four gates (*porta principalis, dextra,* and *sinistra,* and *porta decumana*) survive, that on the north (*porta praetoria*) having long since disappeared. The interior was planned according to a scheme that went back at least to the second century B C. In the central range are the main buildings, the headquarters (*principia*), commandant's residence (*praetorium*), with the rear area in the south (*retentura*) and the front area in the north (*praetentura*) occupied by rectangular barracks, each incorporating a centurion's apartment. There would normally be sixty barracks, one for each of the *centuriae* in the legion of 5,400 men. Outside the northeast corner of the fortress was a military amphitheatre which held about 8,000 spectators. Aerial photographs have revealed traces of an extensive civil settlement (*canabae*) around the fortress, especially along the road leading from the south gate.

About 7 miles (12km) west of the fortress the civil town of Carnuntum lies beneath the houses of Petronell. This became a *municipium* under Hadrian and a *colonia* under Septimius Severus, whose accession to the throne in 193 was first proclaimed there. The most striking monuments surviving from the town are the so-called Heidentor, an arch and two pillars from what was once a four-sided arch about 66 feet (20m) high, but whose purpose remains unknown, and the larger civil amphitheatre built with an area of 223 × 164 feet (68 × 50m) and capacity of 13,000. Two areas of stone buildings have been excavated and preserved, a palace complex and a residential or commercial quarter.

Many of the finds are in the local Museum Carnuntinum, others in Vienna museums and private collections.

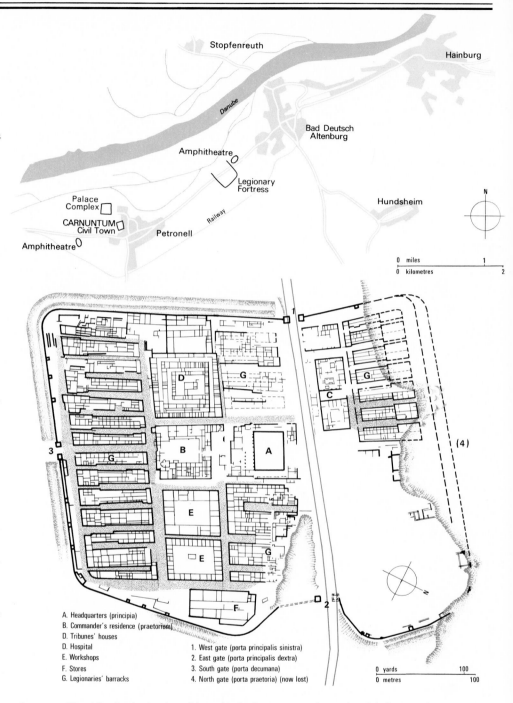

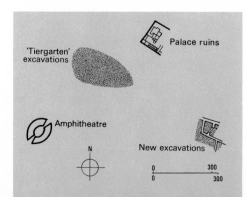

A. Headquarters (principia)
B. Commander's residence (praetorium)
D. Tribunes' houses
D. Hospital
E. Workshops
F. Stores
G. Legionaries' barracks

1. West gate (porta principalis sinistra)
2. East gate (porta principalis dextra)
3. South gate (porta decumana)
4. North gate (porta praetoria) (now lost)

Carnuntum. Top: Map showing locations of the civil and military centres. Above: Plan of the legionary fortress. Below: Remains of the civil settlement

Swoboda, Erich, *Carnuntum, Seine Geschichte und Seine Denkmaler,* 4th ed. and Graz Cologne, 1964
Vorbeck, Eduard, and Beckel, Lothar, *Carnuntum: Rom an der Donau,* 2nd ed., Salzburg, 1973. Remarkable aerial photographs in colour

Left: Tombstone of Roman soldier, Titus Calidius Severus, set up at Carnuntum. The epitaph records his service as optio and decurion (non-commissioned ranks) in the auxiliary cohort Prima Alpinorum, followed by centurion in Legio XV Apollinaris, which was stationed for a period at Carnuntum. He died aged 58, having served for 34 years; the epitaph was set up by his brother Q. Calidius. The three lower panels depict his tunic, helmet and greaves, and his horse, with attendant. Right: Epitaph put up by Illo, son of Itedo, to his wife, Umma, daughter of Tabico, who lived for 45 years. She is portrayed in her native dress.

4 Magdalensberg

This traditionally holy mountain, 3,526 feet (1,058m), about 12 miles (20km) north of Klagenfurt in Carinthia, secure from attack, commanding views of the countryside in all directions, with ample water supply, fertile soil to a high level and iron ore, became during the first century BC an important settlement in the kingdom of Noricum. A Celtic *oppidum* existed on the summit from the second century BC, protected by a *murus Gallicus* type of defence which was replaced by an elaborate *murus duplex* in the time of Caesar, and there

seems little doubt that it can be identified with the Norican capital Noreia, scene of a famous Roman defeat at the hands of the German Cimbri in 113 BC. It was the most extensive settlement in Noricum with an enclosed area of more than 2 square miles (3km²).

Before the end of the second century BC Roman merchants were trading there on a southward-facing settlement at an altitude of 3,018–3,035 feet (920–925m) that occupied an area 374 × 180 feet (114 × 55m). Beginning with timber buildings of around 100 BC, the shops

and offices of individual merchants were arranged around an open space, in the truest sense of a trading *forum*. Later, stone houses and shops were built incorporating cellars serving as storehouses. The period of *c.* 40–20 BC was the most prosperous for the settlement, judging from the fact that some of the residents could afford to have Roman painters decorate their houses with expensive frescoes. Annexation around 15 BC led to a Roman administration being established there, and many new buildings were added.

Numerous inscriptions (mainly tombstones) record the presence of trading families from northern Italy, notably the Barbii from Aquileia. Their most important relic is the so-called Helenenberg Youth (now in Vienna), found beneath the summit in 1502, a life-sized bronze statue dedicated to Mars by a freedman and slave of the family around the middle of the first century BC. The excavated and now preserved buildings of the Roman settlement include a classical temple in its enclosure flanked by a large hall with a tribunal, a council chamber ('house of representatives'), a set of baths and, on the other side of the temple, an area of shops and houses ('commercial quarter'). They all belong to the half century or so following 15 BC. The Roman and Celtic names on the hundreds of tombstones indicate a mixed population. Wall inscriptions still preserved northeast of the trading *forum* record a variety of objects bought from native craftsmen for disposal on the Italian market.

The founding of a new city at Virunum in the Zollfeld below the Magdalensberg in the reign of Claudius caused the rapid evacuation of the latter and none of the great quantity of finds can be dated later than that reign.

Most of the finds from the excavations are to be seen in museums on the site.

Alföldy, Géza, *Noricum*, London, 1974, pp. 44–77. Excellent survey in English

Egger, Rudolf, and others, *Führer durch die Ausgrabungen und das Museum auf dem Magdalensberg*, 16th ed., Klagenfurt, 1973

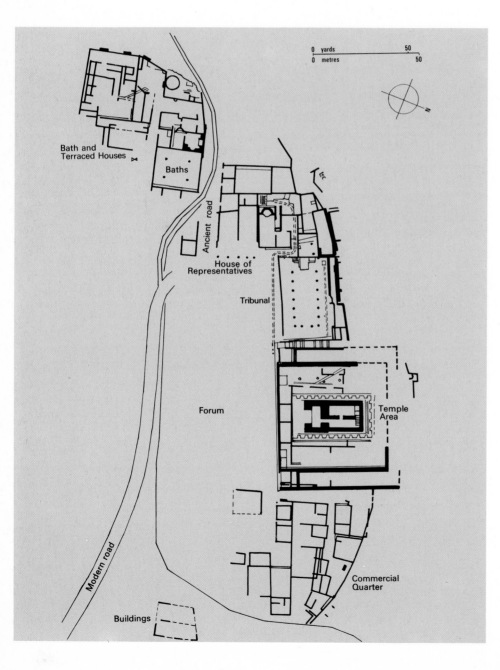

Bath and Terraced Houses

Baths

Ancient road

House of Representatives

Tribunal

Forum

Temple Area

Modern road

Commercial Quarter

Buildings

0 yards 50
0 metres 50

Opposite: The 'Helenberg Youth', a life-size bronze statue of a youth, made in the first century BC in the tradition of Praxiteles' school, found on the Magdalensberg in 1502

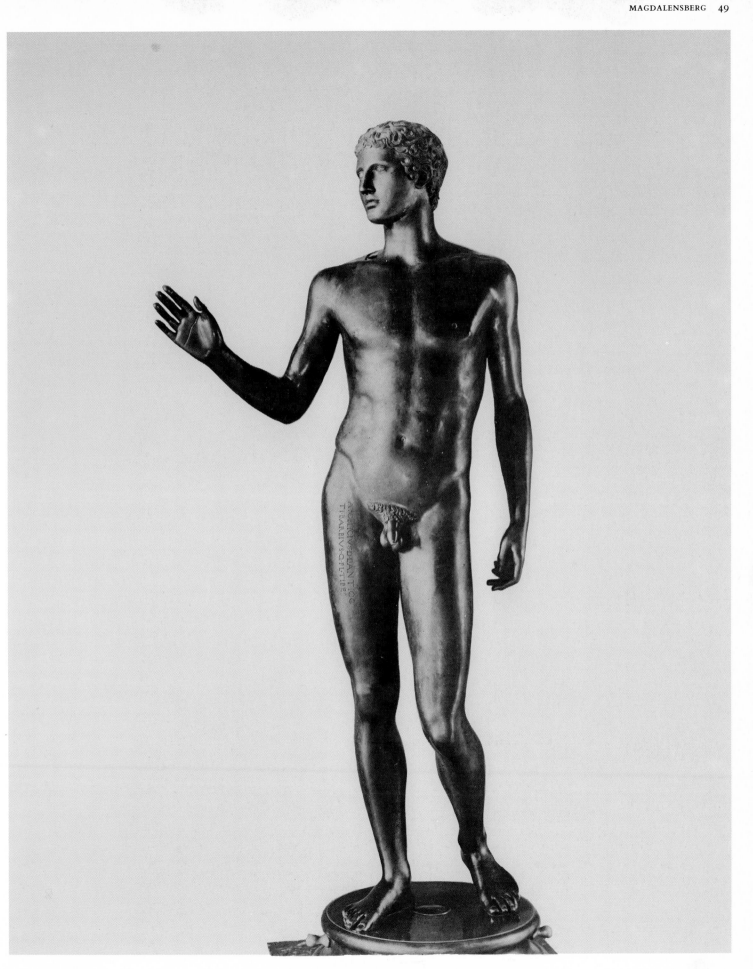

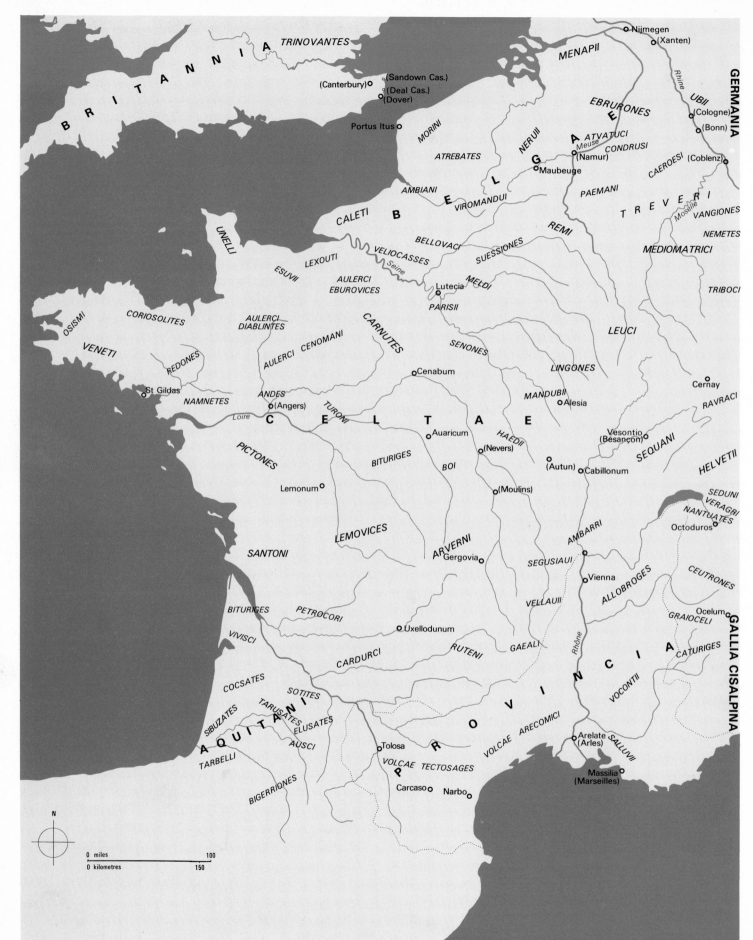

Provence

Provence (Roman Provincia Narbonensis), a hot dry land of sun and sea, cypress, olive, and aromatic herbs, must have reminded Greek colonists of their homeland, whose climate it so closely matches. When the mistral blows down from the north over lagoon and mountain it can be a harsh country, too. Its population at the Roman conquest was about 3,000,000.

A typical native walled *oppidum*, later subject to Greek, Iberian, and Roman influence, is ENSÉRUNE. In due course it came under the influence of Greek Massalia (Roman Massilia, modern Marseille), the oldest city in France, which Greeks from Phocaea in Asia Minor, attracted by its sheltered harbour, founded in about 600 BC. Recent excavation of Massalia has revealed appropriately nautical artifacts: stoppered jars that once contained either fish sauce or pitch for caulking; wooden caulking tools, lead and stone anchors, lead and copper ballast ingots, sounding leads, net weights; also a ropewalk, a Hellenistic haulway, the piles of the Roman port, a ship's keel.

Massalia prospered from the beginning; by 535 BC it had a rich treasury at DELPHI. The city in turn founded Nice and Antibes, and fostered the hinterland's development. It was ROME's ally against CARTHAGE, but failed to compete with Rome commercially, and declined with the founding of the Roman Provincia Narbonensis (118 BC). But Massalia's red mullet was relished by Roman gourmets in exile, and its university by Roman ne'er-do-wells on remittance. It supported the loser, Pompey, against Caesar in 49 BC and suffered siege: Caesar describes elaborate siegeworks. A temple of Artemis underlies the old cathedral; a stretch of towered Hellenistic wall and a theatre were excavated in 1967. At a gate in the wall was found a paved Roman street overlying a Greek dirt road. Under Nero, Crinas, a local physician, subsidized a wall near the harbour; perhaps excavated stretches

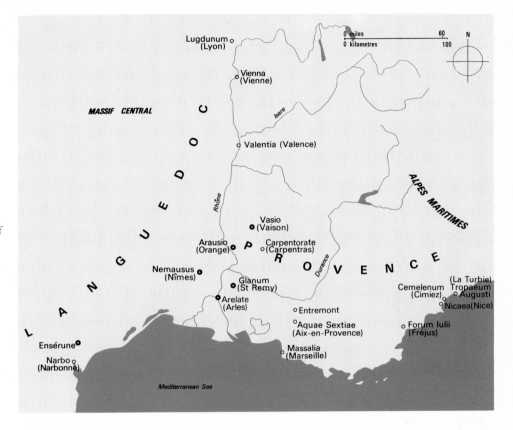

Opposite: The 'Gaul' of Caesar's Gallic Wars, 58–51 BC. The southern district, Provincia (Narbonensis), was already a Roman province

of wall belong to this phase. The walled area would have housed nearly 50,000. It survived until the Visigothic invasions (AD 489).

GLANUM was a Massiliote settlement over a native shrine. Some 33 miles (53km) southeast lies Aquae Sextiae (Aix-en-Provence), a Roman fort established in 123 BC by the general C. Sextius Calvinus near some hot springs under the lee of a Gallic *oppidum*, Entremont. In the plain east of the city, beneath Cézanne's favourite Mont Sainte-Victoire, Sextius beat the Teutones in 102 BC. The blood from the battle (100,000 barbarian dead) allegedly made the field where it was fought extraordinarily fertile. Augustus made Aix a Latin colony; Diocletian made it a provincial capital. Though no major monuments survive, the site of Sextius' camp has been identified in the cathedral area; the *forum* perhaps underlies the Place aux Herbes, near the Hôtel de Ville. The Via Aurelia, 19 feet (5.8m) wide, formed the *cardo* of the colony, whose 35-acre (14ha) area would have held 7,700 – not a very impressive population for a future provincial capital. Probably the colony expanded in the high Empire to include at least the thermal area, 580 feet (177m) west of the crossing of the *cardo* and the *decumanus*; in fact, traces of a circuit wall were found 1,640 feet (500m) west of the baths, enclosing 105 acres

(42ha), which would have held 23,000 inhabitants (modern Aix has 73,000 inhabitants).

In 118 BC the Romans founded a colony, Narbo Martius, in the plain below a Celt-iberian hillfort; it became a river port, a crossroads on the route to Spain, and the capital of Narbonensis. Caesar settled veterans here; Claudius enlarged it. After a fire in AD 145 it was sumptuously rebuilt, with a huge *capitolium*, 160 × 120 feet (48 × 36m), four times the area of the Maison Carrée at NÎMES; an amphitheatre, 400 × 300 feet (122 × 91m) – one-third the area of the Colosseum; baths; a *forum*, 450 × 280 feet (137 × 85m); and a *cryptoporticus*: vaulted subterranean corridors forming a rectangle of 170 × 126 feet (52 × 38m), on which opened 126 rooms probably used for storing grain. At its height the colony occupied 250 acres (about 100ha), embracing a rectangular street grid, and had a population of possibly 55,000. Later, under threat of barbarian invasion, in the early fourth century, it withdrew into a smaller walled area of 75 acres (30ha). The Visigoths sacked it in AD 462.

After ARLES, the Romans founded Vienne: Mark Antony settled veterans there in 43 BC. Its circuit wall enclosed over 500 acres (200ha). Augustus put up Gaul's second largest theatre there, seating 10,800; built on a Greek module, and sumptuously decorated in marble, it survived into Arcadius' reign (A D 395–408). Vienne had also an *odeon* (a covered theatre for music and dance) with a capacity of 3,000, and a third theatre, unique in Gaul, for the mystery plays of the Cybele cult. There was a circus for chariot races, 1,500 feet (457m) long, and a temple to Augustus and his wife Livia (nearly the twin to Nîmes' Maison Carrée); it was remodelled in A D 41. The suburb of Saint-Romain-en-Gal across the Rhône has yielded mosaics, including one of athletes in Olympic events, throwing the discus, running and wrestling.

After planting veterans at Arausio (ORANGE), Augustus in 30 B C used Caesar's port colony of Forum Iulii (Fréjus) as a base for the 300 vessels captured from Antony and Cleopatra at Actium. The artificial harbour, now filled in, covered 54 acres (22ha), had a lighthouse and an entrance flanked by towers and controlled by a chain boom. The adjoining navy yard had warehouses, an arsenal, and two walled and towered camps, with cisterns, granaries, baths, laundry, and elegant quarters with mosaic floors, perhaps for the admiral. Fréjus had a civil as well as a military function – unusual in Gaul. The town wall, 8 feet (2.4m) thick, was 1.71 miles (2.75km) around; the population was possibly 22,000. Within, the street grid had for its *decumanus* the Via Aurelia, which ran from Rome to Arles; its west gate survives. Fréjus has an amphitheatre of Flavian date, measuring 380×270 feet (116×82m) and with a capacity of 12,000, and a poorly preserved theatre, smaller than the one at Arles. An aqueduct served the town and its baths from a source 25 miles (40km) away.

Nemausus (Nîmes) is another Augustan foundation.

In 6 B C, at La Turbie on the Italian frontier, Augustus built a monumental trophy – now partially reconstructed from 3,000 fragments – of his victory over forty-four Alpine tribes named in an inscription on the cubic base. On the cube rests a cylinder surrounded by a colonnade with niches for statues of Augustus' generals, including his stepsons Tiberius and Drusus. On the cylinder rested a pyramid rising in twelve steps to the statue, twice life-size and 161 feet (49m) above the ground, of the godlike victor over these pitiful natives. The décor included kneeling captives, captured arms, and the victorious generals' cloaks. The whole propagandizes Augustus' glory and the Roman peace.

Vasio (VAISON-LA-ROMAINE) flourished in the early Empire, as did Valentia (Valence), a colony of Caesar or the Triumvirs, whose Roman grid plan has been revealed since World War II by air photography. Carpentorate (Carpentras) is famous for the remains of its monumental arch, contemporary with that of Orange. On its east face two muscular Gallic captives, one in a fringed cloak, the other in a sheepskin, are chained to a tree trunk festooned with swords, trumpets, and Gallic helmets suspended from branches. Part of a cuirass, a double axe, and a scimitar with sheath and belt complete this rather gloating décor.

Cemenelum (Cimiez), a former Ligurian *oppidum* above Nice, converted into a garrison town, has one of the Roman world's smallest amphitheatres: 220×190 feet (67×58m) and a capacity of 3,000. Under the Severan dynasty (193–235), baths were built on an adjoining site, one set each for men and women, with stadium and wrestling ground attached. At

the height of the Empire rich villas here exploited the cool air and the view.

Provence was an amalgam of indigenous, Greek, and Roman elements, whose amenities epitomize the material side of Romanization. Rome found there commercial and agricultural advantages, Greek culture, and control of the road to Spain. Provençals lost independence, and gained *fora*, theatres, amphitheatres, baths, and aqueducts; few Gauls felt cheated. Only two major Gallic resistance leaders – both Gallic nobles granted Roman citizenship – were active in Provence. One, Julius Sacrovir, rebelled in A D 21 in resentment at Gaul's heavy indebtedness to Roman financiers: the Orange arch commemorates his defeat. The other, Julius Vindex, a trusted officer, revolted against Nero in 68. Vienne supported him; fear of raids by his partisans apparently halted the building of the amphitheatre at Arles. But he too was defeated and killed, at Besançon. These exceptions prove the rule: most propertied Gauls were pro-Roman: until the Visigoths swept through in the early fifth century, Gauls enjoyed villas like that of Sidonius Apollinaris at Lake Aydat (just outside Provence), where, in the twilight of the Roman culture they had inherited, they sat in their pleasant summerhouses, sipping their snow-cooled wine, while the barbarian prowled at the gates. By 418 the Visigoths had their capital at Toulouse, but in less than a century the Franks drove them out: Provence today is more Roman than Gothic in heritage.

Brogan, O., *Roman Gaul*, London and Cambridge, Mass., 1953
MacKendrick, P., *Roman France*, London and New York, 1972

I Arles

Arles (Arelate), the earliest Roman foundation (46 B C) in Gaul after the conquest, was planted as a colony for veterans. One of its two most conspicuous monuments is its amphitheatre, 450×350 feet (137×107m) with an arena 230×130 feet (70×40m), which is slightly larger than that at Pompeii. The amphitheatre at Nîmes is almost identical; the architect of both was T. Crispius Reburrus. At Arles there are 60 arches on each of two levels, the lower framed with Doric half-columns, the upper with Corinthian. Pierced consoles held the awning masts. Seating capacity was 21,000 to 25,000, with reserved seats (grooves show a 16-inch space allowance) for religious groups such as worshippers of Gallic Silvanus or Egyptian Isis, and also for shipowners, maritime guilds, and local magistrates. Under the arena are beast cages: deer antlers and boars' tusks were found in them. The amphitheatre is well preserved because it became fortified

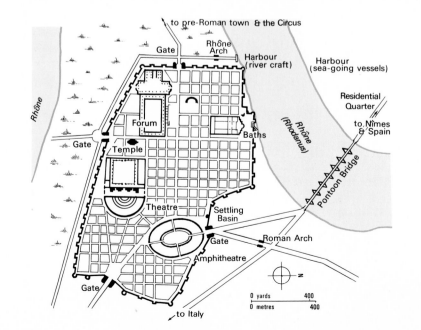

living space in the Middle Ages; two medieval towers appear in the air photograph. After a first phase in wood, part of the colony's circuit wall of 16 BC was demolished to make room for a new stone-built structure. The amphitheatre must be later than the original colony: it is oriented not on the colonial grid but on that of a later quarter. The décor is unfinished, as though interrupted by Vindex's rebellion of AD 68; pottery found under the arena accords well with this date.

The other, more humane monument is the theatre, oriented with the original grid, and therefore built not long after the founding of the colony: a statue of Augustus embellished the centre of the stage building. Between the semi-circular orchestra and the *scaenae frons* was the slot into which the curtain was rolled down before the play began. The sumptuous decoration included green and red marble paving in the orchestra; on the façade were bulls' heads, insignia of Legio VI, for whose veterans Arles was founded. Statues included a Venus, now in the Louvre, Paris, a trio of dancing Maenads, and a Niobid, all illustrating characters in Greek drama. The theatre's size is as impressive as its décor. Its diameter is 335 feet (102m) and it held 7,500, although it was still not as large as the Roman theatres of Lyon or Vienne.

Modern Arles, a city of 30,000, overlies much of the Roman colony. But the *crypto-porticus* west of the theatre, under the *forum*, has been excavated; it consists of three double, parallel tunnels, supported by 50 piers, and arranged in a 'U', measuring 348 × 236 feet (106 × 72m) in length, 13 feet (3.9m) wide and 10 feet (3.3m) high. Waterproofed walls suggest that the tunnels were a grain store; Greek masons – probably Massiliote – left marks in their alphabet cut into the stonework. In the tunnels were found a statue of Augustus and a replica of a shield voted to him in 26 BC, praising his valour, clemency, justice, and piety. A *capitolium* faced the *forum*; the circus lay by the river to the southwest; across the Rhône a portico contained offices like those of the Piazzale delle Corporazioni at OSTIA in Italy. East of the city is centuriation: surveyed plots which made the veterans at Arles men of property.

Constans, L. A., *Arles Antique*, Paris, 1921
Grenier, A., *Manuel d'archéologie gallo-romaine 3*, Paris, 1958, pp. 157–71

Top: Aerial view of the amphitheatre and theatre, Arles, from the northwest
Bottom: The amphitheatre, Arles

2   Nîmes

Nîmes (Nemausus) was an Augustan colonial foundation of about 28 BC on the site of a healing spring. The veterans who settled there apparently came from Egypt: the town's coins – it had its own mint – show a crocodile and a palm tree. Nîmes flourished especially in the reign of Antonius Pius (AD 138–61), whose father's family came from there. The area of the spring was embellished in the second or third century AD with a 'U'-shaped double portico, two temples (to Nemausus, an old water god, and to Rome-and-Augustus), a statue-ornamented fountain house (*nymphaeum*), and a barrel-vaulted building of Hadrianic date (117–38), which may have been a dormitory for pilgrims, as at GLANUM. A small theatre adjoined the spring area in the east; from it stairs ascended to the most striking remnant of Nîmes' circuit wall of 16 BC, one out of nineteen towers: the octagonal Tour Magne, originally 133 feet (40m) high, in three set-back stories. The wall enclosed 550 acres (223ha), but the whole area was not occupied: French archaeologists estimate the peak population at 50,000.

Within the wall, near the crossing of *cardo* and *decumanus*, Agrippa built in 16 BC perhaps the best-known, certainly the best-preserved, Roman temple in France, the Maison Carrée. It rose on the south side of the *forum*, a 460× 230-foot (140×70m) piazza, with the *curia* on the north. Like the *forum*, the temple's length and breadth (86×43 feet; 26×13m), are in the proportion of two to one; its height of 50 feet (15m) was proportionally divided: podium, 10 feet (3m); Corinthian columns, 30 feet (9m); superstructure, 10 feet (3m). The putholes for the bronze letters of the dedicatory inscription make it possible to restore the text: they show that the temple was rededicated in AD 1 or 2 to Augustus' grandchildren Lucius and Gaius, who also had a temple at Glanum. Gaius Caesar was honorary patron of Nemausus. The original dedication, to Rome and Augustus, makes the Maison Carrée one of the earliest monuments of Roman ruler cult in western Europe. The building has since served as assembly hall, dwelling, stable, church, granary, seat of the prefecture, and is now a museum. In Louis XIV's reign it narrowly escaped being moved to Versailles. Thomas Jefferson doted upon it 'like a lover upon his mistress', and copied it for the Capitol of his home state of Virginia.

Nîmes' amphitheatre, about 400 yards (366m) southeast of the Maison Carrée, is nearly the twin of the one in ARLES and was built by the same architect. It was faced with good local stone and laid, without mortar or clamps, over a concrete core. Doric half-columns – not Corinthian as at Arles – flank the arches in the upper tier; 120 pierced consoles held the awning masts. There were 34

rows of seats, in three sections, with 124 exits and 162 sets of stairs. Seats were reserved for the town dignitaries and for the boatmen of the Rhône and Saone. Five radial tunnels facilitated entrance and exit: those on the upper storey have flat arches, giving them a massive, archaic look, though they are of Flavian date. Like that at Arles, the amphitheatre provided fortress-apartments in the Middle Ages.

The water god's city needed more water than his spring could provide. Agrippa brought it from Uzès, 15 miles (24km) away as the crow flies, but the aqueduct covered twice the distance to achieve the right gradient, a fall of 61 feet (18m) in 30 miles (48km). The aqueduct provided Nîmes with about 90 gallons (400 litres) of water per person per day; nowadays 70 gallons is considered enough. About halfway along the aqueduct's course, the arches of the Pont du Gard, by which both pedestrians and water crossed the Gardon river, make up one of the best-preserved, most picturesque, and most famous sections of aqueduct in the Roman world. It stands 176 feet (54m) high; the visitor with a head for heights can walk nearly 1,000 feet (300m) along the topmost slabs, under which ran the water channels, lined with hydraulic cement. Three receding tiers of arches support the channel. The footway,

enlarged for vehicles in the eighteenth century, ran on top of the lowest tier. At each level the arches decrease in width on either side of the central span. The bottom tier, 510 feet (155m) long, consists of six arches, rising nearly 80 feet (24m) above low water; they are 22½ feet (6.7m) thick. The middle tier, 70 feet (21m) high and 868 feet (265m) long, consists of eleven arches, 16 feet (5m) thick. The top tier, 987 feet (300m) long, has 35 arches, 26½ feet (8m) high and 11 feet (3m) thick. The lowest central arch, through which the Gardon flows, is 90 feet (26m) wide. The aqueduct is bowed slightly against the current; the bottom piers, footed in bedrock, have cut-waters. Neither mortar nor clamps are used in the construction: the weight of the stone blocks holds the structure in place. The volume of some of the blocks is as much as 2 cubic yards (about $1.5m \times 1.5m^3$); such a block would weigh 6 tons. The projecting stones visible in the photograph were left on purpose, to support scaffolding for repairs. Letters carved in some of the blocks indicate where they were to be placed in the finished fabric. There are ancient as well as modern graffiti, and one block bears a phallic symbol, a charm against the evil eye. The aqueduct debouches in a settling basin on the *cardo* in Nîmes.

Grenier, A., *Manuel d'archéologie gallo-romaine 3*, Paris, 1958, pp. 143–56; 4, Paris, 1960, pp. 88–101 (Pont du Gard)

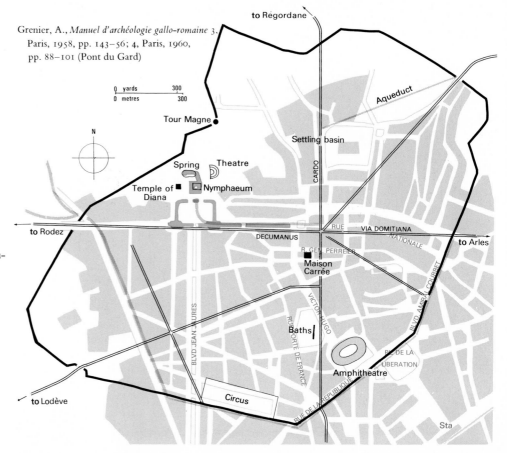

Above: The Pont du Gard

Left: The amphitheatre, Nîmes

3 Orange

Orange (Arausio) was an Augustan colony founded in 36/5 B C for veterans of Legio II. Its most impressive surviving remains are an arch and a theatre. The arch, about 63 feet (19m) high and 65 feet (20m) wide is richly decorated with military and naval motifs: on the voussoirs of the side arches the oak leaves of the civic crown (awarded for saving a fellow soldier's life in battle); in the attic above, trophies: armour, Gallic trousers, harness, saddles, trumpets, battle standards, shields both decorated and inscribed. One motif is Capricorn, Legio II's insignia and Augustus' zodiacal

sign; an inscription reads *Sacrovir*, the name of a Gallic resistance leader who committed suicide in A D 21 after defeat by that legion. These details, plus an interpretation of the put-holes for the bronze letters that once adorned the fascia, date the arch to A D 26, in the reign of Tiberius. Above the inscription on three sides of the arch are friezes of Romans successfully duelling with naked, hairy barbarians. The lateral reliefs above the frieze contain the largest known collection of naval spoils (probably from Actium, a propaganda symbol of Roman defeat of the barbarian):

prows, ramming beaks, figureheads, trident, tillers, anchors, stern ornaments, rigging, gangplanks. Altarlike projections above the naval trophies bear, in relief, sacrificial instruments used in founding colonies. The central voussoirs portray fruit, nuts, ivy, and wheat ears, as on Augustus' Ara Pacis in ROME. Put-holes in and flanking the pediment once supported gilt bronze appliqués – gilt to inhibit verdigris – of a head flanked by cornucopias, and of Tritons. The wide base above the pediment supported a bronze statue of Tiberius in a four-horse chariot. In the relief on the base, infantry and cavalry fight half-naked trousered Gauls, one of whom is trying to hold in his spilled guts with a huge hand. On the arch ends, 30 feet (9m) wide, are reliefs of male and female prisoners chained to trees crowned with arms, as at Carpentras. The overall effect is tumultuous, violent, disorderly, and pathetic, as on the Great Altar of Zeus at PERGAMUM. Here at Orange, Hellenistic realism served the propaganda of Roman power.

The city wall encloses 173 acres (70ha) indicating a possible 38,000 inhabitants. Within it is the theatre, akin in size and date to that of ARLES. Louis XIV called the 121-foot (37m) wall behind the stage – as tall as a ten-storey building – 'the handsomest wall in my realm'. In the permanent architectural stage set there were once 76 columns, a frieze of Amazons, centaurs, a Perseus – all from Greek tragedy; Venus, foundress of the Julian line; Augustus himself, twice life size, as at La Turbie. At his foot is a fragment: a kneeling trousered Gaul appealing to Augustus' well-advertised clemency.

An important find from Orange is a fragmentary marble land survey map of the area around the city, dated A D 77 (Vespasian's reign), decreeing that squatters, often town officials, must restore illegally occupied public land. Frontage, tax per running foot per year, occupant, and bondsman's name were all recorded. Taxes in arrears paid 6 per cent interest. Some of the land was restored to the original owners or their heirs; the most mountainous and least fertile went to native Gauls; some was made communal for grazing. Some uplands, which must have contained quarries, were assessed high; town lots were four times as valuable as farmland. The document, designed to reduce Gallic discontent, well exemplifies the Roman legal mind at work; attention to detail, justice done: the Gauls gained something, the Romans lost very little.

Amy, R., et al., 'L'Arc d'Orange', *Gallia*, Suppl. 16, Paris, 1969

Grenier, A., *Manuel d'archéologie gallo-romaine* 3, Paris, 1958, pp. 172–93

Piganiol, A., 'Documents cadastraux de la colonie romaine d'Arausio', *Gallia*, Suppl. 16, Paris, 1962

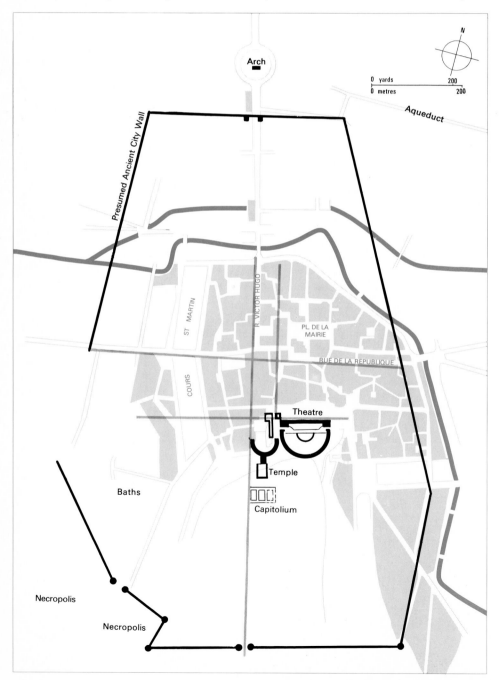

Below: The theatre, Orange

Bottom: Fragment of the theatre frieze, Orange

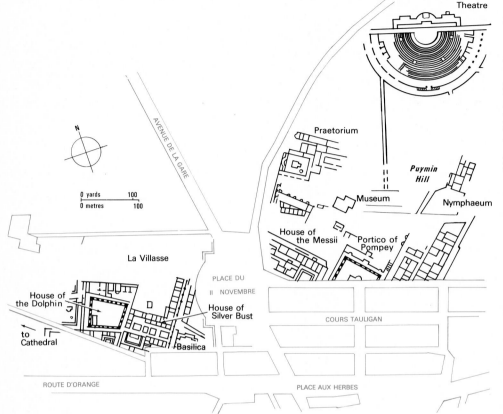

Vaison-la-Romaine (Vasio), a little over 16 miles (25km) northeast of ORANGE, is the Pompeii of Provence. Its excavation was the fruit of nearly 50 years' work by a devoted and gifted amateur, the Abbé (later Chanoine) J. Sautel. The town was the capital of the Vicontii, who lived on the height south of the Ouvèze river, still spanned by a Roman bridge. About 20/19 BC they moved across the river to more level ground, where the Abbé excavated, and there they remained and prospered until the barbarian drove them up onto the height again. Two quarters have been excavated, Puymin and La Villasse.

In Puymin, Sautel excavated the luxurious House of the Messii, with pool, peristyle, mosaic floors, frescoed walls, baths, and latrine. The fresco style is of the first century A D; the baths were added later. The Portico of Pompey is named from an inscribed fragment found in it, recording the gift to the town of this shaded, watered garden, 170 feet (52m) wide, by a municipal officer and priest of Rome and Augustus, the grandson of a Gaul enfranchised by Pompey the Great. The garden has a central pool having in its walls fish nests made of amphoras sawn in half. A niche contained a Roman copy of Polyclitus' Diadumenos, representing an athlete binding back his hair. The marble copy, found in the 1860s, was sold to the British Museum; what the visitor sees

in situ is a plaster cast. The wall in which the Diadumenos stood was originally stuccoed in black, red, and green. Coins range in date from Augustus to Diocletian, i.e., down to A D 305.

There are also blocks of houses that are much more modest in size and décor than the House of the Messii. From the nymphaeum a tunnel led to the theatre. It is smaller than that of ARLES, but was originally adorned with a remarkable number of statues, now in the site museum. One of these is of Tiberius; it has been used to date the theatre in his reign and not later, the argument being that he was so unpopular that statues of him would hardly have been erected after his reign. The year in which the practice of dedicating statues to Tiberius was most in fashion was A D 20/21. There are also statues of members of Tiberius' family; of Hadrian, with a woman who is either his wife Sabina or his mother-in-law Matidia; Venus, Juno, and Apollo; two statues of Bacchus, the patron of drama; and a miscellaneous assortment of hands, arms, feet, legs, and drapery; and various municipal worthies in their best togas.

The theatre has been heavily restored. The restoration provoked allegations of fraud: fake gouges in modern columns, artificial mutilations, ends of blocks deliberately hammered rough, to suggest ancient vandalism. Sautel

rejoined that his restorations saved the theatre from disintegrating, and that only ancient materials had been used in the rebuilding; he made no apology for the planting of shrubs and flower beds. The restoration may have been over-enthusiastic, but the result is charming to the lay eye, and annually brings to Vaison thousands of visitors who would not have crossed the street to see a site austerely left in a condition which only an archaeologist could love. Southwest of the theatre is the praetorium or military headquarters, perhaps incorporating a temple of Isis. It has colourful frescoes in yellow, red, and green. Heaps of oyster shells suggest that the officers had gourmet tastes. Coins show the building was in use as late as A D 244.

La Villasse contained the civil basilica, with an arch, polychrome marble paving, yellow-bordered red frescoes over a green dado, and a latrine with seats for five; the latest coins are of Constantius II, who died in A D 361. Across the cardo is the House of the Silver Bust, with portico and shops facing the street. The bust shows the proprietor as a homely bourgeois. He expanded his holdings westward and swallowed up the adjoining property, adding another peristyle and more rather loud frescoes. An oscilla, which hung in the peristyle, portrays a rabbit eating fruit from a basket. Coins end in 375. The gaily frescoed Atrium House lasted into the reign of Constantius II. One room has a dado with yellow panels bordered in red; above it red panels with white fillets and a black surround; elsewhere, a red or a black dado with a surround of the opposite colour; above, blue panels with red surrounds. North of the large peristyle is the colourful House of the Frescoes, in orange and pink, with representations of animals: leopard, sea horse, deer, lion, wild goat; a man with a doe, and a partridge in mosaic. The House of the Dolphin, with two peristyles and a mosaic floor, is named from a find of a Cupid riding a dolphin. The cathedral, west of La Villasse, is of the sixth or seventh century: its footings are column drums from the Roman city.

The sunlit terraces, green gardens, cool colonnades are typical of Roman urbanism in Provence, 'urban' connoting pleasant living conditions and a sense of community. This civilized urbanity was one of the benefits of Roman rule.

Grenier, A., Manuel d'archéologie gallo-romaine 3, Paris, 1958, pp. 194–210
Sautel, J., Vaison dans l'antiquité, 3 vols. Avignon and Lyon, 1927–42

Street, streetside portico and entrance to the House of The Silver Bust, Vaison-la-Romaine

5   Glanum   **France**

Glanum, just south of Saint-Rémy and 15 miles (24km) northeast of ARLES, began (sixth–fifth centuries B C) as a native shrine. Greeks settled it in the third century B C; the Romans revived it after its destruction late in the second. It lies in a narrow valley below the rocky pine-clad slopes of the Alpilles. Its Hellenistic Greek phase – rarely encountered in the archaeology of Provence – includes the *bouleuterion* (Council House), originally a 40 × 25-foot (12 × 7.5m) building with tiers of seats around the interior wall, as at Hellenistic Priene. The double treasury, opposite the *bouleuterion*, and the Doric portico are proved Hellenistic by coins of the late second century B C from Marseille (Massilia). The portico may have been a dormitory for pilgrims to the shrine. Glanum also has Hellenistic private houses, one two-storied, with a peristyle, pebble-mosaic paving, brightly panelled walls, a latrine flushed with running

water from the pool, and a stable annex. Finds include a statuette of a crouching Negro and an engraved rock-crystal ring.

It was probably the Cimbri who destroyed Glanum. After Marius defeated them, the town revived: it offers one of the few evidences of the Roman occupation before Caesar. There are Roman baths situated to the left of the main street; they resemble the Forum Baths at POMPEII, dated about 80 B C; these, too, have brightly panelled walls, glass windows, a *palaestra*. Excavation also unearthed the *basilica* and the 24 piers of the limestone-faced, porticoed building visible in the upper part of the air photograph. It was stone-paved and measures 135 × 100 feet (41 × 30m). A statue of Augustus adorned the apse. South of it the triumphal monument perhaps commemorated Domitian's German campaign of A D 83. The buildings south of this (9–7 B C) were twin

temples to Augustus' grandsons, Lucius and Gaius. A well between them yielded heads of Augustus' sister Octavia and his daughter Julia. Another building is a shrine to Valetudo (Health) which was dedicated by Augustus' lieutenant Agrippa.

To the north are Roman Glanum's two most important monuments, the Mausoleum and the Arch of the Julii. Under the Mausoleum's conical roof stand the statues of the Julius who commissioned the monument and his wife. He was a rich Gaul, enfranchised by Julius Caesar. The décor he chose advertises him as philhellene: Theseus against the Amazons, Lapiths against Centaurs, the Calydonian boarhunt, the death of Adonis and of the Niobids, the deeds of Patroclus. But all are dressed in the fashion of 40 B C. The arch shows Gallic captives chained to trophies, a Roman freeing a captured Gaul, sacrificial implements.

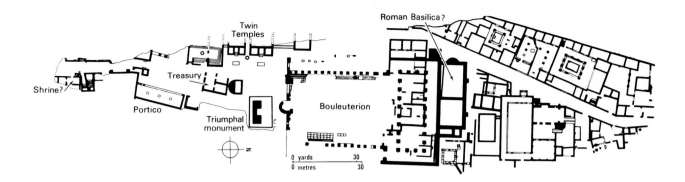

Twin Temples
Roman Basilica?
Treasury
Shrine?
Portico
Triumphal monument
Bouleuterion

0 yards 30
0 metres 30

Framing the archway is a frieze of oak leaves, acorns, grapes and vines, ivy, pine cones, pomegranates, and olive sprays, as on Augustus' Ara Pacis in ROME and on Tiberius' arch at ORANGE.

Rolland, H., *Fouilles de Glanum* I, 1946, II, 1958.
  Supplements to *Gallia* I, II

Arch of the Julii, Glanum

6   Ensérune   **France**

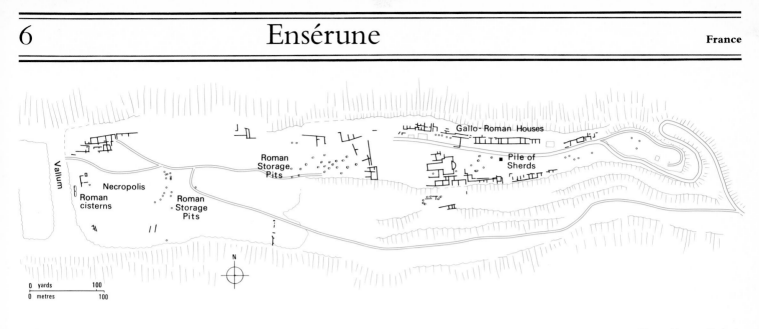

Terraced houses, Ensérune

Ensérune is a typical pre-Roman *oppidum*, on a triangular 37-acre (15ha) plateau 400 feet (120m) above the fertile coastal plain between Béziers and Narbonne. Its earliest level (*c.* 550 BC) was a settlement of wattle-and-daub huts averaging 12 feet (3.6m) across; in the floors were food-storage pits, containing sheep and pig bones, shellfish, loom weights, some stone tools, and handmade pottery. One hundred and fifty years later, in the second phase, the villagers were living in rough stone houses with stuccoed interior walls, on terraces interlinked by stairs. They used waterproof cement to line their cisterns, and built a Cyclopean circuit wall of large irregular stones.

The third phase (from *c.* 225 BC) shows Roman building techniques and pottery, but the language was Iberian. The necropolis yielded weapons (deliberately bent), belt buckles, fibulae, and inexpensive jewelry – but valuable Italian and Greek vases. Influences here were Greek, Celtic, Iberian, and Roman. The earliest pottery is Ionian Greek, then Attic, then South Italian. About 330 BC Roman Campanian ware begins. In the first century BC coins (from Marseille and Béziers) have legends in Greek; later they are in Iberian. The metalwork is both unrestrained and abstract; i.e., Celtic. The use of the Iberian language shows that in pre-Roman times, the Pyrenees were not a cultural barrier.

Roman influence becomes conspicuous after the foundation in 118 BC of Narbo, only 8 miles (12km) away. The natives now imitated Roman building techniques wholeheartedly: waterproof cement, stone paving, tiled roofs, stucco. They did not, however, adopt such Roman comforts as central heating. They used Roman coins and Roman pottery, but not the Latin language. In another century the *oppidum* began to fade away, and it came to an end early in the first century AD.

Jannoray, J., *Ensérune*, 2 vols. Paris, 1955

The Iberian Peninsula

Archaeology in the Iberian peninsula is a record of commercial penetration and slow conquest, hampered by native resistance and by geography. The sea on three sides opens the peninsula to conquest, but inland are stark tablelands, pathless mountains, a severe climate, few roads, and rivers mostly unnavigable. This disunited the natives, but made them harder to conquer, especially by conventional methods. But the peninsula's mineral wealth – gold, silver, copper, iron – made it attractive to trader and conqueror from earliest times.

The cave paintings of Altamira (c. 12,500 BC), with their splendid polychrome animals, probably drawn as hunting magic, show that Spain in the Palaeolithic was as sophisticated as

southwest France (e.g. Lascaux), with which it had obvious cultural links. In Solomon's reign, fabled wealth – gold, silver, ivory, apes, and peacocks – brought ships from the Near East to Tartessus (perhaps Biblical Tarshish), never precisely located, but to be sought somewhere about the mouth of the Guadalquivir (Baetis) river. About 550 BC settlers from Greek Massalia (Marseille), itself a colony of Phocaea in Ionian Asia Minor, founded Emporion (Roman Emporium, modern AMPURIAS).

Punic CARTHAGE had a commercial interest in Spain. Carthaginian interference with ROME's ally Saguntum (modern Sagunto) brought on the Second Punic War, when Hannibal besieged and sacked the city. The Romans rebuilt

it. Its surviving walls show a mixture of native Iberian, Punic, and Roman elements; its theatre (restored), built in the Greek fashion into a hillside behind the city, had a stage sturcture 220 feet (66m) long and seated 6,000.

Rome, spurred on by lust for precious metals, exhausted itself trying to conquer Spain. In 133 BC the centre of Spanish resistance was Numantia, a Celtiberian hill town of 4,000 on the tableland of Old Castile. (Schulten estimates the Celtiberian population before the Roman conquest at about 370,000, half what it is now.) Numantia's Celtiberian level contained adobe huts, thatch-roofed and windowless; these accommodated both men and animals, and had storage cellars. They were

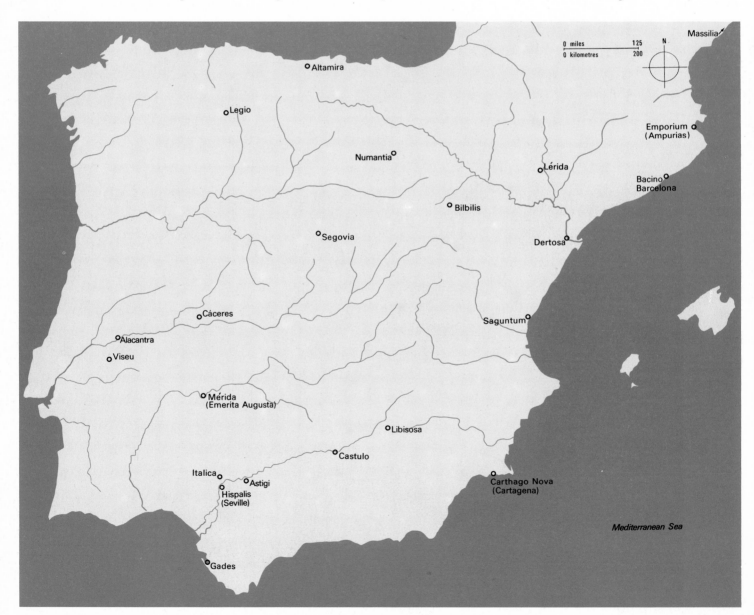

arranged in a rectangular grid and protected by a stone wall 20 feet (6m) thick. Unique pottery portrays horse taming, warfare, duels, dancing, and religious ceremonies. The Roman Scipio Aemilianus enclosed Numantia with works of circumvallation, including seven camps, all of which have been excavated, and starved it out after an eight-month siege. The town survived as a sparsely inhabited shell until Augustus revived it, with tile-roofed houses, drains, mosaics, frescoes, and little peristyles; it lasted until the fifth-century barbarian invasions.

Augustus conquered north of the Tagus river and up to the north coast. The new province of Lusitania (modern Portugal) had MÉRIDA as its capital.

The people of the peninsula lost independence and gained amenities. One of these was the still-functioning aqueduct at Segovia, 60 miles (96km) northwest of Madrid. Its 128 surviving unmortared granite arches run for half a mile (800m) on two levels, rising in the midst of the modern town to over 90 feet (27m). Roman Spain prospered especially under two Spanish emperors, Trajan and his nephew Hadrian, both born in the river port of Italica, 6 miles (9km) northwest of Seville. Italica, founded by Scipio Africanus as a colony for veterans, flourished under its native sons. Its towered walls were nearly 2 miles (3km) around. Its amphitheatre, holding 30,000, was the fourth largest in the Empire, five-sixths the size of the Colosseum at Rome. It was built of brick and stone-faced concrete, with provision for efficient entrance and exit, its stairs were marble-revetted, and there were subterranean cages for the animals that Christians faced here. Italica's grid of streets, 45 to 52 feet (13 to 15m) wide, had drains, sidewalks, and porticoes; its spacious two-storied houses boasted pools, fountains, mosaics, and marble-veneered walls. There were two sets of public baths, fed by a 24-mile (38km) aqueduct. The latest coins date from the fourth century AD, when the barbarians invaded.

The emperor Trajan was responsible for the highest and most famous bridge in the Roman world, across the Tagus at Alcántara, in AD 103: 156 feet (47m) high, on six granite arches. Eleven Lusitanian towns paid for it; a Lusitanian architect built it.

Municipal decline began in the fourth century. Barcino (Barcelona), once a thriving Augustan town, staved off the barbarians with an emergency wall 30 feet (9m) high, with 78 towers, re-using monuments of a more prosperous time, and enclosing 30 acres (12ha), which would have accommodated perhaps 6,600 people. The archaeology of the Iberian peninsula tells a familiar story: the natives resisted; Rome conquered and consolidated by the arts of peace what had been won by the arts of war.

MacKendrick, P., *The Iberian Stones Speak*, New York, 1969
Tovar, A., and Blázquez, J. M., *Historia de la Hispania Romana*, Madrid, 1975
Wiseman, F. J., *Roman Spain*, London, 1956

Ampurias

Spain

I

Ampurias (Greek Emporium, Roman Emporium) on the Gulf of Rosas, Costa Brava, was a Massiliote foundation of about 550 BC. Its polygonal wall, perhaps of the third century, built of huge unsquared stones fitted together without mortar, encloses about 6 acres (2.5ha), and might have held a population of 1,300. Within the wall have been identified a temple of Asclepius, the Greek god of healing, the porticoed *agora* or market place, colonnaded streets, the Council House, a cistern with provision for filtering water through charcoal and sand, a precinct of the Graeco-Egyptian god Sarapis, and peristyled houses. Remains of a catapult show that Greek Emporion did not yield to the Romans without a struggle.

The Romans used Emporium as a base for their interminable Spanish wars. Julius Caesar made it a colony for veterans; the Roman wall, enclosing 48 acres (19ha), would have sheltered over 10,000. On the south, the wall still stands 16 feet (5m) high, built of roughly squared blocks below, concrete above. Outside it was a small amphitheatre, half the size of the Colosseum. Within the wall were shops, a temple of Rome and Augustus, a paved, porticoed *forum* and a *basilica*, combining the functions of law court and covered market. Northeast of the *forum* are two elegant late Republican houses with gardens and mosaics,

Roman mosaic floor of c. 25 BC in one of the excavated houses at Ampurias

the latter restored with trellises, cypress, laurel, and potted aromatic plants. One house had baths, built-in benches, stuccoed walls, and a children's play enclosure. Mosaic motifs include a Greek actor's mask and a partridge pecking at a basket of worms. Part of the city wall was taken down to give the owners a better sea view. This testifies to the security of the Roman peace. In the women's quarters of this house was found the strong-faced portrait of the one-time proprietress, dated, from the hair style, about 25 BC. Another house, though of Roman date, resembles a Hellenistic palace, with its three peristyles, two fountains, and two Greek herms. One peristyle has its stuccoed walls painted black, its columns red, and an altar with a painted cock and snakes drinking from a wine bowl. A third peristyle has a comfortably curved Greek garden seat (*exedra*) a mosaic with black and white stars, and private baths. Roman Emporium adopted Greek sophistication, even here in this little town at the world's end. The barbarians put an end to it about AD 300.

Almagro, M., *Ampurias*, Barcelona, 1967

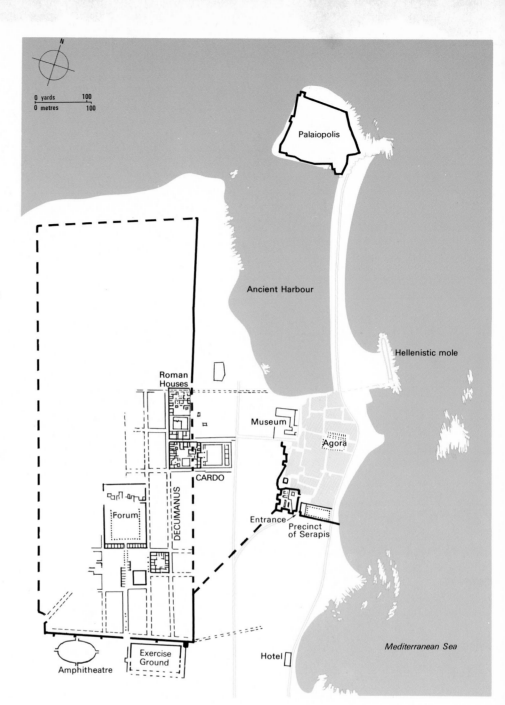

2

Mérida

Spain

Mérida (Emerita Augusta) was the capital of Augustus' new province of Lusitania (northern Portugal). It was founded in 25 BC as a veteran colony by Augustus' lieutenant Agrippa. In the fourth century AD it ranked ninth in size in the Empire, ahead of ATHENS. Its walls ultimately enclosed 123 acres (50ha). The town's monuments include two bridges, a river port, two reservoirs, three aqueducts, drains, temples, theatre, amphitheatre, circus, luxurious private

houses, commemorative monuments, over 200 inscriptions and 70 sculptures. Mérida's main bridge, 2,500 feet (760m) long, has 60 arches. One of the town reservoirs held 350 million cubic feet (10 million m³) of water. The longest aqueduct ran 7 miles (11km); 27 buttressed, cement, brick-faced piers survive, with three stories of arches soaring over 80 feet (24m). Ancient drains, revealed in excavations for new buildings, yield the Roman grid plan. An

inscription of Nero's reign (54–68 AD) identified one temple as dedicated to Mars; the Temple of Concord lies under a building that has been successively convent, prison, and government hotel. Inscriptions and a statue record temples of Sarapis, and of Mithras, the Persian god beloved of sailors and soldiers (Mérida was a river port).

Mérida's theatre, particularly impressive, was built by Agrippa in 27 BC, as an inscription

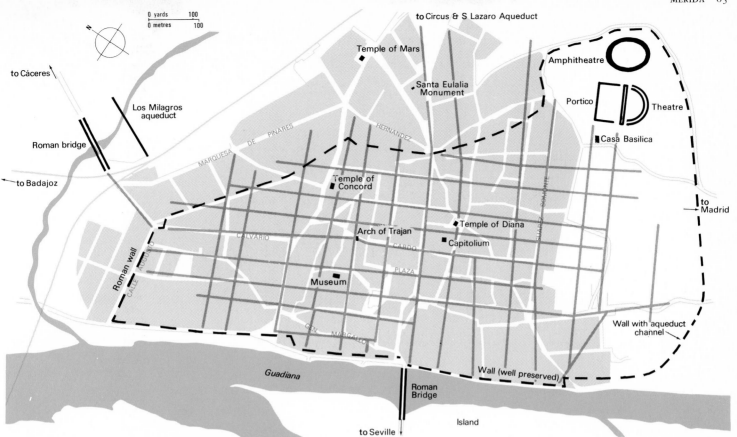

Relief showing woman drawing wine from a barrel, Mérida

over an entrance records. Luxuriously fitted with marble columns, cornices, friezes, statues, and inscriptions, the theatre held 5,500. Upper-class and plebian seats had no intercommunication. The orchestra was paved with blue and white marble. The stage front had alternate rectangular and semicircular niches, with black and white marble mouldings. The ornate stage buildings had three doors and two stories, faced with polychrome marble; its niches held statues of gods and emperors. Behind the stage was the canonical portico for shelter from rain. The adjacent amphitheatre (8 BC) held 15,000; it has rooms for gladiators, and subterranean beast cages. Mérida also had a circus, for chariot races, two-thirds the length of the Circus Maximus in Rome. It seated 30,000, and survived into the fourth century AD. One luxury house was made into a Christian *basilica* and baptistery in the early fourth century. Another house, near the amphitheatre, has an early third-century mosaic of a lively trio treading grapes. Among the finds in the Museo Arqueológico de Mérida is a fine head of Augustus, veiled for sacrifice. In an inscribed relief a tavern keeper commemorates his dead wife, who is portrayed drawing wine into a pitcher from a barrel resting on sawhorses. Mérida, with its luxurious amenities and its humble grave monuments, reveals both the majesty and the earthiness of imperial Rome.

Almagro, M., *Guia de Mérida*, Madrid, 1961

North Africa

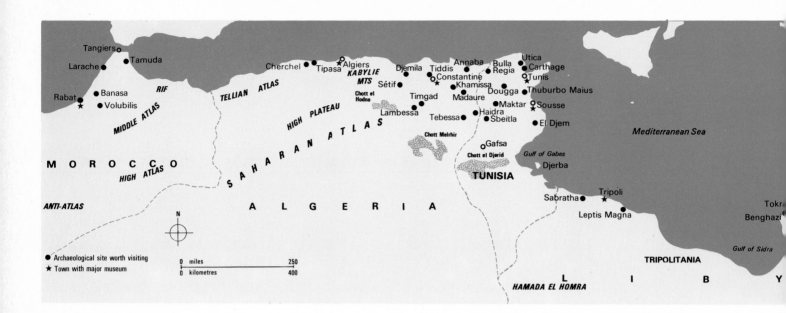

The Phoenicians reached the coast of North Africa in the late second millennium BC. Metal – the silver and tin of Spain – first drew both Levantines and Greeks to the far West and landfalls were made on the coast of the Maghreb from Tunisia to Morocco. Once discovered, such sites became watering places for ships and markets for petty barter with native 'Libyans' (as the Greeks called them). Finally, for a variety of reasons connected with population growth and political unpheavals, from the eighth century BC onward there were quite distinct emigration movements from the Syrian coastal towns, as well as from Greece and the Aegean, toward the west in search of land – to Italy, Sardinia, Sicily, Spain and, to a lesser extent, to North Africa. Thus were born the Phoenician colonies, such as Utica and CARTHAGE in Tunisia, and LEPTIS MAGNA (modern Lebda) and SABRATHA in Tripolitania. At about the same period the Greeks of the island of Thera (Santorin) were settling in Cyrenaica.

By the fifth century BC Carthage had begun to overshadow the colonies within the Phoenician orbit. Then, too, CYRENE, where the first Greek colony had begun to spawn other secondary coastal settlements, first felt the pressure of her neighbour Egypt – an influence that increased until, in the late fourth century BC, the Ptolemaic kings of Egypt controlled the Greek city-states of the African littoral.

The native Libyans not only shared in the early settlements, providing wives, labour, and fighting men, but themselves developed as cohesive, if ephemeral, political forces with their own chiefs and centralized capitals. This was the origin of such inland towns as Cirta

(CONSTANTINE) in Algeria, DOUGGA in Tunisia, and VOLUBILIS in Morocco. While the Libyan kingdoms absorbed Punic (i.e. Phoenician) and later Hellenistic culture, many Punic towns such as Leptis Magna were from the start mixed communities of 'Libyphoenicians'. By the third century BC, as Carthage expanded over much of Tunisia, the Libyan kings, especially Massinissa, acted as the catalyst for Roman intervention in Africa, forming attachments with Roman nobles for their mutual, personal aggrandisement.

The clash between Rome and Carthage, which began in Sicily, ended on the Tunisian plains when Hannibal Barca, greatest of Carthage's generals, was defeated by Scipio at Zama in 202 BC. Eventually Punic Carthage, harassed by Libyan neighbours, was destroyed by Rome in 146 and her possessions formed into the new Roman province of Africa. Soon after, Cyrene, which had been bequeathed as a legacy to Rome by the Ptolemies, was almost reluctantly annexed in the course of the first century BC to form the second North African province.

Although the farm lands of Tunisia and the Tripolitanian coast attracted a stream of Roman and Italian settlers, it was not until the time of Julius Caesar and the emperor Augustus in the late first century BC that a policy of Italian emigration was encouraged. The result was a series of new urban settlements of either Roman military veterans or native communities, granted municipal autonomy. The number of Roman citizens increased dramatically, incorporating Punic and Libyan nobility alongside Roman immigrants. Roman interest in Africa was above all for its agricultural

wealth. Leptis Magna was by the time of Caesar a major olive-oil producer. Tax in kind from the corn lands of Tunisia was a vital supply for the city of Rome by the first century AD. The Roman emperors themselves came to own vast imperial estates, acquired by confiscation.

Meanwhile frontiers pushed southward and westward. Augustus incorporated Numidia (eastern Algeria) into the province of Africa and set up Juba II, a puppet Libyan king, to rule over Mauretania (western Algeria and northern Morocco) with its twin capitals at Cherchel (ancient Caesarea) and Volubilis. Trouble with the Fezzan tribes, followed by a revolt led by a native leader, Tacfarinas, along the southern marches of Tunisia and Algeria, brought Roman arms south and the stationing of a legion at Haidra (Ammaedara), then at Tebessa (Theveste). In the west two new provinces of Mauretania Caesariensis and Mauretania Tingitana were organized after the death of Juba II. During the reign of the Flavian emperors (AD 70–96), after further rebellions, a period of relative peace began. From then on the whole territory was controlled by a single legion, Legio III Augusta, stationed at LAMBESSA (ancient Lambaesis, near Batna) on the line of the Aures mountains. Although further advanced posts were set along the desert routes well to the south and west, civilian Roman Africa stopped at the line of the pre-desert mountains.

As frontiers advanced, so was Roman civilization consolidated by strategically placed towns, some like Tebessa growing because of garrisons, others such as DJEMILA (Cuicul), Sétif (Sitifis) and TIMGAD (Thamugadi), along the edge of problematic, mountain regions, founded as settlements for veterans. Naturally, there were still others (like Dougga) that simply developed out of native centres or (like Khamissa and Madaure on the eastern Algerian border) through a deliberate policy of sedentarization of nomadic tribes.

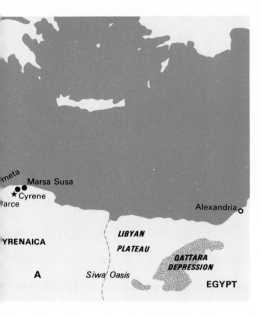

Roman towns were not in the modern sense residential centres. The majority of citizens lived outside the urban area in the rural *territorium*. Only the richer, landed magnates, the local aristocracies who filled the urban magistracies, had town houses – apart from those who serviced the town's amenities and petty industries. The town was essentially a rural centre for markets, religion, entertainment and civil administration. This is why the civic buildings – the law courts, theatres, baths, temples – occupy a disproportionately large sector of the planned sites, sometimes (as at Timgad) as much as a third of the ground plan.

All the towns in Roman Africa tended to develop along uniform lines, becoming, as one Roman writer said, 'a small image and copy of Rome'. The earlier settlements were always based on the *forum*, an open square somewhere near the hub, around which clustered the civic buildings of the court (*basilica*), council house (*curia*) and official temple dedicated to Rome and Augustus or to the Capitoline triad (hence the name Capitol), or to some patron deity. The rest of the town was quartered by the two arterial roads, the *cardo maximus* and the *decumanus maximus*, and parallel minor streets divided the living space into blocks. That, at least, was the theory and the two military colonies of Timgad and Djemila, laid out by military engineers, are examples in different terrain of how such plans were realized. In pre-existing towns like Leptis Magna or Hippo (Annaba), with their harbours and docks, the rigidity of the chequerboard is tempered by curving, irregular, man-made or natural features. Some native settlements, like little Tiddis (near Constantine) or Dougga, never lost their winding streets and confused look.

The greatest period of urban growth came in the later second century and early third century A D under the Antonine and Severan emperors. New town walls and monumental gates often quadrupled the ground area. Large town houses with interior gardens and colonnades were built. Wide colonnaded streets were laid out, linked to the old quarters by triumphal arches and spacious piazzas, abandoning the earlier rigid, criss-cross plan. This is what happened at Timgad, Djemila, Volubilis and – most magnificently of all – at Leptis Magna, home of the African emperor, Septimius Severus.

Later, Roman Africa, although troubled by unrest from the nomadic and mountain regions, was swept by the mass movement of Christianity, which produced new churches and bishops at every community centre. Contrary to a general view, Roman Africa did not go into a decline in the fourth or even the fifth century. In spite of violent episodes, such as the Libyan raids in Tripolitania, huge public baths,

multiple churches and baptisteries, sculptured monuments and luxurious mosaics prove the prosperity of the later empire. Troubles were largely political and social – restless tribes of the interior and the Church split by such heresies as Montanism, Manicheeism and, particularly, Donatism. This was the troubled world of Augustine, Bishop of Hippo in the late fourth century, and the setting for the great Church Council at Carthage in 411 which outlawed Donatism.

In 429 the Vandals crossed from Spain, occupied Carthage, and for a century either ruled or neglected to defend the North African territories against marauding tribes. But in 533 Justinian, emperor of the Byzantine empire, through his generals, Belisarius and Solomon, defeated the Vandal Gelimer in southern Tunisia. For a brief Indian summer the African *diocese*, now divided into seven provinces but much restricted in area, was protected by a series of monumental fortresses built from the debris of the semi-ruined towns. But in the late sixth and early seventh centuries usurpations, church controversies, native attacks and Arab pressure from the east led to a brief transfer of the capital from Carthage to Sbeitla in the south. In 642 Cyrenaica fell, and in 668 the Arab captain, Oqba ibn Nafi, established his camp at Kairouan before sweeping across the southern marches of the Maghreb. It was only a matter of time before 'Ifriqiya' was an Arab country, although the Christian Church remained alive and disputatious until the eleventh century A D.

Broughton, T. R. S., *The Romanization of Africa Proconsularis*, Baltimore, reprint 1968

Charley-Picard, G., *La civilisation de l'Afrique romaine*, Paris, 1959. Details of everyday life under the Roman Empire

Gsell, S., *Histoire de l'Afrique du Nord*, 2nd ed., Vols. I–VIII, Paris, 1929. Still the most respected and detailed work on North Africa up to Augustus

Raven, S., *Rome in Africa*, London, 1969. An entertaining guide by a non-specialist for non-specialists

---

I   # Carthage   **Tunisia**

Carthage is a disappointment. Most successful of the colonial enterprises of the Phoenicians, she dominated the western Mediterranean for centuries as an independent city-state and ultimately as one of the most spectacular cities of the Roman empire. Yet today little remains of her former glory. Located on an easily defensible peninsula of land, much silted up, the site of Carthage and the citadel of Byrsa overlooking the Gulf of Tunis were a natural choice for an immigrant community. Although traditionally founded in 814 by a Tyrian princess, there is nothing archaeologically

earlier than the mid-eighth century B C. Early pottery relics have been found on the foreshore below the Byrsa hill in the *tophet* or burial sanctuary (now romantically named Salammbô after Flaubert's novel), which lies beside the two inland Punic (i.e. Carthaginian) ports. The only other obvious remains of the first city are the chamber tombs scattered over the slopes of the hills adjacent to the Byrsa, stretching from Dermech (region of the present Archaeological Park and Theatre) to the hills of Juno and Ste Monique-Saïda.

Carthage's strength came from her trading

ships, her access to metals and her African manpower which, from the fifth century B C onward, began to dominate southern Spain, Sardinia, western Sicily and the North African littoral from Tripolitania to Morocco.

Carthage's most famous hour was when Hannibal Barca launched his invasion of Italy at the end of the third century B C. But near success turned into disaster and the Punic presence was finally obliterated by the ruthless destruction of the city in 146 B C. Gone are the citadel walls, the multi-storey houses, public buildings, temples and porticoes described by

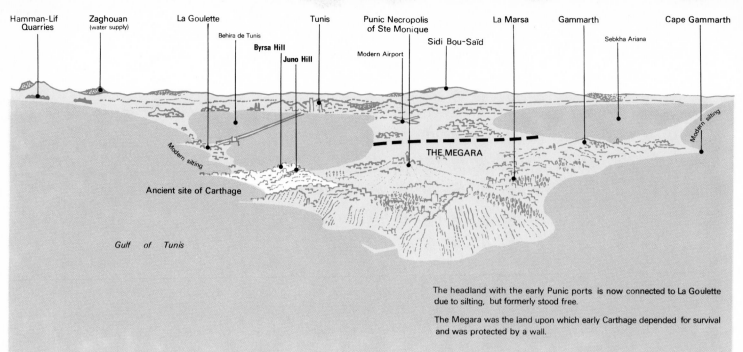

Hamman-Lif Quarries

Zaghouan (water supply)

La Goulette

Behira de Tunis

Byrsa Hill

Juno Hill

Tunis

Punic Necropolis of Ste Monique

Modern Airport

Sidi Bou-Saïd

La Marsa

Gammarth

Sebkha Ariana

Cape Gammarth

Modern silting

Modern silting

THE MEGARA

Ancient site of Carthage

Gulf of Tunis

The headland with the early Punic ports is now connected to La Goulette due to silting, but formerly stood free.

The Megara was the land upon which early Carthage depended for survival and was protected by a wall.

historians. The best of Punic Carthage is now to be found in the museums. For a century the urban site remained empty under a curse, in spite of a semi-abortive Roman settlement in 133 BC.

The new colonization of Carthage, projected by Julius Caesar and carried out by the emperor Augustus at the end of the first century BC, was the beginning of a golden era in which Carthage, now the capital of the Roman province of Africa (roughly Tunisia and part of Algeria), was gradually adorned with all the comforts of Roman civilization, spreading out far beyond the 648 acres (262ha or so) of the original plan. At its peak the population of the built-up urban area, from Byrsa to La Marsa, was about 300,000, although this takes no account of those living in Carthage's unusually extensive rural *territorium*. The period of most intense construction was in the second century AD and early third century, when the great Antonine Baths (*c.* 160) with their accompanying water cisterns, the theatre (mid-second century), the *odeum* or covered theatre (207) and probably many other monumental buildings, such as the amphitheatre and circus, were constructed. Undiscovered yet is the *forum* and administrative centre of the city. The *Capitolium* temple was almost certainly on the site now occupied by the ex-cathedral on the Byrsa hill. Enough of the private residences of the élite of Carthage are preserved in the attractive Archaeological Park and Villa Quarter in the northeastern sector of the grid to give some small impression of the wealth of Carthage, named by some ancients 'the Rome of Africa'. In general, however, we have to be content with artists' reconstructions to imagine such monuments as the Antonine Baths, once the largest Roman baths in Africa and in the world

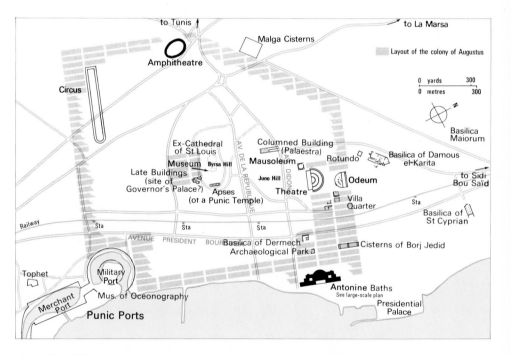

to Tunis

to La Marsa

Malga Cisterns

Amphitheatre

Layout of the colony of Augustus

Circus

0 yards 300
0 metres 300

Basilica Maiorum

Ex-Cathedral of St Louis

Museum

Byrsa Hill

Late Buildings (site of Governor's Palace?)

Columned Building (Palaestra)

Mausoleum

AV. DE LA REPUBLIQUE

Juno Hill

DIDON

Rotundo

Basilica of Damous el-Karita

to Sidi Bou Saïd

Odeum

Theatre

Apses (of a Punic Temple)

Villa Quarter

Sta

Basilica of St Cyprian

Railway

Sta

Sta

Sta

AVENUE PRESIDENT BOUR

Basilica of Dermech

Archaeological Park

Cisterns of Borj Jedid

Tophet

Military Port

Antonine Baths
See large-scale plan

Merchant Port

Mus. of Oceonography

Punic Ports

Presidential Palace

Above: Map of Carthage, showing the Roman town grid. Below: plan of the Antonine Baths

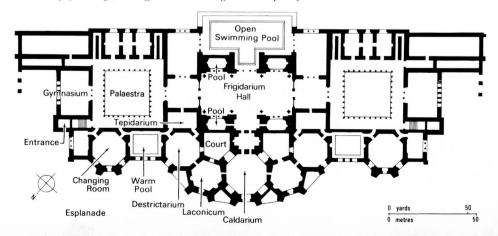

Open Swimming Pool

Pool

Gymnasium

Palaestra

Frigidarium Hall

Tepidarium

Pool

Entrance

Court

Changing Room

Warm Pool

Destrictarium

Laconicum

Caldarium

Esplanade

0 yards 50
0 metres 50

outside Rome, and fed by springs and spectacular aqueducts (still visible) from Zaghouan, but now mere rubble walls of underground cellars.

Almost as prolific in its building activity was later Roman and Byzantine Carthage. In spite of turbulent rebellions and damage in the late third and early fourth centuries A D, docks were reconstructed, public buildings repaired; and, above all, churches were erected. Carthage, the scene of early Christian martyrdoms, influenced a whole progression of church fathers from Tertullian and Cyprian to the great Augustine of Hippo (modern Annaba). Not surprisingly, churches abounded: the Basilica Maiorum, now badly ruined; the magnificently sited Basilica of St Cyprian, where Augustine's mother, Monica, prayed for her son's moral welfare; and, best preserved of all, the Basilica of Damous el-Karita (per-haps a corruption of *Domus Caritatis* – 'House of Mercy').

In 425 Theodosius II ordered the construction of city walls for fear of Vandal and Moorish attacks. But the Vandals swept across Africa in 430 and established an African kingdom, centred on Carthage, that lasted a century, although leaving curiously little mark.

The re-occupation of Carthage by Byzantium in 533 under Justinian's capable generals, Belisarius and later Solomon, led to the Theodosian walls of Carthage being repaired, and the construction of the Mandracium fortress to protect the ports of the city. Its final fall to the Arab invaders in 692 stirred the Byzantine world into brief but vain retaliation.

The Musée National at Carthage on the Byrsa and the Musée National du Bardo in Tunis contain excellent displays of Punic and Roman relics.

Charles-Picard, G., and Picard, C., *Daily Life in Carthage at the Time of Hannibal*, tr. A. E. Foster, London and New York, 1961. Slightly eccentric but good on Punic archaeology

Lapeyre, G. G. and Pellegrin, A., *Carthage latine et chrétienne*, Paris, 1950. The history and archaeology of Roman Carthage

Warmington, B. H., *Carthage*, Harmondsworth and New Orleans, 1964. Mainly a history of Punic Carthage

2 Dougga Tunisia

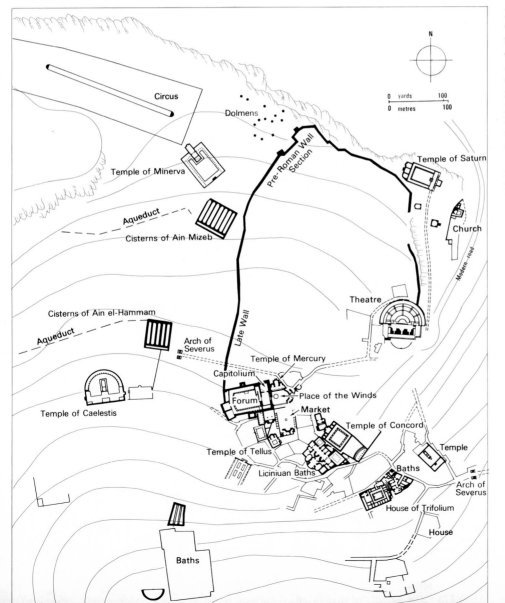

Dougga, about 62 miles (100km) southwest of Carthage, was a prehistoric Libyan settlement that grew in the second century B C to become one of the capital towns of the Libyan king, Massinissa. Thoroughly Punicized in the process, the town was then attached to the administrative district of Carthage in the Roman period and became the centre of the great farming estates of the Medjerda valley, immensely attractive to Roman and Italian settlers who gathered in small communities alongside the native towns. The town, therefore, perched high on the steep side of a valley, is an excellent example of the fusion of Libyan, Punic, and Roman culture in North Africa. Prehistoric dolmens, irregular, winding streets, and Punic-style cult temples and monuments are overlaid by the right-angled regularity of a Roman *forum*, *Capitolium*, market (the 'Place of the Winds'), theatre, baths, and luxury houses. Their excellent state of preservation and the charm of the site itself go some way to make up for the disappointment of Carthage.

Poinssot, C., *Les ruines de Dougga*, Tunis, 1968

Dougga. The Capitolium

3 Volubilis

Situated on a plateau overlooking the fertile Rharb plain and at the foot of the Zerhoun outcrop, Volubilis developed as a strategic meeting point between mountain and plain. The protohistoric tumulus in the centre of the later town was almost certainly a monument venerated by the earliest inhabitants of the site. At least as early as the third century BC, when history records the first 'Mauri' kings in Morocco, there grew a conglomeration of houses, still marked by the irregular line of the pre-Roman walls. Contact with Carthage accounted for the adoption of Punic institutions recorded on early inscriptions. The intervention of Rome in Africa in support of native princes from the late second century resulted in the annexation of northern Morocco and its transfer to the puppet king Juba II in 25 BC. Juba probably established Volubilis as his western capital, enlarging the town to the southwest (mostly unexcavated) and perhaps setting his palace where the 'Palace of Gordian' later stood. Juba's death and the execution of his heir, Ptolemy, provoked a revolt in the western Maghreb. But Volubilis' loyalty to Rome resulted in many grants of Roman citizenship, at the same time as the city became the administrative seat of the newly established province of Mauretania Tingitana.

The earlier Roman buildings were superseded by a building boom that reached a climax in the first half of the third century AD, when the *forum* of the old city was remodelled, the massive triumphal Arch of Caracalla was erected (*c.* 211), the *Capitolium* temple was built overlooking the edge of the *forum* (216), and the superb *basilica* law courts were constructed of grey Zerhoun stone (now being restored) on the east side of the *forum*. At the same time a total reorientation of the city took place, away from the 'primitive incoherence' of the old city of the southern quarter to a new north-eastern residential area of wealthy, Greek-style houses with courtyards and peristyled gardens lining the broad porticoed *decumanus maximus*, which ran out of the 'Tangiers' Gate, and took in the refurbished governor's residence (incorrectly named 'The Palace of Gordian'). The population of the town, however, never reached more than about 10–12,000 and always preserved its essentially rural character – a fact visible today in the many olive presses and grain mills attached to the great houses of the northeast quarter. The fine mosaics and unusual number of excellent bronze statues, from which these and other houses of the city take their names, are preserved in the local site museum or in the Musée des Antiquités at Rabat.

In spite of a dwindling Roman presence in the later empire, Volubilis remained occupied by Romanized Berbers and provided a refuge for Idris I in 788. The site was last known to have been occupied in the tenth century by Spanish refugees; thereafter the stone was robbed to provide buildings for Fez and Meknes.

Étienne, R., *Le quartier nord-est de Volubilis*, Paris, 1960. A detailed study of urban life

Thouvenot, R., *Volubilis*, Paris, 1949

Recent reports in: *Bulletin Archéologique du Comité des Travaux Historiques*, Paris, 1965–6

4   Constantine and Djemila   **Algeria**

Constantine (ancient Cirta), prehistoric refuge, royal Numidian capital, refounded in 44 BC as a Roman provincial capital, has virtually nothing of its history left on view apart from the site itself, perched high on the craggy Oued Rhumel gorge. But the magnificence of that alone, spanned by its bridges, is unforgettable. The Musée de Cirta, however, is filled with discoveries of the region, including a wealth of Roman artifacts from Tiddis, one of several fortified satellite towns ringing Roman Constantine, charmingly situated about 7½ miles (12km) to the north of the city. Although not one of these satellites, Djemila (ancient Cuicul) lay on the road to Sétif some 50 miles (80km) west of Constantine. This native Libyan site on the edge of the Petite Kabylie mountains was an obvious choice for a Roman military veteran colony, founded in the latter years of the first century AD to safeguard the western route through Algeria.

The growth and history of Djemila are largely undocumented but deducible from the layout of the town. The earliest Roman town of the late first and early second centuries AD was clearly that built along the line of the *cardo maximus* running down the ridge of the hillside to the lower north gate. All the other streets would have once been arranged parallel and at right angles to this artery. Central was the porticoed *forum*, shut off by the *basilica*

court on the main street side, and dominated on its north side by the temple of the Capitoline gods (of which only six Corinthian pillars are now preserved). Next to the *forum* was the market, built by a local noble family, where a series of booths opened out into a covered portico, and an official stone table of measures still remains. Many of the local nobility, who were its chief building benefactors, lived in grand houses around the centre, like the House of Europa in the north sector.

The second stage of town development took place in the late second and early third century. It was at this time that the main *cardo* was diverted to a new angle, from the arch of the *cardo* to the south gate, accounting for the curious trapezoidal shape of the temples and houses lining the southeastern side of the *cardo*. But the most important construction of the early third century was the massive and spectacular new town square outside the old south gate. Porticoed on two sides and approached through the great triumphal arch of the emperor Caracalla, it was a perfect setting for the high temple dedicated to the Severan imperial family and it linked up the buildings already constructed in this sector – the theatre, the Great Baths and private mansions, such as the enormous House of Bacchus (named after the large mosaic, now in the museum, found in one of the rooms).

The last phase of expansion was into the southeastern sector – the Christian quarter – much of it dating from the fourth and fifth centuries. Three *basilica* churches, a circular baptistery (fully restored) and the large residential quarters of the bishop, all prove the vigour of the Christian community and the prosperity of the town in a period often supposed to be one of decay.

But for all its splendour, ancient Cuicul always remained unimportant, with a relatively small, mainly rural population of no more than 9–10,000 people, many of them Libyans. Outside the modern museum a collection of religious *stelae* belonging to the temple of Saturn – a cult deriving from worship of Punic Baal – testifies to the strength of native culture.

What happened to Djemila in the period of the Vandal and Byzantine kingdoms is unclear. An inscription suggests Vandals had taken control by 463, and in 553 a bishop of Cuicul is reported as visiting Constantinople. This is our last fixed date, although the town continued to prosper as a market well into medieval times.

Allais, Y., 'Le quartier occidental de Djemila', *Antiquités Africains* v, Paris, 1971, pp. 95–119. A study of new excavations
Février, P. A., *Djemila*, Algiers, 1968

Town plan of Djemila

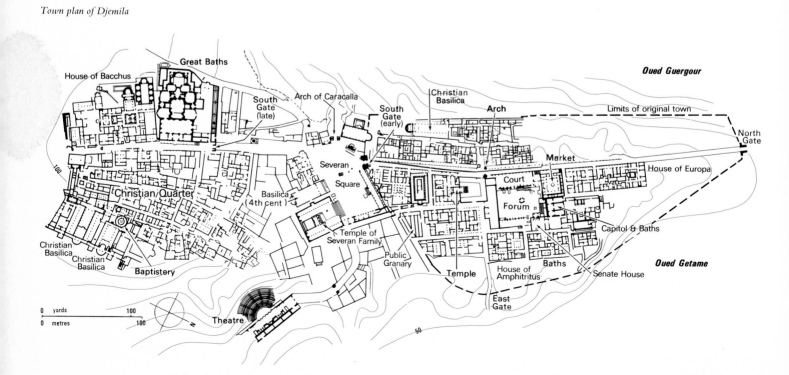

The Oued Rhumel gorge

Djemila. The Arch of Caracalla leading into the new square laid out for the expanding town. The temple of the Severan family is on the right.

5   Timgad   **Algeria**

Timgad (ancient Thamugadi) is the near-perfect model of a Roman provincial town. The 'Pompeii of Africa', its centre resembles a forest of stone, laid out in chessboard fashion almost an exact square of 1,200 Roman feet each side – an archaeologist's paradise but a town without a soul. The town visible today was founded as a Roman settlement for veterans of Legio III Augusta in AD 100 by order of the emperor Trajan and constructed by military engineers from nearby LAMBESSA (Lambaesis). It was only one of a series of strategic towns sited along the corridor plain just north of the Aures mountains to block the passes.

The *cardo maximus* enters from the north gate and runs straight to the *forum*, where it is crossed by the *decumanus maximus*, almost exactly quartering the town, and the building blocks or 'islands' (*insulae*) are absolutely regular in shape and number; yet in spite of this regularity and planned development, the final result was not quite perfect. On the western

side only five instead of six rows of 'islands' exist. Surprisingly enough, although the original plan had its duly allocated sector for such public buildings as the *forum*, *basilica* law court, council house (*curia*), and theatre, within five years of the foundation the huge temple of the Capitoline triad was built outside the urban confines in the southwestern suburbs, completely unaligned with any of the criss-crossing streets. Soon afterward public baths, too, were built outside the main north gates.

Within a hundred years completely new boundaries, today marked by the two distant gateways on the east and west of the town, incorporated a huge area four times the size of the original. In the southern and western suburbs the *decumanus maximus* was extended as a broad porticoed avenue, bending northward but blended into the old chequerboard plan by the most famous of all Timgad's monuments, the so-called Arch of Trajan. This magnificent triple triumphal arch, set at a slight angle to the old *decumanus*, obviously

had nothing to do with Trajan. The southwestern extension was probably part of a unified plan developed in the early third century AD by the wealthy town magnate, Marcus Plotinus Faustus Sertius, whose enormous house occupies the southwestern corner of the old town and who was himself responsible for the large colonnaded market near the great arch.

The population of the town and territory at its greatest was at most no more than 15,000, a fairly ordinary provincial centre, but containing some wealthy citizens who provided the town with its amenities: a charming library in the northeastern quarter, a double-apsed market in the southeastern quarter, and above all its baths; at least twelve public baths, several of considerable size. Scratched into the *forum* paving are the appropriate words 'Hunting, bathing, gaming, laughing – that is living'.

One of Timgad's rare mentions in history was as a centre for the Donatist religious heresy of the later fourth and early fifth centuries,

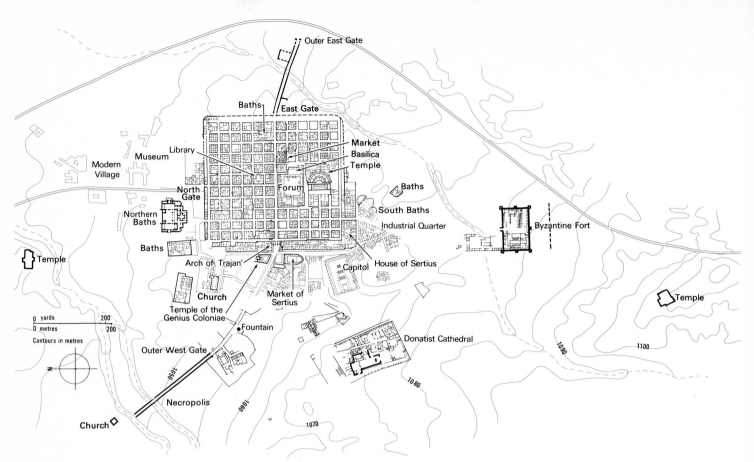

Outer East Gate
Baths
East Gate
Market
Basilica
Temple
Library
Museum
Modern Village
Baths
Forum
North Gate
South Baths
Northern Baths
Industrial Quarter
Baths
Byzantine Fort
Temple
Arch of Trajan'
Capitol
House of Sertius
Church
Market of Sertius
Temple of the Genius Coloniae
Fountain
Outer West Gate
Donatist Cathedral
Necropolis
Temple
Church

0 yards 200
0 metres 200
Contours in metres
N

1050
1060
1070
1080
1090
1100

Below: Timgad. View from the west end of the town, showing the 'Arch of Trajan', forum and theatre, with the Aures Mountains in the background

when Optatus the bishop organized a band of 'Circumcellions' – itinerant harvesters – to attack the Catholic opposition. The enormous cathedral of Optatus, his house complete with an inscription, a baptistery and a whole complex of buildings in the cathedral precinct, have been identified in the southwestern suburbs beyond the *Capitolium*. A second reference was by the historian Procopius to the Byzantine fort of Timgad, relic of the sixth-century revival of Africa by Justinian's general Solomon. This, the finest preserved of all Solomon's constructions, was built on top of an earlier third-century extravagance of water gardens, temples, and porticoes, constructed probably to mark the visit to Timgad of the African emperor Septimius Severus.

The final fate of Timgad is unknown, although life continued to exist there for at least another century.

By the north entrance of the town stands the modern Musée Archéologique, a display gallery for the mosaics of the town, distinctive for their intricate designs and representative of an important local art.

Courtois, C., *Timgad, antique Thamugadi*, Algiers, 1951

Lassus, J., 'Une opération immobilière à Timgad', *Mélanges Piganiol*, III, Paris, 1966, pp. 1221–31. Summarizes recent research.

6 Lambessa

Algeria

Lambessa, the ancient Lambaesis, lies about $12\frac{1}{2}$ miles (20km) west of Timgad. It commands the El-Kantara gap between the Aures and the Hodna ranges, the military heart of Roman Africa, headquarters of Legio III Augusta from the early second century AD until it was disbanded in the late third century. This, the last camp it occupied, is three-quarters exposed to view, presenting a ground plan of barracks, officers' quarters, granaries, and water cisterns. But most striking of relics is the four-way arch, wrongly called the *praetorium*, an enormous rectangular building, 75 × 118 feet (23 × 36m), rising two stories high, built in the mid-third century as the monumental gateway to a large headquarters building complex (*principia*). The *principia* consisted of a large paved and porticoed square lined with various rooms, rising on the south side by steps to a platform which probably opened onto a long *basilica*. This was the sanctuary of the regimental standards, behind which lay a number of rooms (*scholae*) used for the military guilds (*collegia*) that grew up in the third century. Behind the *principia* were baths, shops, and other buildings now covered by a modern prison of French origin. Outside the ramparts are an amphitheatre and yet more baths.

Cagnat, R., *L'Armée romaine d'Afrique*, 2nd ed. Paris, 1912

Lambessa. The Headquarters building (principia) *of the Roman legionary camp. Only the entrance hall remains standing*

7 Leptis Magna and Sabratha

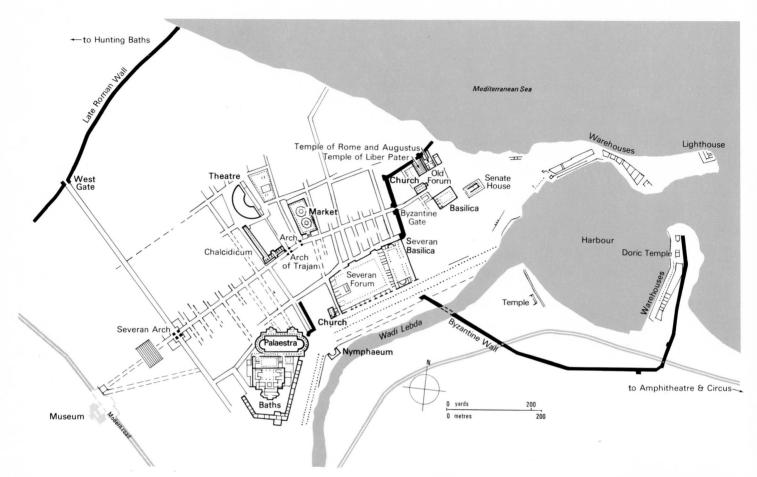

Two basic facts governed the growth and development of Leptis Magna (modern Lebda): its geographical position and its most famous son, Septimius Severus, Roman emperor 193–211. Together with Oea (modern Tripoli) and Sabratha – the Three Cities or Tripolis – Leptis was the entrepôt for the rich corn and olive coastal regions which the ancients named Emporia, as well as a natural outlet for the exports of slaves, semi-precious stones, and wild animals from the Libyan interior.

By the seventh century BC Phoenician settlers first realized the value of this port on the Wadi Lebda, thereby stamping a character on the population that remained long into the Roman period. Otherwise the foundations of an early warehouse, some Punic graves, neo-Punic inscriptions, and statuary are all that survive from six centuries of Phoenician and Carthaginian occupation.

After the fall of Carthage and a period of Libyan rule, the Tripolitanian towns were incorporated into Roman Africa. The earliest Roman buildings clearly replaced the pre-

Above: Town plan of Leptis Magna. Below: Sabratha. The restored stage and proscenium of the theatre

Leptis Magna. The Severan basilica *(left) and one of the carved pilasters (above)*

Roman town centre near the west harbour; that is, the *forum* itself (paved *c.* 5 BC), the two temples on its west side and the old *basilica* on its east side (later rebuilt). From the old *forum* area the Roman city expanded southward along the line of the main road (*cardo*) toward the market (9–8 BC), the *Chalcidium* (probably another market, AD 11–12), and the theatre (AD 1–2). Already one can detect some of the wealth of citizens like Annobal Rufus, who donated the superb market and theatre. The market with its octagonal pavilions, carved display counters, and standard measures, is one of the best in Africa. The theatre can be judged by the famous reconstructed one at Sabratha. Soon after, an amphitheatre (under excavation), the largest in Africa, was built about half a mile (800m) to the east of the harbour.

The second phase of Roman building was in the second century AD (as also at Sabratha), when Leptis expanded still farther south and west, including the four-way triumphal Arch of Trajan on the main *cardo* (called the 'Triumphal Way'), a massive new public baths with colonnaded sports ground (*palaestra*) along the Wadi Lebda and the finely preserved Hunting Baths (so-named after its stucco paintings) on the western edge of the town.

But the greatest phase of building was in the early third-century period of the Severan emperors, when Septimius Severus himself and many important Roman court figures hailed from Leptis or towns in Africa. Severus granted Leptis the status of an Italian (tax-free) city and clearly inspired the magnificent marble-faced complex of *forum*, *basilica*, and colonnaded street along the Wadi Lebda. The whole work was crowned by the triumphal four-way Arch of Severus at the southern entrance of the town (there is a model in the local museum). Marble for the new Severan *forum*, *basilica*, and arch was carved by Levantine Greek master craftsmen (probably from Aphrodisias in Asia Minor), the best of which is now in the Archaeological Museum, Tripoli. Most, however, is laid out along the ground or, like the 'lacework' of the *basilica* pilasters, is still *in situ*. Severus, too, may have been responsible for the fine harbour warehouses, the lighthouse, and the new circus for horse racing, near the amphitheatre.

So much of Leptis remains unexcavated that generalizations about a decline or about population sizes are unwise. The late Roman wall on the west side is evidence of raiding Libyan tribes in the late third and fourth centuries,

but the 'Nile mosaic' from a seafront villa of the fourth century proves that luxury spending continued. Leptis was briefly occupied and damaged in the later fourth and fifth centuries by Libyan tribes and invading Vandals. When Belisarius landed in Tripolitania in AD 533, the sand was encroaching on the buildings. The Byzantine walls and monumental gateway, visible around the *forum* area, were part of the fortifications of the strategically important harbour, incorporating the Severan *basilica* (converted into a church).

After a century of Byzantine rule, the Tripolitanian towns were occupied by the Arabs. Stone columns and blocks were robbed to adorn nearby mosques and tombs until European adventurers began to export them. And finally the sand took over.

Bianchi Bandinelli, R., *The Buried City: Excavations at Leptis Magna*, tr. Ridgeway, D., London and New York, 1966. Excellent pictures and information on recent discoveries

Haynes, D. E. L., *Antiquities of Tripolitania*, London, 1955

New work in the reports of: The Society for Libyan Studies, London

8 Cyrene

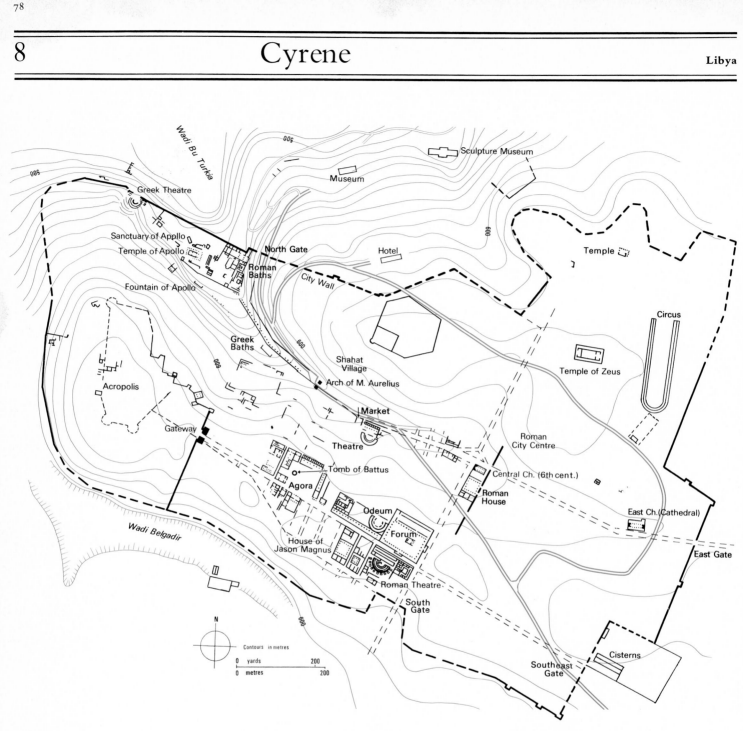

Wadi Bu Turkia

Greek Theatre

Sculpture Museum

Museum

Sanctuary of Apollo

Temple of Apollo

North Gate

Hotel

Temple

Roman Baths

Fountain of Apollo

City Wall

Greek Baths

Circus

Acropolis

Shahat Village

Arch of M. Aurelius

Temple of Zeus

Gateway

Market

Theatre

Roman City Centre

Tomb of Battus

Agora

Central Ch. (6th cent.)

Roman House

Wadi Belgadir

Odeum

East Ch. (Cathedral)

House of Jason Magnus

Forum

East Gate

Roman Theatre

South Gate

Cisterns

N

Contours in metres

0 yards 200

0 metres 200

Southeast Gate

The story of Cyrene's foundation by Greek emigrants from Thera (Santorin) led by their king 'Battus' in about 631 BC, is recounted by the Greek historian, Herodotus. The charming site, high on the terraced hills overlooking the fertile agricultural plain, was revealed by friendly Libyans, whose early assimilation and assistance provided the colony with wives, rural labour, and a valuable barter in the wild, medicinal herb (now extinct) called *silphium*. The great Doric temple of Apollo, whose fine columns of local limestone have been partially restored, marks the earliest site in a cleft between two spurs of a plateau alongside the life-giving spring, named after the nymph Cyrene. The sanctuary of Apollo, as the religious centre of the colony, was linked by a Sacred Way to a

southern spur of the plateau above, where the *acropolis* (fortified refuge) and *agora* (civic and market centre) were located.

Once established, Cyrene gave rise to other colonies in Libya, such as Euhesperides (Benghazi) and Apollonia (modern Marsa Susa, the port for Cyrene), which all became known as the 'Five Cities' or Pentapolis in the third century BC, when the whole of the region was brought under the control of the Ptolemies of Egypt. Most interesting of all the Hellenistic or Ptolemaic buildings is the Greek baths, cut into the rock behind the portico that lines the Sacred Way.

Cyrenaica passed bloodlessly from Egyptian to Roman hands in the first century BC, but her part as a province in the Roman empire was

of small significance. The major episode in her history was the bloody outbreak of the great Jewish Revolt of AD 115, fired by the large Jewish communities of the diaspora along the Levantine coast, which swept through Cyrene, creating immense damage still traceable today.

The empire was a period when the Greek and Hellenistic city took on Roman dress and mores, but without ever losing her essential Greekness. Many of the older sites such as the sanctuary of Apollo and the *agora* were reconstructed, the Greek theatre was turned into an amphitheatre, and a new entrance *propylaeum* to the sanctuary was designed to accommodate the large Roman Baths of Trajan (early second century AD). After the Jewish Revolt the centre of the city shifted from the *agora* and

acropolis toward the east and north where the major Roman roads crossed. The circus on the North Hill and the massive temple of Zeus (in spite of its archaic Doric appearance) were probably both constructed at this time. Adjoining the *agora* the large house of the Cyrenian magnate, Tiberius Jason Magnus, demonstrates the wealth of the city's élite. Finally the porticoed *forum* (or Caesareum, now impressively restored) and law court was constructed together with the Roman theatre, to form the eastern end of a monumental complex of buildings, stretching from the *agora* and approached by the two Roman *propylaea* (gateways) at either end. At its greatest, however, the city never covered more than about 9 square miles (24km²) nor exceeded an urban

and rural population of roughly 30,000.

Cyrene's loss of status as provincial metropolis in the later empire, followed by a terrible earthquake in 365, was responsible for a good deal of permanent damage. Christian churches and private houses, however, continued to display signs of wealth. The cathedral church (and baptistery) at the extreme east end of the area was one of a number in the later city. But the Byzantine city of the sixth century was under pressure from the Berber tribes and contracted behind walls surrounding the market area. It finally fell into Arab hands in 643, although it remained relatively unchanged until the Hilals swept across North Africa in the eleventh century.

Apart from the city itself, there are thousands

of tombs surrounding the site, some still used as houses by the poor. Especially interesting are the Doric and Ionic façades of those tombs cut into the rock, which, together with the monumental sculpture in the Museum of Antiquities, testify to the essential Greekness of Cyrene for all its Roman veneer.

Chamoux, F., *Cyrène sous la monarchie des Bathades,* Paris, 1953. Mainly concerned with the early history of Cyrene

Goodchild, R. G., *Cyrene and Apollonia,* 2nd ed., London, 1963

Sicily

Sicily is an island just under 10,000 square miles (26,000km²) in area, not much bigger than nearby Sardinia. In antiquity it was famous for its fertility – wheat, olives, vines, fruit – and for its forests, especially in the mountainous regions stretching from Mount Etna west and south to AGRIGENTO. It is otherwise poor in natural resources, lacking metals and hard building stone; it is subject to earthquakes; and in Mount Etna (10,750 feet; 3,270m) it has the highest volcano in Europe, never completely dormant.

The fertility of the island coupled with its crossroads location in the Mediterranean – 2 miles (just over 3km) from Italy at the Straits of Messina, less than 100 miles (160km) from Africa at the nearest point in the west – have given it an otherwise surprising historical importance. Greeks, Phoenicians, Italians, Jews, Vandals, Saracens, Normans, Spaniards and others have at one time or another migrated to Sicily or seized control of it. Prehistoric settlements began in the Stone Age, perhaps before 20,000 BC, but its history began with the arrival of the first Greeks and Phoenicians in

the eighth century BC. They found three peoples in possession: Sicels in the eastern half, Sicans in the west, and Elymians in the northwest. Eventually the island became fully Hellenized, and it remained Greek in its language and culture until the Arab conquest in the ninth century AD. Great poets and playwrights, such as Pindar and Aeschylus, visited Sicily as an integral part of their Greek world; it produced one great philosopher, Empedocles of Acragas (AGRIGENTO), in the fifth century BC, and the greatest Greek scientist, Archimedes of SYRACUSE, in the third; its Christian communities had close affinity with the Eastern church.

The monumental remains of ancient Sicily are, therefore, largely Greek, despite Roman and Christian modifications to individual buildings, and apart from the characteristically Roman amphitheatres. Their distribution, however, does not give a correct picture of the dominant pattern of settlement and power in antiquity. Messina and Catania, for example, both old Greek cities, lack ancient remains because of massive destruction by earthquake (Messina most recently in 1908) or by the

eruption of Mount Etna (Catania in 1693). Palermo, on the other hand, a Phoenician foundation, did not become significant until the Roman period (when it was Panormus), and from Arab times it has been the capital of Sicily, repeatedly built and rebuilt on a scale and in a style appropriate to its status and growing size (more than 500,000 inhabitants today).

Greek immigrants began to establish themselves in Sicily before 750 BC, and more came in successive waves for two centuries. Although historians call this movement 'colonization', the new communities were politically independent from the start, and they were characteristically Greek: in their location on, or just off, the coast, their political organization and their development, their desire for local autonomy. During the sixth century BC most of the communities were ruled by 'tyrants', as in Greece itself, men who managed to seize power and who tried to establish dynasties. But then the histories of Sicily and Greece diverged – except for the second half of the fifth century BC, tyrants were the norm in Greek Sicily.

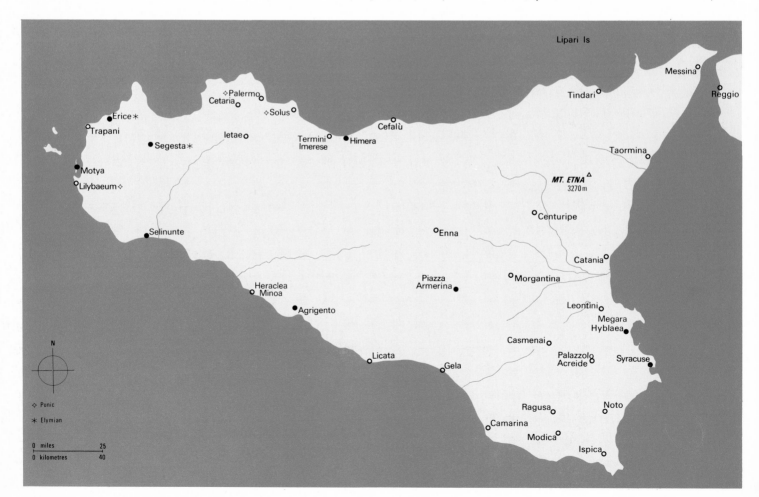

Although it may be true, as Voltaire remarked contemptuously, that under its tyrants Sicily 'at any rate had counted for something in the world', the price was high. Sicilian tyranny meant continuous violence, in both internal and external affairs: wars of expansion; massacres, expulsions and transplantations of people; the injection of mercenaries, a disruptive force, into the communities. By the mid-fourth century BC, for example, the island had become so depopulated that, when Timoleon of Corinth, starting with a small mercenary force, succeeded in unseating most of the tyrants and taking power in Syracuse himself, he had to sponsor a large new immigration into Sicily, perhaps as many as 60,000, in order to re-create a viable, prosperous society. Tyranny was eventually converted into monarchy, on the model of the new Hellenistic states to the east, and then the Romans put an end to independence in 212 BC. Never since has there been an independent Sicily, except in the remarkable years of Norman rule (1071–1194).

Tyranny received much impetus in Sicily from its crossroads position, its attraction for powerful neighbours, Etruscans, Carthaginians, and finally Romans. Although actual Phoenician settlement in Sicily was severely restricted to small coastal points in the west, selected as ports of call between North Africa and southern Europe, there were moments when Carthage seemed on the verge of controlling the whole island. Indeed, Carthaginian invasions were frequent enough to tempt historians into seeing the struggle against Carthage as the main thread of Greek Sicilian history, as an irrepressible 'racial' conflict. The temptation must be resisted. There were long periods of peace, during which trade with North Africa was essential for the wealth and prosperity of Selinus (SELINUNTE) and Acragas, for example, and during which there were enclaves of Carthaginians in Syracuse, of Greeks in MOTYA. And Greeks who felt themselves threatened by other Greeks did not hesitate to call on Carthaginian military assistance (as they later appealed to the Romans and the Arabs).

Thus, the first Carthaginian invasion was in response to a request from Terillus, who had been unseated as tyrant of HIMERA, supported by Rhegium and probably by Selinus, against the growing power bloc of Syracuse and Acragas. The scale of the Carthaginian effort is probably to be explained by unsettled conditions in the western Mediterranean as a whole. A great armada, which took three years to prepare, was virtually destroyed at the battle of Himera in 480 BC. In the same year, a similarly massive Persian invasion of Greece was defeated in the Bay of Salamis, and the legend grew that the two Greek victories occurred on the same day: 'gathering back Hellas from the weight of slavery' the poet Pindar wrote. Carthage returned to the attack late in the fifth century, wreaked much destruction, and by 378 BC more or less divided authority over the island with Dionysius I of Syracuse. A generation later, Timoleon barely rescued Sicily from total Carthaginian rule, and at the end of the fourth century, Agathocles of Syracuse turned

the tables and invaded North Africa, but was compelled to abandon his effort in 306 because his home base had become insecure. The final episode began when Roman legions came to Sicily in 264 on the invitation of the Mamertines, mercenaries from Campania in Italy who controlled Messina. That step initiated two long, savage wars with Carthage, known as 'Punic Wars' from *Poeni* (Phoenicians), the Latin name for the Carthaginians. The first (264–241) was fought in Sicily, at great cost to the islanders, the second (218–201) in Spain, Italy and Africa as well, and it left Sicily wholly in Roman control after the capture of Syracuse in 212.

Sicily thus became the first Roman possession outside Italy, the first Roman province. The chief Roman interest, apart from power itself, was in grain and in land. The tithe, paid in kind, became a major source of food for Roman armies and later for the populace in the city of Rome. Confiscations of land, especially during the Roman civil wars, led to large holdings by some Romans, usually as absentees, with the emperor himself by far the most prominent in the end. And eventually, by a process we cannot trace, the popes matched the emperors in their Sicilian possessions. The majority of the landowners, however, like most townsmen, remained Greek Sicilians, some among them also owners of large estates. One consequence was that Sicily saw two of the three great slave revolts of antiquity, the first *c.* 139–132, the second *c.* 104–100 BC. The numbers involved may have approached 100,000; though they failed, they had sufficient temporary success, even against Roman legions, briefly to establish monarchies modelled on the Hellenistic.

As in all their provinces, the Romans allowed much local autonomy, so long as taxes were paid and no opposition arose, and they did not interfere in cultural matters. Roman Sicily was a quiet, fairly prosperous backwater for several centuries, until it became involved in the turbulent last centuries of the Roman Empire. For example, it suffered raids by the Vandals and even fell briefly, but loosely, under their control. Then, when the Byzantine emperor Justinian began to reconquer some western imperial territories, Sicily fell easily to his general Belisarius in 535, and became a Byzantine province. That strengthened the attachment of Sicily to the Greek East and the Greek church, though the popes were left to enjoy their landed estates, until they were confiscated early in the eighth century. One Byzantine emperor, Constans II, faced with a near civil war, even moved his capital to Syracuse, where he was assassinated after five years, in 668.

The early centuries of Sicilian Christianity are poorly documented. There are few authenticated Christian personalities in the first three centuries, other than three or four martyrs, and no Christian burials can be dated much before 200. However, the rapidity with which Christianity spread after Constantine's 'Edict of Toleration' (313), especially in the cities, suggests that there was a strong foundation in the period of illegality. Bishop Chrestus of Syra-

cuse attended the Council of Arles in 314, and by the end of the sixth century there were at least twelve bishops on the island. Catacombs and other burial places are so numerous and well developed that Sicily has been called 'the classic land of early Christian funerary architecture'.

The end of ancient (or, at least, Byzantine) Sicily was the work of the Arabs of North Africa and Spain. In 827 the Aghlabid emir of Tunisia was invited to accept Sicily as a province by a rebel against the Byzantine emperor. He accepted, and a pitiless war followed for half a century, ending with the capture of Syracuse in 878. Although Taormina held out until 902, and Rometta in the mountains west of Messina until 965, Syracuse was the key, as always in antiquity.

Finley, M. I., *Ancient Sicily to the Arab Conquest*, London and New York, 1968

Führer, J., and Schulze, V., *Die altchristliche Grab-stätten Siziliens*, Berlin, 1907

Guido, M., *Sicily: An Archaeological Guide*, London and New York, 1967

Koldewey, R., and Puchstein, O., *Die griechischen Tempel in Unteritalien und Sicilien*, 2 vols, Berlin, 1899

Pace, B., *Arte e civiltà della Sicilia antica*, 4 vols, Rome and Naples, 1936–49 (2nd ed. of Vol I, 1958)

Touring Club Italiano, *Sicilia*, Milan, 1968. A model, 791-page guidebook

Founded in the middle of the eighth century BC, in a district in which human habitation went back to Neolithic times, Syracuse was throughout antiquity the first city of Sicily, until the Arab conquest in AD 878 gave the pre-eminence to Palermo. Its economy rested on the splendid double harbour, a fertile hinterland and the limestone subsoil, which was extensively quarried. (The ancient quarries, known by an Italianized form of the Greek word, *latomie*, are now among the attractions of the city.)

From the outset, Syracuse was aggressive and expansionist in a way not easy to explain. Alone among the early Greek settlements on the east coast of Sicily, Syracuse adopted a hostile policy toward the native Sicels, subjecting those in their immediate territory to compulsory labour, driving others into a 'reservation' in the southeastern corner of the island, and founding three strongpoints, at Acrae (now Palazzolo Acreide), Casmenae, and Helorus, to hold them in check. Steady growth in population required an early expansion from the original base, on the narrow island of Ortygia, 1,750 yards (1,600m) long, to the mainland, with which Ortygia was linked by a causeway about 550 BC. Growth continued, as is archaeologically demonstrated by the cemeteries as well as the monumental remains, until Syracuse eventually rivalled Athens as the most populous city-state of the classical Greek world, with perhaps 250,000 inhabitants. On the mainland the centres of population were the districts of Achradina and Neapolis (New Town'), the latter containing the major monuments.

Little is known about the detailed history of Syracuse until Gelon, tyrant of Gela, seized the city in 485, transferred his base and more than half the population of Gela there, and made himself the most powerful individual in the Greek world, perhaps in all Europe. In 480 he led a coalition in a famous victory over the Carthaginians at HIMERA. In celebration, Gelon began the construction of two great Doric temples, one at Himera itself, the other, dedicated to the goddess Athena, in Ortygia. The latter has columns $28\frac{1}{2}$ feet (8.7m) high, resting on a platform $170\frac{1}{2} \times 72$ feet (52×22m); it extends over roughly the same area as two older, narrower, and architecturally far less mature temples in Syracuse, one to Apollo in Ortygia, built about a century before, the other to Olympian Zeus in the Anapus valley outside the city, begun about 560. Built of local limestone, the temple of Athena was richly decorated with imported marble; later, panel paintings and doors studded with gold nails and ivory carvings were added, creating an effect of great sumptuousness and wealth. In the seventh century AD, perhaps under Bishop Zosimus, the temple, already turned

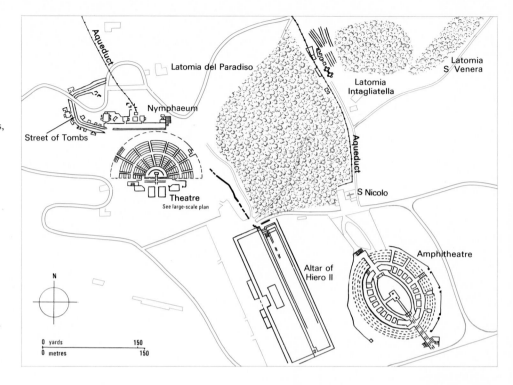

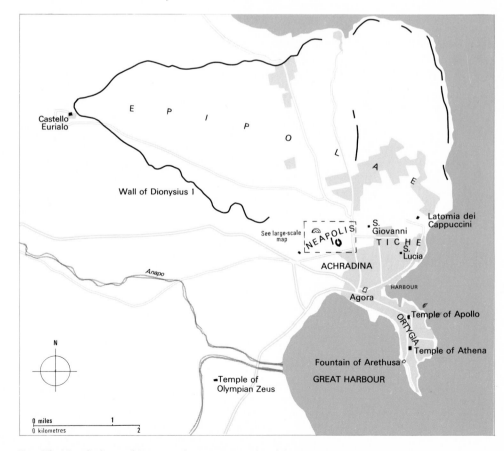

Top: The Neapolis district of Syracuse. Above: Syracuse. Plan of the city area

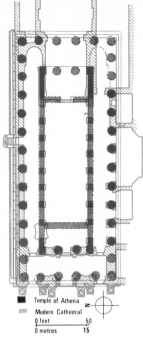

Temple of Athena
Modern Cathedral
0 feet   50
0 metres   15

Above: Plan of the cathedral of Syracuse, incorporating the fifth-century BC *Doric temple of Athena. Left: An aisle of the cathedral of Syracuse, retaining the colonnade of the original temple. The pavement and iron gateways date from the Renaissance.*

into a Christian church, was completely rebuilt to serve as a cathedral, though some of the original columns were retained both in the interior and in the outer walls, where they are still visible.

Gelon was succeeded in 476 by his brother Hiero, who continued the policy of conflict with other Sicilian communities and who also won a great victory over 'barbarians', in a naval battle against the Etruscans in the Bay of Naples in 474. His death in 467 was followed by a quick conflict, sparked off by popular hostility to the tyrants' enfranchised mercenaries, which ended in the establishment of a democratic regime in Syracuse (and soon in most of Sicily), lasting until 405. Unavoidable involvement in the great war between Athens and Sparta, during which the Syracusans barely

defeated a massive Athenian invasion after two years (415–413), was followed in 410 BC by a series of Carthaginian invasions which were also thrown back only at the last moment, and these conflicts brought tyranny back to Syracuse in the person of Dionysius, the general who succeeded in making peace with the Carthaginians by conceding the western end of Sicily to them.

Dionysius ruled until his death in 367, at one time controlling more than half the island as well as some of the Greek communities in southern Italy, almost permanently at war with Carthage, raiding the Etruscans, even trying to intervene in Greece, ruthlessly deploying both his mercenaries and the civilian population. Not surprisingly, he became the model, for Plato among others, of the evil tyrant. Never-

theless, he had considerable popular support and he continued the fifth-century tyrants' tradition of patronage for poets and playwrights. He was not, however, a builder of monuments: his efforts were directed to fortification (though the keystone of the system, a complex and technically advanced fortress now known as Castello Eurialo, on the northern edge of the territory of Syracuse, is in its present state largely the work of subsequent rulers).

Dionysius' constant wars and depredations, together with Carthaginian invasions, debilitated and gradually depopulated Syracuse along with the rest of the island. Under his son, Dionysius II, a quarter century of civil strife set in, after which there was remarkable recovery, initiated by Timoleon and continued by another tyrant, Agathocles. The latter seized power in Syracuse in 317, and took the title of king (*basileus*) in about 305, following his return from a four-year invasion of North Africa. Then, under King Hiero II, who reigned in Syracuse from 269 to 215, Rome entered the scene. Hiero and Syracuse benefited greatly from his alliance and friendship with Rome, but after his death there was a mysterious about-face, leading to a two-year Roman siege. The city surrendered in 212 and was looted on a massive scale. From that date, wrote the Roman historian Livy, began the Roman admiration for Greek works of art.

As the principal city of the Roman province of Sicily, Syracuse was a prosperous centre for

Above: The Roman amphitheatre at Syracuse, from the air. Left: Marble sarcophagus of Adelfia, wife of 'Count' Valerius, found in the San Giovanni catacomb in 1872, and now in the Museo Archeologico Nazionale, Syracuse. Below: Original plan of the Greek theatre at Syracuse, third century B.C. Opposite: Ground plan of the San Giovanni catacomb, Syracuse

many centuries, and a tourist attraction, though it appears never to have reached the size and populousness of its Greek heyday in the fifth and fourth centuries B C. The outstanding Roman monument is the amphitheatre, one of the largest in existence, an elliptical structure, 460 × 390 feet (140 × 119m), built not before the late second century A D. Before that, glad-iatorial shows were held in the theatre: what the visitor now sees, one of the finest examples of a Greek theatre, is a structure for some

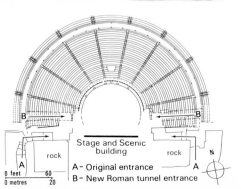

Stage and Scenic building

rock   rock

A - Original entrance
B - New Roman tunnel entrance

0 feet   60
0 metres   20

N

15,000 spectators designed in the later years of Hiero II, but altered in the first century A D and on several later occasions, not for the better. Nearby are the remains of an outstanding example of ancient Sicilian 'megalomania', an immense, highly decorated stone altar, 650 × 75 feet (198 × 22.8m), built by Hiero for the public sacrifices at the feast of Zeus Eleutherios.

The existence of a Christian community can be traced back to about A D 200, thanks to their practice, which continued well into the sixth century, of burying their dead in catacombs. The oldest and largest is Santa Lucia (a modern name after the saint martyred soon after 300), but the later San Giovanni catacomb is more elaborate, laid out like a Roman town on the gridiron principle, with its axis a wide central corridor along the bed of a disused aqueduct. Taken together, the Sicilian catacombs are larger and more grandiose than those in Rome. Whereas Santa Lucia reflects the modesty of the early Christian community, San Giovanni catered for class distinctions, with carefully cut cubicles and even 'rotundas' for sculpted stone sarcophagi.

Finds from the entire period, beginning with the prehistoric, are in the Museo Archeologico Nazionale, Syracuse.

Drögemüller, H.-P., *Syrakus. Zur Topographie und Geschichte einer griechischen Stadt*, Heidelberg, 1969
Guido, M., *Syracuse*, London and Chester Springs, Pa., 1958. A short guidebook
Loicq-Berger, M. P., *Syracuse. Histoire culturelle d'une cité grecque*, Brussels, 1967

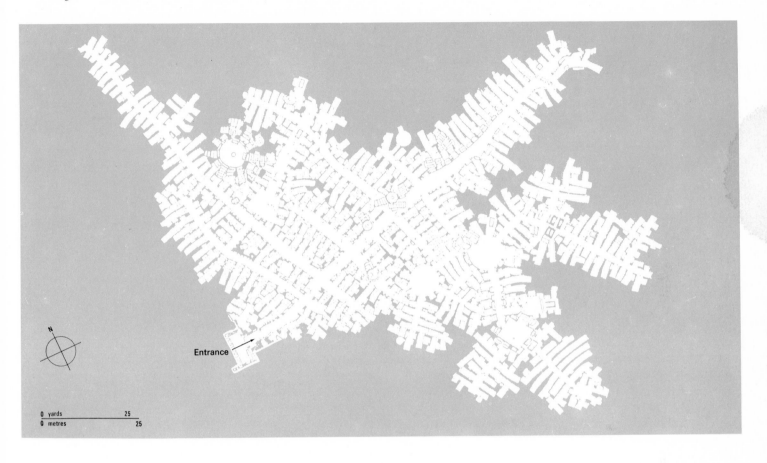

Entrance

0 yards 25
0 metres 25

2

Megara Hyblaea

Sicily

Megara was the last, the smallest, and the poorest of the settlements established on the east coast of Sicily by immigrants from Greece, in the mid-eighth century BC. The site is a coastal plain a little over 9 miles (15km) along the sea and generally about 4 miles (6–7km) deep, lying just behind the promontory of the modern harbour town of Augusta (not settled until the thirteenth century AD). It was un-occupied when the Greeks arrived, and they established themselves in peaceful relations with the native Sicels in the surrounding hills by agreement with a Sicel chieftain, Hyblon (according to tradition, hence the name Megara Hyblaea). Further growth was blocked by two somewhat older and more powerful Greek cities, each less than 10 miles (16km) distant, SYRACUSE to the south and Leontini to the west. By about 630 BC, therefore, a portion of

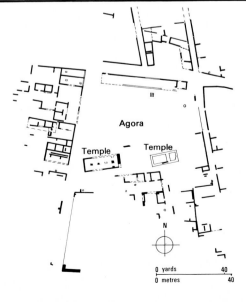

Agora

Temple   Temple

N

0 yards 40
0 metres 40

the population left Megara and led in the foundation of Selinus (SELINUNTE) on the south coast. In 483 the city was destroyed by Gelon, tyrant of Syracuse. It was re-established in about 340 by Timoleon, who expelled the tyrants of Syracuse and organized an extensive resettlement programme in western Sicily. Then it was destroyed once more by the Romans in 213 BC, in the course of the Hanni-balic War; thereafter it survived for another century or two only as the home of squatters.

Thanks to its small scale and its desertion, Megara is the one western Greek settlement that archaeologists have been able to recon-struct, at least in the main outlines, from the earliest period. That is its main interest. The urban centre, at the coastal end of the plain (which lacks an *acropolis*), began with a regular layout of one-room houses on streets running

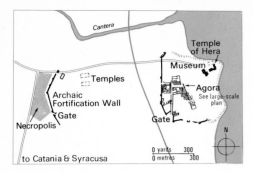

alongside or toward an open trapezoidal space, roughly 215×245 feet (65×75m). This permanently unpaved space was apparently set aside from the start as the future town square, the *agora*, and was kept free until the day when the little settlement would be able to erect the temples, *stoas* and civic buildings that characterized a proper Greek *polis*. That day came, with a burst of construction, in the second half of the seventh century BC: all the ruins of the *agora* can be dated to that short period. Although not every building can yet be identi-

fied, the over-all effect is clear from the plan of the *agora*.

The finds, including a surprising amount of sculpture, are housed in the Museo Archeologico Nazionale, Syracuse, and in a small museum on the site.

Vallet, G., 'Mégara Hyblaea', *Kokalos*, Palermo, Vols XIV–XV (1968–9), pp. 468–75

Vallet, G., and Villard, F., *Mégara Hyblaea*, Paris (so far published: II, 1964, on pottery; IV, 1966, on the fourth-century temple)

3   Selinunte   Sicily

Selinus ('celery' in Greek) was the ancient name of (Marinella) Selinunte. Situated on the south coast it was the westernmost of the archaic Greek settlements in Sicily. Established by about 630 BC on the initiative of emigrants from MEGARA HYBLAEA, who secured a 'founder', named Pammilus, from their own 'mother city' (Megara) in Greece, it soon became one of the wealthiest Sicilian city-states. It minted silver coins (with the celery leaf as emblem) in some profusion in the sixth century – ahead of SYRACUSE, for example – and it was notable for the number and scale of its temples. Its prosperity was presumably based on its extensive, fertile territory, from which agricultural products were exported to North Africa.

Remarkably little is known of the city's history. It was in continuous conflict with its northern neighbour, Elymian SEGESTA, and also involved in the endless warring among the Sicilian Greeks. The Carthaginians captured the city in 409 BC, massacred the male population and gutted the place. A much-reduced and impoverished settlement was quickly re-created, with marked Carthaginian elements. In the next century and a half, Selinus was normally in the Carthaginian sphere of influence, but during the First Punic War the Carthaginians again razed the city, in 250, and transferred its population to Lilybaeum (modern Marsala). It has been no more than a centre for squatters ever since, perhaps because the swampy mouths of the two small rivers that frame the site were malarial.

At the southern coastal end of the city was the *acropolis*, a plateau of some 8 acres (3.25ha), artificially reinforced, laid out on a rectangular grid system, and heavily walled; about one-third of it was set aside for the gods. After an initial period of primitive, chiefly wooden constructions, the Selinuntines embarked before the middle of the sixth century on a vast programme of building in stone: four Doric temples on the *acropolis*, three on a site about 1,100 yards (1km) to the east, and a sanctuary of Demeter Malaphorus across the river to the west. (As the gods to whom the

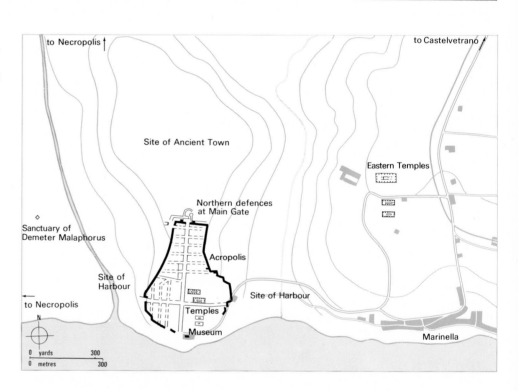

individual temples were dedicated are in most instances unknown, the temples are conventionally identified by letters of the alphabet.) Local soft stone was used, much of it quarried at Rocche di Cusa, some 6 miles (10km) to the west, where rough, abandoned column drums can still be seen lying about. Temple C, the largest and oldest on the *acropolis*, has a platform 78×209 feet (24×64m), framed by 6×17 columns. It is almost puny when compared with Temple G (dedicated to Apollo) in the eastern group, 8×17 columns on a platform 164×361 feet (50×110m), so wide that interior columns were required to support the *cella* roof. This colossal temple, like some others on that scale elsewhere, was still unfinished when the Carthaginians destroyed it in 409, a century after construction began. The Selinuntines had set out deliberately to erect a colossus; it has few equals in the Greek world, and in Sicily

Right, above: Three metopes from temple C, Selinus, now in the Museo Archeologico Nazionale, Palermo. Right, below: The centre metope, which shows Perseus cutting off the head of Medusa

it was exceeded in size, fractionally and by calculation, only by the temple of Olympian Zeus at Acragas.

The temples reveal an unusual freedom in many details and an uncommon exuberance, exemplified by the few surviving painted *antefixes*. Some of the temples had charming sculpted *metopes*, rare in Sicily, portraying mythological scenes. Archaeologists have suggested native influence, but there is no positive evidence. Certainly the sanctuary of Demeter Malaphorus, a Megarian cult, in a precinct which may already have been sacred, is purely Greek. Demeter was the Greek goddess of fertility (*malaphoros* means 'apple-bearing'), and more than 10,000 terracotta female figurines have been found in the ruins.

An earthquake in late Roman times shattered the temple remains, but modern reconstruction on the *acropolis* has created a haunting ghost town. The *metopes* are displayed in a special room in the Museo Archeologico Nazionale, Palermo.

Gàbrici, E., 'Studi archeologici selinunti', *Monumenti antichi*, Rome, Vol. 43 (1956), pp. 205–407

White, D., 'The Post-Classical Cult of Malophorus at Selinus', *American Journal of Archaeology*, New York, Vol. 71 (1967), pp. 335–52

4 Agrigento

The last major Greek settlement in Sicily was Acragas, founded in 580 just off the south coast, between Selinus (SELINUNTE) and Gela, by a combined effort from Gela and Rhodes. It became Agrigentum in Roman times, then Gergent (Girgenti) from the Arab conquest in 827 until 1927, when Mussolini restored the Roman name. The site slopes southward from a steeply rising plateau (1,060 feet; 325m) to a narrow east-west ridge some two miles (just over 3km) down (and that distance again from the sea). It commands an extensive territory fertile in fruit and cereal, which made Acragas,

through trade with North Africa, the only rival in Sicily to SYRACUSE and perhaps the fourth city of Europe for a time. At its peak the city's population was about double the present 50,000; its wealth is symbolized by the triumphal welcome accorded the Olympic sprint winner Exaenetus in 412 BC, escorted into the city in a procession of 300 chariots.

Although the settlers at first clung to the plateau and its slopes, within a generation they had built a defensive perimeter wall that embraced the whole area down to the ridge. A large precinct at the western edge of the ridge,

already sacred to the native Sicels, was converted into a sanctuary of Demeter, the goddess of fertility, as was another native shrine at Rupe Atenea in the northeast, which rises to 1,160 feet (355m). Two or three temples, now unknown, were constructed on the heights. The embezzlement of funds designed for that purpose, says a late writer, enabled Phalaris to seize power about 570 BC: his greatest claim to fame was the hollow brazen bull in which he roasted his opponents alive. Later in the sixth century two temples were begun, but abandoned, in the precinct of Demeter. Finally,

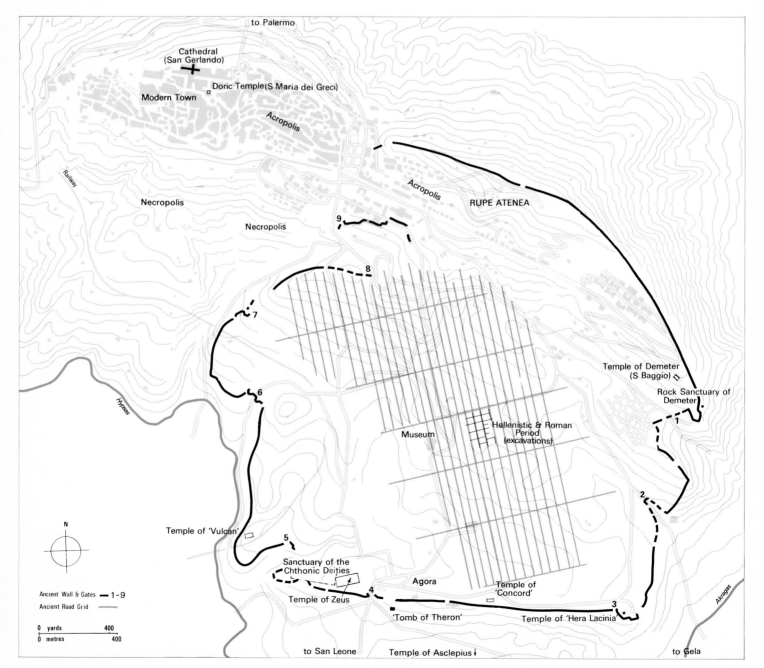

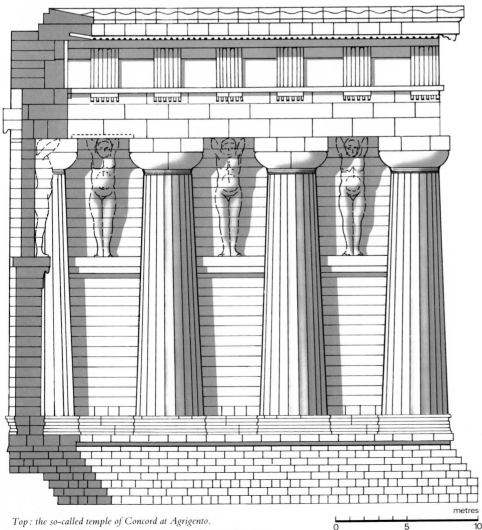

Top: the so-called temple of Concord at Agrigento.
Above: Restoration of the temple of Olympian Zeus at Agrigento

metres
0   5   10

before 500 B C, the earliest surviving monumental temple was begun on the ridge, near the main southern gate, a mature Doric temple, the size of which, 200 × 83 feet (61 × 25m) on the ground, suggests a deliberate attempt to outdo Selinus and perhaps Syracuse. (It is known as the 'temple of Heracles', but that attribution, like a majority of the familiar temple names in Agrigento, is false.)

It was another tyrant, Theron (488–471 B C), who initiated Acragas's unrivalled building programme. Like Gelon in Syracuse, Theron's stimulus came from the victory over the Carthaginians at HIMERA in 480; he shared undeservedly in the glory, the numerous captives, the booty and large indemnity. Far outstripping Gelon's commemorative building activity, Theron and the democratic regime which followed his overthrow embarked on eight or nine temples. Theron himself was responsible for starting three: a little temple to Demeter on the Rupe Atenea, without a frame of columns, later incorporated into the medieval church of San Biagio; a second temple to the goddess, on the ridge, now a complete ruin, one corner of which was reconstructed in 1836 in a fanciful pastiche, familiar as the city's emblem under the incorrect name of 'temple of Castor and Pollux'; and a third, a colossus dedicated to Olympian Zeus. The latter was 9 feet (2.75m) wider than Temple G at Selinus, then the largest structure in the Greek world, and it too was unfinished (lacking its roof) when the Carthaginians sacked the city in 406 B C.

The architect took a revolutionary approach to the task of erecting such a gigantic structure. For the traditional frame of columns he substituted solid walls of engaged half-columns, about 60 feet (18m) high and over 13 feet (4m) in diameter, adding a sense of massivity to the vastness of scale. A heavy moulding was introduced slightly more than half way up the walls, on which stood naked muscular Atlas-like figures between the columns supporting the entablature with their upraised arms and heads (whether they were structurally necessary or primarily decorative is a subject of controversy). The columns, furthermore, were constructed from small blocks, not from full drums, and pedimental sculpture was introduced (the only instance in Acragas) illustrating two legendary themes, the war of the gods against the giants and the capture of Troy.

After Theron the city returned to more conventional building, and in the small temple of 'Concord', to be dated probably between 460 and 450, they achieved a work that stands comparison in its delicate curvature and its proportions with the Parthenon. Not much more than half the size of the latter, it is even smaller than the altar outside the temple of

Zeus (which measured $57\frac{1}{2} \times 178\frac{1}{2}$ feet; 17.5×54.4m). It is also, with the Hephaesteum in Athens, the best-preserved Greek temple anywhere, thanks to a local bishop, San Gregorio, who in AD 597 converted it into a church by opening up the *cella*, creating a basilica with three naves. In the end, there were five major temples on the ridge and a sixth, the 'temple of Asclepius', near mineral springs outside the walls. Why the Acragantines chose to concentrate so many shrines at the edge of the city, rather than in the centre or on the *acropolis*, is a puzzle. So is their liking, shared with Himera, for finely carved lion's-head spouts.

After the Carthaginian sack, the city had a fluctuating history, determined largely by the activities of others. During the wars between Rome and Carthage, it was captured by the Romans in 261 BC (25,000 inhabitants were sold into slavery), burned by the Carthaginians in 254, and seized once more by the Romans in 211 (who again sold off the population). Thereafter it was a second-class city, Agrigen-

tum, in the Roman province of Sicily. In 197 BC the Roman senate ordered the provincial governor to build up Agrigentum by transplanting people from elsewhere in the island. The subsequent centuries saw a steady increase in population and prosperity, evidenced by the orderly residential layout in the space between the northern heights and the temple ridge and by the appearance from about 100 BC of Roman-style housing. Under the Roman emperors, a further boost to the economy came from the exploitation, perhaps for the first time, of the nearby sulphur mines, apparently an imperial monopoly.

The finds are mainly in the new Museo Archeologico Nazionale at Agrigento, including a reconstruction of one of the 'Atlases' of the temple of Zeus (another lies in the open alongside the temple).

Marconi, P., *Agrigento*, Florence, 1929
Waele, J. A. de, *Acragas Graeca* I, The Hague, 1971
  (II forthcoming)

5 Himera

Sicily

Founded about 650 BC by migrants from Zancle (later Messina) and refugees from SYRACUSE, Himera offers good anchorage but has a restricted hinterland, and it is puzzling that it should have been among the first Sicilian cities to mint silver coins. It has long been famous for the ruin (hardly more than the foundation) of a large, classical Doric temple just off the main coastal road. Excavations begun in the 1960s have now revealed the settlement itself, over the hill to the south, including three earlier, smaller temples, one of them dating from the late seventh century.

Himera's claim to fame rests on a single battle. In 483 BC Theron of Acragas seized the city from a local tyrant, Terillus, who called in the Carthaginians. The latter responded and in 480 BC were totally defeated by a coalition under Gelon of Syracuse. The temple of Nike (Victory) was erected in commemoration, and the unusual location, outside the city proper, may have been selected because it was the battle site. The Carthaginians returned in 409, destroyed the city, massacred half the population, and then transferred survivors to Thermae (now Termini Imerese). Himera itself was never rebuilt.

Finds, including the best of the splendid lion's-head rainspouts, are in the Museo Archeologico Nazionale, Palermo.

Himera I (published by the Istituto d'Archeologia, Univ. di Palermo, Rome, 1970)
Marconi, P., *Himera*, Rome, 1931

---

6   Segesta   **Sicily**

The most important Elymian centre in the northwest, Segesta is 985 feet (300m) above sea level, and 10½ miles (17km) by modern road from Castellammare del Golfo, where its ancient harbour presumably was to be found. Little is known of its internal history, or of its foreign affairs apart from its persistent conflict with Selinus (SELINUNTE), beginning early in the sixth century BC. On more than one occasion Segesta turned outside Sicily for help, first to Carthage, then in 416 BC to Athens (provoking the disastrous Athenian expedition against SYRACUSE), again to Carthage in 410 (provoking the Carthaginian expedition that destroyed Selinus), eventually, in the First Punic War, to Rome. Effectively Segesta ceased to be autonomous after 410: it then became dependent on Carthage, except for a brief period in the second half of the fourth century BC when its population is said to have reached 10,000, until it went over to the Roman sphere. The material remains show a rapid Hellenization in the sixth century BC, symbolized by the issuance of Greek-style silver

The fifth-century BC Doric temple at Segesta

coins and the employment of the Greek alphabet (though the Elymian language, still unidentified, remained in use), and the conclusion of an agreement with Selinus (surprisingly) recognizing intermarriage between members of the two communities.

Two monuments have made Segesta a major attraction, both for themselves and because of the terrain in which they are situated. The first is the shell of an unfinished Doric temple built outside the city, to the west, on an isolated hill in an extensive, uninhabited valley. The structure must almost certainly be the work of a major Greek architect, so sophisticated and advanced are the existing elements. The suggestion has been made that it was begun in 416 in order to impress Athens – that is at least the right sort of date – and that the project was abandoned after the Athenian defeat removed its reason for existence. The other monument is a semi-circular Hellenistic theatre, modified in Roman times, 207 feet (63m) in diameter, on the highest point of the city and facing north, giving marvellous views of the mountains and the sea.

Burford, A., 'Temple Building at Segesta', *Classical Quarterly*, Oxford, Vol. XI (1961), pp. 87–93

Van Compernolle, R. 'Ségeste et l'Hellénisme', *Phoibos*, Brussels, Vol. V (1950–1), pp. 183–228

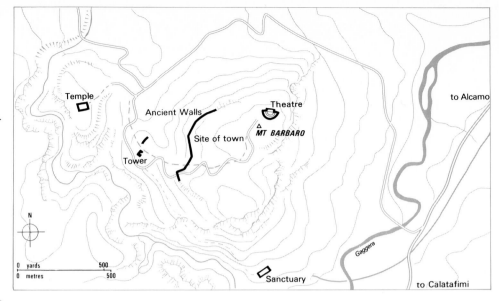

7 Erice Sicily

An Elymian settlement on an isolated mountain, 2,460 feet (750m) above sea level, $3\frac{3}{4}$ miles (some 6km) from the port of Trapani (ancient Drepana), Erice (Eryx in antiquity) is perhaps the most panoramic and the most mysterious site in Sicily. It was the centre of a native cult, of which no archaeological traces have been found, and became sacred to the Carthaginian goddess Tanit (or Astarte), and then to Greek Aphrodite, who, with her doves, flew from Eryx to North Africa for a few days every year. There a daughter-shrine was established at Sicca Veneria (modern El Kef), inland near the western border of Carthaginian territory in Tunisia. According to a dubious ancient source, sacred prostitution became a feature of both shrines. During the Second Punic War, the Roman general Fabius Maximus vowed to dedicate a temple in Rome to Aphrodite of Eryx if the goddess aided the Roman armies. He did so in 215 BC, and the temple was placed on the Capitol. During another war, a second temple was erected for Venus Erucina (the goddess's Latin name) outside the Colline Gate, where 'the day of the whores' was celebrated. Thereafter we hear little of ancient Eryx, though it remained a centre of habitation. The Normans used the temple stone to build a fortress, the ruins of which can still be seen, and in 1167 changed the name from Eryx to

Monte San Giuliano, as it was known until 1934. Nothing of antiquity survives on the ground except for parts of the city wall.

Fragments of sculpture and other ancient objects are housed in the local museum.

Cultrera, G., 'Il "temenos" di Afrodite Ericina e gli scavi del 1930 e del 1931', *Notizie degli scavi*, Rome, 1935, pp. 294–328

Kienast, D., 'Rom und die Venus vom Eryx', *Hermes*, Wiesbaden, Vol. XCIII (1965), pp. 478–89

Below: A silver tetradrachm of Eryx, c. 400 BC. Left, obverse: a four-horse chariot galloping, while Nike (Victory) flies to crown the driver. Right, reverse: Aphrodite seated; a dove alights on her right hand, while a winged Eros raises his arm towards her

8   Motya

Motya (now San Pantaleo) is a low-lying island, 1½ miles (2.4km) in circumference, in a shallow lagoon off the northwest coast of Sicily. It was the first Phoenician station on the island, from about 700 BC, contemporary with their earliest posts on the coasts of Sardinia, to be followed in a few decades by Palermo. Thanks to intensive archaeological excavation (still in progress) for much of the present century, Motya is our best source of information outside North Africa for Punic culture traits in the West.

There were Greek products and Greek inhabitants in Motya from an early date, and peaceful coexistence was the rule for most of its history. The little island was fortified, a breakwater was constructed at the entrance to the lagoon, and by the fifth century BC the growing population required a new cemetery, developed in the Birgi district on the mainland of Sicily, with which Motya was linked by a causeway more than a mile long. Then came the war between Dionysius I of SYRACUSE and Carthage. Motya was the tyrant's first objective; he captured the island after a siege of some months, in which he employed for the first time advanced siege equipment his military engineers had invented, massacred the inhabitants and destroyed the town. Those Greeks of Motya who remained loyal – their existence is worth noting – were crucified.

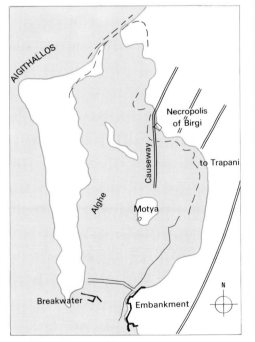

Above:
A section of the Punic tophet (sacrificial burial ground) of Motya, excavated in 1965

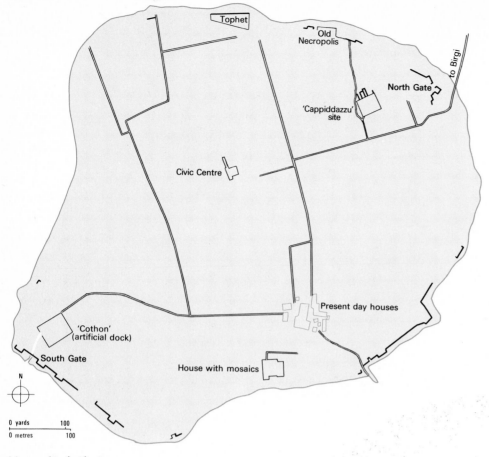

Motya and its fortifications

Carthage soon regained the area, but now established Lilybaeum (Marsala) as its main fortified outpost, and Motya resumed an insignificant existence for another century or so.

The pottery and other small finds are both Greek and Carthaginian, but the walls and more monumental architecture are basically Greek, though with alien elements. However, the administration and the cult were predominantly Punic. The main religious centre was apparently a walled sacred precinct, 90 × 116 feet (27.4 × 35.4m), in the north, near the Birgi causeway, called Cappiddazzu by archaeologists: the oldest building can be dated to the seventh century B C; it eventually included a largish temple, and many animal bones remain from the sacrifices. Some 109 yards (100m) west is the sacrificial burial ground, the best example of a *tophet* known today, with its characteristic contents: special gravestones, terracotta masks, and cinerary urns containing traces of the bones of infants and small animals. Although the Greeks boasted that after his victory at HIMERA in 480 B C, Gelon compelled the Carthaginians to abandon human sacrifice, the *tophet*, in continuous use from the sixth to the mid-third century B C, demonstrates that the practice disappeared gradually around 400 B C.

Finds are housed in the local museum.

Mozia (published irregularly by the Centro di Studio per la Civiltà Fenicia e Punica, Rome; the latest is No. VIII, 1973)

Whitaker, J. I. S., *Motya*, London, 1921

---

9   Piazza Armerina   Sicily

In a wooded valley at Casale, 3¾ miles (6km) south-by-west of Piazza Armerina (a medieval foundation on the main road from Gela to Enna), there are the well-preserved remains of a palatial hunting villa of the early fourth century A D. Erected on several levels, as required by the terrain, the villa had nearly fifty rooms, courts, galleries, baths and corridors, arranged in four complex groupings approached by a monumental entrance. It was occupied until the Arab conquest and again briefly for a time under the Normans, when it was destroyed by King William the Bad late in the twelfth century. Archaeological interest, and plundering, began in the eighteenth century, and it is only in the present century that the villa has been systematically excavated and preserved. It is now covered over and open to visitors.

Little remains of the marble architectural elements, the sculpture and the murals, but much survives of the elaborate mosaic pavements, which originally covered nearly an acre (over 4,000m²) of floor space, far exceeding in

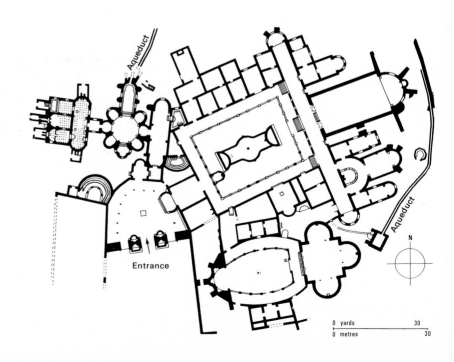

A section of one of the pavement mosaics of the villa at Casale (Piazza Armerina), depicting the end of a chariot race. The whole composition is very elaborate and filled the room, more than 65 feet (20 m) in length

scale and cost anything else of the kind known today. The original ownership and the exact date of construction are controversial. The official guidebook retains the view that this was an imperial villa of the emperor Maximian and his family. The more probable alternative is that it was a private villa, somewhat later in date, perhaps belonging to the owners of the nearby *massa Philosophiana*, one of the greatest estates in Roman Sicily, identified in a late Roman itinerary as a staging point on the inland road from AGRIGENTO to Catania.

The mosaics were almost certainly the work of craftsmen imported from North Africa, and it has been estimated that ten teams would have required half a century for the job. There is a basic unity of style – which may be called 'Roman imperial' – but a great diversity of subjects. Hunting and fishing scenes are naturally much in evidence, but the range runs the gamut from geometric patterns through bathing and dancing to complicated pictorial and narrative compositions, most of them drawn from Greek mythology or Greek games.

The whole was ostentatiously pagan and Greek.

Ampolo, C., and others, 'La villa del Casale a Piazza Armerina', *Mélanges de l'École française de Rome*, Vol. LXXXIII (1971), pp. 141–281

Cagiano de Azeveda, M., 'Questioni vecchie e nuove di Piazza Armerina', in *Rendiconti* of the Pontifica Accademia Romana di Archeologia, Rome, Vol. XL (1967–8), pp. 123–50 (defends late fourth-century date)

Carandini, A., *Ricerche sullo stile e cronologia dei mosaici della villa di Piazza Armerina*, Rome, 1964

Italy

The central position of Italy in the Mediterranean makes it one of the most important archaeological areas of the classical world that came to be dominated by the Roman Empire. Not that Italy is a corporate geographical or political entity. Most of its history until A D 1870 attests that truth. Geographically Italy falls into two distinct units: first the northern plain flanked by the Alps and second the Apennine peninsula running down to Sicily. Today the division is implicit in the rivalry between ROME and Milan, the one the traditional seat of political and religious power and the other the centre of industrial progress; the former with its Mediterranean interests, the latter open to more European influences.

In the north the Po valley between the foothills of the Alps and the Apennines offered rich alluvial soils to settlers. Nor was access from the north and east as difficult as it might appear to be, for well-defined passes such as the Brenner provided relatively low-level routes to the Veneto and the head of the Adriatic. The northwestern passes, such as the Little St Bernard (preferred to the Great St Bernard in antiquity), were more difficult but there was coastal access from Provence. Nowadays the north claims a greater intensity of agriculture than peninsular Italy but in antiquity its rich, well-watered soils were perhaps not exploited to the same degree. Peninsular Italy, over 620 miles (1,000km) long and normally over 125 miles (200km) across, had the Apennines as its predominantly limestone backbone. The mountains, reaching a height of 9,560 feet (2,914m) in the Gran Sasso, and their outliers combined with the major river valleys of the Arno and the Tiber to compartmentalize the peninsula into a series of units on a larger scale than in Greece. Although in terms of area the mountains account for some three-quarters of the countryside, the plains are particularly rich and enjoy, with the exception of the notoriously parched coastal plain of Apulia, a higher rainfall than comparable areas. The strength of peninsular Italy always lay in the richness of the agricultural hinterland of such cities as CHIUSI (Clusium) and indeed Rome itself, where the fertile volcanic soils of the Campagna supported intensive cultivation.

Farther south the fertility of the plain of Campania, with the town of Capua as its centre, was famous and ultimately combined with the attractive climate and scenery to give the BAY OF NAPLES probably the highest population density in Italy. Yet the very fertility of the area created conflict as Greeks, Etruscans, Samnites and finally Romans sought to gain predominance in its exploitation. Farther south still, Greek colonial activity enjoyed a freer rein. Many coastal sites suffered,

however, from the perennial problem of the lack of adequate deep-water harbours. Coastal lagoons made much of the western coast malarial even under the empire, and the silt carried down by the Tiber rendered attempts to create an artificial harbour for Rome only a qualified success.

These developments, however, occurred long after the dawn of the Neolithic Age in Italy. The period is noteworthy for the advent of large-scale settlement in the southeast which has left its trace on the Apulian Tavoliere and presumably reflects the development of cultural links across the Adriatic. Equivalent population movements must also have taken place southward into the northern plain, most likely as offshoots of Balkan and Danubian cultures but perhaps also of Alpine lake dwellers. What all these brought or encouraged among the existing population was the development of primitive agriculture. During the second millennium the spread of Aegean contacts brought Mycenaean trade to Sicily, the Lipari Islands and southern Italy. At the same time the development of the so-called amber route opened up the Brenner and led to the exploitation of Austrian copper deposits. Indeed it was their skill in metalwork that distinguished the various cultural levels by the middle of the millennium. The inhabitants of the *terremare* in the Po valley lived in villages practising relatively advanced arable, as well as pastoral, farming and enjoying some expertise in the working of bronze. To the south their contemporaries of the Apennine culture relied more exclusively on hunting and the pasturing of livestock.

The beginning of the first millennium saw rapid advances based on the mastery of iron working which, together with a distinctive kind of cremation burial, formed the technological development underlying the indigenous Villanovan culture, so termed from a type site near Bologna. While the Apennine culture continued across much of the peninsula, its Villanovan contemporary spread (with local variations) across the southern Po valley and down the western coast as far as the Tiber to include what became the heartland of Etruria. The reasons for, and the manner of, the transition from the Villanovan to the Etruscan period starting in the eighth century are problems that exercised historians in antiquity no less than modern archaeologists, as is the problem of Etruscan origins. Both can be argued in terms of the two conflicting accounts from antiquity, the prevailing view perhaps being that they were immigrants from Asia Minor. There remains, nonetheless, a strongly indigenous content and continuity of ideas. The 'canopic' jars of such northern centres as Chiusi, wherein a disproportionately large but realistic terra-

cotta head dominates a small representation of the body, are the basis for the later portrait effigies on stone or terracotta sarcophagi. The funerary hut urns from southern Etruria, early Rome, and the Alban Hills of Latium point to the development of the celebrated house-tombs painted at TARQUINIA or carved in relief at CERVETERI. There undoubtedly were, however, developments involving increased wealth and new burial customs and from the mid-seventh century the use of a language with no basic affinity to the Indo-European dialects of the rest of Italy set Etruria apart and ahead of the rest of the peninsula. At one stage Rome was simply a small city state under Etruscan political control.

The growth of Etruscan political power had differing results. To the north the gridded plan of Marzobotto between Florence and Bologna shows that in the layout of Etruscan colonies town planning reflected the more advanced ideas of the day, like Georgetown or New Delhi in a latter-day empire. At the head of the Adriatic the gridded layout of SPINA, anticipating the canal systems of medieval Venice, shows an Etruscan trading colony with strong Greek elements. To the south, though, geography brought Greek and Etruscan into a direct conflict of interest. Greek colonization in Italy followed the routes pioneered initially by traders in the second millennium but involved far more concerted effort from about 730 B C when the first colony was established on the Italian mainland at Cumae. The site marked the most northerly Greek post on the maritime trade route to the copper and iron deposits of Elba and the Etruscan coast. Later Greek colonies became common along the coastline of southern Italy. Some, like PAESTUM, can still be seen in approximately their original form with little later superimposition. Others, like METAPONTUM, were laid out on so large a scale, with a land-division system linked to the city road grid, that research has only recently uncovered the true nature of their extent and the achievements of town and country planning by the sixth century B C.

It was the fertility of Campania that brought Greek and Etruscan into direct conflict. The Etruscans held Capua by 650 B C but successive defeats at the hands of patchwork Greek alliances in 524 B C and 474 B C curbed any further Etruscan expansion into the area. Greek expansion, however, never materialized because of internal divisions among the city-states at a time when the Etruscan league was showing itself incapable of determined unified action, notably over the problem of supporting VEII against the growing power of Rome. Thus, while in the first instance in Campania it was the Samnites of the interior with their capital at BENEVENTO who benefited from the

Alps

Augusta Praetoria

Comum

Mediolanum
Brixia
Verona

Ticinum
Patavium

Placentia
Adige

Fidentia
Po

Augusta Bagiennorum
Veleia
Parma

Regium Lepidum
Mutina
Spina

Bononia

Marzabotto
Forum Cornelii

Luca
Ariminium

Arno
Florentia
Iader

A p e n n

Chiusi

Asculum

Adriatic Sea

Cosa

Acqua Rossa

Tarquinia
Veii

Cerveteri
Alba Fucens

Tiber
Roma

Ostia

Norba

i n e

Capua
Beneventum

Cumae
Neapolis
s

Herculaneum
Pompeii

Poseidonia

Metapontum

Heraclea

Tyrrhenian Sea

Thurii

Ionian Sea

Lipari Is.
Caulonia

Zancle
Locri

Mediterranean Sea
Rhegium

Selinus

Carthage

Megara Hyblaea

Simitthu

N

0 miles 125
0 kilometres 200

power vacuum in the south, ultimately the continued growth of Rome saw the absorption of the Campanian plain.

The rise of Rome from a small satellite of its larger Etruscan neighbours to the major power in Italy, and ultimately the metropolis of an empire, is a fascinating historical story. This brief survey is concerned primarily with the archaeological side. The corporate results of excavations on the Palatine and beneath the Forum confirmed that the essentials of the legendary foundation of Rome in 753 BC contained a factual core. This is not the place to discuss the development of Roman political institutions during the remote regal period (753–509 BC) or the early days of the fledgling republic. Although the struggle against some neighbours, such as the great Etruscan city of Veii, was long and bitter, the achievement of Rome in the early and middle republican period lay in giving Italy a unity that was not repeated until the late nineteenth century. The key probably lay in the way that, whatever the actual bloodshed involved, Rome's leaders never lost sight, particularly with her southern neighbours, the Latins, of the fact that they were dealing not with conquered aliens but with fellow Italians and ultimately potential allies. By the end of the third century BC, Rome had weathered the invasion of Italy by King Pyrrhus of Epirus and the Second Punic War in which Hannibal too failed to break the power of Rome in the peninsula. Strategic control of the peninsula was assisted by the planting of colonies such as Cosa (273 BC) and the early castrum at OSTIA to protect Rome's maritime interests on the western seaboard. In the second century Rome's influence began to assert itself southeastward and by the end of the first century the Hellenistic kingdoms were under her control.

To the north, expansion into the Po valley was based on the Via Aemilia. This strategic route was protected to the south by the establishment of centres such as VELEIA on a mountain road to the southwest. To the far northeast the early establishment of a colony at AQUILEIA ensured not only strategic control of the area but also important trade links both across the Alps and into the Danubian area. In the west much of Spain had fallen to Rome after the Punic Wars, while Caesar had gained control of Gaul. By this stage the mechanisms of a city-state were ill-equipped to cope with the management of an empire and the struggles between leaders such as Pompey, Caesar and Crassus in the first century BC reflected the need for strong centralized rule, ultimately established when Caesar's heir Octavian defeated Mark Antony at the Battle of Actium in 31 BC. His assumption of the title of Augustus marked the foundation of the Roman Empire and the Julio-Claudian dynasty.

The middle republican period saw Rome absorbing artistic and architectural influences from the Greek and Etruscan worlds. The triumphs of the Roman generals in the Hellenistic world during the second century fed an increasing mania among the rich for Greek art treasures, culminating in 133 BC when the

bequest of the kingdom of Pergamum to Rome brought the treasures of the Attalids to Rome. What was not supplied by conquest was provided by the influx of Greek artists often reproducing earlier classical statuary or painting. The Round Temple of the Forum Boarium is a product of this movement.

Yet with space at a premium, the crowded republican metropolis is not the place to examine Roman ideas of architectural design. For exotic elements imitating the extravaganzas of the Hellenistic monarchs but incorporating advances in the use of concrete vaulting, we may move outside the city to such places as the Sanctuary of Fortuna Primigenia at Palestrina. There growing competence in concrete vaulting combined with an increasingly less functional and more decorative use of the classical orders, a change that finds further development in the free-standing Roman theatre. The traditional buildings of the Roman world, the fora, basilicas, theatres, and amphitheatres all drew on the classical tradition and were being built in the late republic. What gave these types of buildings their impact on the architecture of the empire as a whole was the great increase in building programmes initiated by Augustus. He claimed to have found Rome a city of brick and left it a city of marble. Yet the endless development of Rome itself does not make it the easiest place to appreciate his claim. It is in the centres of northern Italy, such as VERONA, and above all in the provinces that we can best appreciate the advances made in integrated town planning.

Although as the empire developed Italy became of decreasing importance and after the Severan emperors was treated very much as another province, archaeologically it continued to be of great interest. At Ostia, for instance, we can observe the transition of a whole town from first to fourth century AD in architectural and social terms, something that cannot be appreciated at POMPEII and HERCULANEUM, however spectacular and informative the detailed survivals from their destruction in AD 79. Although Rome brought advances to the fields of portraiture and mosaics the majority of her art, rather than her architecture, clung essentially to the classical tradition, a tendency reaffirmed by the at first wholly traditional motifs on sarcophagi used to bury the well-to-do after Hadrian. In the second century standards in the execution of the classical tradition declined; in this sense the column of Marcus Aurelius in the Campus Martius at Rome represents a decline (particularly in the modelling of the human figures) from the column of Trajan. The famous Arch of Constantine beside the Colosseum is the most complete of its kind but the re-use of earlier sculpture for much of the reliefs was in a sense an admission of the decline in standards.

Yet it would be wrong to talk of decline without realizing that there were also fresh developments that corporately represent an attempt to diversify away from the classical tradition. Artistically it can be seen in the treatment of internal decoration. The greater tonal range of mosaics rested on the availability

of material from all over the empire. Not only by the fourth century had taste changed in the use of marbles but attention had turned away from floor decoration to walls, vaults, and domes. The mosaics decorating the vault of Santa Costanza, probably built as a mausoleum at Rome in AD 354, anticipate the fresh, incisive splendour of Byzantine mosaics. Likewise the creation of a Christian sarcophagus tradition replacing the motifs of classical mythology added a new dimension to medieval Christian art. The realism of Roman portrait painting was also transmitted to Christian paintings like the Christ in Majesty from the Catacomb of Domitilla, a picture that combines a hard outline drawing with an impressionistic presentation.

In architecture there was also change from purely classical tradition and a fresh impetus toward structural innovation. The economic conditions of the later empire naturally restricted the amount of major building, particularly in the metropolis. Nonetheless internal spacial treatment became increasingly ambitious. The enormous main hall of the Baths of Caracalla had cross-vaulting supported on eight massive piers. In the Diocletianic Baths the space enclosed was even greater. Likewise the plan of the Basilica of Constantine (actually begun by his predecessor Maxentius in AD 306–10) rejected the traditional basilican form relying on columns to adopt the layout of the great halls of the baths. So on the one hand in the later empire the traditional form of the basilica led to the basilican churches of RAVENNA. On the other hand the latest Roman experiments in the construction of the vault and the discovery of the spherical pendentive, which allowed the transition from vertical wall to domed roof, made possible the development of the rotunda churches exemplified by San Vitale at Ravenna, and ultimately such masterpieces as St Irene and St Sophia at ISTANBUL. The catalyst throughout was, of course, the growth and practice of Christianity, a theme too large for this brief summary but one that ultimately gave art and architecture fresh character, purpose and sources of inspiration until the rediscovery of the classical tradition in the Renaissance.

Barfield, L., Northern Italy before Rome, London, 1971; New York, 1972

Boethius, A., & Ward-Perkins, J. B., Etruscan and Roman Architecture, London and New York, 1970

Brunt, P. A., Italian Manpower 225 BC–AD 14, Oxford and New York, 1971

Chilver, G. E. F., Cisalpine Gaul, Oxford, 1941

Frank, T. (ed.), An Economic Survey of Ancient Rome, vols. I, v, Baltimore, 1933, 1935

Guido, Margaret, Southern Italy, an Archaeological Guide, London, 1972; Park Ridge, N.J., 1973

Kähler, H., Rome and Her Empire, London and New York, 1963 (in Art of the World series).

Paget, R. F., Central Italy, an Archaeological Guide, London and Park Ridge, N.J., 1973

Salmon, E. T., Samnium and the Samnites, Cambridge and New York, 1967

Scullard, H. H., The Etruscan Cities and Rome, London and Ithaca, N.Y., 1967

The Roman colony of Aquileia at the head of the Adriatic was deliberately and carefully chosen to block the movement of invaders through the Carnic Alps to the north and the Julian Alps to the east. In 181 BC under the command of P. Scipio Nasica, Gaius Flaminius, and L. Manlius Acidinus (whose tombstone has been found) a force of 6,000 cavalry and foot soldiers founded the city as a Latin colony, the importance of which was quickly recognized by the infusion of a further 1,500 settlers in 169 BC. A relief sculpture shows the cutting of the ritual furrow associated with the foundation of the colony, which was soon linked to the rest of northern Italy by the Via Annia and the Via Postumia. Its strategic position rapidly made Aquileia the base for second-century BC campaigns in the northeastern corner of Italy, then a major trading base with Noricum, (modern Carinthia) and Istria. Augustan expansion beyond the Alps gave the city assured importance and prosperity shaken only by the Marcomannic invasion of AD 167 and the so-called War of Aquileia that ended with the murder of Maximinus Thrax outside the walls of the besieged city.

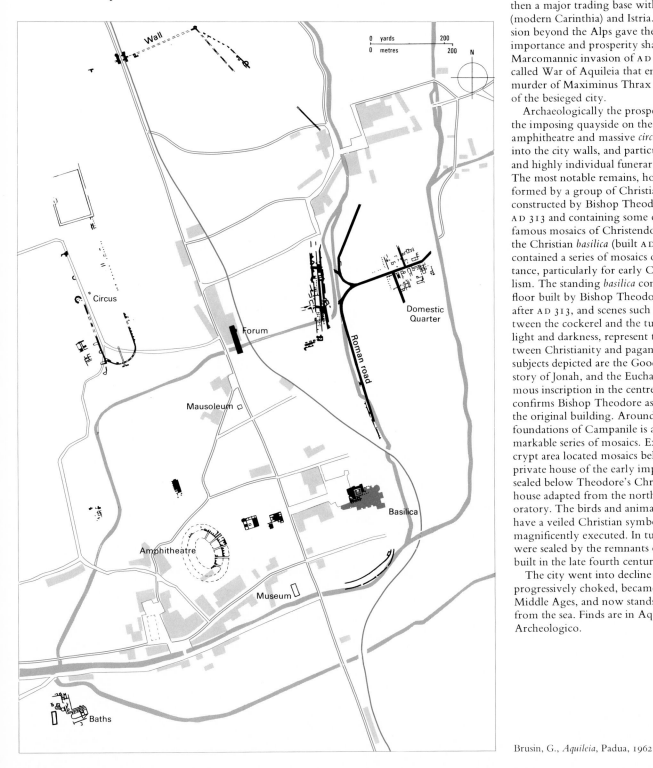

Archaeologically the prosperity is shown by the imposing quayside on the Natisone, the amphitheatre and massive *circus* incorporated into the city walls, and particularly by the rich and highly individual funerary monuments. The most notable remains, however, are formed by a group of Christian buildings constructed by Bishop Theodore shortly after AD 313 and containing some of the most famous mosaics of Christendom. The area of the Christian *basilica* (built AD 1021–1031) contained a series of mosaics of great importance, particularly for early Christian symbolism. The standing *basilica* contains a mosaic floor built by Bishop Theodore immediately after AD 313, and scenes such as the fight between the cockerel and the turtle, symbols of light and darkness, represent the conflict between Christianity and paganism. Other subjects depicted are the Good Shepherd, the story of Jonah, and the Eucharist. A posthumous inscription in the centre of the choir confirms Bishop Theodore as the instigator of the original building. Around the excavated foundations of Campanile is an equally remarkable series of mosaics. Excavations in this crypt area located mosaics belonging to a private house of the early imperial period, sealed below Theodore's Christian meeting house adapted from the north end of the oratory. The birds and animals represented have a veiled Christian symbolism and are magnificently executed. In turn these remains were sealed by the remnants of a large church built in the late fourth century.

The city went into decline as the harbour progressively choked, became malarial in the Middle Ages, and now stands several miles from the sea. Finds are in Aquileia's Museo Archeologico.

Brusin, G., *Aquileia*, Padua, 1962

One of the most remarkable results of modern Italian archaeology has been the discovery and exploration of the Etruscan settlement at Spina on the ancient coastline of the Adriatic close to one of the former mouths of the Po. The settlement represented an outpost of Etruscan expansion and its position made it an entrepôt of great importance at the head of the Adriatic before the Gallic raids of *c.* 390 BC and changes

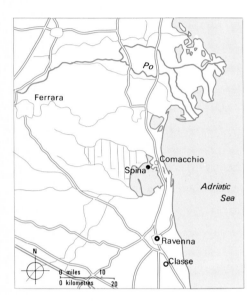

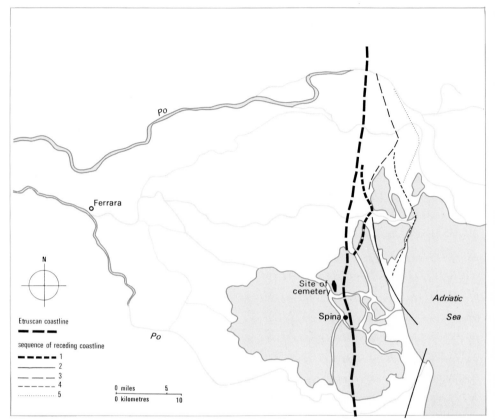

in the coastline stranded the city inland. Archaeologically, however, that gives it great importance as a unique survival of its kind.

    Little excavation has been carried out within the interior of the city. Attention was concentrated in 1922 on the cemeteries where, buried beneath alluvial deposits, an extraordinarily rich series of grave goods has been recovered from 1,213 tombs in very difficult waterlogged conditions that have, for instance, preserved wooden coffins for detailed analysis. The pottery and other objects from the cemetery of Valle Trebba attest the strong connections with the Greek world represented not only by its ceramics, including some priceless black and red figured ware, now housed in the Museo Archeologico di Spina at Ferrara, but also Greek *graffiti* with the names of the deceased owners alongside their Etruscan equivalents. Further excavation in 1953 in the Pega valley to the south produced 1,195 other tombs and in 1956 air photography showed the location of the associated city covering the enormous area of over 700 acres (283ha). As in Venice, canals, including a *decumanus* about 98 feet (30m) across, created a gridded series of building plots that await archaeological investigation.

Changing coastlines also affected the growth of the city of Ravenna in the classical period.

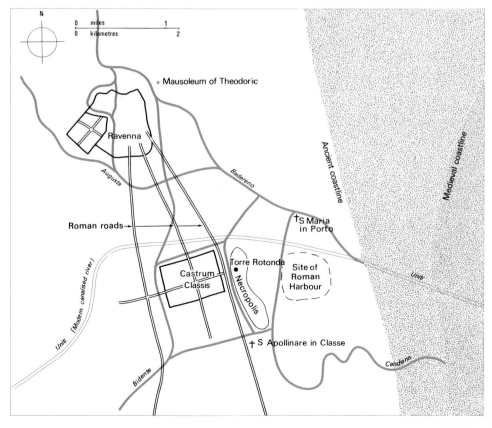

Below: Ravenna. The mausoleum of Galla Placidia
Bottom: Detail of ceiling mosaic
Opposite, above: Location map of Spina
Opposite, below: Area map of Ravenna in the late Roman
period

Below: Ravenna. The tomb of Theodoric (died 526),
restored in 1719

Today perhaps Ravenna is most famous for
its wealth of late buildings stretching into the
Byzantine period. This late blossoming has
historical reasons prompted by the geographical security of the walled town. The city was
capital of what remained of the Western
Roman Empire under Honorius and Galla
Placidia (403–76), then the seat of barbarian
kings governing in the name of the Eastern
Emperor (476–540) and later the seat of the
exarchs representing the Eastern Emperor
(540–751). During the period from the first
half of the fifth century AD to the second half
of the sixth, from Honorius to Justinian, a
series of churches of basilican and circular plan
were erected, the richness of which is without
parallel in Italy. The great basilicas of San
Giovanni Evangalista (heavily restored), San
Apollinare Nuovo, San Michele in Africisco,
and San Apollinare in Classe each has three
naves and an apse but no transept, a longitu-
dinal plan that has close affinities with early
Christian basilicas in Rome. The Neonian
Baptistery and San Vitale were based in contrast on a circular plan familiar in later Byzantine churches. The latter is famous for its
mosaics, notably that of Emperor Justinian
and his Empress Theodora at the dedication
of the church. Mosaics too decorate the domed
interior of the brick-built mausoleum of Galla
Placidia.

Most of the noted buildings lie within the walls of the city which date back to the early empire. Little is known of the early town save elements of its street grid, but the area had by then already taken on strategic and commercial importance following the construction by Octavian on the ancient coastline of the defended harbour at Classe (*classis*='fleet' in Latin) to safeguard his fleet in the Adriatic. Despite further substantial changes in the coastal configuration, recent aerial photography has revealed the position of the fort and harbour basin at Classe, nearly 2 miles (3km) to the southeast between the modern town and the church of San Apollinare in Classe. Apart from the mosaics, other finds are in the Museo Nazionale at Ravenna.

Alfieri, N., & Arias, P. E., *Spina*, Florence, 1958.

Aurigemma, S., *Il R. Museo di Spina in Ferrara*, Ferrara, 1936

Bovini, G., 'Il Problema della ricognizione archeologica del "Portus Augusti" di Ravenna e del "Castrum Classis",' *Atti del I. Congresso Internazionale di Archeologia dell'Italia Settentrionale*, Turin, 1963

Chierichetti, S., *Ravenna*, Milan, 1958

Mansuelli, G. A., *Geografia e storia di Ravenna Antica*, Corsi di Cultura sull'Arte ravennate e bizantina XIV, Ravenna, 1967. pp. 157–90

---

3   Verona   **Italy**

The city owes its importance to its position as a trade and communications centre controlling the crossing of the Adige river (the ancient Athesis) close to the northern edge of the Italian plain. It thus controlled the southern exit of the trade route across the Brenner Pass and lay across the east–west route along the northern edge of the Po valley toward the entrepôt of AQUILEIA. It has generally been assumed that in the protohistoric period the native Rhaetian *oppidum* that formed the antecedent of the Roman city lay under Castel San Pietro, the hill to the northern side of the

Adige. The Roman city was formally laid out as a grid across flat, alluvial land to the south within a loop of the river which, it has been conjectured, followed a broader curve in antiquity than today. Initially a Latin colony was founded at Verona in 69 BC under Pompeius Strabo. Of this town, where the famous poet Catullus was brought up, all trace appears to have been obliterated by a later, Augustan reorganization along standard lines familiar from several other Augustan settlements in Gallia Cisalpina.

The regular grid of streets from the Roman

city is still traceable today in the modern road pattern and two gates mark the position of the southern and eastern walls. Topography dictates the line on the other sides and the whole circuit, which was both partially restored and extended on the southeast to incorporate the amphitheatre under Gallienus in AD 265. The modern street system, where it clearly derives from a Roman antecedent, points to the existence of a regular grid layout of which the Corso Porta Borsari and the Corso Cavallotti form the *decumanus* (north–south axis) and the Via Cappello (and the Via S. Egidio) the *cardo* (east–west axis). As at Turin, the individual *insulae*, or street blocks, measured 260 Roman feet square, indicating that the city was intended to be divided into units of two *iugera*. The amphitheatre was laid out with an axis parallel to the *cardo*. The integrated plan was extended by the position of the *circus* between the north wall of the city and the river. A bridge linked the area with the site of the theatre built into the hillside of San Pietro, although no extensive settlement is known on that side of the river. More than Turin perhaps, Verona represents a north Italian city that shows its ancient origins in present-day layout. Like Turin, the Augustan layout stems from a phase in the conquest of the southern Alps in 28 BC and 15 BC respectively.

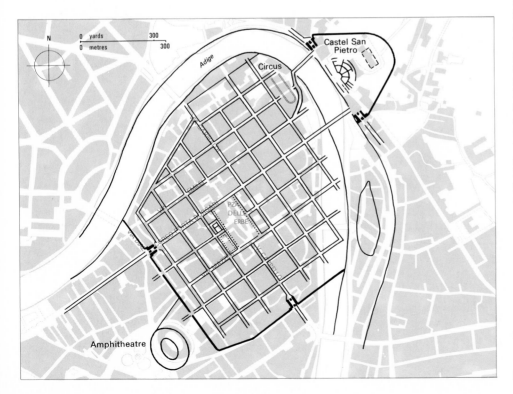

Richmond, I. A., and Holford, W. G., 'Roman Verona: the Archaeology of its Town Plan, *Papers of the British School at Rome*, XIII (1935) pp. 69–76

Zorzi, F., *et al.*, *Verona e il suo Territorio*, vol. I (1961)

4 Veleia

Veleia was a Latin colony founded in 89 BC on the slopes of the Apenninal south of Piacenza and overlooking the valley of the Chero. Its strategic position was such that it blocked the mountain route from Parma to Luni on the coast. Excavations began at the site in 1760 under the Bourbons and give us a useful picture of the layout and organization of a small provincial centre in northern Italy. The *forum* was aligned on the points of the compass; measuring 236 × 164 feet (72 × 50m) overall, the interior comprised a colonnaded portico and paved central courtyard. To north and south respectively lay the *capitolium* and *basilica*. Modern buildings partly overlie the baths to the southwest but the amphitheatre to the southeast has been completely excavated.

The town has a further special interest. It yielded an inscription on bronze tablets dating from AD 109–12 that, along with similar evidence from BENEVENTO, shows how the emperor Nerva had promoted a scheme 'for girls and boys born of needy parents to be supported at public expense throughout the towns of Italy'. The policy, designed to foster the prosperity of Italy, was known as the *alimenta* system. The imperial treasury, or *fiscus*, made loans to owner-farmers up to a small fraction of the total value of the property. The resulting interest was earmarked for a municipal fund that supported poor children. The system both made capital available to farmers at below market rates and supported the continuation of family life, and thus a continuing agricultural labour supply. In the register from Veleia the loan is 8 per cent of the value of the land listed as security. Yet the register provides a further insight into the declining state of Italian agriculture, largely through the development of the large estates or *latifundia*. In the Veleia register the 300-odd farms listed belong to a mere 48 landowners, some of them absentee landlords.

Atti del III. Congresso di Studi Veleiati, Milan, 1969
Calvani, M. M., *Veleia*, Parma, 1975
Duncan-Jones, R. P., *The Economy of the Roman Empire*, Cambridge and New York, 1974, chapter 7

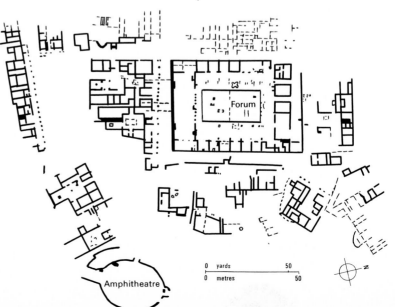

Above, right: The forum, *Veleia. Right: Plan of Veleia showing the area around the* forum

Forum

Amphitheatre

0 yards 50
0 metres 50

The site of Rome lies in the middle of an eroded plain forming a broad saddle in the volcanic plateau between the Monti Albani to the south and the Monti Sabatini to the north. This geographical unit extends from the Tyrrhenian Sea at the mouth of the Tiber some 30 miles (50km) inland to the Sabine Hills, limestone outliers of the Apennine system. To north and south the plain is bounded by the Tolfa hills and the edge of the Pomptine Marshes. Geologically the whole area comprises an upper layer of volcanic ash, or tufa, through which the bed of the principal river, the Tiber, has eroded down to the Eocene clays beneath. The Pleistocene period saw the formation of a trough forming a lake extending some 22 miles (35km) to the limestone outlier of Monte Soracte. An outlet, now followed by the final stages of the Tiber, was formed beside Monte Gianicolo overlooking the Vatican across the saddle between the two most southerly volcanoes, the craters of which are now represented by Lago Bracciano and Lago Albano. Subsequently the river eroded its bed some 165 feet (50m) below its original level, and radial streams from the volcanic cones to south and north further dissected and lowered the surface. The geomorphological effect was to leave flat-topped spurs between the valleys, spurs that became further eroded and often isolated when abutting the main river valley through the action of small wet-weather streams. On the south side of the river a small group of such detached hills, not otherwise distinguished from their fellows, forms the site of early Rome. The principal hills involved are the Palatine and the Capitoline, the latter controlling a river crossing at the island in the Tiber bend.

In the long-standing tradition the site of Rome was first settled from Alba Longa, now identified near Castelgandolfo in the Alban Hills, in the year 753 BC. In the developed literary version the poet Virgil pictured Aeneas entertained by the local leader Evander and lodged in a modest hut on the Palatine. Archaeologists have been able to confirm elements of the story, without, of course, the characters traditionally involved. The similarity of pottery from Alba Longa and chance finds from the area of the Forum and Palatine had already been noted in the last century. There remained the question of date. Two excavations this century located clear evidence of timber and wattle huts on the Palatine from the presence of their foundation trenches cut in the volcanic tufa. The earliest assemblage of material belongs to the eighth century BC and ties in well enough with the traditional date.

The next two centuries of occupation attested by this material take us through to the so-called regal period, when Rome was a poor satellite of the flourishing Etruscan cities to the north and was ruled by an Etruscan king. Part of the evidence stems not from the Palatine itself but from a necropolis found to underlie the centre of the Forum to the northeast. By the sixth century, but prior to the creation, c. 575 BC, of the *cloaca maxima*, the main drain of central Rome, the marshy valley floor was taken over as a cemetery for the population on the Palatine and perhaps some of the other hills nearby. The graves take the form of cremation burials in the main, the funerary ashes being inserted within a hut-shaped urn set in a recess in the bed rock, a practice attested at Alba Longa and also in several sites to the north.

This evidence for the earliest phase of Rome's existence needs to be kept in perspective; the cultural level was well below that of the rich Etruscan cities of Etruria proper. Yet Etruria lay on the doorstep. The great city of VEII lay only some 12 miles (20km) away, CERVETERI little more. In this period Etruscan influence saw its greatest expansion southward along the Cassino corridor into Campania. Although Rome lay off the principal communication route, its proximity meant that it inevitably fell under Etruscan influence. Broadly speaking this is represented by the regal period extending from c. 700–509 BC when the names of the successive monarchs illustrate their Etruscan origins. If literary tradition is to be believed, the popular anti-monarchical movement that swept them away implies that they were aliens planted on a native populace. Few of the kings were received with any favour. The exception was Servius Tullius, to whom tradition again assigned the construction of Rome's earlier wall circuit chiefly visible today beside the main railway station (Stazione Termini). Archaeology, however, now places its construction later, in the mid-republican period, c. 378 BC, but its extent serves to show the area of the pre-imperial city.

Unfortunately very little of republican Rome survives. The exceptions are principally the group of four temples at Largo Argentina and in the Forum Boarium. The Round Temple built at the beginning of the first century BC is of particular importance as the oldest marble building surviving in the city. Greek architects imported a structure of Hellenistic type, built in the appropriate material, Pentelic marble, and representing a complete break with Italic tradition. The temple is a splendid precursor of Roman architecture in marble which preponderated after Augustus, who boasted that he had found a city of brick and left one of marble; his claim to have built or restored no less than eighty-two temples lends weight to his statement.

The main elements of imperial architecture in the city appeared at this stage. By and large

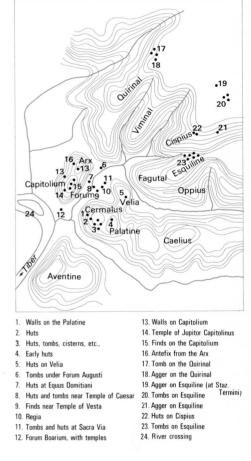

Above: Map of early Rome. Below: Map of Rome in the time of the Republic

1. Walls on the Palatine
2. Huts
3. Huts, tombs, cisterns, etc.,
4. Early huts
5. Huts on Velia
6. Tombs under Forum Augusti
7. Huts at Equus Domitiani
8. Huts and tombs near Temple of Caesar
9. Finds near Temple of Vesta
10. Regia
11. Tombs and huts at Sacra Via
12. Forum Boarium, with temples
13. Walls on Capitolium
14. Temple of Jupitor Capitolinus
15. Finds on the Capitolium
16. Antefix from the Arx
17. Tomb on the Quirinal
18. Agger on the Quirinal
19. Agger on Esquiline (at Staz. Termini)
20. Tombs on Esquiline
21. Agger on Esquiline
22. Huts on Cispius
23. Tombs on Esquiline
24. River crossing

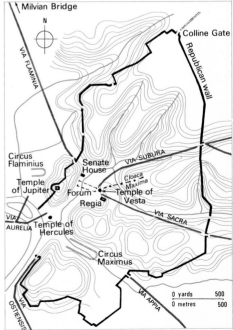

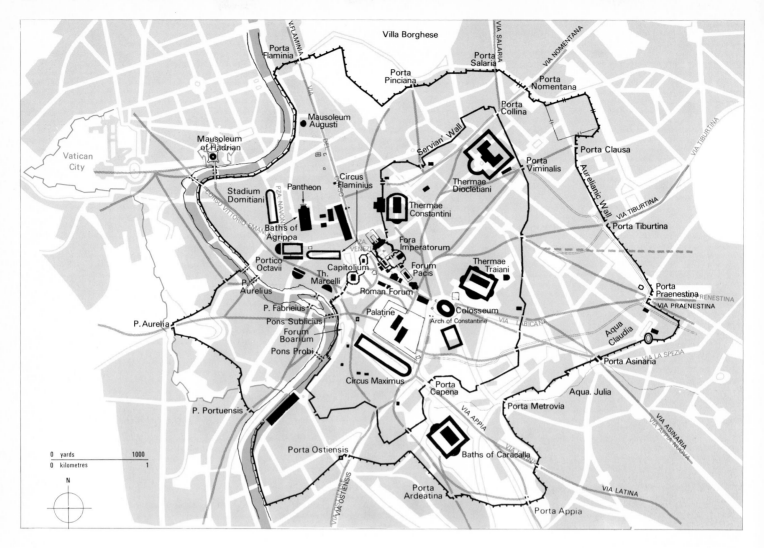

Above: Map of Imperial Rome (the modern city is shown in brown). Right: The temple of Portunus (the Round Temple) in the Forum Boarium. Opposite: The temple of Romulus in the Roman Forum

there was no room for expansion in the old *forum* where alongside and opposite the republican *curia*, or senate house, space was preempted by the older *basilicas*, and the House of the Vestal Virgins fronting the Via Sacra. Imperial monuments were inserted in the *forum* but they tended to be small in size like the triumphal arches of Titus, with its famous depiction of the sack of Jerusalem in AD 70, and of Severus. The imperial *fora* developed elsewhere to the north, where Augustus' own *forum* was later to be dwarfed by the tiered

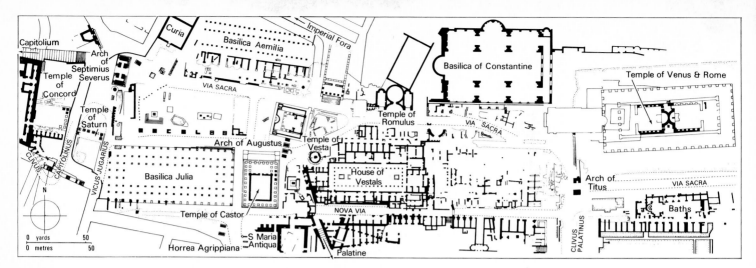

The Roman Forum

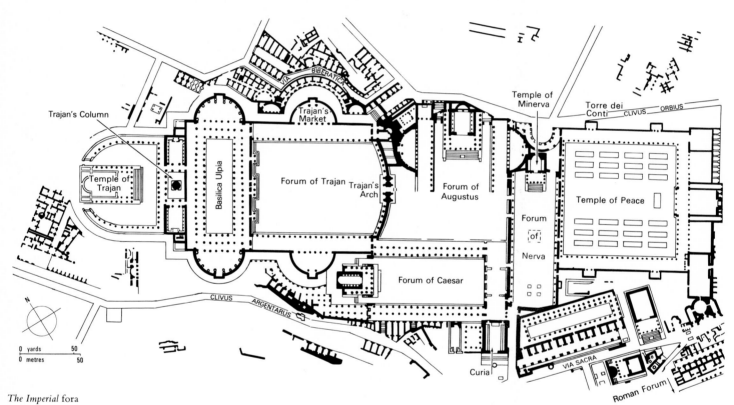

The Imperial fora

forum and market of Trajan with his column depicting the Dacian Wars as its centrepiece. To the east the megalomaniac plans of Nero, given free rein by the great fire of AD 64, involved the construction of the Golden House fronting onto a lake dominated by a colossal statue of the emperor. The Flavian dynasty that succeeded him was quick to obliterate the obvious traces of these ventures, first by the construction of an amphitheatre, the Colosseum capable of containing at least 60,000 under Vespasian, and the baths of Titus that incorporated the Golden House in their foundations and were again superseded by those of Trajan.

Imperial baths were indeed a feature of the later development of the city's architecture.

The little-known baths of Antoninus were followed by the famous baths of Caracalla, Diocletian, and ultimately Constantine. All served as social centres, and the plan of the Caracallan example, for instance, reveals not only the circulation pattern of the bathers through baths of increasingly high temperature, but also the presence of libraries and recreation areas.

During this time the Palatine Hill had changed beyond all recognition. While Augustus had confined the imperial quarters to relatively modest proportions, his successors covered the hilltop with a maze of palaces starting under Tiberius and Caligula, and ultimately more formalized in the shape of the

Domus Flavia, or Palace of Domitian, built as an integrated unit with the so-called stadium across the centre of the hill, and with a range of terraces overlooking the Circus Maximus below. Now the Arch of Constantine marks the northeastern corner, but in antiquity the exotic Septizonium of the emperor Severus crowned the southeastern tip of the hill.

Away from the main core of the city, in the area contained by the Tiber bend and known as the Campus Martius, many fragmentary buildings survive in modified form in much the same way that the Capitolium, the temple of Jupiter, is encapsulated beneath later buildings on the Capitoline Hill. The Theatre of Pompeii, for instance, is reflected

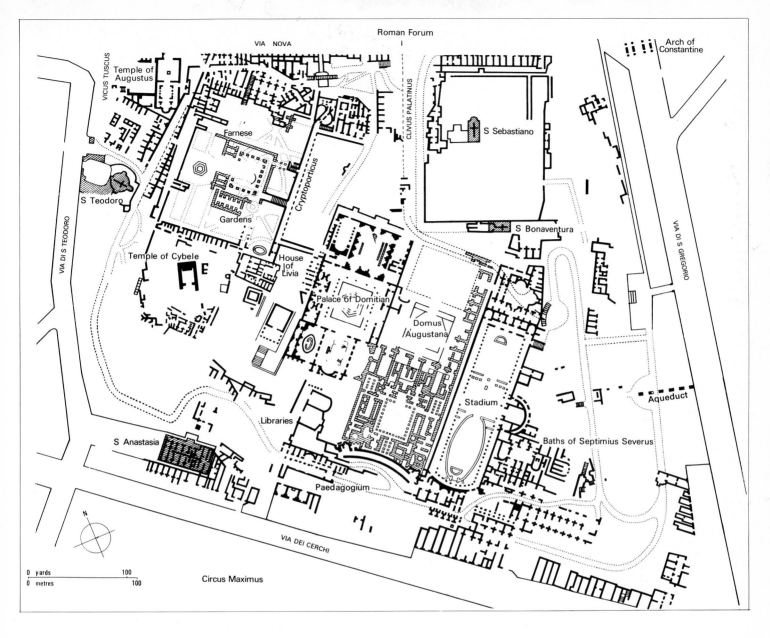

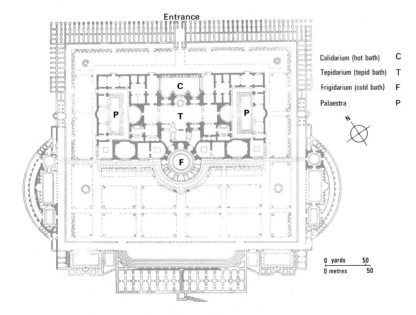

Calidarium (hot bath)   C

Tepidarium (tepid bath)   T

Frigidarium (cold bath)   F

Palaestra   P

Above: Plan of the Palatine. Below left: Plan of the Baths of Caracalla

in the modern street plan, while the Piazza Navona represents the *stadium* of the emperor Domitian. The major standing structure, however, is the Pantheon erected by Agrippa in 27 BC, restored by Domitian after a fire in AD 80, and further reconstructed under Hadrian in AD 126. The building consists of a huge rotunda of brick-faced concrete, fronted by a pedimented portico. The ancient bronze doors are still preserved although other bronze decoration was stripped in the seventeenth century.

Elsewhere imperial tombs are represented by the Mausoleum of Augustus. Nearby is reconstructed the relief altarpiece known as the *Ara Pacis*, celebrating the establishment of

peace in the empire and dedicated in 9 BC.
Across the Tiber in the Vatican stands the
Mausoleum of Hadrian, now better known
as Castel Sant'Angelo. Both imperial tombs,
with their massive cylindrical drums, derive
from the Etruscan tradition seen at Cerveteri.
On the opposite side of the city, near the
station, stands the so-called Temple of Minerva
Medica, in reality a *nymphaeum* believed to
belong to the Gardens of Licinius. Structurally
the building, which is of third-century date, is
of great importance in anticipating certain
features of later Roman/Byzantine architecture.
The ten-sided structure is crowned by a ribbed
vault and has circular projections on two sides.
It stands in the line of development that led to
such circular buildings as San Vitale at RAVEN-
NA. The Imperial Guard was housed nearby in

*Top: Rome in the time of Constantine, from the Palatine
to the Baths of Caracalla. Reconstruction by I. Gismondi.
Right: The Arch of Titus (detail)*

the *Castra Praetoria* whose barracks were later incorporated in the curtain on the imperial city wall built by the emperor Aurelian (AD 270–75). The original battlements were modified by Maxentius (AD 305–12) by the addition of an upper level and more elaborate gateways, many of which were further remodelled under Honorius (AD 395–423).

The gateways of the city have received much medieval modification but the Porta Appia (Porta San Sebastiano) exemplifies an original simple gate plan with later modifications. The Porta Asinaria at St John Lateran is now well displayed and shows an Aurelianic plan modified under Maxentius. The gates of the city lead us naturally to the famous aqueducts that entered Rome at these points. It is on the southern side of the city that the visible remains of the aqueducts can be seen running on columns of arches across the Campagna, particularly toward the Porta Praenestina at the eastern tip of the city. The gates, of course, took their names in most cases from the destination of the road leading out of them. All the routes were originally flanked by tombs, but it is the Via Appia where the best examples of such a linear cemetery survive today and where some ôf the Christian catacombs can be visited close to the Porta Appia.

Although thousands of remains are known in the Roman Campagna, attention must focus in particular on the port of Ostia. The seasonal flooding of the Tiber has always created difficulties for river transport and the site of the port of ancient Rome now lies some 3 miles (5km) from the present seashore at Ostia. The original settlement took the form of a *castrum* or camp that can still be recognized in the core of the town, probably founded in the mid-fourth century BC and now occupied by the area of the *forum* and *capitolium*. In archaeological terms Ostia is in many ways more informative than Rome itself, so far as everyday life is concerned. North of the theatre on the principal *decumanus* lies the Piazzale delle Corporazione. This colonnaded enclosure round the Temple of Ceres contained the offices of many of the merchants operating in the town. Mosaics outside each office indicate each merchants' guild concerned and the principal imports involved. While the corn supply to the metropolis was the prime concern, the mosaics demonstrate the import of wine, timber and even exotic animals for the amphitheatres of Rome. Toward the river there are surviving examples of the granaries used to store corn during transshipment: the Horrea Epagathiana represent an example of one such granary, presumably reflecting the name of the merchant (of eastern Mediterranean origin) involved in the corn trade.

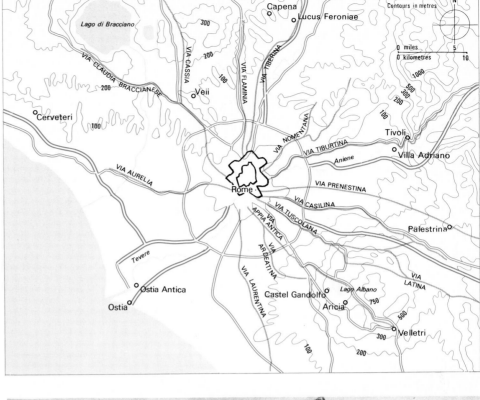

Top right: Map of the environs of Rome
Right: The Horrea Epagathiana, Ostia

The town also gives us a picture of the development of all kinds of bath houses across some four centuries of time, while the eleven *mithraea*, or temples of Mithras, are the best group of their kind and reflect the addiction of the predominantly slave-based proletariat to mystery religions derived from the eastern Mediterranean. Further, while only one example of housing survives in Rome (beside the market of Trajan), Ostia abounds in the cramped and noisy tenements, such as the Casa di Diana, that housed its poorer population, many of whose humble graves can be seen flanking the road to the north at Isola Sacra. That road led to the harbour installations of the imperial period.

The alluvial deposits of the Tiber floods led the Roman emperors to attempt the creation of an artificial harbour nearly 4 miles (6km) to the north. The first attempt under the emperor Claudius was known only from literary sources until the construction of Fiumicino Airport revealed parts of a lengthy breakwater. The scheme, however, was unsuccessful in avoiding the problems of silting and Trajan created a smaller harbour in the southeastern corner of the Claudian basin. The main octagonal basin of the Trajanic harbour, surrounded by its warehouses, is still visible (but not accessible) today in the grounds of the Torlonia Estate.

Above: Ostia. Latrines on the via della Forica

Top: Façade (reconstructed) of an insula in the via di Diana, Ostia, with a tavern on the ground floor.
Above: Interior of the tavern

Opposite, top: Plan of ancient Ostia. Bottom: Ostia. Block of houses in the via di Diana

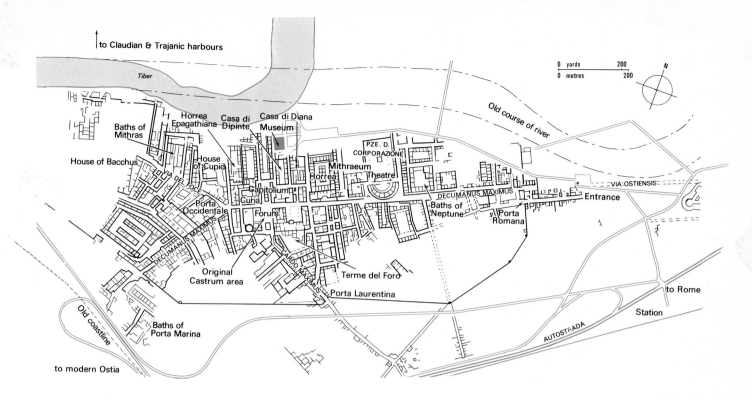

to Claudian & Trajanic harbours

Tiber

Old course of river

0 yards 200
0 metres 200

N

Baths of
Mithras

Horrea
Epagathiana

Casa di
Dipinte

Casa di Diana
Museum

PZE. D.
CORPORAZIONE

House of Bacchus

House
of Cupid

Mithraeum
Horrea

Theatre

VIA OSTIENSIS

VIA DEL FOCE

Capitolium

Curia

DECUMANUS MAXIMUS

Entrance

Porta
Occidentale

Forum

Baths of
Neptune

Porta
Romana

DECUMANUS MAXIMUS

Original
Castrum area

CARDO MAXIMUS

Terme del Foro

Porta Laurentina

to Rome

Station

AUTOSTRADA

Old coastline

Baths of
Porta Marina

to modern Ostia

In total contrast with the teeming streets of
Ostia, Tibur, the modern Tivoli, lay where
the foothills of the Apennines meet the Campagna. Many remains of temples and villas
occur around the town but none like the
unique and idiosyncratic villa of the emperor
Hadrian, which represents the most remarkable
architectural pot-pourri of all imperial villas.
Hadrian was passionately interested in architecture himself and probably was personally
responsible for the choice of the baroque
agglomeration of buildings comprising the
villa. The structure, which is 1,100 yards (1km)
long by approximately 550 yards (500m)
across at one point, contains palatial reception
rooms, a *basilica*, pavilions, a naval theatre, and
libraries, as well as a private palace and baths.
Projecting from these were the celebrated
Poikile, or painted portico, and Canopus, an
elongated pool axially aligned on a rock-cut
temple of Serapis. It was an expression of one
man's mind and the Roman world never saw
its like again.

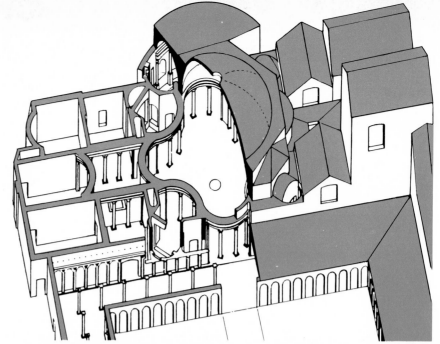

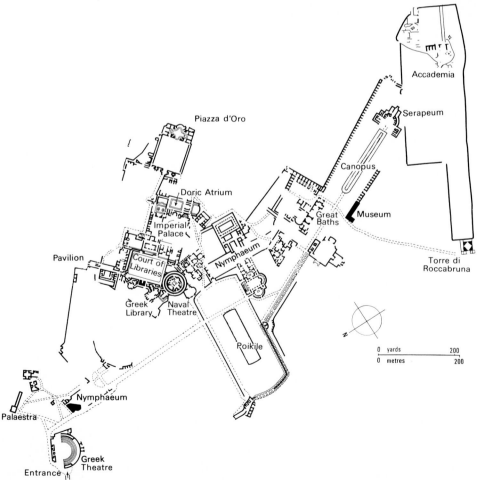

Hadrian's Villa, Tivoli. Opposite, above: Axonometric plan of the Piazza d'Oro. Opposite, below: The 'Naval Theatre'. Above: The Canopus. Left: Ground plan of the complex of the villa

Ashby, T., *Aqueducts of Ancient Rome*, Oxford, 1935

Aurigemma, S., *Villa Adriana*, Tivoli, 1955

Calza, G., & Becatti, G., *Ostia* (Official Guidebook), Rome

Dudley, D. R., *Urbs Roma*, London 1967. A source-book of classical texts on the city and its monuments

Gjerstad, E., *Early Rome*, vols. I–IV, Lund, 1956–63

Kähler, H., *Hadrian und seine Villa bei Tivoli*, Berlin, 1950

Lugli, G., *I Monumenti Antichi di Roma e Suburbio*, I–III, Rome, 1938

Meiggs, R., *Roman Ostia*. 2nd ed. Oxford and New York, 1974

Nash, E., *Pictorial Dictionary of Rome*, 2 vols, London and New York, 1968

Platner, S. B., & Ashby, T., *A Topographical Dictionary of Ancient Rome*, Oxford, 1929

Richmond, I. A., *The City Wall of Imperial Rome*, Oxford, 1930

In 1964 archaeologists excavating at Pyrgi, the port of the Etruscan city of CERVETERI, found several gold scrolls, two of which were inscribed in different languages but clearly expressed the same meaning. One was written in Etruscan, the other in Phoenician, a language that has been deciphered. Unfortunately, neither text was sufficiently long to make a major contribution to understanding the Etruscan language, but this kind of discovery shows the basic gap in our knowledge of the Etruscans, the greatest people to dominate the Italian peninsula before the rise of ROME. Nearly 9,000 Etruscan inscriptions exist but the great majority simply give the name of the deceased on a tombstone. Of the three longer texts, one survives by the strangest of chances on a mummy wrapping (now at Zagreb), another on an inscribed tomb scroll at TARQUINIA, and a third on a tile from Campania. None is long enough to establish the grammar of the language, although the meaning of individual words can be deciphered.

The culture known as Etruscan becomes clear by the end of the eighth century B C in the region between the Tiber and the Arno, the area of ancient Etruria. Etruscan culture at one stage spread to SPINA in the Po valley and into Campania to the south. It gradually contracted, losing its special character during the later Roman period, the emperor Claudius actually writing an antiquarian treatise on the subject. The Romans, their close neighbours, and long their inferiors, both feared and learned from them. Later they acquired an aura of mystery, even in antiquity, and historical curiosity revived in the Renaissance has since been fanned by the prospect of tomb looting, first documented as early as 1489. Ironically, therefore, while practically no Etruscan towns have been archaeologically investigated, the splendid weapons, gold ornaments, and beautiful vases that enrich the major museums give a vivid, if biased, picture of Etruscan life. Most impressive of all perhaps one can admire the paintings on the walls of underground tombs at Tarquinia or the relief sculptures on the rock-cut tombs at Cerveteri.

This century archaeologists have formulated, and in some measure elucidated, the problem of the Etruscan origin, and partly revealed the nature of their cities, their religious beliefs, and the character of their everyday life. The evidence for Etruscan origins is based on ancient literature, linguistics, and archaeology. The historians in antiquity were unsure of Etruscan history. The Greek historian Herodotus implies that they came from Asia Minor and his view was supported by several other ancient writers. Dionysius of Halicarnassus says on the contrary that the Etruscans were indigenous natives of Italy. The value of these statements is not very great because the classical

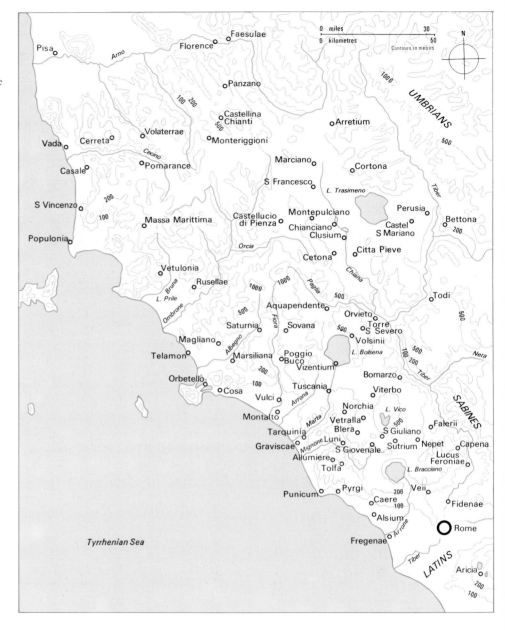

authors themselves were generally relying on speculation and legend. The linguistic evidence is more trustworthy, especially as it was not open to slanted interpretation. We know what the Etruscan language was like as far back as the seventh century B C. We also have a fair knowledge of other languages spoken in Italy at the same time. None of them, save Faliscan, was related to Etruscan; nor was Greek, nor, so far as we know, was Lydian, Lydia being the region of Asia Minor from which (according to Herodotus' version) the Etruscans derived.

The archaeological evidence is gradually receiving modern synthesis, though it is difficult to draw a coherent archaeological sequence of cultural development. It appears that in the eighth century B C and earlier an Iron Age culture known as Villanovan existed in and beyond Etruria. It is generally regarded as the product of a native Italian culture that had attained an Iron Age level, but had not progressed greatly toward urbanization. By the end of the eighth century, however, a much richer culture began to emerge on the sites of Etruscan cities. The Etruscan culture exhibits a wider variety of grave goods and the Villanovan artistic tradition was improved and supplemented by Greek and Oriental influences. At first Greek and Oriental influences were about equally visible, but during the seventh century the Greek prevailed, and

Opposite: Map of Etruria. Below: The Etruscan necropolis, Cerveteri.

gradually even Greek deities and mythological figures were accepted into Etruscan art and belief.

Roughly speaking the theories now fall into two camps. One asserts that the Etruscans were immigrants, the other claims that they were natives or at least naturalized before 'Etruscan culture' began. That the latter was brought or developed by invaders is the traditional view. It is supported by the sudden or rapid appearance of the Etruscan culture, its superiority over the other contemporary cultures of Italy, its strong artistic connections with the eastern Mediterranean, its elaborate and perhaps Oriental ritual, and its probably non-Italic language. The arguments are alluring but there are many difficulties of detail, just as the theory that the Etruscans were native breaks down principally over the fact that the rise of the Etruscan culture was too sudden to have been achieved almost overnight by Villanovan peasants. Nor is it remotely clear why the Villanovans alone of the native Italians should have made such progress.

The Etruscans were organized politically in the form of city-states such as VEII, Tarquinia, CHIUSI (Clusium), and Cerveteri. The twelve principal centres were united in a politico-religious league, although distance and divergent interests greatly hindered cohesive action and each city clearly prized its independence. Yet, first under a regal system, then under an aristocracy Etruscan power spread throughout peninsular Italy. Militarily no doubt this was due to the development of improved heavy body armour and bronze chariots. Geographically it brought Etruscan rule to Rome and Praeneste for a time, and expansion into Campania brought control of Capua by *c.* 650 B C. To the north Etruscan colonies were established at Marzabotto in the northern Apennines and as far away as Spina close to the mouth of the Po at the head of the Adriatic. Internal disunity, the rise of the Romans and Latins, defeats at the hands of Greek fleets off Cumae in 524 B C and 474 B C, and the loss of Capua in 440 B C all curbed Etruscan dominance. The invasion of marauding Gauls in the late fifth century B C finally disrupted the Etruscan heartland and eventually the piecemeal expansion of Rome saw the absorption of the Etruscan states, often initially under allied treaty arrangements. Despite their dwindling power in the historic period the cultural influence of the Etruscans had a lasting effect, just as many aspects of Roman technical achievement, particularly in the realm of hydraulics, may derive from Etruscan origins. However much it may have derived from Greek or other Oriental influences (and this is very much a matter of subjective debate), Etruscan art in the form of statuary, metalwork, and painting made an important contribution to the cultural development of peninsular Italy under the aegis of Rome.

Banti, Luisa, *The Etruscan Cities and their Culture*, London and Berkeley, Cal., 1973

Bloch, R., *The Etruscans*, London and New York, 1958

—, *Corpus Inscriptionum Etruscarum*, Leipzig, 1936

Dennis, G., *Cities and Cemeteries of Etruria*, 2 vols., London, 1883

Hencken, H., *Tarquinia and Etruscan Origins*, London and New York, 1968

Pallottino, M., *The Etruscans*, new ed., London, 1975

Randall-MacIver, D., *Villanovans and Early Etruscans*, Oxford, 1924

Trump, D. H., *Central and Southern Italy before Rome*, London and New York, 1966

6a   The Etruscans: Veii

The great Etruscan city some 12 miles (20km) to the northeast of ROME far outshone its humble neighbour in the seventh and sixth centuries BC. One of the major sites of Etruria Tiberina, and the southernmost of the major Etruscan cities, it grew in importance as Etruscan trade and political influence developed down the Cassino corridor to Campania. This may explain why Veii shunned the gradual move toward oligarchy discernible in other cities and is known to have been one of the latest Etruscan monarchies, thus placing her in political isolation from other Etruscan states that goes a long way to explain eventual defeat by Rome in 396 BC.

Despite proximity to the modern city the site is still largely intact; and is so extensive that its very size is difficult to appreciate. Two deeply entrenched streams, the Fosso Cremera and the Fosso del due Fossi, come close together near the village of Isola Farnese, swing away from each other and unite beneath the citadel of Piazza d'Armi nearly 2 miles (3km) to the south. The whole of the plateau thus enclosed formed the ancient city. Ultimately it was completely walled, although the citadel, it is assumed, was defended earlier than the rest. Some surviving remains can be identified on the plateau but most date to the later Roman period, while the principal earlier features survive outside. Pride of place goes to the Portonaccio temple, where the famous statue of the Apollo of Veii was recovered. The gateways can be related to a series of roads that radiated from the city and these in turn to some of the richest cemeteries in southern Etruria, notably that of Quattro Fontanili which has established associations between imported pottery of Greek type and the Etruscan funerary urns and other grave goods. The environs provide some of the finest examples of Etruscan engineering, particularly in hydraulics. There is possible evidence for a watermill, and the so-called Ponte Sodo represents a diversionary tunnel for the Cremera. To the east, however, lie corporately perhaps the most impressive remains of all, miles of *cuniculi*, or underground drainage channels, that checked topsoil erosion in the fertile valleys on which Veii depended for its crops.

The Roman sack of Veii in 396 BC marked the first stage in the northward expansion of Rome into Etruria, rapidly followed by the conquest of Capena and Falerii. The circuit wall of Veii, which still stands over 16 feet (5m) high in places, is known to have been built after 450 BC and is doubtless connected with the impending conflict. At issue was control of the Tiber trade route and the strategic river crossing at Fidenae between Rome and Veii at the end of the Cremera valley, and Rome's victory gave her a firm base for further expansion within Etruria.

Ward-Perkins, J. B., 'Veii: The Historical Topography of the Ancient City', *Papers of the British School at Rome*, XXIX (1961)

The Etruscans: Cerveteri

The Etruscan city of Cerveteri (which the Greeks called Agylla, the Romans Caere and the Etruscans Cisra) lay some 5½ miles (9km) inland from its port of Pyrgi (Santa Severa) along the coast north of ROME. Little is known of the once flourishing city which was absorbed by Rome in 351 BC and went into gradual decline. Yet the famous and extensive necropolis on the hill of Banditaccia, covering at least 670 acres (270ha), testifies to the richness of the site. The city itself lay to the south on a steep-sided, flat-topped plateau between the Fosso del Manganello and the Fosso della Mola which came together, like the situation at VEII, to restrict easy access from the northeast. There is evidence for at least a partial wall circuit but little is known of the city interior except for six temples, and a wealth of architectural fragments. There is, however, no doubting the city's importance and wealth which should be viewed in relation to TARQUINIA. The latter was in the eighth century the major centre for copper and bronze working, thanks to the rich Tolfa mining area. By the early seventh century, however, Cerveteri had achieved more exploitation of these mineral deposits, heralding the city's most prosperous period of development when it developed trade contacts with Greece and Asia Minor.

The Etruscan city lay underneath the area of the modern town and, as at Tarquinia, interest centres on the magnificent cemetery remains. The main cemetery area lay on Banditaccia, a ridge to the north. Many of the tombs were grouped along streets and were carved as great cylindrical drums from the tufa rock. While practically nothing is known of the city, the tombs give us a remarkable picture of everyday life and artifacts. The unique Tomb of the Stuccoes contains not only niches with beds for the spirits of the departed but also representations of tools, weapons, and domestic animals on the central pillars and around the walls. Many other of the circular tombs, which reached up to a diameter of 44 yards (40m), contained internal arrangements of archaeological interest. Yet the standing tombs are in a sense only the tip of the iceberg. Aerial photography and geophysical exploration, as at Tarquinia, have shown that the whole ridge was honeycombed with rock-cut and simpler graves that go back to the Villanovan period. The date of the cemetery appears to extend into the third century BC.

To the south of the site there are further cemetery areas. The famous Regolini-Galassi tomb is renowned for its gold jewelry (now in the Vatican Museum) and dates from the late seventh century BC. Farther southeast on a separate ridge lies the Campana Tomb on Monte Abetone where aerial photography has

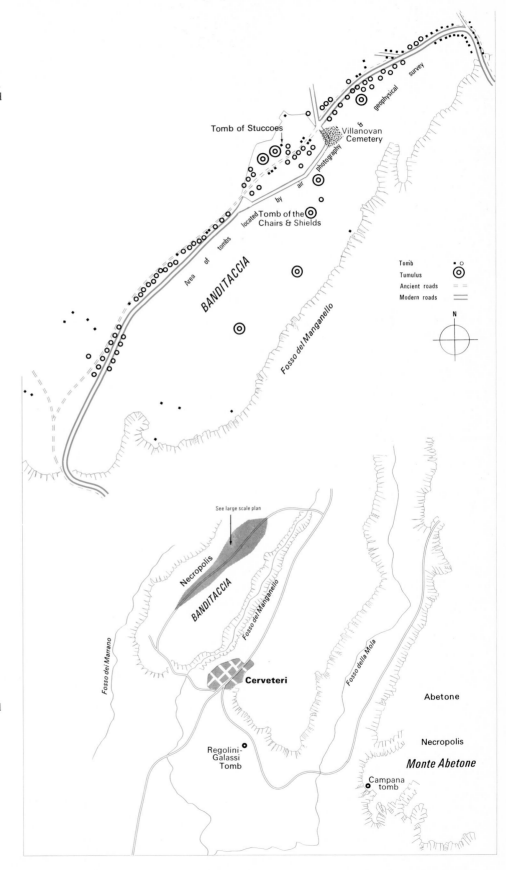

Above: Cerveteri. The Tomb of the Stuccoes

again shown the presence of a cemetery.

Of Cerveteri's two ports that of Pyrgi, to the west of Santa Severa, is of greater interest. Recent excavations yielded a bilingual gold tablet in Etruscan and Phoenician, while re-mains of the harbour installations are also visible under suitable conditions. The site, lying beside the Via Aurelia, continued in occupation throughout the Roman period. There is a museum on the site at Cerveteri.

Pallottino, M., *Cerveteri* (Official Guidebook), Rome

6c   The Etruscans: Tarquinia   Italy

Some 43 miles (70km) northwest of ROME lay Tarquinia, one of the most important Etruscan cities, and one whose famous painted tombs have attracted attention for several centuries. The very extensive site comprises a city area even larger than that at VEII and extensive cemeteries running southeast from the modern town along the Monterozzi ridge.

The city site lay on a ridge-top plateau some 1¼ miles (2km) east of the Marta river and is known to have developed from Villa-novan nuclei. By the third century B C, 5 miles (8km) of walls enclosed the defended area, although in certain places the natural scarp edge may have been left undefended. It is, however, unlikely that all the site area was ever occupied simultaneously. Although there has been relatively little work within the wall circuit, the core of the site probably lay on the western side. In the rest of the enclosed area the principal feature visible today is the massive temple foundation known as the Ara della Regina.

In total contrast the cemeteries along the Monterozzi ridge are among the richest in Etruria. Graves are known to extend for at least 3 miles (5km) southeast from the modern town along the ridge. Archaeologists have been able to locate the original Villanovan nucleus at Arcatelle. From this developed a

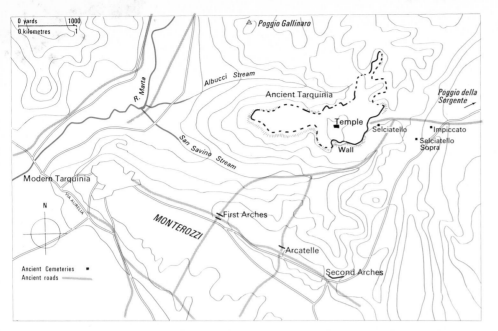

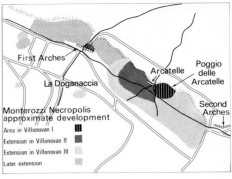

late Villanovan extension to the west and ultimately some 2 miles (3km) of the ridge was extensively filled with tombs. The number of tombs is continuously being extended by geophysical survey and aerial photography. Principal interest, however, centres on the painted tombs of the necropolis which date predominantly from the sixth to the third century B C. In contrast to the relief sculpture of many tombs at CERVETERI, the practice at Tarquinia was to paint the rock-cut burial chamber with frescoes depicting such topics as funerary banquets, athletic contests, and scenes from mythology or combat. Most of the tombs are preserved in excellent state and the contents of the paintings are normally happy in character. This extends even to the depiction of the funeral ceremonies of the deceased; in contrast the figures of the Underworld, which appear in some of the latest tombs, are depicted in very sombre fashion.

The wealth of material from this outstanding necropolis also contains certain scenes such as fishing and wild fowling from everyday life and serves to counterbalance the relative absence of information from the great city site to the north. The most important finds from the latter are perhaps the great terracotta horses derived from the façade of a temple and housed in the Palazzo Vittelleschi. This now contains the museum whence a guide will conduct visitors to some of the tombs. The tombs are naturally kept blocked to prevent vandalism, and techniques have recently been developed to photograph the interiors of newly discovered chambers by means of a periscope camera, thus obviating the immediate need for excavation.

Hencken, H., *Tarquinia and Etruscan Origins*, London and New York, 1968
Pallottino, N., in *Monumenti Antichi*, 36, 1, (1937)
Romanelli, P., *Tarquinia: la necropoli e il museo*, Rome, 1954

Top left: General map of Tarquinia. Top right: Map showing detail of the Monterozzi ridge. Above left: Frescoes in the Tomb of the Augurs. Left: The sarcophagus of a magistrate, now in the local museum

6d   The Etruscans: Chiusi   Italy

The most famous city of northern Etruria and the home of the legendary king Porsenna lay at Chiusi (ancient Clusium) south of the lake of the same name in the upper valley of the Chiana river. Around Chiusi and the Val Chiana to the west of Lake Trasimene a dense concentration of Villanovan and Etruscan settlement is known, principally from finds made in the associated cemeteries. The main settlement, Chiusi, is lost beneath the present town but the yield of sepulchral and other archaeological material has been enormous and forms the basis of much of the collection in the Museo Archeologico, Florence.

While there is evidence of a substantial Villanovan settlement at Poggio Renzo to the north it appears that by the seventh century BC Clusium (sometimes called Clevsin, it would appear, in some Etruscan inscriptions and Camars by the Roman historian Livy) had

attained pre-eminence in northeastern Etruria. Its hinterland was extremely fertile, with navigable contact with the Tiber to the south, and the city's prosperity was based on the richness of its agriculture. By the seventh century imported tomb material shows that artistic influences were filtering through from the great coastal cities as well as from the south. Among the Greek imports is the famous 'François vase' discovered at Fonterotella. By the sixth century BC the city was a centre of great artistic activity principally known to us through artifacts recovered as grave goods.

There is evidence of flourishing workshops producing terracotta and other statuary, painting and metalcraft. A particular feature is the number of urn statues produced between the sixth and fourth centuries BC, following a severe archaic style. Standing statues are few but there are many examples of reclining

figures, such as the magnificent Thanunia Tlesana sarcophagus, and husband and wife composite sarcophagi. For its paintings Clusium and its artists appear to have drawn heavily on the Tarquinian tradition. The painted tomb chambers exhibit themes and motifs familiar from sixth- and fifth-century TARQUINIA, though with perhaps less Greek influence. Among the surviving painted tombs two deserve to be visited, one on Casuccini and the other the *Tomba della scimmia* (the Tomb of the Monkey). Both date from the middle of the fifth century; their painted figures shown in the familiar routines of banqueting and dancing form a frieze around the chamber. Elsewhere the Tomb of the Grand Duke belongs to a later date and exemplifies the small rock-cut *hypogaea* that honeycomb so much of the surrounding area.

Although there is no doubting the prosperity and artistic richness of Clusium in the Etruscan period it does not have the more dramatic remains of its seaboard equivalents. Yet the city played a major role in the development of the area and its richness can best be appreciated by the treasures on display in the Florence museum. There is also a local museum.

Left: Lid of a cinerary urn, 650 BC, now in the local museum

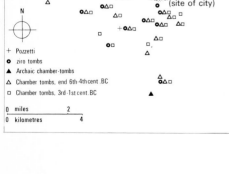

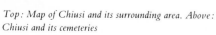

Top: Map of Chiusi and its surrounding area. Above: Chiusi and its cemeteries

On the coast of the BAY OF NAPLES beneath Vesuvius lay the ancient sites of Pompeii and Herculaneum, the latter now largely covered by the modern town of Resina. Both ancient towns were shaken by the earthquake of AD 63, but in the final catastrophe of AD 79 they suffered different fates, which had important archaeological consequences. Herculaneum (in Greek *Herakleion*), closer to the centre of the eruption, was engulfed by up to 23 feet (7m) of mud lava instead of the volcanic ash that buried Pompeii. The effect of the lava was to act as an airtight seal that has often preserved internal architectural details such as timber to quite a remarkable degree, while sometimes allowing structures to survive to roof height.

The remains that survived at Herculaneum are also very different in character from those at the far larger site of Pompeii. Exploration by tunnelling during the last few centuries, although motivated by the hope of recovering treasure or *objets d'art*, located considerable areas of the town, notably the theatre, first discovered in 1719 when the King of Naples' cavalry commander dug a well in his garden! Altogether the area of the town may not have exceeded 50 acres (20ha). The excavated area comprises a largely residential southern quarter close to the foreshore. The visible remains, exposed since the start of modern excavation in 1927, begin at the line of a main *decumanus* north of which the edge of the *forum* was located, and the area was divided by a series of narrow streets. The resulting *insulae* contain the public baths and on the southeast a large *palaestra*. The remaining area is taken up by shops and, as one approaches the foreshore, increasingly opulent houses. All survive substantially and in places to the top of the first storey; the casements and projecting balconies of the shops overlooking the streets conjure up a remarkable picture of town life. The richer villas dominating the south wall of the town are reminiscent of those to be found in the northern quarter of Pompeii.

Elsewhere, below the town wall, the foreshore now some 220 yards (200m) from the sea was occupied partly by a cemetery and partly by the recently excavated Suburban Baths, remarkable for their early imposition of arches directly upon columns in the central hall. It is perhaps in these baths that one gains the greatest impression of the effect of the eruption. The impact of the mud stream of lava had pushed down doors and engulfed the interior, but left the building substantially intact down to the complete boiler system for the hot plunge bath. In this way it is perhaps the most evocative of all the buildings in the town. At the same time, even though excavation has probably only exposed a quarter of its full extent, the town proper gives us a

picture to counterbalance that from Pompeii. Relatively small in size, its character was notably more residential and indeed more refined than its neighbour to the southeast. The town plan, so far as it is understood, reflects pre-Roman planning reminiscent of the street grids at OLYNTHUS in Greece, and architecture and internal decoration survive to a degree that is rarely paralleled at Pompeii.

Continuity with the pre-Roman period is represented structurally by the *Casa Sannitica* (Samnite House) which must once have been the predominant style of housing *c*. 200 BC. It contains a magnificently preserved *atrium* decorated in the first style with a marble-lined

impluvium set in a decorated floor. This Italic design was enhanced by an Ionic-style loggia and walkway on the upper floor, a feature that was ultimately walled in. The whole design looks back to the early days of the town's development (although formally conquered in 307 BC the town only came under strong Roman influence after 89 BC) and forward to the loggias of Italian Renaissance houses. Nearby, and sharing many of the features mentioned above, stands the *Casa del Tramezzo di Legno* (House of the Wooden Partition), probably the most completely preserved house in either Pompeii or Herculaneum. This large house, originally occupied

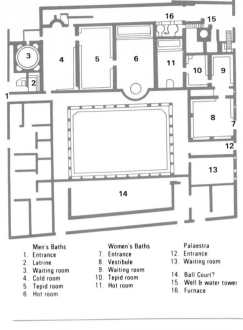

Men's Baths
1. Entrance
2. Latrine
3. Waiting room
4. Cold room
5. Tepid room
6. Hot room

Women's Baths
7. Entrance
8. Vestibule
9. Waiting room
10. Tepid room
11. Hot room

Palaestra
12. Entrance
13. Waiting room

14. Ball Court?
15. Well & water tower
16. Furnace

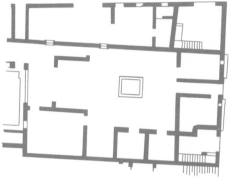

Opposite: The Suburban Baths, Herculaneum. Top left: Plan of the Forum Baths. Above: Plan of the House of the Wooden Partition. Above, right: House of the Neptune Mosaics. Right Residential street, Herculaneum. The House with the balcony is the House of Opus Craticium. Adjoining it on the far side is the House of the Wooden Partition

by a single well-to-do family, was later divided to accommodate smaller groups. The house takes its name from the large partition separating the *atrium* from the *tablinum* and constructed of three beautifully panelled double doors. In the same area stand the public baths which are in an exceptionally good state of preservation. Although dark and ill-lit (see below in the section on Pompeii), one can readily understand the water-heating arrangements for both men and women that controlled the movement of people from *apodyterium* (changing room) to *caldarium* (hot plunge).

On the southwestern wall overlooking the foreshore stood five very substantial villas. They give a detailed picture of the life of the well-to-do. The *Casa dell' Atrio a Mosaico* (the House of the Atrium with a Mosaic) stands to the height of the eaves in most places. The *atrium* survives almost completely as the formal reception room, while at the other end of the house, south of the formal garden, the family rooms overlooking the terrace include a large dining room and sun loggia. Sites like this made the town a quiet seaside resort in comparison with its more populous neighbour.

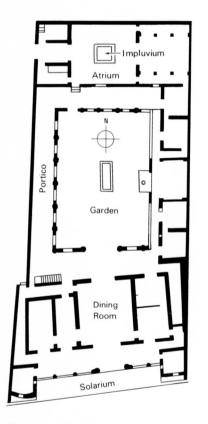

Herculaneum. The House of the Atrium with a Mosaic

In origin the famous site of Pompeii on the bay of Naples was a small native town founded in the sixth century BC close to the mouth of the Sarno river. Its position, therefore, placed it at a point of contact between the Greeks and Etruscans. In the last quarter of the fifth century BC it fell under Samnite domination and eventually became a Roman colony *c.* 80 BC. Like Herculaneum, it was totally destroyed by the eruption of Vesuvius in AD 79, and indeed many of its buildings had suffered extensive damage in another earthquake some seventeen years earlier. Unlike Herculaneum, however, the site was engulfed not with mud lava but with a protracted hail of cinders that killed, among many others, the elder Pliny, who had sailed out across the bay from nearby Stabiae to observe the phenomenon of the eruption at close hand. The effect of the ash and cinders was often more damaging to the remains that it engulfed, and timber work in particular does not survive to the same extent as at Herculaneum. Indeed, archaeologists have come to recognize that some of the voids in the compacted cinders represent the contorted forms of humans and animals that died of asphyxiation in the eruption.

The overall plan of the town is one of the fullest known of any classical site. Although the details in some cases still await precise elucidation, it is generally agreed that the nucleus of the town lay in the southwestern angle and comprised a roughly orthogonal plan based on small intersecting street grids. The rapid subsequent development of the site was probably contemporary with the creation of the much larger visible wall circuit. This probably dates to the aftermath of the Battle of Cumae in 474 BC, and the irregularities in the plan reflect the incorporation of preexisting roads within the larger layout.

In one respect the greatest importance of Pompeii as an archaeological site lies in the complete range of public buildings that are preserved within its walls. In the state that it survived at the time of the eruption, the *forum* gives us a picture of the formal centre of a provincial town in the middle of the first century AD. The northern end was dominated by the Temple of Jupiter, where in AD 79 damage from the previous eruption was still being repaired. Along the western side, behind the imposing two-storeyed colonnade flanking the *forum*, lay the *macellum* and Weights and Measures Office. This was followed by the Temple of Apollo which looked across to the remarkable *basilica* projecting from the southern side of the *forum*. This building could have served as law court and public meeting centre alike. The three buildings at the southern end of the forum were the meeting place of the town council (*curia*), two of whose number formed the annual magistrates of the town. The eastern side of the *forum* is of exceptional interest in that it preserves two small temples related to the imperial cult. They give us a clear impression of the way in which emperor worship, though stopping short of personal deification of the living, infiltrated itself in

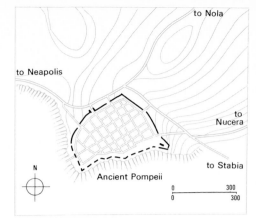

acceptable form into everyday life in Italy.

In the southern quarter of the town lay the theatre and *palaestra* complex. This carefully integrated group of buildings comprised a large conventional theatre and beside it an *odeum* for smaller audiences. The complex linked directly on to a *palaestra* that extended to the south wall of the town. The far eastern extremity of the walls enclosed the remains of the large *palaestra* and a massive amphitheatre. At the time of the eruption it had lain vacant for several years because the emperor Vespasian had forbidden its use after several fatalities during rioting between Pompeians and visitors from the neighbouring town of Nuceria.

The town is also remarkable for its range of bath buildings which provide a useful corrective to the common impression of such structures. The truth is that in the early first century AD most baths were still cramped, claustrophobic, ill-lit places, rightly stigmatized by Seneca for their unsavouriness. Pompeii and Herculaneum provide the proof of this in contrast with the later establishments at OSTIA. The Forum Baths have survived in considerable detail with their roof intact. Of even greater interest perhaps are the Stabian baths which tell us something by implication about sexual equality in the city. The baths were divided into separate male and female sections but the men had the better accommodation and water-heating arrangements, leaving the ladies with the dark, inferior portion of the building. At the time of the eruption, however, change was at hand. The New Baths toward the east of the town represent a complete change. The large airy windows created a well-lit interior, and sophisticated water-heating systems were being installed throughout the building.

The northern quarter of the town was the largely residential area. The parallelogram-shaped *insulae* contained a series of villas whose architecture tells us much about aesthetic feeling of the time. Tall walls in *opus incertum* pierced only by the occasional doorways preserved from prying eyes the internal courtyards of the well-to-do such as the Vettii, Vesonius Primus, and Lucretius Fronto. The plans of such villas are comparable with those at Herculaneum, and there is evidence from

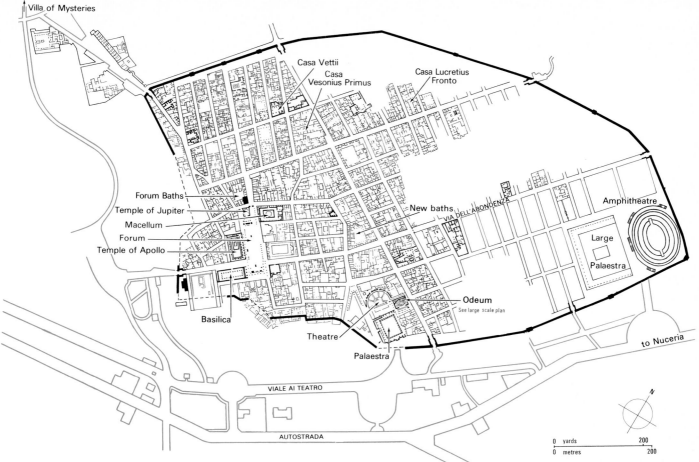

Labels on map (clockwise/as positioned):

Villa of Mysteries

Casa Vettii
Casa Vesonius Primus
Casa Lucretius Fronto

Forum Baths
Temple of Jupiter
Macellum
Forum
Temple of Apollo

New baths
VIA DELL'ABONDENZA
Amphitheatre
Large Palaestra

Basilica
Odeum
See large scale plan

Theatre
Palaestra

to Nuceria

VIALE AI TEATRO

AUTOSTRADA

0 yards 200
0 metres 200

Opposite, top right: Map of early Pompeii

Above: Map of Pompeii. Below: The Forum Baths, Pompeii, the hot-plunge room

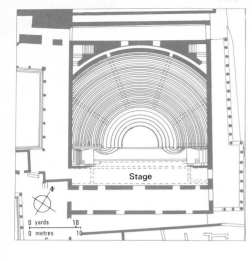

Above: Plan of the odeum, Pompeii. Right: Pompeii, the atrium, *House of Menander*

the Villa of the Mysteries, with its famous but enigmatic Dionysiac paintings copying a Greek original, that even larger sites existed on the fringes of the town. In complete contrast the main shopping street, the Via dell' Abbondanza forming the east–west axis of the town, gives us a glimpse not only of commercial life behind the shop fronts, but also of the thoughts and feelings of the citizens. In many places wall plaster has survived with political or sporting slogans, love poems, doggerel, and other obscenities of the day. With this wealth of material Pompeii is the town that gives us the greatest insight into everyday life in provincial Italy.

Becatti, C., *Pitture murali campane*, Florence, 1955
Buren, A. W. van, *A Companion to the Study of Pompeii and Herculaneum*, Rome, 1938
Carrington, R. C., *Pompeii*, Oxford, 1936
Diehl, E., *Pompejanische Wandinschriften*, Berlin, 1930
Diess, J. J., *Herculaneum*, London and New York, 1966
Gerkan, A. van, *Stadtplan von Pompeji*, Berlin, 1940

Maiuri, A., *Herculaneum* (Official Guidebook), Rome.
—, *Pompeii* (Official Guidebook), Rome.
—, *Pompei ed Ercolano: tra case e abitanti*, Milan, 1958
Tanzer, H. H., *The Common People of Pompeii*, Baltimore, 1939
Zuntz, C., *On the Dionysiac Fresco in the Villa dei Misteri*, Proc. British Academy, No. 49, Oxford, 1963

8   Paestum   **Italy**

In the seventh century BC colonists from the Greek metropolis of Sybaris farther south founded this city, now justly famous for its temples. There is evidence that the area had been settled previously in the Bronze Age. Originally known by its Greek name of Poseidonia, the city was conquered by the Lucanians in the late fifth century and refounded in 273 BC as Paestum, a military colony of Rome. Our knowledge of the city derives partly from modern excavation and aerial photography but principally from the remarkably well-preserved condition of the walls and temples that survived in an area that remained malarial until modern times. The walls belong

either to the late Greek or the Lucanian period and represent a partial reduction in size of the original street grid. The latter is probably of late-sixth-century date in its surviving form. The alignment of the temples, however, and the displaced position of the northern gate suggest the existence of an earlier street grid a few degrees off the later layout, a situation attested in more obvious form at MEGARA HYBLAEA, and precisely paralleled at SELINUS in Sicily.

There, as at Paestum, the central strip of land was utilized for public buildings of which the temples are the most outstanding element. At Paestum the oldest of the three, misnamed

the Basilica by early antiquaries, dates from the middle of the sixth century and was probably dedicated to the goddess Hera. Exceptionally, an odd number of columns front the building and the ambulatory is abnormally broad. The limestone columns taper with a marked bulge or, to use the technical term, *entasis* below wide, flat capitals of an early type familiar at Paestum. Immediately to the north stands one of the best preserved of all Greek temples. This example, known as the Temple of Neptune, dates to around 475 BC. The interior *cella* is remarkable in that its two-storey colonnade is partially preserved along with the lower part of a staircase. Beyond

Opposite: The temple of Neptune seen from the temple of Hera

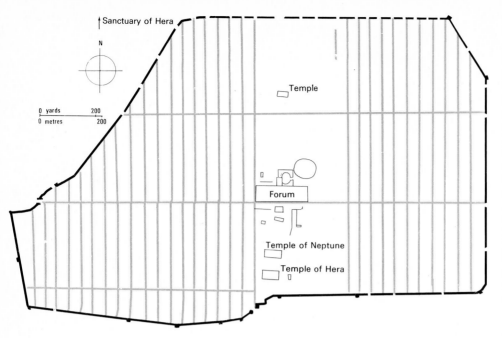

Sanctuary of Hera

N

0 yards 200
0 metres 200

Temple

Forum

Temple of Neptune

Temple of Hera

these two Doric temples lies the *forum* (which in its excavated form relates to the later Roman period) and the small temple of Ceres (though the ascription is not certain) toward the north gate. Complex details of carving and decoration give the temple an individuality without parallel in Magna Graecia. As an entity in the central area of the city, the three temples with their mixture of the classical tradition and local decorative features form a group unique in the classical world, not least in their degree of preservation. Beyond the north gate lies the prehistoric necropolis of Contrada Gando first discovered in 1943 and of Neolithic date. At the mouth of the Sele river, $7\frac{1}{2}$ miles (12km) from the city, the famous and long-sought sanctuary of Hera, traditionally founded by Jason, the leader of the Argonauts, was finally located in 1934. It apparently dates from the seventh century BC with principal buildings comprising a temple 128×61 feet (39×18.5m) and a *thesaurus* from which almost the entire Doric frieze was recovered.

Bradford, J. S. P., *Ancient Landscapes*, London, 1957
Castagnoli, F., *Orthogonal Town Planning in Antiquity*, London and Cambridge, Mass., 1972
Sestieri, P. C., *Paestum* (Official Guidebook), Rome
Zancani Montuoro, P., & Zanotti Bianco, P., *Heraion alla Foce del Sele*, Rome, 1951

9 Benevento

Italy

The expanding power of Rome in the fourth century BC brought conflict with the principal nation of south central Italy, the Samnites, particularly over control of the northern Campanian plain and Capua. The first (343–341 BC) and second (326–304 BC) Samnite Wars brought first moderate Roman successes and then the disaster of the battle of the Caudine Forks where the consuls and 40,000 Roman soldiers surrendered in 321 BC. When fortune changed for the better by 312 BC, Appius Claudius Caecus built the Via Appia, the major road to the south that ultimately ran through Benevento – ancient Beneventum (or rather Maleventum as it was known to Romans at the time) – to Brindisi. The third Samnite War (298–290 BC), in which Rome's enemies in Etruria also joined, reduced the Samnites to dependent allies and saw the adoption of the more propitious name for a colony whose position on the route to the south always ensured its importance.

Today, with one major exception, little of archaeological importance survives. Elements of the ancient town plan can be traced and the theatre has been heavily restored for modern use. A city gate is also visible together with the Ponto Leproso nearby on the Via Appia. Under Trajan the Via Appia was replaced in its southern section by a more

easterly route across Apulia known as the Via Traiana. The commemorative arch was dedicated at the head of the new road between 10 December 113 and 9 December 114 by the Roman senate and people at the start of Trajan's Parthian campaigns. In design the arch bears strong links with the Arch of Titus in the Roman Forum and it was apparently not completed until after AD 117 when Hadrian had succeeded to the throne. It may be from Hadrian's more pacific policies that the themes on the Benevento Arch derive, in total contrast with the unquestioning expansionism implicit in Trajan's Column in Rome, the memorial to the Dacian Wars. While some of the panels relate to the creation of the new highway and others are of direct local interest, the two principal façades proclaim mutually balanced themes. Travellers approaching from the east were faced with panels outlining the benefits of Roman provincial policies. Those heading from Rome, or the inhabitants of the town, were faced with panels proclaiming the benefits of internal policy in Italy and indeed in the Benevento area. One panel shows the emperor (probably accompanied by his successor, Hadrian) making a dedicatory sacrifice at the inauguration of the new road. This is associated with another in which Trajan and his court are shown distributing relief to

the poor and needy families of the region. A local inscription actually attests the process which was part of the *alimenta* system also identified at VELEIA. While certain other scenes relate to the political prelude to, but not the military events of, the Parthian War, the arch is unique in being limited to showing, albeit in the grand manner and sometimes in allegorical form, the peaceful achievements of the 'best of emperors'. In depicting these themes it is perhaps the finest piece of imperial propaganda in both impact and artistry. Finds are in the local museum.

Pietrangeli, C., *L'Arco di Traiano a Benevento* (Documentario Fotografico Athenaeum), 1943
Hassel, K. J., *Der Traiansbogen in Benevent*, Berlin, 1966

Opposite: Benevento. Trajan's Arch

The Bay of Naples is one of the richest archaeological areas of Italy, where the fusion of Greek and Italian influences is fundamental to an appreciation of the history of the region. The present geography is dictated by a number of extinct volcanoes and the now quiescent Vesuvius, encircling the eastern and northern sides of the Bay and extending beyond Baiae and Cape Misenum in the form of an island chain comprising Procida and its larger neighbour, Ischia. To the south the island of Capri forms an outlier of the limestone Sorrento peninsula. This great bowl, backed by the fertile Campanian plain, must have attracted human settlement from earliest times, although little is known of the early prehistory. Toward the other end of the time scale the twin towns of POMPEII and HERCULANEUM, buried by the eruption of Mount Vesuvius in A D 79, form two of the most informative sites in Italian archaeology.

For the proto-historic period the area is of the greatest importance. The more precise chronology now available for Greek pottery enables some of the initial points of contact between Greece and mainland Italy to be analysed; it has also decided among conflicting traditions in favour of the account that the great *acropolis* of Cumae had been established from the earliest Greek settlement, Pithecussae on the island of Ischia. The cemetery excavated in the Valle San Montano beneath the presumed settlement site of Pithecussae at Monte di Vico on Ischia has produced pre-colonial Greek material belonging to the first third of the eighth century B C. Whatever the precise nature of the settlement, it appears to have been associated with the commerce generated by the smelting of iron ore.

Although it lacked an adjacent harbour, the *acropolis* of Cumae was too inviting a strategic strongpoint not to have been occupied in the prehistoric period. Around 730 B C, however, the Greek colony was founded on the *acropolis*, eventually dominated by a temple (the so-called Temple of Jupiter) dating· back at least to the fifth century B C (although extensively refurbished and later damaged). The so-called Temple of Apollo lay on a lower terrace and the *acropolis*, despite its natural strength, was further defended by a rampart circuit of probably fifth-century date. Although the area round about the site abounds with archaeological remains, its earlier cemeteries are still of unknown extent and it was not until 1932 that Cumae's most famous feature, the gallery and grotto of the Sibyl, or prophetess, was found cut through the tufa bedrock and leading to a chamber made famous by the poet Virgil as the place where Aeneas had received the Sibyl's prophecy.

Much of the archaeology of Cumae still awaits detailed examination. Nonetheless, her historical role is clear as the focus of opposition to growing Etruscan power in Campania. Cumae's strength was based on maritime power and she twice defeated Etruscan forces, once on land in 524 B C and later with the allied forces of Greeks in Sicily and Campania in 474 B C. By that time Neapolis (Naples) and presumably Puteoli (Pozzuoli) were in her control. At Naples the original settlement lay on the promontory of Pizzofalcone on the western side of the modern harbour. In the middle of the fifth century a new town (which

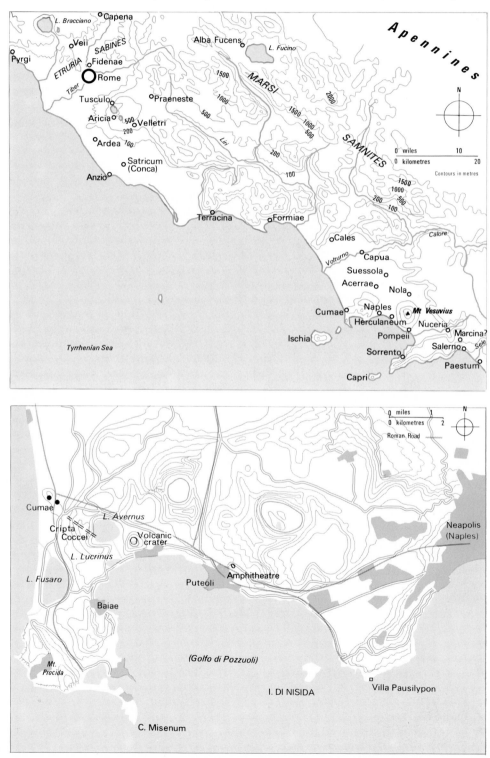

Top: Bay of Naples. Above: Cape Misenum

explains the name of the city) was created north of the port; the street plan of much of the medieval city still shows three of the four east–west roads and many of the smaller north–south divisions that must have made the town plan closely comparable with a near contemporary example at Thurii.

The Greek cities of the coast passed gradually under first Samnite (421 BC), and ultimately Roman (338 BC) control. The period of the Civil Wars at the end of the Republic saw a phase of intensive military activity at the hands of Octavian's lieutenant, Agrippa. The Greek description for the area between Naples and Misenum was the Phlegraean (fiery) Fields, a name that reflects the vivid relics of its recent volcanic past. Hot springs and the crater of the Solfatara near Pozzuoli demonstrated that, apart from the obvious extinct craters, Lake Avernus and the double bays of the harbour at Misenum represented flooded craters. In the search for secure naval bases Agrippa set aside the sombre legends of Lake Avernus and made it a naval base connected by a canal and dock to the Lucrine lake and the sea. As part of the same large-scale operations the mountain between Naples and Pozzuoli was pierced by a road tunnel known as the *Crypta Neapolitana* cut through the ridge extending south to Cape Pausilypon. The poet Virgil was buried nearby but the precise site is a matter of dispute. Agrippa's constructional feats were further extended west of Lake Avernus by another road tunnel (the so-called Crypt of Cocceius, named after Agrippa's architect) through the intervening ridge of Mount Grillo toward Cumae. Underneath the *acropolis* itself there also ran another tunnel along an east–west line which formed part of the same strategic system. Later in the first century AD the difficult approach to Cumae across the marshes to the north was made possible by the construction of the Via Domitiana.

Around the bay there were a number of towns other than Naples, HERCULANEUM and POMPEII. Pliny the Elder, for instance, had a villa overlooking Stabiae, modern Castellamare di Stabia. Puteoli, originally the Greek Dicaearchia, was a natural harbour settled in 529 BC; it enjoyed great prosperity throughout the Roman period with a polyglot population reflecting its trading connections with the

southern and eastern Mediterranean. The town was the principal commercial port of Campania and for three centuries prior to the construction of the artificial harbours at OSTIA on the mouth of the Tiber perhaps the most important port in Italy. This goes a long way to explain the wealth of monuments surviving in the town. The monuments of the lower town include part of the mole and the so-called Temple of Serapis, in reality the *macellum* or market, familiar in plan from such places as TIMGAD and DJEMILA in North Africa. The remarkable feature of the structure is geological because the building is a precise indicator of slow seismic changes in the level of the earth's crust caused by underground volcanic changes since the Roman period. Sometime between the thirteenth and sixteenth centuries the floor of the *macellum* was submerged to a depth of nearly 19 feet (5.7m). After a period of rise, the monument is again sinking at the rate of approximately four-fifths of an inch (2cm) per year. The upper town contains the remains of the baths and two amphitheatres of Augustan and Flavian date respectively, the latter worth visiting to inspect the lifting arrangements for the animal cages. Farther round the coast toward Cape Misenum, named after Aeneas's mythical companion, lay the resort of Baiae whose therapeutic springs and mild climate made it the most famous spa in Italy. In the late Republic Marius, Pompey, Caesar, Varro and Cicero all owned luxurious villas there, property that was gradually transformed into an imperial residence. It was in one such villa that the empress Agrippina met her death. Now the shoreline is littered with the remains of thermal establishments much damaged by earthquake and subsidence. Their effect on the visitor explains the geographer Strabo's comment that 'at Baiae another city has come into being, with one mansion on top of another.' He referred in particular to the great multi-level construction built on the slopes of the Sella di Baiae and dominated by the three domes of the so-called Baths of Diana, Mercury and Venus. The former was the *sudatorium* of a bath unit, as perhaps were the others: the so-called Bath of Mercury, although at not quite 71 feet (21.55m) less than half the diameter of the Pantheon (147 feet;

44.8m), is earlier in date and therefore of great architectural interest for the evolution of the dome. The complex of assorted buildings goes back to the Hellenistic period and, it has been argued, eventually became the Severan palace at Baiae. That of the Julio-Claudians lies largely lost on the slopes toward the present castle. Farther along the coast the double basin of Misenum offered a secure fleet base, with a large water supply from the great reservoir known as the Piscina Mirabilis overlooking the bay.

On the opposite side of the bay other villas of the rich abounded, notably around Stabiae and Surrentum (Sorrento). Inland from Pompeii the neighbouring establishments at Boscoreale and Boscotrecase give some idea of the agricultural wealth that supported the rich. The island of Capreae (Capri), however, holds a special place because it received unique developments from Augustus and particularly Tiberius. The Villa of Damecuta on the plateau beneath Mount Solaro, originally accessible only by sea, was a superb *porticus*-style villa centred on a magnificent belvedere. The similarity of part of the design suggests that it may have been conceived at the same time as the *Villa Iovis*, Tiberius' eyrie perched on a cliff 1,050 feet (320m) high at the northeastern apex of the island. The villa, with its elaborate water-supply system, was intended for year-round residence commanding a panoramic view of the Bay of Naples. To the imperial recluse it must have appeared as it did to Strabo at approximately the same time, as an unbroken series of towns, residences and plantations – one continuous city.

The main museum for the area is the Museo Archeologico in Naples.

Buchner, G., *Metropoli e colonie di Magna Grecia*, Naples, 1964, pp. 263–74.

D'Arms, J. H., *Romans on the Bay of Naples*, Cambridge, Mass., 1970.

Maiuri, A., *Capri: Storia e monumenti* (Official Guidebook), Rome.

—, *The Phlegraean Fields* (Official Guidebook), Rome.

McKay, A. G., *Ancient Campania*, Hamilton, Ont., 1972.

Ridgway, D., 'The First Western Greeks', *Greeks, Celts and Romans* (ed. C. F. C. & S. C. Hawkes), London and Totowa, N. J., 1973, pp. 5–37.

11   Metapontum   Italy

Metapontum was a native Messapian centre when Greek colonists arrived there probably in the latter half of the eighth century BC. Destroyed by the Samnites toward the middle of the seventh century, it was later recolonized by the Achaean Leucippus whose effigy appears on the city's coins during the fourth century BC. The city's prosperity was due to

the fertility of the coastal area between the Bradano and the Basento, a fact also symbolized by the appearance of wheat on its coins. The city enjoyed a chequered history; first a refuge for the philosopher Pythagoras, the city was involved in the Pyrrhic War and the Second Punic War, when it was for some time the headquarters of Hannibal and his army. Eco-

nomic decline set in as the aftermath of the Hannibalic wars and later perhaps the effects of the slave revolt of Spartacus. When Cicero made a pilgrimage to the house of Pythagoras in 50 BC urban disintegration was advanced. By the middle of the second century AD only the walls and theatre appear to have survived relatively intact.

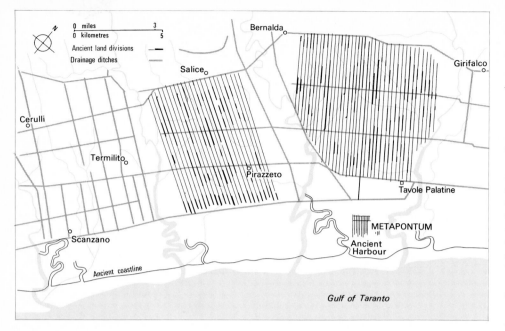

The plan of the city is known from some trial excavation supplemented by aerial photography. Like the extensive grid at Ptolemais in Cyrenaica, the city layout comprises broad east–west avenues intersected by numerous streets creating elongated *insulae* aligned north–south. The street complex is set within an irregular wall circuit overlooking the site of the ancient harbour now completely silted and more than 1,100 yards (over 1km) from the present coast. An elliptical area identified near the centre probably represents the *agora*, and to the east a concave depression marks the site of the theatre. Nearby stand the confused remains of the temple dedicated to Apollo Lycius, measuring 136×74 feet (41.5 ×22.5m) and distinguished by imposing architraves and metopes, some of which are displayed in the museum at Potenza.

The most important ruins lie outside the city at the so-called *Tavole Palatine*, a temple just over 1 mile (nearly 2km) to the northeast. The site is that of a Doric hexastyle temple of the late sixth century BC. It measures about 112×44 feet (34×14m) with ten and five columns surviving on the north and south sides respectively. Several nineteenth-century excavations uncovered much of the structure and yielded many painted terracotta fragments, sixth- and early fifth-century votive statuettes, and also the right arm of a cult statue. Recently traces of an early and extensive land division have been explored. Two zones, extending over 40 and 35 square miles (104 and 91km²) respectively, were divided longitudinally by drainage ditches about 224 yards (205m) apart. Individual plots were then created by latitudinal boundaries every 380 yards (323m), creating land units of 60 Greek *schoinoi*, perhaps representing the land grant to the colonists. These discoveries establish the application of advanced surveying techniques by the Greeks by 470–60 BC, but the ditch systems appear to have refurbished some elements of an orthogonal land-division system established in the mid-sixth century.

Ugerri, R., in *Parola del Passato*, XXIV (1969), pp. 51–71

Right: Doric Temple at the so-called Tavole Palatine

Illyricum, Moesia, and Dacia

Across the north of the Balkan peninsula, roughly from Vienna to the Black Sea, and between Macedonia and the Adriatic and the Carpathians, the Romans established four large provinces, all controlled by imperial governors of the highest grade for all or most of their existence. On the west, Illyricum had been conquered by Augustus and around A D 9 was divided into the separate provinces of Pannonia in the north and Dalmatia in the south. Territory farther east along the lower Danube, extending southward as far as the Balkan mountains, was organized about the same time as the province of Moesia. Dacia, north of the Danube and roughly equivalent

Dacians and Getae, in the east. Although both of these groups had long been in contact with the classical world, neither was noted for a rapid assimilation of Graeco-Roman culture, either in social order or material possessions. Except where large-scale mining was carried on under imperial supervision, for example in Dalmatia (gold, silver-bearing lead, copper, and iron) and Dacia (gold), the economy remained pastoral and agricultural with the population scattered throughout the countryside. Some areas, notably Pannonia and Dacia, were very fertile, but large parts of Dalmatia and Moesia could support no more than a simple pastoral economy. Advanced agriculture

sponsible for the creation of cities throughout all four provinces. From Caesar to Hadrian colonial settlements were established, normally of veterans discharged from the Roman army. This was the origin of the larger coastal cities in Dalmatia (SALONA, Iadar, Narona, Epidaurum, and others); some in the interior of Pannonia (Emona, Savaria, Scarbantia, Siscia, SIRMIUM, and Poetovio); in Moesia (Scupi, Ratiaria, Oescus, Ulpianum, and Nicopolis); and Dacia (Apulum, Napoca, Porolissum, Romula, Sucidava, ULPIA TRAIANA (SARMIZEGETUSA) and probably others). At the time all these provinces, except for Dalmatia which lost its legions before the end of the first century

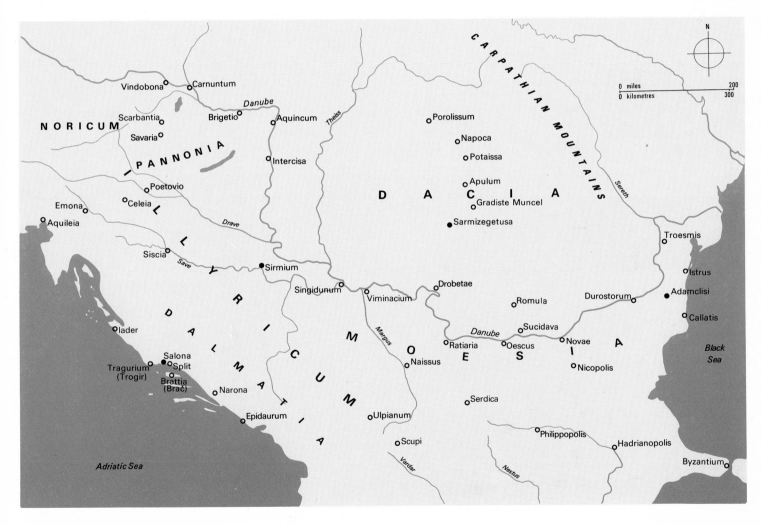

to Transylvania within the Carpathians, was conquered by Trajan in 105.

The natives of these lands spoke varieties of two languages belonging to the Indo-European family: Illyrian in the west (in Pannonia and Dalmatia, although both contained Celtic areas); and Thracian, including the speech of

could support wealthy landowners, and rich villas in Pannonia and Dacia reflect this. Except for isolated pockets along the Adriatic coast of Dalmatia and a few favoured areas in the larger valleys of Moesia this was not the case south of the river.

It was the Roman presence that was re-

A D, held standing armies of legionaries and *auxilia*, up to 50,000 men in each case, deployed along the Danube or, in the case of Dacia, in a defensive network watching the routes for the once expected move forward or, as time went on, the routes by which barbarian invasions might be expected. The road system linking north Italy, the Rhineland and the northwest with the Aegean, Asia Minor, and the East, was planned for military needs: as far as the imperial government was concerned the commercial importance was quite incidental. Later on, even some of the larger native centres remote from major roads became Roman cities, as much under pressure from the central government as from any genuine advance toward an urbanized society among the local population.

Ironically it was the relative backwardness of these provinces that enabled the Empire to recruit large numbers of tough Illyrians and Thracians to defeat the many invaders who crossed the Rhine and Danube during the middle decades of the third century. Dacia had to be abandoned (c. 274) but the Empire as a whole recovered largely through the efforts of some capable and hard-headed emperors who came from humble families in the Illyrian provinces, Claudius Gothicus (from Dalmatia or Dardania), Aurelian (Dacia Ripensis, formerly Moesia), Probus (Sirmium, Pannonia), Diocletian (Salona, Dalmatia), Maximian (Sirmium), Galerius (Serdica), Constantius I and his son Constantine (Naissus, Moesia). After this crisis the provinces remained more or less intact until the early fifth century when invasions destroyed Roman authority in Pannonia. Dalmatia was lost in the sixth and early seventh centuries to Slav invaders, but much of Moesia remained under Byzantine authority for many years afterward.

Wilkes, J. J., *Dalmatia*, London, 1969

Mócsy, András, *Pannonia and Upper Moesia*, London, 1974

Hoddinott, R. F., *Bulgaria in Antiquity: An Archaeological Introduction*, London, 1975

MacKendrick, Paul, *The Dacian Stones Speak*, Chapel Hill, N. Car., 1975. Brief but clear survey of ancient sites and their history

Salona and Diocletian's Palace · Yugoslavia

I

Salona (modern Solin, near Split) lay at the eastern extremity of a large bay in the central part of the Dalmatian coast, at the foot of steep hills that rise to form the mountains Kozjak and Mosor, closing off the coast from the interior. Originally a stronghold of the Delmatae, it was captured by the Romans in 118–117 B C and again in 78–76 B C. By 47 it had become a settlement of Roman traders strong enough to take Caesar's side in the civil war against Pompey. Soon after this it became a colony (Colonia Martia Julia Salona) and under Augustus the provincial capital of Dalmatia.

Apart from small villages that have grown up on its eastern and western fringes, the site of Salona has remained unoccupied since antiquity. Despite large-scale excavations the evolution of the city and its principal monuments remains unclear. The circuit of walls 2½ miles (4km) long encloses an area 4,590 × 2,300 feet (1,400 × 700m) and consists of two circuits joined along one side, a western city labelled *urbs vetus* by archaeologists and an eastern *urbs nova*. The earlier western circuit may date from the time of Caesar, although the so-called *porta Caesarea* leading from the *vetus* into the *nova* is demonstrably Augustan, rebuilt extensively in the early fourth century. The defences of the eastern *urbs nova* were apparently added in the reign of Marcus Aurelius, and further overhauls of the entire perimeter, including the addition of massive projecting towers, are recorded for the early fifth and the mid-sixth centuries. Other monuments of the city still visible include the amphitheatre built in the late first or second century to hold about 15,000, and later incorporated into the defences of the city as a vast bastion, and a small theatre of Roman semi-circular design with a raised-up stage and an adjoining temple precinct.

By far the most remarkable structures, however, are those of the early Christian era. In the northwest angle of the *urbs nova* were a basilican church and a cruciform church, rebuilt on more than one occasion in the fourth, fifth, and sixth centuries, together with their baptisteries. Outside the city were at least four great Christian burial grounds, associated with memorials of martyrs of the great persecution under Diocletian (c. 303–4), of which that at Crkvina has been completely destroyed by cement digging. Others at Manastirine, Marusinac and Kapljuč have all been scientifically excavated and the architectural evolution of the shrines understood. They come to an end before the early decades of the seventh century.

Perhaps the most famous native of the area was Diocletian, born of humble parents somewhere near Salona in 246. After reigning successfully for twenty-one years (284–305), he deliberately abdicated and withdrew to private life, for which he built a villa on the coast near Salona, where he lived until his death in 315. Later, part of the imperial residence was converted into an imperial textile factory (*gynaecium*). During the sixth century when the advancing Slavs were threatening Salona, it became a haven for refugees and from it grew the medieval city of Spalato (Split), whose houses and shops until recently obscured much of the Roman structures.

The Palace occupied an area of about 7½ acres (3ha), an irregular quadilateral 709 × 590 feet (216 × 180m), 574 feet (175m) on the north. The walls were of plain ashlar limestone quar-

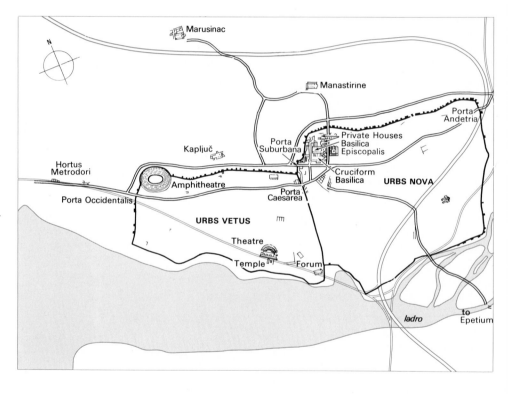

ried from the island of Brattia (modern Brač) or from near Tragurium (Trogir), 56 feet (17m) high on the north and 79 feet (24m) on the south, with an arcade screening a walk at the upper level on the north, east, and west sides. On the south a gallery with three loggias ran the length of the wall at the upper level. Gates in the north, east, and west sides were flanked on the outside by octagonal towers; at the corners and intervals were square towers, three of which still survive to near their original height, along with most of the curtain. Inside, a road flanked with rows of columns between the east and west gates divided the Palace. Little is known about the arrangement or function of buildings in the northern half, which probably contained accommodation for bodyguard and attendants, workshops and the like. South of the road was the octagonal Mausoleum of Diocletian (now the cathedral of Split) and a classical temple within its enclosure, on either side of an open paved area flanked with colonnades and now called the

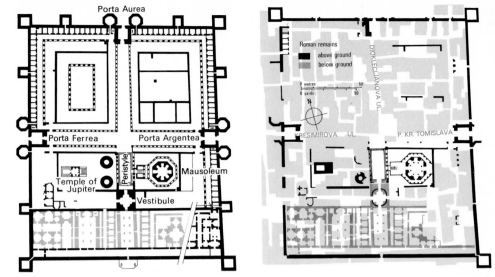

Diocletian's Palace. Above left: Restored plan. Above right: Roman remains surviving above and below ground level. Below: Model following the reconstruction of E. Hebrard

Peristyle. From this one entered the private apartments, raised above ground level on a substructure of vaults to a height of nearly 26 feet (8m). Of the original halls, corridors, vestibules, suites of rooms, almost nothing survives except for the great circular vestibule, although the original arrangements may be deduced from the plan of the underground chambers that supported them.

Finds are in the Archaeological Museum, Split.

Marasovic, J. and T., *Diocletian Palace*, Zagreb, 1968.
Wilkes, J. J., *Dalmatia*, London, 1969.

Sirmium, modern Sremska Mitrovic, lay on the north bank of the Sava river in southeast Pannonia not far west of its confluence with the Danube at Belgrade. It became a Roman military base during the conquest of Illyricum under Augustus and under the Flavians a colony was settled there (Colonia Flavia) where, unlike earlier colonial settlements, an important role was retained by the native population. Situated at the crossing of major routes across the Danubian provinces, Sirmium became strategically important during the

Below: Sirmium. Plan of the city
Right: Sirmium. The southern part of the city

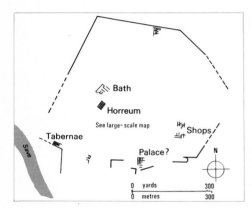

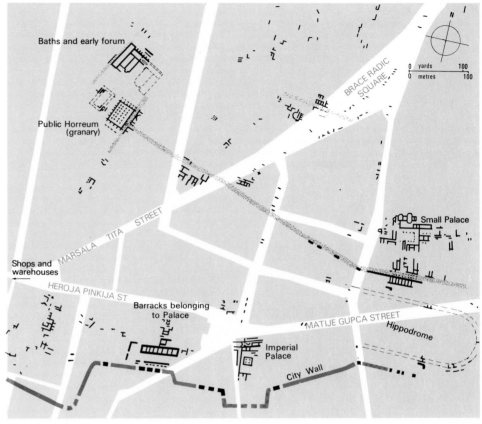

emergency of the third century, and from the reign of Galerius was a permanent residence for emperors. Sirmium was finally destroyed by the Avars in the years before 582, from which time there survives a dramatic appeal for help written on the surface of a building brick.

Today Sirmium is far from devoid of impressive ancient remains but their interpretation is uncertain, and it is still difficult to make much sense of the topography of the city as a whole. It seems clear, however, that when Sirmium became an imperial residence it be-

gan to acquire monumental buildings, constructed in brick apparently almost regardless of cost. Apart from a huge set of baths there is a vast storehouse with floors raised on stone pillars in the normal fashion of a granary (*horreum*), remains of a building that may have been part of an imperial residence, a row of shops possibly belonging to a city market, a hippodrome also connected to the imperial palace, and some rich private houses, also built in brick that may have belonged to imperial officials. The inscriptions attest a population that was then predominantly Christian.

Finds before 1918 are in the Archaeological Museum, Zagreb; others are in the Vojvodina Museum, Novi Sad, and the National Museum, Belgrade.

Hoffiller, Viktor, *VI. Int. Kong. für Arch. Berlin 1939*, Berlin, 1940, pp. 517–26.
Mócsy, András, *Pannonia and Upper Moesia*, London, 1974, 321f.
Ochsenschlager, E., and Popović, V., *Sirmium*, I–III, Belgrade – New York; 1971–3

Ulpia Traiana, the original capital of Roman Dacia, lay at Haţeg about 5 miles (8km) east of the Transylvanian Iron Gates. The site of a Roman military base during the Trajanic conquest, the civil settlement that grew up then was the basis for a veteran colony settled there between AD 108 and 110 (Colonia Ulpia Trai-

ana Augusta Dacica). Under Hadrian it acquired the name of the old Dacian capital Sarmizegetusa which lay in the hills about 37 miles (60km) to the east. Ulpia Traiana was the residence of the imperial finance officer (*procurator*) for the three provinces of Dacia. Under Severus Alexander (222–235) it acquired the

unusual title *metropolis*, but after the middle of the third century fell into a rapid decline and has since remained unoccupied.

The central area of the colony was enclosed by stone walls within a rectangle of approx. 1,970 × 1,770 feet (600 × 540m) with rounded corners, inside which some substantial buildings have been excavated. The *forum*, partly explored, included a *basilica* 280 × 33 feet (85 × 10m) in which three periods of construction have been noted. Along its north side some statue bases have been discovered, including one of the second-century governor M. Sedatius Severianus. At the end of the *basilica* a flight of steps led up to a heated room which was probably the *curia* where the city council, and, in the third century, the provincial assembly of the three Dacian provinces met. South of the basilica was the open forum area, about 280 × 138 feet (85 × 42m), paved with flagstones and surrounded by a covered portico. North of the *forum* are the remains of a great rectangular building, originally two storeys high and with buttressed walls, measuring overall 280 × 213 feet (85 × 65m). It appears to have been the centre for that branch of the imperial cult reserved for rich freedmen (*Augustales*) as a compensation for their ineligibility for normal municipal office, and it has been labelled *aedes Augustalium*. Behind this lay the shrine of *Roma et Augustus* with underground cisterns beneath.

Outside the walled area are remains of the amphitheatre built up from ground level to hold 5,000 people. Over a dozen temples are known, more than two-thirds of them outside the walls, dedicated to a variety of classical and oriental gods. Also striking is the private mausoleum of the Aurelii family, a circular monument 69 feet (21m) in diameter about 660 yards (600m) east of the city. It probably dates to the middle of the second century when the family was prominent in local politics. Farther away from the city the flourishing economy of the second century is reflected in

the rich variety of finds from excavated Roman farms (*villae rusticae*) in the vicinity.

Finds are in the museum on the site, at Deva and Cluj, and now also in the National Museum, Bucharest.

Daicoviciu, C., and H., *Ulpia Traiana (Monumentele patriei noastre)*, Bucharest, 1962.

Below: Ulpia Traiana. Plan of the city

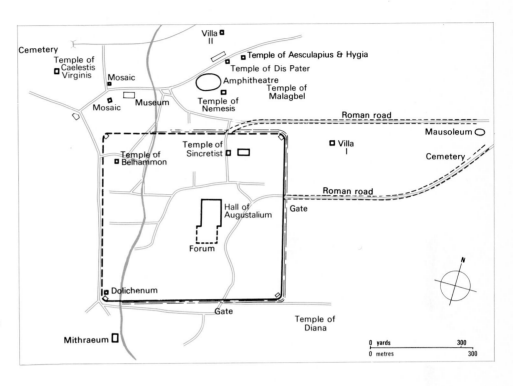

---

4   Adamclisi   **Romania**

This most famous of Roman war memorials commemorates Trajan's conquest of Dacia in the form of a monumental *tropaeum*, about 37 miles (60km) southwest of Constanţa, and 10 miles (16km) south of the Danube in Moesia Inferior. Why it was built there is not clear but it was probably connected with an early altar, some hundreds of yards east of the *tropaeum*, which listed Roman casualties in a Dacian war, either that of Domitian (AD 86–8) or Trajan. An inscription, which appeared twice on the hexagonal pedestal supporting the 26-feet (8m) high stone trophy, records that the *tropaeum* was dedicated in 109 to Mars the Avenger (*Mars Ultor*). It consists of a solid concrete drum nearly 100 feet (30m) in diameter set upon a stone platform with nine steps. Originally it was encased with ornamental friezes and seven courses of plain limestone that framed a series of 54 metopes placed either halfway up or at the top beneath the cornice. The precise details of the reconstruc-

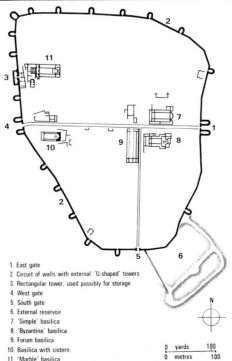

1. East gate
2. Circuit of walls with external 'U-shaped' towers
3. Rectangular tower, used possibly for storage
4. West gate
5. South gate
6. External reservoir
7. 'Simple' basilica
8. 'Byzantine' basilica
9. Forum basilica
10. Basilica with cistern
11. 'Marble' basilica

tion and in particular the original order of the metopes is still a matter of argument. The most recent arrangement, followed in the permanent display now on the site, by Florea Bobu Florescu, is based on analysis of the constructional details of the metopes and the ornamental friezes, together with a study of the positions in which the metopes had fallen off the monument after a major earthquake. A variety of subjects is treated through the individually framed relief on each metope, including battle scenes between Romans and Dacians (with their German and Sarmation allies). Trajan appears more than once with his staff. Dacian wagons are shown and Dacian women and children appear as prisoners after a defeat.

In the valley below there grew up a city which became known as Tropaeum Traiani. Most of the impressive remains on the site belong to the period of Constantine I and later, when the city was completely rebuilt following destruction by the Goths, a recon-

Below, left: Roman war memorial (tropaeum) built at Adamclisi by the emperor Trajan and dedicated in A D 109 to commemorate Roman victories over the Dacians. Right: Plan of Trajan's monument

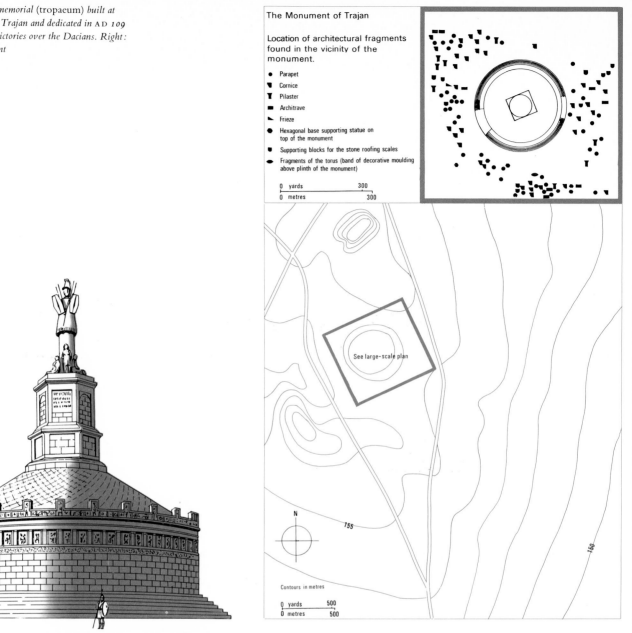

The Monument of Trajan

Location of architectural fragments found in the vicinity of the monument.

- • Parapet
- ◤ Cornice
- ⊤ Pilaster
- ■ Architrave
- ◣ Frieze
- ● Hexagonal base supporting statue on top of the monument
- ▪ Supporting blocks for the stone roofing scales
- ◗ Fragments of the torus (band of decorative moulding above plinth of the monument)

| 0 | yards | 300 |
| 0 | metres | 300 |

See large-scale plan

N

155

150

Contours in metres

| 0 | yards | 500 |
| 0 | metres | 500 |

struction commemorated in a verbose inscription of A D 316. The city walls were 13 feet (4m) thick and had twenty-two projecting rounded towers enclosing an area of 25 acres (10ha). Of the three gates the east and west were flanked with towers, but that on the south was no more than a narrow postern. The paved road between the two main gates was flanked by covered porticoes. In the angle with a side road leading to the south gate was the great *basilica*, 197 × 85 feet (60 × 26m), with two rows of eighteen columns. Four other similar buildings have been identified as Christian churches, one of which was extensively rebuilt in the sixth century. The city was supplied by three aqueducts, one of which drained into a reservoir outside the city walls on the southeast. At the end of the sixth or early in the seventh century the city was destroyed once again by invaders and has since remained unoccupied.

Finds are divided between the museum in Constanța and the Archaeological Institute, Bucharest.

Florescu, Florea Bobu, *Das Siegesdenkmal von Adamklissi*, Bonn, 1965. German ed. of his detailed description of *tropaeum*

Richmond, I. A., *Papers of the British School at Rome*, XXXV, 1967, pp. 29–39

Vulpe, R., and Barnea, I., *Din Istoria Dobrogei*, 2, Bucharest, 1968, pp. 383–6, 507–9. Romanian summary of present knowledge of site

Greece

Greece is the most easterly of the southern extensions of Europe. It is formed of mountain ranges mainly of limestone and with crests often over 5,000 feet (1,500m) high, which run between south-southeast and southeast and continue in chains of islands across the Aegean Sea. Only about a fifth of the terrain is cultivable and travel is often difficult by land and restricted by sea, since apart from storms, which are frequent in winter, good harbours may have poor access to the interior. Earthquakes occur, especially along the line of the Gulf of Corinth, and there are volcanoes still active off Thera (Santorini) and on Nisyros, though such natural hazards never deter human habitation. Physically the most notable change since ancient times is an uneven rise in sea level, averaging perhaps 6–7 feet (2m), enough to submerge many harbour installations. The climate, in spite of some fluctuations, seems to have been much the same two or three thousand years ago as it is now, with hot summers and an annual rainfall, mostly in winter, of around 20 inches (500mm) on the east coast and 40 inches (1,000mm) or more on the west; but since limestone is porous, much of the country gets little benefit from it and few Greek rivers are perennial and none navigable. The main crops – before the modern introduction of tobacco and citrus – were corn, olives, and grapes, grown in the plains and on stony terraces along hillsides, and higher up there was summer pasturage for sheep and goats. Other livestock were cattle (serving for traction) and pigs, but horses were not used for farmwork. There was more wood than now on some mountains, though deforestation began early, especially near the larger settlements. To judge by census records of the late nineteenth century AD, when agricultural methods were still primitive and two generations of peace had let the population fill up, Greece as far north as Thessaly – its ancient limit – might have produced enough food to support about 2,000,000 people near subsistence level.

Although a Greek language was spoken in Greece in the Late Bronze or Mycenaean period, it would be misleading to call the civilization of that period 'Greek'. Mycenaean civilization had an elaborate and autocratic organization, centred on a few big palaces, usually fortified, and with an appetite for luxuries and busy contacts abroad. When the palaces were destroyed – mainly in the thirteenth century BC – the higher techniques of craftsmanship as well as of administration were no longer wanted; and the embryonic Greek society that emerged after much loss and movement of population inherited some religious beliefs, legendary memories, and necessary or inexpensive skills, but its standards and aspirations were hardly higher than those of peasants. This new society was composed of a hundred or more communities, mostly small and at their level of culture nearly self-sufficient, which might share festivals with their neighbours at a common sanctuary but were jealously independent; nor is this surprising, since there was no economic motive to amalgamate and coercion by a more powerful neighbour could often be prevented by alliance with some other old enemy of that neighbour. Exceptionally SPARTA managed to subjugate the rest of Laconia and by 700 BC Messenia as well, though to hold these conquests its own society became abnormally militarized; and ATHENS somehow and at some unknown time absorbed the other communities of Attica in a harmonious and equal union.

Each independent community, however small and rural, was dignified by the name of *polis* or 'city-state'. Its standard form of government was tripartite, executive, council, and general assembly of all adult male citizens; but the composition and powers of these parts varied. Originally the executive was a king, the council – of aristocrats – was advisory, and the assembly had shadowy rights of approval. In most states kingship gave way fairly soon, anyhow by the eighth century BC, to an annually elected board of aristocratic officers – a system intended to prevent concentration and continuity of individual power – and effective control passed to the council, though the assembly might be allowed to elect the officers. Later, as conditions changed, aristocratic rule in its turn was challenged and generally, often with an interlude of dictatorship (in Greek terminology 'tyranny'), it was replaced by 'oligarchy', a modification by which wealth instead of noble birth was the qualification for political power, or by 'democracy', where a larger proportion or in extreme cases all of the citizens were eligible for office and, though an elected council prepared business, the assembly was dominant. Yet, even when government became more public and more complex, it did not require much apparatus – small rooms for the officers, a council chamber (*bouleuterion*), perhaps a separate repository for records, an open-air meeting place (which might also be the theatre) for the assembly and, if special provision was wanted, an enclosure for law courts. As far as was practicable, these structures were in or near the *agora*, the recognized meeting place for citizens and later often a market place too. Citizenship, especially in a democracy, was a valuable privilege and generally Greek states became strict in confining it to the male offspring of citizen marriages.

Very little is known of the Early Iron Age (the eleventh to the eighth centuries BC). It was largely ignored by the oral traditions that came down to the first Greek historians in the fifth century BC and, except for the painted pottery, its material remains have till recently been neglected by archaeologists; but a little may be extrapolated from later institutions and the society described by Homer is evidently not Mycenaean, so that it should be based on something later. At the beginning there was emigration to the west coast of Turkey, which became fringed with Greek city-states, mostly new though some had Mycenaean predecessors; but though Greeks kept in touch across the Aegean Sea, commerce with more distant and foreign countries was now slight. At home the level of civilization was low and there was a continuing danger of attack by land and sea (as is shown by the location of such sites as ZAGORA and EMPORIO). During this period there was no building with architectural pretensions, sculpture did not exist, the small clay figurines were crude and those of bronze not much better (before the eighth century when metalwork became more ambitious), and the painted pottery was content with simple, but harmonious decoration.

Still, things were changing. By the early eighth century the population of some states was reaching the limits of local production of food, the wealthy were looking for more sophisticated luxuries, imported from countries farther east, and Greek traders were becoming active in Syria and also in Italy. From Syria they obtained objects of luxury in ivory and precious metals and of course more perishable materials, and these stimulated the artisans of Greece itself; another borrowing was the alphabet, which reintroduced writing – a skill lost after the Mycenaean collapse – and in an easier form. In Italy trade was probably in the main for Etruscan iron and bronze, but it was soon followed by emigration, and by the later eighth and earlier seventh centuries much of the coast of southern Italy and Sicily was occupied by Greek 'colonies' (as they are called, though in fact they were independent new city-states). Later there was more 'colonization' in the north of the Aegean Sea, along the Sea of Marmara, and finally round the Black Sea. Most of these colonies were agricultural and produced surpluses, especially of corn, which were exported to the motherland, and so such cities as Corinth could expand, paying for food with manufactures (among which painted pottery is often overestimated because it survives). These economic changes had vigorous and various effects in political development, speculative thought, craftsmanship, art and literature, and during the archaic period – from the mid-eighth to the beginning of the fifth century BC – the character of 'Greek' civilization became fixed. The material

0 miles 50
0 kilometres 80
Darker tint shows land over 200 metres

N

Dyrrachium

I L L Y R I A

M A C E D O N I A

Philippi

Pella

Thasos

Thessalonica

Samothrace

Olynthus

Corcyra

E P I R U S

Dodona

T H E S S A L Y

Lémnos

A e g e a n

Lesbo

A E T O L I A

E U B O E A

Sea

PHOCIS

Chalcis

Delphi

Eretria

Chios

Thebes

Empo

B O E O T I A

A C H A E A

A T T I C A

Megara

Athens

Andros

Corinth

Aegina

ARCADIA

Argos

Zagora

Olympia

Epidaurus

Delos

P E L O P O N N E S E

MESSENIA

Paros

Naxos

Sparta

LACONIA

Melos

Thera

Mediterranean Sea

C R E T E

T H R

remains of this period are impressive, since both private and public wealth were increasing and craftsmen catered eagerly for the new demands.

While the states of European Greece had only each other to fight, those in Asia met foreign enemies too and by 550 BC were subjects of the Lydian and soon after of the Persian kingdom, which also advanced into Thrace. Then in 490 BC a small Persian force crossed the Aegean to punish Athens and Eretria for helping the Asiatic Greeks in an unsuccessful revolt. Eretria was taken and its inhabitants were deported to Mesopotamia – more humane treatment than they might have expected from a Greek victor – but the Athenians with the Plataeans (who depended on Athens for protection against Thebes) defeated the Persian troops at Marathon. In 480 BC the Persians came back in strength, this time overland and intending to annex all Greece. The states north of the Isthmus of Corinth surrendered prudently, except for Athens and Plataea which had nothing to gain by surrender; but under the leadership of Sparta most of the Peloponnesians, except Sparta's rival Argos, decided to resist at the Isthmus. So Attica was evacuated and – to the great benefit of archaeology – devastated systematically. Luckily the Greek navies, of which that of Athens was far the largest, enticed their enemies into the strait of Salamis and defeated them decisively, and the next summer at Plataea the united Greek infantry somehow beat the Persian army, which then retired to Asia.

Sparta, more interested in keeping its own subjects down, would not take the war further, but Athens was not only a naval power but had recently become a democracy and democracies (where the poor could decide) were readier for adventures that might be profitable. So the Athenians set about liberating the Greek subjects of Persia, enrolling them and other threatened states in a league for mutual protection and soon turning the league into a subject empire. The revenues made Athens the richest and largest of Greek cities and, as a by-product, the centre of intellectual activity and art. Attempts at further aggrandizement led in 431 BC to a war with Sparta and its allies, ending in 404 with total defeat and the loss of the empire and its income. For the next thirty years Sparta dominated Greece, then Thebes had its turn, and finally in 338 BC Philip II, king of the Macedonians – a people not recognized as Greek nor all perhaps even Greek-speaking – made himself master of Greece. In this 'classical' period, from the early fifth to the late fourth century BC, ancient Greece was at the height of its prosperity and its art and architecture reached maturity. By lucky chances the most accomplished classical buildings – those on the acropolis of Athens – have survived unusually well: during the Middle Ages and on to the last century the acropolis was garrisoned and so moderately safe from depredation.

Philip was assassinated in 336 BC. His son, Alexander the Great, suppressed the inevitable Greek rebellion and then attacked the Persian Empire, conquering Asia as far as Pakistan as well as Egypt, and imposing Greek culture. When he died in 323, he left an infant heir and several talented generals, who were soon fighting over his inheritance. Eventually four main 'Hellenistic' kingdoms survived – Macedonia, Pergamum (in western Turkey), Syria with dwindling extensions eastward, and Egypt. Greece itself, again independent enough for cities to fight each other, had become peripheral, though a useful source of personnel for the Syrian and Egyptian kingdoms and, partly because of its impotence, a venerated repository of culture. In the second century the Romans moved in, annexing Macedonia and erratically controlling Greece, till in 27 BC (when for archaeologists the 'Roman' period begins) the emperor Augustus organized it as a province with Corinth as capital. The rich soon became willing partners; the poor, deprived of earlier privileges, had to be content with the benefits of peace. Till the mid-second century AD some ancient cities and sanctuaries continued to receive the munificence of rich admirers, though others declined or disappeared; and then, as the prosperity of the Roman Empire began to fail, Greece was left more and more to its own weak resources. A raid by the Germanic Herulians in AD 267 added widespread destruction and, though in 330 the Roman capital was moved to Greek Byzantium (ISTANBUL), the acceptance of Christianity as the official religion robbed Greece even of its cultural prestige. When the modern Greek kingdom was inaugurated in 1832, what survived from the ancient past was a dwindling stock of ruins, locally regarded as no more than a convenient source of building materials.

The art of the Early Iron Age was based on simple but well-judged arrangement of abstract patterns and it was not till near the middle of the eighth century that figures were attempted seriously and then in an abstract manner. The principal media were painted pottery and metalwork. In the second half of the eighth century new animal and vegetable motives became popular, copied and adapted from Oriental art, particularly that of Syria: the new Greek style is called 'Orientalizing'. Sculpture was added early in the seventh century and sophisticated architecture appeared about the same time. At first the human figure, in sculpture and painting, conformed to the primeval system of showing each part in strictly profile or frontal view – the views most easily recognizable – but the Greeks' continuing interest in anatomical accuracy, unimpeded by any religious or court dogma, led them around 500 BC to develop the representation of twisting and oblique poses. This progress can be followed most clearly on the painted pottery, since it was produced in large quantity (so that it provides excavators with much of their evidence for dating) and till the early fifth century was abreast of the more expensive arts. Sculpture in the fifth century achieved a serene balance between the formal and the natural, in the fourth interested itself more in texture and momentary phenomena, and in the third and second tried various innovations from the baroque to the sentimental till copying and adapting earlier works for Roman customers replaced invention. The Greeks had an enormous appetite for statuary of marble and bronze, set up in sanctuaries and other public places, though relatively very little of it has survived. For the effect it should be remembered that marble was painted, with increasing naturalism, and that on bronze (which was kept shiny) eyes, lips, and nipples were inlaid.

Greek architecture had a strongly sculptural character and was often more concerned with beauty than utility. Its principle was that of lintel and post, which meant that spans of much more than 20 feet (6m) needed intermediate supports, and for material it preferred large blocks of squared stone fitting precisely without mortar: the arch and the vault, fired bricks, and concrete were rarely tolerated before Roman times. The main styles were the Doric, with its appearance of structural logic, and the lighter and more decorative Ionic. The leading type of building was the temple, an oblong block surrounded by a colonnade: its purpose was largely civic ostentation, since worship was conducted at an altar outside and the temple itself was used to store ceremonial apparatus and valuable offerings, though often housing an impressive statue of the patron deity as well. Treasuries, frequent in sanctuaries, were smaller storehouses with a columned porch. The *propylon*, a monumental gateway, had a similar porch on each side; and the fountain house might have a single one in front of the water spouts. The *stoa* – the restricted use of the word is modern – was a regular feature of an *agora* or a sanctuary. Its norm was a long shed with an open colonnade on one side – a sheltered promenade, sometimes with shops behind. The *palaestra* was a square space for athletic exercise, enclosed by colonnades with rooms behind them, and a larger version with running tracks about 200 yards in length is commonly called a *gymnasium*: these establishments were often in the outskirts of a town. Council chambers were squarish rectangular buildings, which might have a columned porch. Theatres, for economy, were set in a convenient hillside and depended aesthetically on nicety of plan rather than ornamental embellishments: it was not till the Roman period that the auditorium and the stage building were combined. Private houses, if of any size, faced inward on a courtyard and in time acquired architectural features, usually of inferior quality.

Generally old towns that had grown up from villages remained unplanned, but new foundations were laid out on rectangular grids, if at first only for easy allocation of plots. The *agora* and sanctuaries too, if old, were irregular in outline, though as building progressed their sides tended to straighten out. City walls, a necessity in independent Greek life, had to follow natural lines and not much could be done about the contours of its *acropolis* or citadel. Further, within any area the relation of one building to another was hardly studied, at least before the second century BC, when examples of axial planning occur, nor (unless imposed by a grid) was regular alignment thought desirable. To Greek architects it was the unit that was important.

Survival has depended on material, location, and luck. So wood and mud brick normally have perished, metal unless concealed was melted down as scrap, and except in remote places marble has often been burned for lime and other building stone robbed or broken up for re-use. Further, many important sites are now built over and elsewhere excavation has rarely been complete.

Burn, A. R., *The Pelican History of Greece*, Harmondsworth and Santa Fe, 1966. A useful one-volume account

Cook, R. M., *Greek Art*, London and New York, 1972; paperback 1976. A short survey

Kirsten, E., and Kraiker, W., *Griechenlandkunde*, 5th ed., 2 vols, Heidelberg, 1967. The best short account of the sites

Wycherley, R. E., *How the Greeks Built Cities*, 2nd ed., London and Totowa, N.J., 1962. Lucid on planning and types of units

Annual surveys of archaeological work in Greece are published in *Archaeological Reports* (a suppl. to *Journal of Hellenic Studies*, London) and *Bulletin de correspondance hellénique*, Paris

I Zagora

Greece

The site now known by the Slav name Zagora is on a rocky promontory on the west coast of the island of Andros. It is surrounded by impracticable cliffs on three sides and dips toward its neck, on each side of which there is a small bay. The area of the top, which is over 500 feet (150m) above sea level, is roughly 16 acres (6.7ha). It has no natural supply of water and the nearest good springs are about a quarter of a mile (400m) away. So habitation was unlikely except when there was a constant danger of attack, and fortunately the town of Zagora existed only in the ninth and eighth centuries BC: when its inhabitants left, voluntarily it appears from the remains, it was presumably because more peaceful conditions allowed the use of a more genial site.

The town was defended by a stone wall about 470 feet (140m) long and not less than 6½ feet (2m) thick, with a well-protected gate near its southern end. How dense occupation was within is not yet known, but in the excavated areas houses clustered together and the population may have been more than 1,000. Building was mostly with the local schist, presumably packed with mud, floors were of

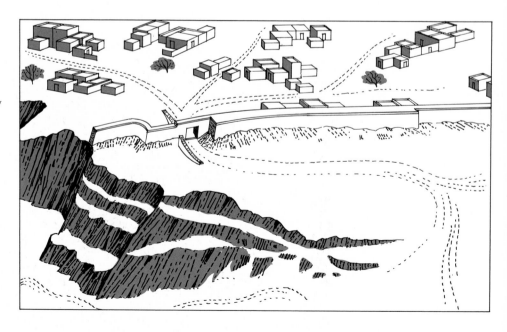

Above: Zagora. Tentative reconstruction, from the east

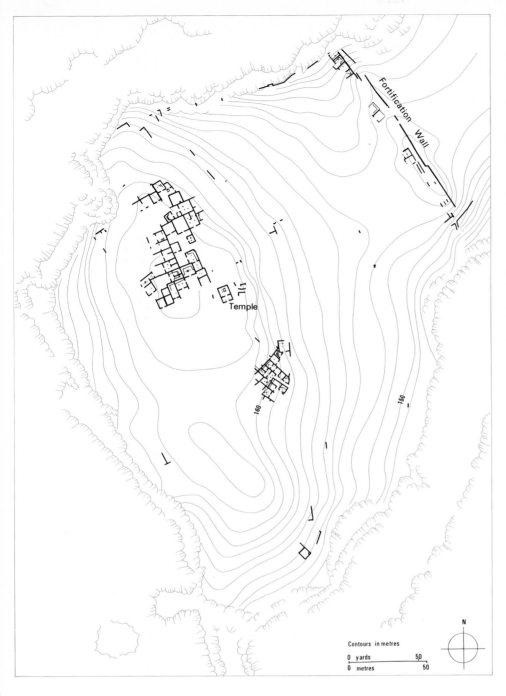

Temple

Fortification Wall

160

150

Contours in metres

0 yards 50

0 metres 50

N

earth and roofs flat and covered by stone slabs and mud. Rooms were squarish, varying in area from 60 square feet (5.5m²) to more than twelve times that size; many houses had several rooms; there were probably no upper storeys. The ideal plan seems to have been at first a single large room and later a more complex arrangement of courtyard, one or more living rooms and store (recognizable by a platform hollowed to hold big jars) with perhaps a shed for animals, but there is no regular arrangement of the units. Size varies, but no house yet discovered is so much larger than the others as to indicate a pre-eminent head of the community. The space round the temple was the town's sanctuary, but the temple itself was no earlier than the mid-sixth century BC: this suggests that the inhabitants of Zagora did not move far away, so that they and their descendants were able to visit and honour the old precinct. Though probably dependent on farming and fishing, Zagora appears to have been moderately prosperous: at least painted pottery, imported from Euboea, ATHENS, and CORINTH, has turned up in the houses. These and other small finds are still in the excavation storehouse.

Cambitoglou, A., etc., *Zagora* I– , Sydney, 1971–
Report on the excavations

2   Emporio   **Greece**

Emporio – its ancient name remains uncertain – is near the south end of the eastern side of the island of Chios. Here there is a good small harbour with a fertile valley running inland, a small hill on the south and a bigger one on the north. This northern hill, which rises steeply to more than 700 feet (220m), was the site of a village in the late eighth and the seventh centuries BC. The top was fortified by a rough stone wall, a good 6½ feet (2m)

thick and about equally high: the circuit, half a mile (800m) long, enclosed a space of about 6 acres (2.5ha). Within it, near the entrance, there were a big house (the 'Megaron Hall'), about 60 × 22 feet (18 × 6.5m) overall, and a simple temple. On the slope below more than fifty small houses stood on terraces. They were of two types: one oblong with a porch supported by two posts (the '*megaron*' type), and the other square and without a porch

(the 'bench' house, so-called because it contained a raised platform used – by modern analogy – to sleep on). All the houses, even the big one, were very simple, with only one room, earth floors, rubble walls and – to judge by the irregular placing of the bases of posts – flattish mud roofs. The *megaron* type may be the older. The temple succeeded an open precinct in the middle of the sixth century BC, when the settlement had been deserted.

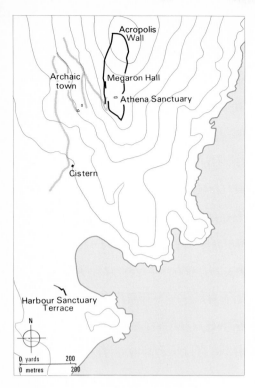

Though never impressive, this village is important historically: few settlements of its period have been examined and only ZAGORA as completely. The population is not likely to have been more than 500, engaged presumably in agriculture and fishing: there is no sign of specialized craftsmen and, to judge by the painted pottery, manufactured articles were obtained from the town of Chios. The choice of site is familiar in the Aegean islands in insecure times – not too near to or accessible from a landing place for a surprise attack by a small party of pirates; and the apparently peaceful evacuation about 600 BC (since there are no signs of violent destruction) suggests that such dangers were past and the inhabitants could move down to the more convenient locality of the harbour, where there already was a sanctuary. Politically it may be inferred that the village was controlled by the occupant of the 'Megaron Hall', a landed aristocrat. That his house alone was inside the fortification can hardly mean that he needed defence against the villagers, since the circuit was much too large for one household to man: perhaps, if water had to be fetched from the well halfway down to the harbour, only he had the spare labour – free or slave – to make the extra haul worthwhile. The standard of living, of the aristocratic family too, was very simple; but this Emporio was a very minor community. The finds, interesting to specialists, are in the Chios Museum.

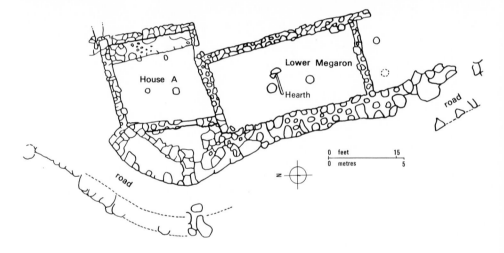

Above: Emporio. House 'A' and 'lower megaron'. 'A' is of 'bench' type, the other of 'megaron' type

Top right: Emporio from the north, tentative restoration. (The temple, dedicated to Athena, was not built until the settlement had been abandoned; all the houses may have had flattish roofs)

Boardman, J., *Excavations in Chios, 1952–1955: Greek Emporio*, London, 1967. Comprehensive report and study

Attica was the southeast corner of continental Greece with an area of about 1,000 square miles (say 2,500km²), two-fifths of it mountainous. It had good natural boundaries – on the west the rough hills between Eleusis and Megara, on the north the range of Parnes about 4,700 feet (over 1,400m) high, and to east and south the sea; only Oropus at the northeast was geographically and sometimes politically extraneous. There were four plains, those of Athens, Eleusis, the Mesogeion, and Marathon, which by Greek standards were moderately fertile. Other assets were silver in the Laurion hills, marble (which, though not important economically, was handy for Athenian sculptors and architects) and – as in many parts of Greece – good clay. Because of the size of Attica much of the population lived at a distance from Athens, and there were some small country towns that were worth fortifying.

The eminence of Athens is accidental. It was not on a main route, by land or sea, though this was an advantage for a weak settlement in unsettled times. More positively, its *acropolis*, though originally less sheer than now, was by ancient standards the best natural refuge in the plain of Athens. Then, as the capital of the central, largest, and presumably most populous district, it managed to absorb the rest of Attica. This unification, early enough for its details to have been forgotten by the fifth century BC, was not inevitable geopolitically, since Boeotia remained divided and Argos did not control all its plain till the 460s BC; but as a result Athens became an abnormally large Greek state. Later, in 492 BC, Themistocles persuaded his fellow citizens to make Athens a naval power, with the unexpected result after the defeat of the Persians in 479 that it established an empire in the Aegean and

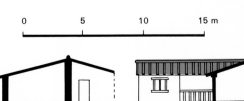

Above: Map of Attica. Left and below: Plan and reconstructed drawing of a country house near the Dema wall, Attica, about 420 BC. The purposes of the rooms are conjectural

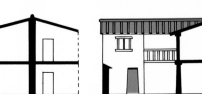

along the west Turkish coast. The profits made
Athens not only the richest of Greek states
with a population of perhaps 300,000, about
half of it in the city and Piraeus (now joined
by the Long Walls), but also the artistic and
intellectual centre of the Greek world; and
when in 404 BC the empire was lost, its cultural
eminence and the architectural monuments of
imperialism survived. Though the number of
inhabitants fell and eventually Corinth, because of its natural position, became the busiest
city in Greece, Athens had the sheltered status
of a hallowed university town, surviving looting by the Romans in 86 BC and to a lesser
extent devastation by the Herulians in AD 267,
until its pagan culture was finally prescribed
by militantly Christian emperors. So through
the Middle Ages and till the 1830s it was no
more than a local market town of perhaps
around 10,000 and its resurgence as the capital
of modern Greece was not due to any economic importance, actual or potential, but because European statesmen with a classical
education thought of Athens as the cradle of
their culture.

The best-explored parts of ancient Athens
are the Acropolis and the Agora together with

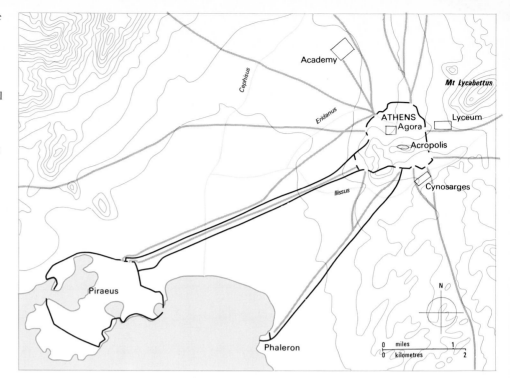

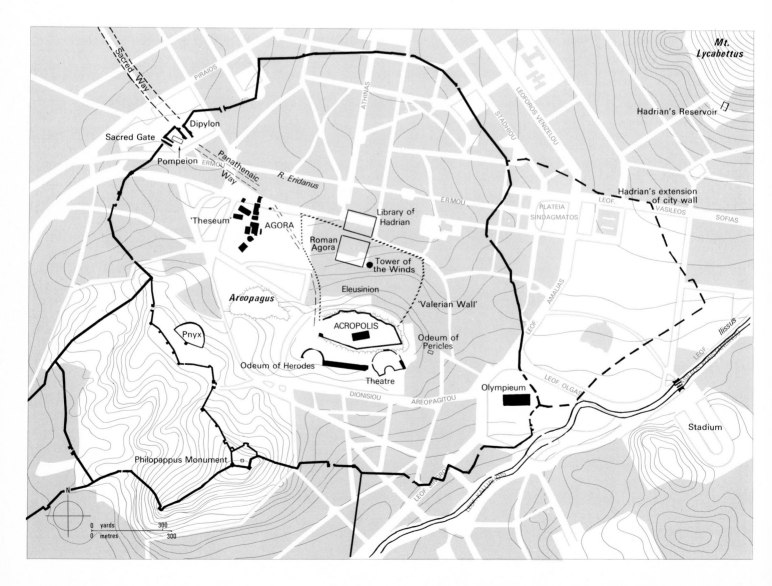

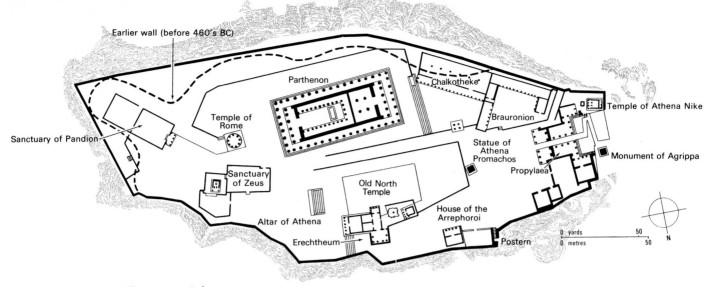

Earlier wall (before 460's BC)

Parthenon

Chalkotheke

Temple of Athena Nike

Temple of Rome

Brauronion

Sanctuary of Pandion

Statue of Athena Promachos

Monument of Agrippa

Propylaea

Sanctuary of Zeus

Old North Temple

Altar of Athena

House of the Arrephoroi

Erechtheum

Postern

0 yards 50
0 metres 50

N

Left: Athens and Piraeus, later fifth century BC. Left below: Athens. Plan of city. Above: Plan of the Acropolis of Athens, first century AD. Below: Model of the Acropolis, in the fourth century BC, seen from the northwest

their groups of public buildings. The Acropolis was fortified in the Late Bronze Age, when presumably there was a Mycenaean palace on it. In the Early Iron Age the defensive wall was maintained and sanctuaries were marked out inside it. Yet no traces of buildings remain that are older than the sixth century B C. These were two Doric temples (one just south of the later Erechtheum and the other on the site of the Parthenon), some treasuries, and a *propylon*: all these were destroyed by the Persians in 480 B C. Thirty years later rebuilding began on a grander scale. The Parthenon, in the dominant situation, though in cult not the principal temple, was of Doric style but with eight instead of the standard six columns at the ends and measured 101 × 228 feet (30.9 × 69.5m) in plan: it was built in 447–432 B C and housed Phidias's colossal statue of Athena. Next came the Propylaea (437–432 B C), an exceptionally complex Doric entrance. The Erechtheum (*c.* 421–406 B C), Ionic of very irregular plan, contained the principal shrine and the holy idol of Athena. More buildings were put up close to the defensive wall, now straightened and extended – of these only the little Ionic temple of Athena Nike survives. Though parts of one programme, the main buildings of the Acropolis were on different alignments and the great altar of Athena remained in front of the site of the old temple south of the Erechtheum; and the statues and other dedications so frequent in major sanctuaries were set up here and there with little regard for the general effect or each other. Similarly, the approach was by an unassuming zigzag path, not the present monumental stairway, which was a Roman improvement.

At first the meeting place of citizens may have been near the west end of the Acropolis, but by the sixth century the Agora was on fairly level ground down the slope to the north, an irregular open space some 500 feet (150m) across each way. On the west and also the south side a few public buildings were constructed, gradually becoming more pretentious, but these were destroyed by the Persians in 480 B C. Though some were patched up, replacement was necessary, since government had become more complex and for civic pride; and by 400 B C the west side was nearly filled, the so-called 'Theseum' (a temple of Hephaestus) had been erected on the eminence behind, and *stoas* and other public buildings closed north and south sides. The two-storeyed Stoa of Attalus on the east was a benefaction of around 150 B C: it has been restored reliably and gives a good impression of the purpose and convenience of such structures. The Panathenaic way, for ceremonial processions, crossed the Agora diagonally on its way from the Dipylon Gate to the Acropolis: part of it was used for races till the Stadium was made in the later fourth century B C.

The Pnyx, for meetings of the assembly of citizens, was on the hillside opposite the entrance to the Acropolis. It was created presumably at the end of the sixth century B C, when Athens became a democracy, and was abandoned in the later fourth for the theatre, when

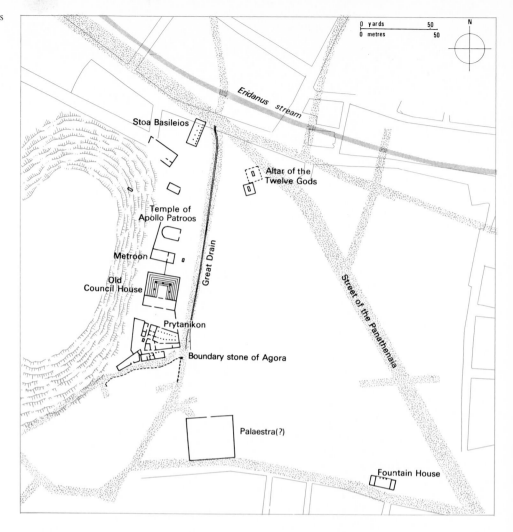

that was improved. This theatre, on the south side of the Acropolis, goes back at least to the early fifth century, but was remodelled several times. The Odeum, farther west, was built by Herodes Atticus in the mid-second century A D and has a Roman grandiloquence. The Olympieum, east of the theatre, was an unusually large temple, 135 × 354 feet (41 × 108m) in plan; it was begun near the end of the sixth century B C, continued in the second B C and completed – by Hadrian – in the second A D. Interruption of building was not uncommon: the Propylaea for instance never got its intended eastern wings nor, as often happened, was all its detail finished.

The streets of ancient Athens were mostly narrow, winding, and unpaved. The houses varied in size and comfort and, though often irregular in shape, were planned if possible around an inner court. Water was provided by a few springs, connected to public fountain houses, and there were many private wells: a good supply was not available till the second century A D, when Roman emperors built an aqueduct, and this did not last long. Sewerage disposal was rudimentary.

The city was fortified before the Persian destruction of 480 B C and afterward a new wall was built farther out. In the 460s Athens was connected by long walls with the Piraeus,

itself fortified, as a corollary of its naval policy and an insurance against attacks by land. (The so-called Valerian Wall was put up after the Herulian sack of A D 267 and shows how much the city had shrunk by then.) Beyond the city gates were cemeteries, clustering along the roadsides, with the best plots at the front: some notion of their original appearance can be got from the excavation of the Ceramicus cemetery outside the Dipylon gate. The *stadium* also was outside the walls, not surprisingly since the track had to be a *stade* – about 200 yards (180m) – long and there was seating for about 60,000 spectators; it was built in 331 B C, done up in marble by Herodes Atticus in A D 144 and restored by another benefactor about 1900.

Eleusis, 10 miles (16km) west of Athens and presumably once independent, was a small fortified town with its own plain and the most famous of Greek sanctuaries of the agricultural goddess Demeter. The site is now unattractive because of industrial development, but the low ruins of the Telesterion (where the mysteries were performed) show well how Greek architects of the mid-fifth century B C roofed a big hall. On the east coast of Attica, Sunium had sanctuaries and part of a temple of the 440s survives, perhaps by the same architect as the 'Theseum'. At Thoricus and in the hills

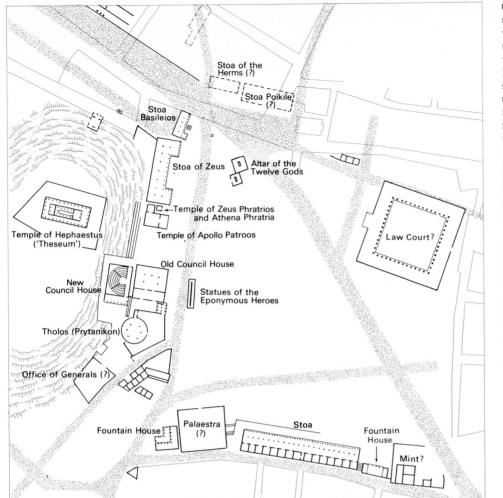

to its west there are clear remains of ancient mining installations. Brauron had a sanctuary where the dormitories of the girls brought up there can still be seen. At Rhamnus there were two temples and another fortified town. Near Oropus the Amphiareum was a healing sanctuary with lodgings for visitors and a theatre. The other sites of Attica are now less impressive, except for some of the border fortresses: of these the most accessible is Gyphtokastro (perhaps the ancient Eleutherae) which gives an excellent impression of the principles of defence in the fourth and third centuries B C. Very few farmsteads have been found: one of the later fifth century B C, which can be restored on paper, is near the Dema wall between Athens and Eleusis.

In art, Athens was exceptionally successful. In the so-called Protogeometric and Geometric styles of Greek painted pottery its school was the most accomplished and inventive and, though Corinth took the lead in the later eighth century, Athens recovered its primacy toward the middle of the sixth and for over two hundred years dominated Greek markets, except latterly in Italy and Sicily. For sculpture we have nothing from Attica before about 600 B C, but in the sixth and early fifth centuries (from which, thanks to the Persian destruction, many originals survive) Athenian products seem to have been as good as any. In the classical period and later it is hard and perhaps wrong to think of local rather than personal

Opposite: Plan of the Agora, Athens, 480 B C. Left: Plan of the Agora, 300 B C. Below: Model of the west side of the Agora in the second century A D, seen from the southeast

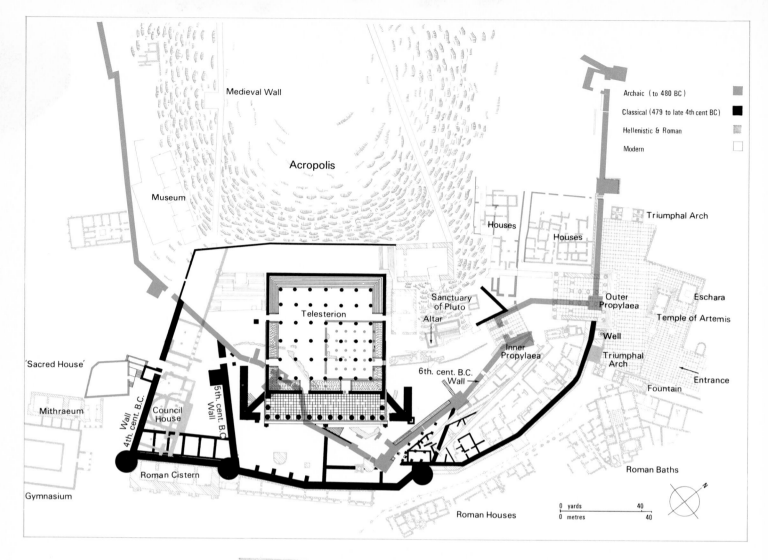

Archaic (to 480 BC)
Classical (479 to late 4th cent BC)
Hellenistic & Roman
Modern

Medieval Wall

Acropolis

Museum

Houses

Houses

Triumphal Arch

Telesterion

Sanctuary
of Pluto
Altar

Outer
Propylaea

Eschara

Temple of Artemis

Inner
Propylaea

Well

6th. cent. B.C.
Wall

Triumphal
Arch

Entrance

'Sacred House'

Fountain

Mithraeum

4th. cent. B.C.
Wall

5th. cent. B.C.
Wall

Council
House

Roman Cistern

Roman Baths

Gymnasium

Roman Houses

0 yards 40
0 metres 40

schools, but several eminent sculptors (such as Phidias and Praxiteles) were Athenian by birth and residence. Afterward the workshops of Athens were more concerned with remembering the past than with innovation. Of picture painting little is known, but Athens was probably the principal centre in the fifth century BC and still important in the fourth. As for architecture, the Athenians were ambitious enough in the later sixth century; and when the Persian destruction was more than made good in the second half of the fifth, they set new standards of subtlety and finish for the Doric style and disciplined and refined the Ionic. In later developments of Greek architecture Athens had a diminishing part.

The Acropolis Museum at Athens has the rich finds of sculpture buried after damage by the Persians in 480 BC and also architectural sculpture from structures of the fifth century, though much of that from the Parthenon was removed by Elgin. The National Archaeological Museum is the most important in the world for Greek art, drawing on other parts of Greece besides Attica; in sculpture it complements the Acropolis Museum and in painted pottery has a complete series of the Attic school. The Agora Museum (Stoa of Attalos) is more informative on less artistic subjects. The Parthenon, Erechtheum, Propylaea, Temple of Athena Nike, 'Theseum', Choregic Monument of Lysicrates, and 'Tower of the Winds' are all well enough preserved to rank as museum pieces. Not much sculpture from Athens is to be seen outside Greece, except for the Elgin Marbles in the British Museum, London; but most big Western museums have collections of Attic pottery, some with finer selections than there are at Athens of the work of the sixth and fifth centuries BC, when export to Etruria and elsewhere was busy.

The Athenian Agora, Princeton, 1953– . A series of definitive reports

The Athenian Agora: A Guide, 2nd ed., Athens, 1962. A clear account, but needs a little modification for more recent discoveries

Hesperia, Princeton, 1932– . Includes various reports on the Agora and other sites in Athens

Hill, I. T., *The Ancient City of Athens*, London and Cambridge, Mass., 1953. A convenient survey, but no longer up to date for the Agora

Travlos, J., *Pictorial Dictionary of Ancient Athens*, London and New York, 1971. A well-illustrated short account of most of the sites of primary and secondary importance

Opposite, above: Plan of the sanctuary of Demeter at Eleusis. Left: Part of the east frieze of the Parthenon, Athens showing assembled gods, marble, c. 440 BC. (The photo is of an old cast: the original is now more damaged.)

Above: Votive relief, set up on the Acropolis, Athens, showing Athena contemplating the new wall of the Acropolis (?), marble, c. 460 BC

4 Corinth

Corinth was strategically and commercially the best-placed site in southern and central Greece, but because of the disruptive system of the independent city-states, its importance was realized in full only by the Macedonians and the Romans. The Isthmus, less than 4 miles (6km) wide, is both the only connection by land between the Peloponnese and continental Greece and also at the head of two deep gulfs of the western and eastern seas; and Acrocorinth (which has its own water supply) is much the best natural stronghold near it, even if too high for convenient occupation except as a citadel and rather large for a small community to defend. For a long time the settlement at Corinth, round the low headland where the temple of Apollo stands, was merely one of several villages in the district. In the southern part of the Corinthia there is a fertile coastal plain about 2 miles (3km) wide, bounded by the steep scarp that is the edge of a plateau shelving up to Acrocorinth. This plateau was composed of limestone and conglomerate, both porous strata, and below them clay, so that there are good springs where the clay is exposed, as in the ravine of Pirene. Security for Corinth was possible only when the population had become big enough to build and man fortifications that extended far enough south to include Acrocorinth, and this did not happen till the archaic period.

To judge by finds, Corinth had little more than local interests, presumably agricultural, till the eighth century BC. Then trade by sea became important, both westward and eastward, and prosperity began. By now the Corinthia was united, with ports at Lechaeum and Cenchreae, though the little state of Cleonae managed to keep its autonomy through alliance with, of course, ARGOS. Early in the sixth century the *diolkos* was constructed, a paved or rock-cut track of 5-foot (1.5m) gauge by which ships or their cargoes could be wheeled across the Isthmus on bogeys, and before 400 BC two parallel walls were built to link the city with Lechaeum: by this time the total population, mostly in the fortified area, may have reached 90,000. In 338 BC the Macedonians made Corinth the meeting place of their league of Greek states and had a garrison on Acrocorinth till 243 BC. In 146 BC the city was destroyed thoroughly by the Romans and the site left deserted till 44 BC, when they refounded it as a 'colony', many of the colonists being Italian, though soon assimilated to the surrounding Greeks. In 27 BC this new Corinth became capital of the Roman province of Achaea, that is Greece as far north as Thessaly. It remained relatively prosperous in the Middle Ages. The Corinthia also contained the sanctuary of Poseidon on the Isthmus, where – as at Nemea in the territory of Cleonae – one of the four great athletic festivals of the Greeks

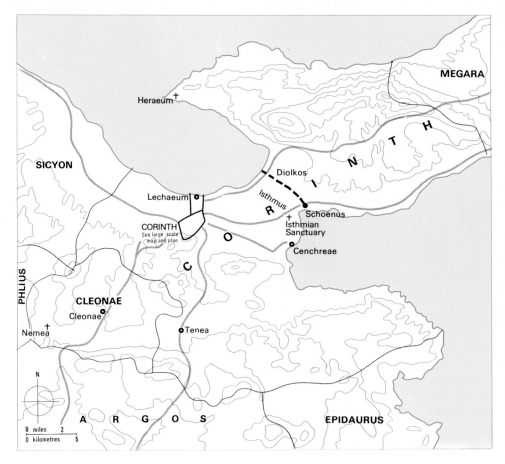

was held. The promontory of Perachora, with a fortified post near the little sanctuary of Hera at its tip, had the negative value of a position which the Corinthians, when maritime and still independent, could not let another state occupy; it was naturally neglected under the Romans.

Not much of the Greek city remains. The oldest considerable structure is the temple of Apollo, in a good Doric style of *c.* 540 BC; it was of local limestone and measured about 70×177 feet (21.5×54m) in plan. Before the cuttings for later buildings, the rise on which it stands had gentler slopes. To the north were a *stoa* and baths, to the east in the Pirene ravine a market building (with small fish tanks in the shops), a sanctuary of Apollo, and the fountain house of Pirene, remodelled time and again and augmented by long tunnels cut back into the clay. To the south there were various small sacred buildings and the 'Northwest Stoa'. Beyond them a race track has emerged, with starting grooves for the runners, and still farther south was the 'South Stoa', about 540 feet (165m) long, a two-storeyed block of taverns and lodgings put up soon after 350 BC: the original ground-floor arrangement survives at the west end. The theatre, first constructed

in the fourth century BC but altered in Roman times, seated about 18,000. The sanctuary of Asclepius, a quarter of a mile (400m) to the north and against the city wall, has buildings of the fourth century BC, but its healing cult was older, to judge by the votive terracotta limbs and members found there. Beside it, at a lower level, was a court (known as Lerna) with dining rooms round it. The Roman builders restored or remodelled the 'South Stoa', the 'Northwest Stoa', and the fountain house at Pirene, but elsewhere ignored the old alignments. The Lechaeum road became more regularly monumental and the area to the south was developed as the city centre (which it may not have been in Greek times): characteristically the surface was levelled and paved, with a row of shops dividing it into two terraces, basilicas to the east and south, and a row of temples at the west. Other notable Roman

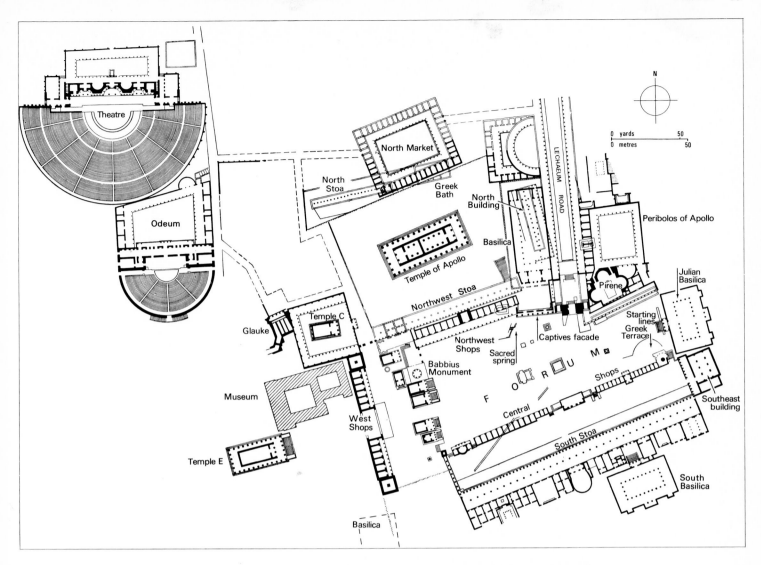

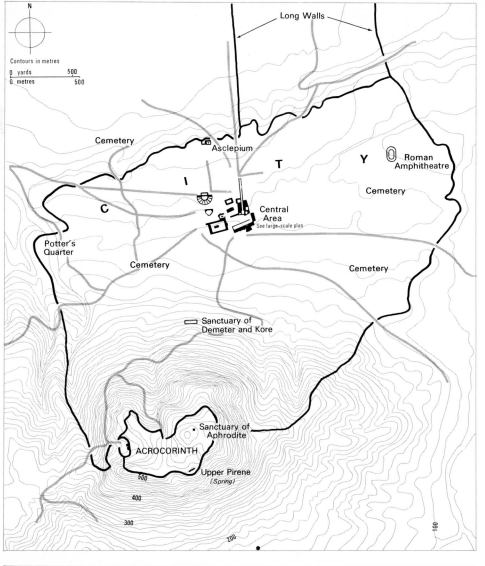

constructions are the *odeum* near the theatre and, unique in Greece, an amphitheatre three-quarters of a mile (1.2km) to the east.

In the Early Iron Age Corinthian art was unassuming, but after 750 B C it broke away decisively from the Geometric tradition and developed with rapid assurance. In painted pottery, the best known of its products, Corinth set standards for the other Greeks till the early sixth century; in architecture it appears to have been the pioneer of the Doric style; it was probably important in early sculpture too; and its bronze work was of high quality. We know much less of Corinthian art in the classical and Hellenistic periods, but its craftsmen seem to have kept a metropolitan reputation. Corinth never became an intellectual centre, though Diogenes retired there: the reason was perhaps not so much the conservative climate of a usually oligarchical government as the lack of the opportunities and attractions that were available in Athens, thanks to its imperial wealth in the fifth century.

The pleasant museum on the site of Corinth has most of the finds from the American excavations there (which have been in progress since 1896) and from the Isthmian sanctuary: they are not spectacular. The finds from Perachora are mostly in the National Archaeological Museum in Athens. Other Corinthian works, especially painted pots unearthed in Italy, are on view in all important museums in western Europe and America.

Sakellariou, M., and Faraklas, N., *Corinthia-Cleonaea*, Athens, 1971. A soundly conceived ecological study

Corinth, Princeton, etc., 1929– . Series of definitive reports on the excavations

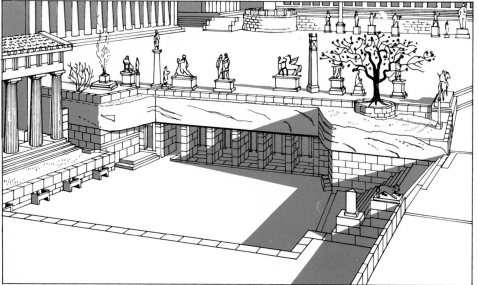

Top: Corinth. The city and Acrocorinth. Above: Reconstruction of the Fountain of Pirene at Corinth in the second century B C. The draw basins of the fountain are inside the piers; on the left of it is the end of a Doric stoa, and on the right the Lechaeum road. The bottom of the 'south stoa' appears in the background. Opposite: The 'Apollo of Tenea', a marble grave statue from Tenea, c. 560 B C. (Only the upper part is shown here.)

The Argolid consisted of a sizeable plain and parts of the mountains that enclosed it on three sides: much of the coast was swampy, but there were good beaches at the east end. In the Early Iron Age this region was divided between five states – Argos, Mycenae, Tiryns, Nauplia, and Asine. Of these Argos was very soon the largest and most aggressive. It conquered Asine toward 700 B C, Nauplia a century later, and Tiryns and Mycenae in the 460s: Nauplia was kept as a port, but the others were destroyed and, though resettled in the third century B C, were deserted again by the second A D, presumably because (as elsewhere in Greece) big private estates had acquired their territories. Argos also had wider ambitions and from the seventh to the fourth century B C was in conflict with SPARTA, without much success but avoiding its own destruction.

Before Roman times the city of Argos was the largest in the Peloponnese with a free population of up to 50,000 and perhaps as many unfree. Its position on a main route to the central and southern Peloponnese was probably not so important, since its economy was dominantly agricultural; but it had good supplies of water and room for defensible expansion with both a small, low *acropolis* (the 'Aspis') and, convenient when numbers grew, a much bigger one (the 'Larisa'). The most spectacular remains are round the *agora* – the theatre, constructed about 300 B C but remodelled later and holding about 20,000 spectators, the Roman baths of the second and fourth centuries A D, and a Roman *odeum* (or covered theatre) built over the meeting place of the Argive assembly, to which the straight rows of seating belong. There are also remains of a sanctuary of Apollo on the slope of the Aspis.

Of Greek Mycenae and Tiryns little is known, since the earlier excavators were more interested in Bronze Age discoveries. At Mycenae occasional repairs to the earlier walls are or were evident; in the seventh century B C a temple was built at the top of the earlier palace, and in the third a little theatre cut into the 'Tomb of Clytemnestra'. At Tiryns, too, traces of a seventh-century temple were found. At Nauplia parts of the wall of Itch Kale go back to 300 B C and the position was much stronger than appears now, since half of the area of the old town below was not reclaimed till modern times, as also much of the passage below the higher hill of Palamidhi (a site of no strategical value till the range of artillery was improved a few hundred years ago). At Asine the most intelligible remains are again of Hellenistic fortifications. The Argolid also had a rich sanctuary of Hera, the Argive Heraeum, presumably at first shared by all the nearby cities. It lies on the east side of the plain, about 3 miles (5km) south of Mycenae. This sanctuary began to become important in the later

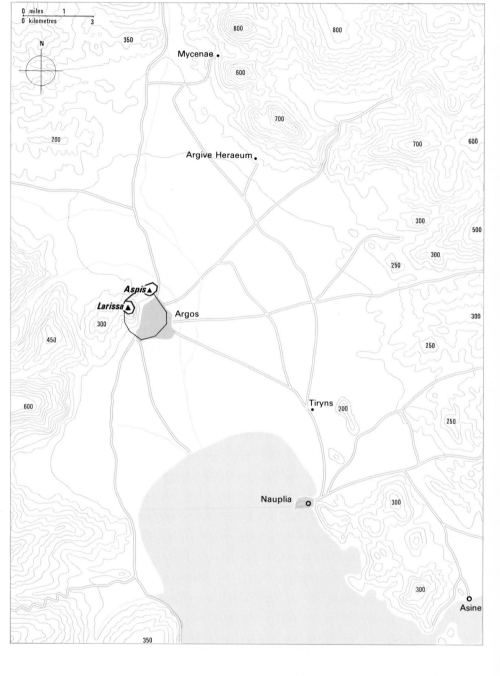

eighth century and acquired a big Doric temple perhaps rather before 600 B C, and after its destruction in 423 B C another lower down the slope; other early buildings, mainly of the sixth and fifth centuries B C, included various *stoas*, a four-aisled hall, and a courtyard with dining rooms round it – a frequent amenity of Greek festive life – and in the Roman period a set of baths was added.

Argos was an important artistic centre. In the ninth and eighth centuries B C its Geometric school of vase painting was inferior only to

that of Athens; from as early as 600 B C it produced sculptors of distinction, among them Polyclitus who was one of the great masters of the mid-fifth century; and there were Argive architects too. Of the finds made in the Argolid, which generally are disappointing, much is in the National Archaeological Museum at Athens, but the local museum of Argos has a fine series of Geometric pottery and that at Nauplia a puzzling collection of grotesque terracotta masks from early seventh-century Tiryns.

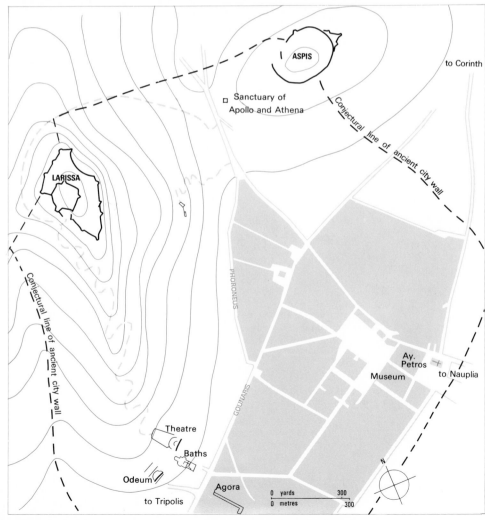

Top: Argos. View from the southeast, showing the 'Larisa' in the centre, and part of the 'Aspis' to the right. Left: Argos. Plan of the city. Above: Part of a relief panel, perhaps from an altar, limestone, c. 635 BC; from Mycenae

Bulletin de correspondance hellénique, LXXVII–   , Athens and Paris, (1953–   ). Current reports on excavations in Argos

Waldstein, C., *The Argive Heraeum,* Boston, Mass., 1902. Detailed report on main excavation

6   Epidaurus

Epidaurus. View northwest across the theatre, toward the sanctuary of Asclepius

The territory of Epidaurus, east of the Argolid, was poor and remote. The city was on the coast facing Aegina and its sanctuary of Asclepius was some 5 miles (8km) inland. When near the end of the fifth century BC Asclepius became a popular healing deity among the Greeks, the Epidaurian sanctuary found itself a centre of pilgrimage and needed appropriate buildings. These were provided at intervals over the next 100 or 150 years. The temple of Asclepius, about 39×76 feet (11.8×23m) in

plan, was built of limestone in a Doric style perhaps in the 370s: an inscription with the accounts shows that the work took four years and eight months and cost the equivalent of about 140,000 days' wages for a skilled man. The rather later *tholos*, a round Doric structure 72 feet (22m) in diameter, cost more than twice as much, but was of marble: its purpose is unknown. Nearby a couple of *stoas* formed the *abaton*, where patients slept for dreams to cure them, supplemented by sounder advice from

the priests. To the southeast was the *katagogion* or hotel, 250 feet (76m) square, with 160 rooms round four colonnaded two-storey courts. The annual festival also gained in importance and acquired a *stadium* and a theatre, which holds about 14,000 spectators and is an excellent and well-preserved example of the Greek type. Its date is disputed: some think it mainly of the late fourth or early third century BC, others that the upper part of the auditorium was added in the second. The sanctuary had a

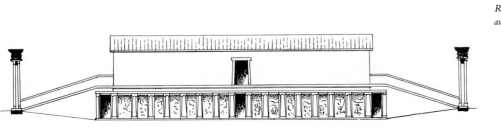

Above: Plan of the sanctuary of Asclepius, near Epidaurus.
Left: The theatre at the sanctuary of Asclepius.
Reconstruction of the original stage, as seen from the
auditorium

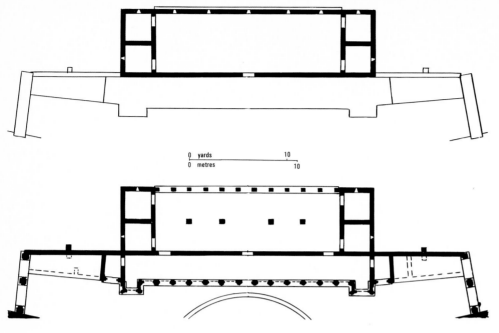

The theatre stage, Epidaurus. Top: Plan of ground floor. Above: Plan of upper floor

revival in the second century A D, as some of its buildings show. The setting has changed little since ancient times, except for the lusher effects of irrigation. Traces of a much smaller sanctuary of Apollo, who probably preceded Asclepius in the main sanctuary, have been uncovered on a spur about 1,100 yards (1km) to the east.

Epidaurus had no artistic school of its own and hired sculptors and architects from elsewhere. Much of the statuary has perished, but there are some good figures (now in Athens) from the temple of Asclepius. Useful reconstructions of parts of that temple and of the *tholos* are exhibited in the museum on the site.

Burford, A., *The Greek Temple Builders at Epidauros*, Liverpool and Toronto, 1969. Useful mainly for the building contracts

Cavvadias, P., *Fouilles d'Épidaure*, I, Athens, 1891. Account of the main excavation

Pharaklas, N., *Epidauria*, Athens, 1972. An ecological survey of the territory of Epidaurus with useful plans of the Asclepieum

Roux, G., *L'Architecture de l'Argolide*, Paris, 1961. Includes detailed studies of several buildings of the Asclepieum

7 Sparta

Greece

Sparta and Mount Taygetus, from the east

Sparta, which stood beside the river Eurotas in a rich plain, was the ruling city of the Lacedaemonians. In the Early Iron Age it reduced the other communities of Laconia to serfdom (the helots) or political dependence (the *perioeci*), by 700 B C had conquered Messenia too, and then imposed alliances on most other states in the Peloponnese. To hold this position the small élite class turned themselves into a military society and became much the most efficient heavy infantry in the Greek world, till in 371 B C the Thebans by new tactics crushed them decisively. For the next two hundred years Sparta remained a nuisance with dreams of regaining its lost power, but afterward had to live off its own little plain, sentimentally reviving some of its more repulsive rituals. Around 400 B C the population of Laconia with Messenia may have exceeded 200,000, of whom perhaps a third were free and only 8,000 of the Spartiate élite.

Its freakish development made the city as well as the citizens of Sparta abnormal. While the military regime lasted, there was no need for other defences and the first city wall was built about 192 B C. So the settlement did not need to be compact and, since government was controlled by a few officials and austerity was publicly (if not privately) admired, there was not much fine architecture. This was noted by Thucydides in the late fifth century B C, with the comment – which archaeologists should remember more often – that one cannot judge the importance of a city by its remains.

Ancient Sparta sprawled over the area of the modern town and northward as far as the low hill which was the *acropolis*. Here excavation has uncovered part of a temple of Athena, built in the sixth century B C. Below it are the theatre, not earlier than Hellenistic, and farther east the *agora* and a *stoa*, also late. To the south there was a small temple, now popularly called the 'Tomb of Leonidas', though its date is the third century B C. To the northeast the

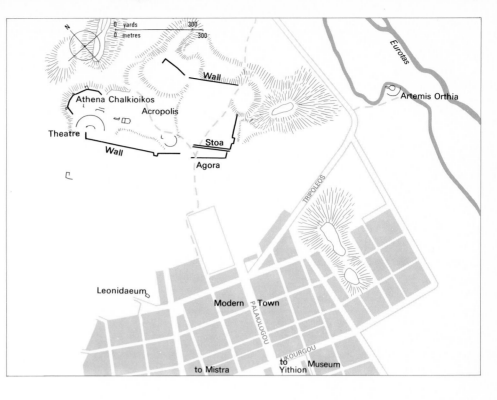

little sanctuary of Artemis Orthia lies by the river: it has a primitive temple and altar, which were incorporated in a small theatre in the third century A D. Here and there remains of comfortable Roman houses have been found, some with mosaic floors.

Laconia, thanks presumably to the *perioeci*, had in the archaic period provincial, but often attractive schools of painted pottery, bronze figurines and utensils, sculpture and architectural terracottas, not of course made by Spartiates. The Archaeological Museum at Sparta shows a fair selection of this work, though the best examples of pottery and bronzes are scattered in mueseums outside Greece.

Annual of the British School at Athens, XII–XVI and XXVI–XXX, London, 1906–32. Contains various papers on the excavations at Sparta

Dawkins, R. M. (ed.), *Artemis Orthia*, London, 1929. A full account of this site and the finds

Forrest, W. G., *A History of Sparta, 950–192 B C*, London and New York, 1968. The best short account in English

---

8   Olympia   Greece

The sanctuary of Zeus at Olympia is about $7\frac{1}{2}$ miles (12km) inland from the western shore of the Peloponnese in the wooded valley of the Alpheus, a perennial river. The district, which was rural and politically unimportant, belonged first to Pisa and then to Elis. In the Early Iron Age there was a local athletic festival here, which gradually attracted competitors from farther afield, till in the seventh century B C it became the premier sporting occasion of the whole Greek world. The festival, as now organized, was held every four years in the hottest time of summer and lasted five days; and the events were the one-*stade* race – about 210 yards (a little more than 190m), the two-*stade* race, a longer distance race (perhaps 24

stades), boxing, wrestling, *pankration*, the pentathlon (one-*stade* race, long jump, javelin, discus, and wrestling), horse races and a chariot race (in which the owner got the prize and the credit): later a race in full armour was added. Entries were by individuals, who had to be free-born Greeks, and not, as in the modern revival, by states, and the prizes were only wreaths of wild olive; but states took great pride in the success of their citizens and often rewarded them substantially, so that it is misleading to speak of a purely amateur spirit. During the fourth century B C professional athletes became common, to the disgust of the rich gentry who had had a monopoly. Still, the Olympic Games continued to flourish and

their suppression – in A D 391 – was to placate Christian consciences.

The prestige of the Games enriched the sanctuary with buildings and dedications and, though the Romans removed many of the statues, there were plenty left for Pausanias to record in the mid-second century A D. Of the buildings many were demolished in A D 267 for material for a defensive wall round the temple of Zeus and some adjacent structures, and the rest either decayed or were thrown down by earthquake, probably in the sixth century. Afterward floods and landslides covered nearly everything with sand, gravel, and mud. As a result the component parts of buildings have survived unusually well, but most of the statu-

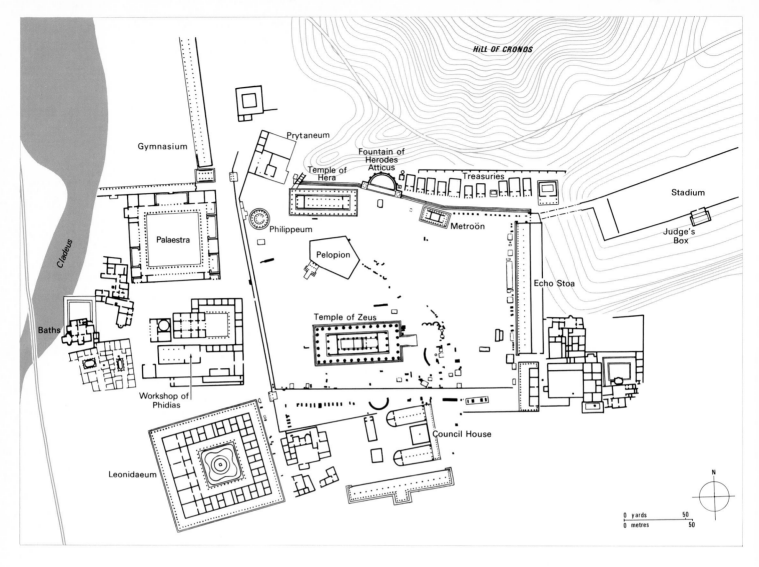

Above: Plan of the sanctuary of Zeus, Olympia

ary – even in this remote place – was retrieved by medieval scrap merchants to melt down, if of bronze, or to burn for lime, if of marble.

The sanctuary itself, the 'Altis', was a quadrilateral of about 650 × 500 feet (roughly 200 × 150m), shaded by plane trees. Its oldest ruins are those of the temple of Hera, presumably conjoined with Zeus, since both had statues inside: it measured $61\frac{1}{2} \times 164$ feet (18.75 × 50m), is in an early and perhaps provincial Doric style of the beginning of the sixth century BC and always had mud-brick walls and a wooden entablature and for a while some wooden columns. The temple of Zeus, also Doric but much grander and larger (about 91 × 210 feet or 28 × 64m in plan), was built around 460 BC of a shelly conglomerate coated with stucco: it contained Phidias's colossal seated statue of Zeus, 40 feet (12m) high, with ivory for the flesh and gold sheeting for the drapery and – for its spiritual quality – one of the most admired achievements of classical sculpture. Between the two temples was the 'Pelopion', a mound of earth supposed to be the burial place of Pelops, a legendary hero of Olympia, and near it was the simple altar of Zeus. At the northwest of the Altis the *prytaneum* was the office of the principal magistrate with a dining

room for victors in the Games and other notables. In front of it was the 'Philippeum', a handsome round building put up in the 330s BC to celebrate the supremacy over Greece of Philip II of Macedonia. The 'Exedra' of Herodes Atticus, just east of the temple of Hera and at the foot of the steep little hill of Cronus, was a fountain house of fired brick faced with marble, which about AD 160 provided the first piped supply of water in Olympia, till then dependent only on wells – a typical example of the different attitudes of Greeks and Romans to public services. Farther on were the 'Metroön', a temple of the Mother of the Gods of about 400 BC; above it on a terrace a row of treasuries of the sixth and fifth centuries BC, erected by Greek states mostly of Sicily and South Italy; and closing the east side the 'Echo' *stoa*, mainly of the later fourth century BC.

The early *stadium* had extended into the Altis, but in the mid-fourth century it was shifted farther east: the track, very narrow by modern standards, was surrounded by an embankment of earth on which more than 40,000 spectators could have stood. Of other buildings outside the Altis the most notable were, proceeding clockwise from the *stadium*, a big Roman house (perhaps prepared for the em-

peror Nero when he competed embarrassingly in AD 67), a pair of linked apsidal halls of the sixth and fifth centuries BC (thought to have formed the Council chambers), the 'Leonidaeum' (a hotel for distinguished visitors) built by the architect Leonidas in the later fourth century BC but remodelled in the second century AD, the workshop of Phidias (where his statue of Zeus was constructed), various baths (both Greek and Roman), a *palaestra* of the third century BC and a *gymnasium* of the second. The hippodrome, the racecourse for horses and chariots, was somewhere to the south of the site.

Olympia never had an artistic school of its own, except perhaps for the unenterprising figurines of the Early Iron Age found and presumably made there. Later dedications of any quality were in general either imported or made by craftsmen trained elsewhere and – anyhow for statuary – visiting only to execute a particular commission. Most of the objects found at Olympia are in the Archaeological Museum there. It is especially rich in bronze work of the eighth to the sixth century BC and also has the marble architectural sculpture, much more complete than usual, of the temple of Zeus.

Berichte über die deutschen Grabungen (Olympia Berichte), 1– , Berlin, 1937– . Reports on the renewed excavations and finds

Curtius, E., Adler, F., and Dörpfeld, W., *Olympia, Ergebnisse der Ausgrabungen*, Berlin, 1890–7. A detailed report of the main excavation

Finley, M. I., and Pleket, H. W., *The Olympic Games: The First Thousand Years*, London and New York, 1976. A helpful wide-ranging survey

Mallwitz, A., *Olympia und seine Bauten*, Munich, 1972. A good general account

Opposite: Head from a statue of a boxer, bronze, later fourth century BC, from Olympia. Above, left: Bronze statuette of a runner in starting position, from Olympia, early fifth century BC. (The inscription on the thigh records its dedication to Zeus.) Above right: The Nike of Paionios, marble, c. 420 BC. The statue, set on a triangular base about 30 feet (9m) high, was dedicated by the Messenians and Naupactians from spoils from an intra-Greek war

9   Delphi

Delphi, on a minor route along the south flank of Mount Parnassus and nearly 1,900 feet (570m) above sea level, was a city-state the size of a village, but it possessed what became much the most famous of Greek oracles. How this happened is not known, though the insignificance of the city must have helped. To judge by finds, the Delphic oracle did not have a wide clientele before the late eighth century BC, but then its reputation grew fast, even attracting the interest of some non-Greek powers; and in 590 BC it was guaranteed protection by the Amphictyonic League, an association of mostly neighbouring Greek states. Though there are traces of earlier deities, the oracle as we know of it belonged to Apollo, who answered inquiries through a 'priestess', whose utterances in turn were edited by attendant officials. Questions might be political, asking approval for a colonial venture or a change in a city's constitution or even action against another state, and here answers needed to be discreet or ambiguous; or they might be about religious matters, on which the oracle tended to humane solutions, or even about the personal problems of individuals. Partly from gratitude, but also for self-advertisement in the religious centre most respected by Greeks, cities and rulers made impressive dedications and the better parts of the sanctuary were soon being crowded with expensive buildings and monuments. This advertising service helped the Delphic establishment to survive the loss of its political influence when it wrongly forecast Persian victory in 480 BC. Though around 350 BC the sanctuary was robbed systematically by the Phocians, and later on and off by Romans, new benefactions were still coming in till the second century AD. Then it shared in the general decline of Greece and in AD 391 the suppression of paganism was the final blow.

The sanctuary of Apollo was in a re-entrant of a steep shelf on a mountainside, exposed to falls of rock and landslides but with good springs of water so that it has always been an attractive site for a settlement. The boundaries of the sanctuary, as enlarged in the later sixth century, enclosed a terraced quadrilateral of about 430×600 feet (just over 130×180m). In the centre, on the largest terrace, stood the successive temples of Apollo. One, not necessarily the earliest, was burned down in 548 BC; the next, which was larger, was destroyed or demolished in 373 BC; and the last, apparently on the same foundations, was completed by 330 BC. Both the second and third of these temples, which were of Doric style, were paid for by contributions from the Greek states, and from the accounts of the third we know that the cost of stone imported from Corinth was in the ratio of 1 for work at Corinth, $3\frac{3}{4}$ for shipping to the port below Delphi and 7 for haulage up to the site. The oracle was

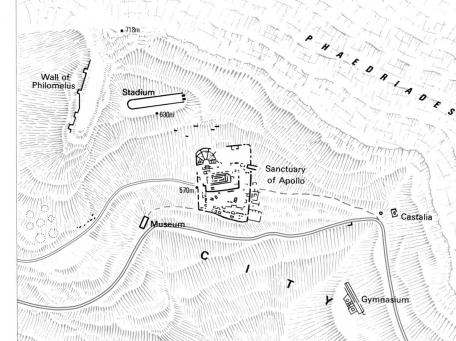

housed in the temple, but details of the arrangements are not evident. The big altar in front of the temple was given by Chios about 475 BC, replacing a less elaborate predecessor.

Most of the other dedications were near the temple or to the south, since the entrance was there. Some were 'treasuries', that is small and often exquisite buildings with a columned porch, which housed valuable and movable offerings: that of Athens, put up about 500 BC and now restored, is fairly typical, measuring a little less than 22×32 feet (nearly 7×10m) in plan and of marble. Among other dedicators of treasuries were Corinth (which seems to have initiated the fashion about 650 BC), Sicyon, Thebes, Cnidos, Cyrene, and – in the sanctuary of Athena Pronaia – Marseilles. There were also large numbers of statues, some single and some in rows on the same base, as well as of metal 'tripods' (three-legged bowls), much fancied by the early Greeks. The series of monuments just inside the present entrance to the sanctuary is instructive about the developed purpose of some of these dedications. Here Athens put up a memorial of its defeat of the Persians at Marathon in 490 BC; at the end of the century Sparta broke Athenian power,

which depended on its navy, and put up figures of its own mostly inferior admirals on a neighbouring site; and a little later the Arcadians celebrated nearby the defeat of the Spartans in 369. These statues have disappeared, as have almost all of the thousands there once were, but the bases often remain with informative inscriptions or holes for the attachment of their feet. The buildings have done better, since many of their blocks have survived and the rules of Greek architecture allow fairly safe inferences about the whole from some of the constituent parts.

Of structures of other types than those mentioned there are the primitive shrine of Ge (the Earth goddess) who seems to have preceded Apollo at Delphi; the 'Halos' (Threshing Floor) where some sort of ritual performances were held; the *stoa* of the Athenians against the

Opposite, above: Model of the sanctuary of Apollo at Delphi, as in 150 BC, seen from the southeast. Opposite, below: Part of the north frieze of the Siphnian Treasury, Delphi, showing the battle of the Gods and the Giants, marble, c. 525 BC

terrace wall below the temple and an important example of Ionic architecture in the 470s B C; a small theatre probably of the fourth century B C but much remodelled and seating about 5,000; and in the northeast corner the 'Lesche' of the Cnidians – a sheltered sitting place of the early fifth century B C with pictures by the first great Greek painter, Polygnotus. In this area, which was too remote to attract dedications, excavation has uncovered ruins of poor Early Iron Age houses. Outside the sanctuary there was a Hellenistic *stoa* on the west and another on the east (which projected within the wall) and, lower down, ruins of baths and shops which are recognizable as Roman because of their brickwork. Farther east, beside a ravine, is the Castalian spring with the intelligible remains of a fountain house, mainly of the sixth and fourth centuries B C.

About half a kilometre to the southeast of the sanctuary of Apollo a separate sanctuary belonged to Athena (Pronaia). It contained a row of buildings on a narrow terrace – a priest's house (perhaps), a temple of Athena of the mid-fourth century B C, the *tholos* (a fine round building of about 400 B C), two treasuries, an older temple of Athena (built about 500 B C to replace an earlier one and itself abandoned after a landslide) and of course an altar.

There was also provision for the Pythian Games, organized about 590 B C on the pattern of those at Olympia, but adding musical to athletic competitions. For these a *gymnasium* was constructed in the fourth century B C and remodelled in Roman times; it lies between the sanctuary of Athena and the Castalian spring and had two practice tracks a *stade* long, one inside a *stoa* and the other in the open, and on a lower terrace there were a *palaestra* and baths. The *stadium* was at first, it seems, on the valley floor far below, but about the middle of the fifth century B C a new one was made to the northwest of the sanctuary of Apollo: the stone seating, for only about 7,000, was added in the second century A D. The course for chariot and horse races stayed down in the valley. As for the city, settlement was originally in the area of the sanctuary of Apollo but, as that grew, moved farther down the slope, to return to its old place in the Middle Ages: there were no springs on the safer site of the modern village, to which – to clear the ground for excavation – the inhabitants were removed, protesting, in the 1890s. Because of its situation the ancient city could not have an effective circuit of walls, though the Phocians when occupying Delphi around 350 B C put up a stretch of fortification on the ridge to the west of the *stadium*.

Delphi, like Olympia, had no artistic school of its own and the objects found there were

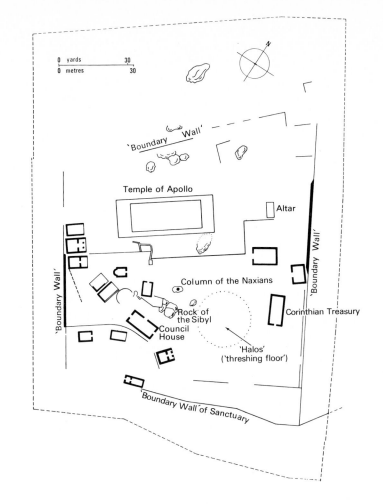

Above: Plan of the sanctuary of Apollo, Delphi, 550 B C. Opposite: The sanctuary in 150 B C. Right: Metope from the Athenian Treasury, Delphi, showing Heracles and the hind, marble, c. 500 B C

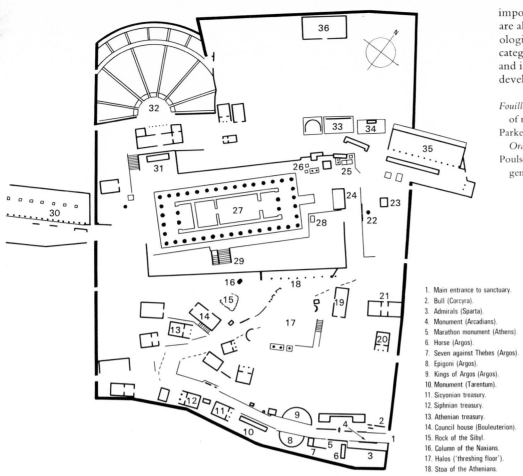

imported or made by visiting craftsmen. These
are almost without exception in the Archaeological Museum near the site. Of the various
categories, the sculpture is the most imposing
and important and illustrates conveniently the
development of that art in Greece.

Fouilles de Delphes, I, Paris, 1904– . Detailed reports
  of results of the excavation
Parke, H. W., and Wormell, D. E. W., *The Delphic
  Oracle*, 2 vols, Oxford, 1956. Comprehensive
Poulsen, F., *Delphi*, London, 1920. Still the best
  general account in English.

1. Main entrance to sanctuary.
2. Bull (Corcyra).
3. Admirals (Sparta).
4. Monument (Arcadians).
5. Marathon monument (Athens).
6. Horse (Argos).
7. Seven against Thebes (Argos).
8. Epigoni (Argos).
9. Kings of Argos (Argos).
10. Monument (Tarentum).
11. Sicyonian treasury.
12. Siphnian treasury.
13. Athenian treasury.
14. Council house (Bouleuterion).
15. Rock of the Sibyl.
16. Column of the Naxians.
17. Halos ('threshing floor').
18. Stoa of the Athenians.
19. Corinthian treasury.
20. Cyrenaean treasury.
21. Prytaneum (?).
22. Serpent column.
23. Chariot of the Rhodians.
24. Altar of the Chians.
25. Tripods of the Dinomenids.
26. Pillar of Prusias.
27. Temple of Apollo.
28. Pillar of Aemilius Paulus.
29. Spring.
30. Hellenistic stoa.
31. Dedication of Craterus.
32. Theatre.
33. Monument of Daochus.
34. Precinct of Neoptolemos.
35. Stoa of Attalus I.
36. Lesche of the Cnidians.

10   Delos   Greece

The island of Delos, half-way across the Aegean
Sea, has two reasons for fame, both accidental.
It is small and narrow – with an area of less
than $1\frac{1}{2}$ square miles (about 3.5km²) – infertile
and short of natural supplies of water, so that
often it has not been inhabited; but it had a
fairly sheltered landing place and in the Early
Iron Age acquired holiness as the birthplace of
Apollo and Artemis. By the seventh century
BC its annual festival was bringing in Greeks
from the neighbouring islands and even from
the mainland, and buildings and statues began
to embellish the sanctuary. At first Naxos
appears to have been dominant, but after the
defeat of the Persians in 479 BC the Athenians
made Delos the official centre of their league,
though twenty-five years later they moved its
treasury to ATHENS. In the late fourth century,
backed by one Hellenistic power or another,
Delos became nominally independent and,
since the sanctuary was rich enough for money-
lending, of commercial importance too, so that
by the mid-third century BC Italian merchants
were moving in. Then in 166 BC Rome – to

injure Rhodian trade – declared Delos a free
port, a privilege still more lucrative after the
destruction of Corinth in 146. The next fifty or
sixty years were the acme of commercial Delos;
its population may have reached 25,000 and
its slave market is said to have been able to
handle 10,000 sales a day. The end of this artificial prosperity came in 88 BC, when Mithridates, King of Pontus in Asia Minor, seized the
island and massacred or enslaved its residents,
and after a partial recovery pirates completed
the job a few years later. In the new, more
rational order of the Roman Empire Delos
was not wanted; by the second century AD
its only inhabitants were the guardians of the
sacred places.

The sanctuary of Apollo, close to the landing
place, was eventually an irregular quadrilateral
of about 500 × 600 feet (roughly 150 × 180m).
In it were three temples of Apollo, side by
side. The earliest and most venerable was the
'Poros' (limestone) temple of the second half
of the sixth century BC. Next to it was the
temple of the Athenians of about 420 BC. The

largest, known as the 'peripteral' temple of
Apollo (since it alone had colonnades on the
sides), was started soon after 477 and completed, more or less, in the third century BC:
it measured about 41 × 94 feet (12.5 × 28.5m)
in plan. The first was Ionic in style, the second
Doric, and the third began as Ionic and ended
Doric. To the southwest the 'House of the
Naxians', of the early sixth century, replaced a
still earlier building: it was a simple hall with a
line of Ionic columns down the middle. Against
its north wall stood a marble statue of a naked
male, originally about 30 feet (9m) high; its
date is the late seventh century BC and pieces
of it survive, badly weathered, the two largest
being on the site near the temple of Artemis.
This temple, to the northwest, was rebuilt in
the early second century BC, but had a probably seventh-century predecessor. Before the
third century BC the sanctuary of Apollo was
unimpressive architecturally, but Hellenistic
kings made more imposing additions. The *stoa*
of Antigonus, nearly 400 feet (120m) long,
closed the north side of the precinct and on the

east the so-called Sanctuary of the Bulls, measuring about 220 × 30 feet (67 × 9m) overall, was probably a glorified shed to preserve a warship, dedicated as a memorial of a naval victory: both were of the mid-third century BC.

Outside the sanctuary on its south side was the old Agora of the Delians and to the north the chief early sites are those of the temple of Leto, the mother of Apollo and Artemis, which was built in the sixth century, the 'Sacred Lake' (now drained and encircled by a low wall), and a terrace overlooking it with a row originally of at least nine lions, of the seventh century BC and perhaps inspired by Egyptian avenues of sphinxes. Most of the other remains belong to the period of commercial prosperity and illustrate its cosmopolitan basis. The 'Hypostyle Hall', near the shore, of the late third century BC and about 185 × 112 feet (56 × 34m) in area, had nine rows of five columns inside, interrupted below a central clerestory, and may have been a corn ex-

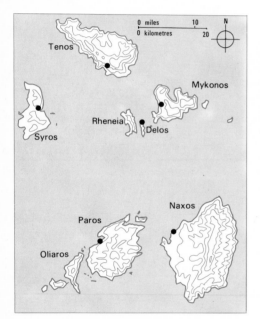

change. The 'Agora of the Italians', enclosed by two-storey colonnades and some 330 feet (100m) long by 230 feet (70m) wide, was erected in the late second century; about the same time the merchants of Berytus (Beirut) built their private 'agora', for worship and business, and there were other Hellenistic agoras and stoas round the sanctuary. Beyond them there were some large private houses and on the north side a couple of palaestras, again Hellenistic; and across the island to the northeast traces can be seen of a gymnasium, a stadium, perhaps a Jewish synagogue, and more houses. The top and slopes of Mount Cynthus, to the southeast of the sanctuary of Apollo, had a few modest holy places in the seventh century BC; but here again Hellenistic expansion is evident, with the improvement of old shrines and the addition of new, some of them specifically for Egyptian and Syrian gods.

The main residential area, remarkably well

preserved though only partly excavated, was south of the Apollo sanctuary and is largely of the second century BC, though some bits go back to the third. It contains substantially built houses often of irregular shape, is densely crowded, and has narrow winding streets: presumably it was developed privately and, unlike Olynthus and Priene, without much civic control. The typical better-class house had a central court with a colonnade round it and rooms behind the colonnade: windows were probably usual on the upper floor or floors, but rare below, though the street front was often broken by small lock-up shops, not accessible from the house itself. Walls were of roughly squared stone, faced with plaster, and columns of inferior marble; and important floors were decorated with mosaics. For water it was usual to have a deep cement-lined cistern under the court, fed from the inward-sloping roof. At the far end of the agglomera-

tion was a theatre of the third century BC with seats for perhaps 5,000 and a few small Hellenistic sanctuaries. Along the shore southward from the sanctuary of Apollo the harbourage was divided into five basins and there was a long line of warehouses and the usual amenities for sailors. Farther on more sanctuaries have been found, of various dates.

Delos was too small to support artists or expensive craftsmen before its commercial boom. Then and especially in the later second and earlier first centuries BC sculptors on Delos helped to form Roman taste, developing more

Above, left: Delos and the neighbouring islands. Above: Plan of the sanctuary of Apollo and town. Opposite: Delos. View south across the Terrace of Lions

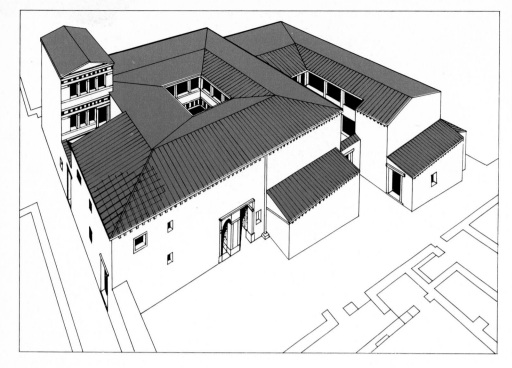

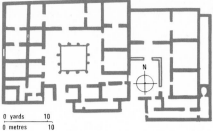

Left and above: Reconstruction and plan of block of three houses on Delos, northwest of the lake. The drawing shows: top left 'House of the Pediments' (its street door visible halfway along the side wall); forward and centre 'House of the Comedians'; right 'House of the Tritons'. Only the 'House of the Comedians' is of strictly normal type. Opposite: Mosaic in the 'House of Masks', Delos: Dionysus riding a panther, later second century BC

Above: Plan of part of the town of Delos, north of the theatre

lifelike ('veristic') as well as ideal portraiture, and copying and adapting old masterpieces. There was a demand too for architecture, public and private, and for mosaics (some of high quality); but whether Delos contributed anything novel here is unknown. Of objects found the seventh-century statues, apparently Naxian, and the Hellenistic sculpture and mosaics are the most remarkable. Some of the best are in the National Archaeological Museum in Athens, the rest in the Delos Museum. Further, of interest to specialists, there is a large assortment of painted pottery, found in a repository on the facing shore of the island of Rheneia, to which they were removed

when the Athenians 'purified' Delos in 425 BC (and perhaps also a century earlier), clearing out the graves there: these pots are now in the museum on the neighbouring island of Mykonos.

Bruneau, P., and Ducat, J., *Guide de Délos*, Paris, 1965. A good summary account of the site and the finds

Exploration archéologique de Délos (briefly *Délos*), I– , Paris, 1909– . Detailed studies

I I   Dodona   **Greece**

Dodona, in a broad valley in the territory of the Molossians of Epirus, had an oracle of Zeus, which the Greeks thought the oldest of their oracles; but because of its remoteness it was not much visited except by those who lived near, mostly individuals with personal problems. Answers, normally yes or no, were obtained from the rustling of the leaves of the sacred oak tree, the sounds of the doves in its

branches, the jangling of bronze cauldrons set up round it, or even the utterances of a priestess. Till the early fourth century B C the sanctuary remained very simple, without even a temple – so it seems – and further buildings were not added till the early third, when King Pyrrhus was making the still-tribal Epirots into a formidable power. Most of these were destroyed by the Aetolians in 219 B C, but the

damage was soon more than made good. Fifty years later and again in the early first century B C Dodona was plundered by the Romans. Recovery began late in that century and continued till the second century A D. The final devastation came at the end of the fourth century.

The oak tree was always the centre of the cult. Soon after 400 B C a plain little temple was put up beside it and rather later a courtyard was enclosed in front, including the sacred tree. Early in the next century, Pyrrhus built a bigger temple and enlarged the enclosure, giving it also an interior colonnade. After 219 BC there was further enlargement and a new temple, with columned porch but still modest in dimensions (about 18 × 31 feet; 5.6 × 9.5m). Pyrrhus also provided three small temples nearby (for Dione and perhaps Heracles and Aphrodite), a Council chamber for the representatives of the Epirot tribes (measuring about 107 × 143 feet; 32.5 × 43.6m), and a theatre with seating for some 18,000: in Roman times the lowest rows of seats were removed to give a high wall to an enlarged orchestra, so permitting contests of gladiators and wild beasts. In front of the theatre was one end of the *stadium*, instituted or at least improved in the late third century BC. The hill above was fortified with a wall and towers: this goes back to the later fourth century BC.

The objects discovered, which include fine bronze figurines and lead strips on which questions to the oracle were written, are mostly in the National Archaeological Museum at ATHENS.

Right: Plan of the sanctuary of Zeus and the acropolis *of Dodona*

Carapanos, C., *Dodone et ses ruines*, Paris, 1878. An account of the early excavation and finds

Praktika tes Archaiologikes Etaireias, 1952– , Athens. Current reports on the new excavations

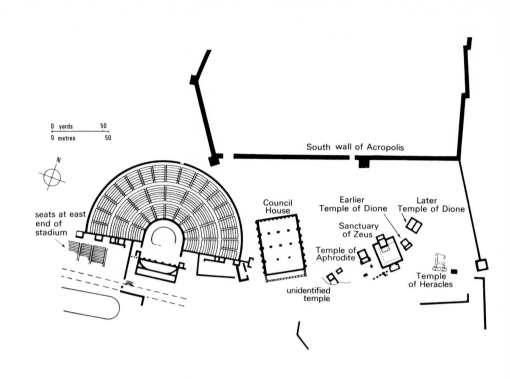

Olynthus

12

The new city of Olynthus was founded in 432 BC as the centre of the Chalcidians, who had united to form a single state. The venture was successful, till Philip II set about consolidating and enlarging his kingdom of Macedonia and, since the Chalcidians were in his way, he attacked and destroyed their Olynthus in 348 BC. Since then the site has never been inhabited.

The city, about 1½ miles (roughly 2.5km) inland, was on a hill standing around 100 feet (30m) above the surrounding countryside and strengthened by a wall of mud brick on stone foundations. With its eastward extension down the slope, also walled, it occupied an area of some 110 acres (45ha). Except at the southwest, where the ground rose steeply, it was planned on a north-south grid, with main streets about 23 feet (7m) wide and minor ones 16 feet (5m). The blocks so formed were normally of about 275 × 115 feet (84 × 35m), divided by a narrow lane into two rows of five well-to-do houses, though in the extension some of the plots were larger. The standard house had a court, sometimes with a colonnade, entered from the street and with rooms on three sides; the main suite was on the north, shaded from the high sun of summer but open to it in winter when it was low, and above this suite was an upper storey; there were also a kitchen with flue and a bathroom with terracotta tub. Construction of

walls was in mud brick on stone footings, roofs were tiled, inner walls were painted (often in imitation of masonry), and important floors had pebble mosaics, some figured. Shops set into house fronts were uncommon; these and the accommodation of artisans were in the southwest district, which also had a market. The scarcity of official buildings is remarkable: there was a public open space in the middle of the west side, with a *stoa*, probably a council hall, and a fountain house. Nor, curiously, have the indispensable sanctuaries been found. Water was brought in terracotta pipes from a source nearly 10 miles (15km) distant. The city

was more residential than commercial, with a population that may have reached 15,000.

Though plundered thoroughly in 348 BC, many small or less valuable objects have survived, so that Olynthus gives exceptionally full information about life and artistic trends of its time. The portable finds are in the museum at Thessaloniki, but the mosaics were left in place and reburied.

On the surface of the site not much more than the plan is visible.

Robinson, D. M., etc., *Excavations at Olynthus*, I– , Baltimore, 1929– . A detailed account

The 'House of Good Fortune'. Below: Plan. Bottom: Model. Note courtyard (the central feature) and first floor balcony around it.

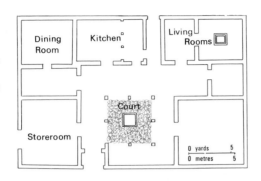

Below right: Plan of house A.vii.4 (the second from the southwest corner of block A.vii)

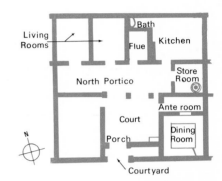

13   Philippi

Philippi in Thrace is about 9 miles (15km) inland from Kavalla (in ancient times Neapolis). Here, between a marsh (later drained) and the mountains, there was a Greek settlement called Crenides, intended to exploit the nearby gold mines. This was taken over by Philip II of Macedonia in 356 BC, for its strategic as well as economic value, fortified and renamed Philippi. After the exhaustion of the mines the city declined, but when in the second century BC the Romans arrived it became a position on the Via Egnatia, the military high road from Dyrrachium (Durresi in Albania) to Byzantium (ISTANBUL). In 42 BC, in the civil war following the assassination of Julius Caesar, Octavian (Augustus) and Mark Antony crushed Brutus and Cassius outside Philippi and celebrated the event by settling discharged soldiers in the city, so enlarging its size and making it a privileged Italian enclave. Its prosperity seems to have increased further around AD 170, when there was much re-building, and continued till the sixth century. The population is not known, but the theatre, as enlarged in the Roman period, held only about 8,000.

Much of the site has not been excavated and very little is known of the Macedonian period. To it belong parts of the walls of the city and its *acropolis*, a few small sanctuaries or houses and the theatre, though this was remodelled in the second and third centuries AD. Nor has much of the Roman city been found that is older than the AD 160s. This is the date of the visible buildings of the *forum*, the Roman equivalent of the Greek *agora*, which measured roughly 490×230 feet (148×70m). On its long north side there was a tribune flanked by fountain houses, on each short side a temple and a colonnade with various rooms behind, and on the south side a colonnade. South of the *forum* excavation has uncovered the remains of a more or less contemporary *palaestra* with a 50-seater latrine and of a covered market (below a sixth-century Christian church). Still farther south, in a residential district, a big set of baths was built about AD 250 on the site of an earlier Roman sanctuary. The Via Egnatia ran immediately north of the *forum* and on the hillside above were a miscellaneous collection of mostly minor sanctuaries and the channel for the Roman water supply.

Much sculpture has been found, of Roman date and generally mediocre.

Collart, P., *Phillippes*, Paris, 1937. A detailed account, though much can now be added

Lapalus, E., in *Bulletin de correspondance hellénique*, Paris, LVII (1933), pp. 438–66 and LIX (1935), pp. 175–92. On the sculpture

Lazaridis, D., *Philippoi-Romaiki Apoikia*, Athens, 1973. An ecological study with brief account and plans of later discoveries

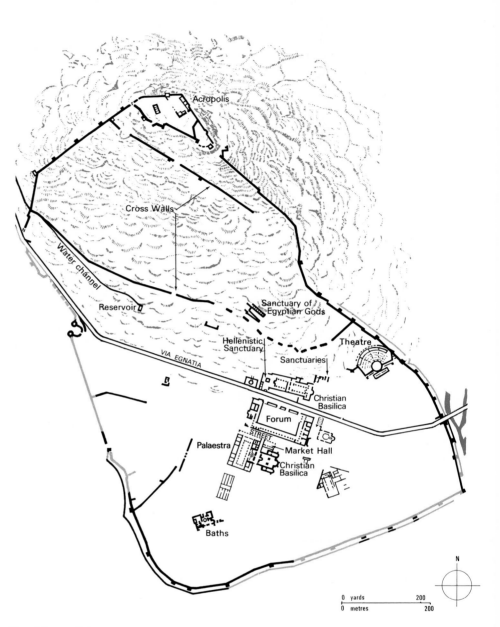

Plan of the city, Philippi

14 Thasos

Thasos is a roughly circular island with an area of about 150 square miles (400km²) and 5 miles (8km) distant from the coast of Thrace. It had well-watered and fertile land, which produced one of the better Greek wines, useful timber on its mountains, which rose to about 4,000 feet (1,200m), veins of gold and silver, and good fishing grounds. Besides these natural advantages, it was conveniently situated for trade with the backward Thracians of the mainland. So the Greek city of Thasos, founded from Paros about 680 B C, very soon became prosperous; and it increased its prosperity by conquering and securing with walled settlements a 45-mile (70km) strip of the coast opposite it, the 'Thasian Peraea', so procuring more fertile land and richer sources of gold and silver.

During the seventh and sixth centuries B C, while free from interference, Thasos was probably at its most affluent, with an income from mining and the Peraea of – so Herodotus says – 200–300 talents a year, more than half as much as the total annual tribute that ATHENS levied from its empire around 450 B C. The fifth century was less happy. After a short spell of Persian suzerainty Thasos joined the Athenian alliance but suffered from Athenian encroachment and, when it resigned from the alliance in 465, was besieged for two years and forced to submit, though to judge by its assessment for tribute it was soon one of the richer subject cities. After the destruction of the Athenian empire at the end of the century Thasos contrived to keep in with the dominant powers, except for a wrong but luckily not disastrous choice in the Roman civil war in 42 B C, and it remained successful till the late fourth century A D. The size of the ancient population of the island is not known, but should have been considerably more than the 16,000 of the census of 1961.

The city, an unusually intelligible specimen of its type, was on the northeast coast. It was built round a good harbour, divided by moles into two basins, one almost completely enclosed: an inscription of the third century B C sets out regulations for its busy traffic. The fortification wall follows the natural line of the ridges of the hill above and is about 2½ miles (4km) long. It was constructed, it seems, around 500 B C – presumably before then the Thasian navy was protection enough – and in parts was faced with marble and still more unusually had sculpture in relief on some of its gates. The *agora* was close to the harbour, in its final form a rhomboid about 360 feet (110m) across each way. The colonnaded structures round it, of which substantial remains are now visible, date from the fourth century B C to the first A D, but must have had predecessors. Near the east corner, later enclosed in a long hall of the first century A D, was the monument of

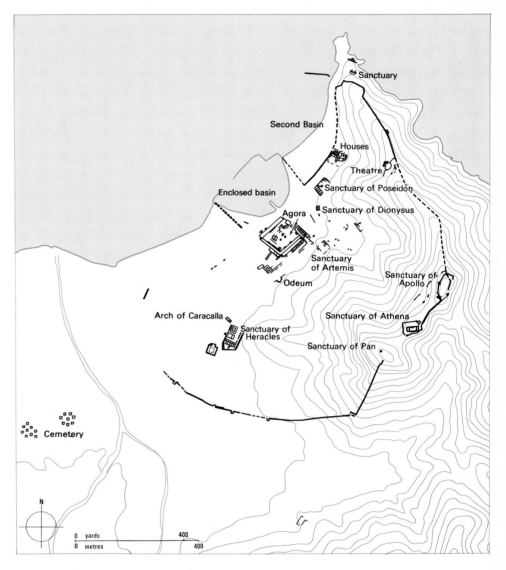

Above: Plan of Thasos. Below: Thasos and its Peraea

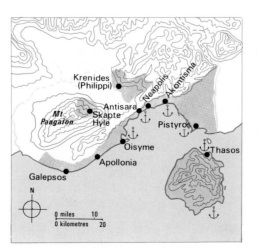

Glaucus, one of the founding fathers, put up in the seventh century B C; and among other structures in the *agora* there were toward the north a sanctuary and temple of Zeus of the early fourth century B C and a sanctuary, no later, of the athlete Theogenes, who was said to have won 1,300 victories up and down Greece around the 470s. To the east and north of the *agora* were more sanctuaries of Artemis, Dionysus, and Poseidon – the first going back to the seventh century B C and the other two, it seems, to the fifth or fourth. Still farther north part of a residential quarter has been uncovered. Here some sort of grid plan existed in the sixth century B C and presumably from the beginning, but because of continual rebuilding details of the earlier houses are not clear. Farther on, still more sanctuaries have been discovered, three – of Apollo, Athena, and Pan – on the peaks within the wall and one of Heracles below to the south: that of Pan is of the fourth century BC, the rest were earlier. Other notable public buildings were to the northeast a theatre, initially of the fifth century BC, and south of the *agora* an *odeum* of the second century AD. Outside the city on the west a cemetery has been found.

So rich and large a state could afford its own artists. In painted pottery there may have been local manufacture in Cycladic and East Greek styles in the earlier sixth century and there certainly was local imitation of Attic later. For sculpture Thasos had its own supply of fine marble and there is evidence of local work from the late seventh century BC till at least the first AD. In painting the earliest Greek great master, toward the middle of the fifth century BC, was the Thasian Polygnotus, but his training (like his activity) may have been elsewhere. In architecture the quality of craftsmanship in Thasos was good, though perhaps a little old-fashioned. Since the island belonged to Turkey till 1912, the earlier finds went mainly to ISTANBUL and the Louvre, Paris; later finds are in the Thasos Museum.

Bulletin de correspondance hellénique, Athens and Paris, LXXIII– (1949–). Current reports on excavations in Thasos

Études thasiennes (Paris), I– (1944–). Detailed studies

Guide de Thasos, Paris, 1967. A good summary account of the site and the finds

Lazaridis, D., *Thasos and its Peraia*, Athens, 1971. An ecological study

15 Samothrace

The island of Samothrace in the northeast Aegean is small and mountainous, with an area of about 70 square miles (180km²) and a highest point of well over 5,000 feet (1,600m). Its natural resources were poor, though it had good timber, and its position may have been at times important for naval strategy. Greek settlers, it seems, arrived around 700 BC and mixed peacefully with Thracians already there. The state soon acquired territory on the mainland to the north, languished in the fifth century under Athenian domination, and was annexed by Philip II of Macedonia about 340 BC. From then on its sanctuary flourished under the patronage of Hellenistic kings and by the late second century BC of Roman notables, who saw there the origin of one of their own oldest cults. About AD 200 an earthquake devastated the site, but there was some recovery till the spread of Christianity in the late fourth century. The Samothracian sanctuary was famous for its *mysteries*, a form of religion that required initiation, and (as with other Greek *mysteries*) ancient writers were tiresomely conscientious about keeping its secrets. The deities were the 'Great Gods', with a dominant female partner; initiation – at two levels – was open to all, male and female, slave and free, Greek and non-Greek; the principal benefit was protection against shipwreck, though some students claim immortality too. The cult, which appears to have changed with time, was partly Thracian in origin; but ancient religion was accommodating and exotic beliefs could be combined with pious acceptance of the orthodox divinities.

The sanctuary, about a quarter of a mile (400m) from the shore, was on a ridge just outside the city wall, which runs up the hill to the east and in part is as old as the sixth century BC. The earliest remains, some pre-Greek, are scrappy and unimpressive. Monumental buildings appeared in the second half of the sixth century: the Anaktoron for the first initiation ceremony – a simple hall with an interior area of about 90×40 feet (27×11.6m); a sort of *stoa* of Doric style and rather smaller, which served for the display of votive gifts; and the earliest *hieron* for the higher stage of initiation. Then after a long interval the Temenos was constructed about 340 BC, with a fine Ionic *propylon* of marble, now for the first time used at Samo-

Samothrace. Reconstructed view of the Arsinoeum from the south

thrace. The 'Altar Court' followed, and near the end of the century a new much larger *hieron* was begun – Doric, of marble and with an interior apse. The Arsinoeum, given by Queen Arsinoe in the 280s, is the largest Greek rotunda yet known (over 66 feet or 20m across). It was of marble, enlivened in its upper part with pilasters outside and half-columns inside. Shortly afterward Ptolemy II of Egypt built a bridge and an imposing marble *propylon* to give the sanctuary an entrance from the east. Finally, about 200 B C, the sanctuary was extended across the stream to the west and the extension used for a theatre, a *stoa* perhaps of two storeys and about 330 feet (100m) long, and the landscaped fountain above which stood the Nike (Victory) of Samothrace now in the Louvre, Paris.

Samothrace had no artistic school of its own, but in the early Hellenistic period, for which it is remarkably informative, commissions brought able architects and sculptors there and perhaps encouraged them to experiment. The older sculptural finds went mostly to ISTANBUL and Vienna. Recent finds are in the museum near the site.

Conze, A., etc., *Archäologische Untersuchungen auf Samothrake*, I–II, Vienna, 1875–80. Detailed report of the older excavations

Lehman, K., *Samothrace: A Guide to the Excavations and the Museum*, 4th ed., Locust Valley, N.Y., 1970. A good summary

—, etc., *Samothrace: Excavations*, I–   . London, 1959–   . Detailed studies of results of new excavations

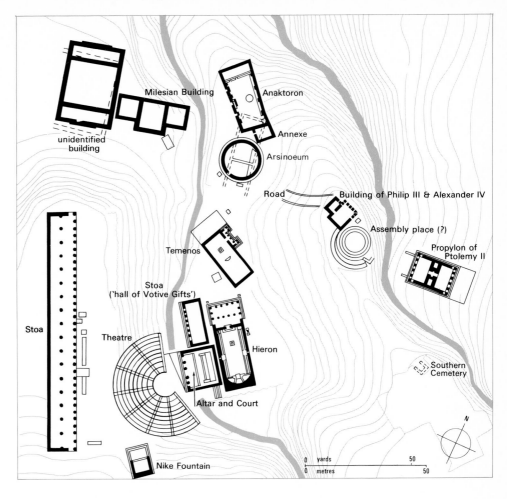

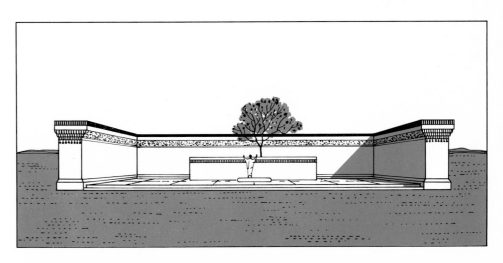

16   Samos   Greece

Samos, 28 miles (45km) long and 12½ miles (20km) wide and less than 1½ miles (2.4km) from the Turkish shore, is one of the more fertile Aegean islands: its wine was in demand in antiquity. Greek settlers arrived around 1000 B C and Samos was soon one of the richer states of Ionia. When in 546 B C the Persians reached the coast, Samos for a time not only kept its freedom, but under its brilliant and unprincipled tyrant Polycrates (*c.* 538–22 B C) created an empire over other islands. Afterward, though rarely independent, it was usually prosperous down to the third century A D. Its population in good times may have reached 50,000.

The city, at modern Tigani (or Pythagoreion) near the east end of the south coast, had a small harbour with moles and beside it an *acropolis*. The walls, over 4 miles (6.7km) in circuit, may be a reconstruction of those of Polycrates. An aqueduct, constructed under Polycrates by Eupalinus and one of the wonders of its time, brought water from a source outside the wall. It began with an underground pipe about 930 yards (853m) long and continued through the mountain in a tunnel of over 1,140 yards (1,045m): work was begun at both ends and the error was less than 7 feet (2m) horizontally and 10 feet (3m) vertically –

Reconstructed drawing of the altar of Hera in the Heraeum of Samos in the mid-sixth century B C. Behind the altar proper is the sacred 'lygos' (chaste tree)

a surprising feat with ancient surveying instruments.

The principal sanctuary, the Heraeum, was about 3 miles (5km) west along the shore, in marshy ground which has helped the survival of offerings. The first altars are said to date to the tenth century BC and the first temple of Hera ('Hekatompedon I') to the early eighth. This was a shed of 21 × 110 feet (6.5 × 33m), later surrounded by wooden posts to support the roof. 'Hekatompedon II', a little more extensive, succeeded it around 650. Rather before 550 BC it in turn made way for a new limestone temple by the local architects Theodorus and Rhoecus; novel in size – about 170 × 350 feet (52 × 105m) – and in elaboration, it had a double colonnade on all four sides. Some twenty years later, whether or not because of a fire, Polycrates demolished the Rhoecus temple and began a slightly larger replacement some 130 feet (40m) farther west, but his grandiose project – which included some use of marble – was never completed. The altar, too, had its improvements, the most important in the time of Rhoecus, when it was shifted into alignment with the temple and received a staircase about 100 feet (30m) wide. There were of course other temples, *stoas*, treasuries, and dedications around the sanctuary, the great building period being the time of Polycrates, though some additions were made in the early Roman period.

Samos was a notable centre of culture, particularly during the sixth century BC. In art and architecture it was a leading partner in the Archaic East (that is Asiatic) Greek school and till the Hellenistic period its sculpture may perhaps have had some flavour of its own. Finds at the Heraeum include sculpture, figurines of bronze and ivory and even wood, architectural members, and painted pottery. Some earlier pieces were diverted to Berlin – the statues now in the East sector and the small objects in the West – but Samos has most of the others, especially in the museum at Vathy.

Mitteilungen des Deutschen Archäologischen Instituts: Athenische Abteilung (briefly *Athenische Mitteilungen*), Athens, IX, pp. 163–92 and LIV– , (1884 and 1929–). On the aqueduct of Eupalinos and current reports on work at the Heraeum

Samos, I– , Bonn, 1961– . A series of definitive studies of finds from the Heraeum

Tolle, R., *Die antike Stadt Samos*, Mainz, 1969. A short description of the city

before mid 6th cent BC
mid 6th cent BC
later 6th cent BC
Roman period

Above, right: Plan of the Heraeum, Samos. Right and far right: Ivory figure of a kneeling youth, originally the sidepiece of a cithara. From Samos, late seventh century BC

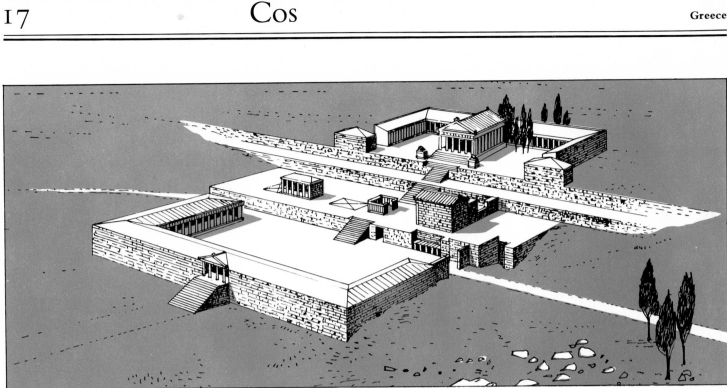

The island of Cos, about 28 miles (45km) long and on average 4 miles (6.5km) wide, has some good and well-watered land. In the fifth century BC it was subject to Carians of the adjacent mainland and then to ATHENS. In 366 BC its separate communities united and chose the site of the present town for their city. Near the end of the century Ptolemy I of Egypt used Cos as a naval base and his son Ptolemy II, who was born there, afterward became a generous benefactor. Cos also had a specialized manufacture of fine dress material, mineral springs, and a medical school, the most notable member of which was Hippocrates (allegedly 460–357 BC). In the Hellenistic and Roman periods the city was fortunate, except for the earthquakes of 6 BC and AD 142; and its final devastation, again by earthquake, was not till 554.

In the city the principal Hellenistic remains are the third-century *agora* near the harbour, a *stoa*, a couple of temples, and a theatre. From Roman times there are two sets of baths, an *odeum* and private houses with mosaics and wall paintings. The Asclepieum, about 2 miles (3.2km) to the southwest, has been excavated more comprehensively: besides having a curative function – Asclepius was a healing god – it was also the principal sanctuary of the island, where state records were kept. No foundations have been found older than the second half of the fourth century BC, that is after the establishment of the new city, and any earlier structures must have been simple. Nor were any of the buildings appropriate for the medical

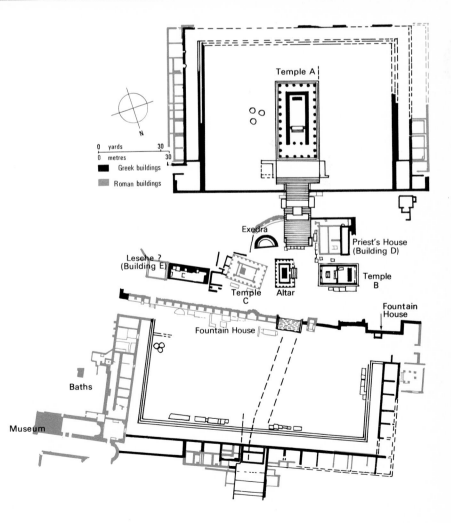

Sanctuary of Asclepius, Cos. Top: Reconstructed view from the north, as in the first century AD. Right: Plan

school, which anyhow relied not on religious ritual or faith but on clinical observation and rational treatment. The sanctuary covered eventually three terraces, each more than a hundred yards (or metres) wide and fifty deep, though not strictly parallel. The middle terrace had priority. There, near the centre, an altar was constructed around 340 BC, and soon after a small Ionic temple on its west side; beside this a simpler edifice was put up around 300 BC and on the east another small temple and what may have been a *lesche* (a place to sit in), these two on different alignments. About the same time the lower terrace was enclosed by *stoas*. An attempt to impose formal symmetry came about 160 BC with the development of the upper terrace, on which stood a grove of cypresses: a peripteral Doric temple was put in the centre, measuring in plan about 53 × 102 feet (16 × 31m) and much the tallest building in the sanctuary, with *stoas* set back on three sides (replacing timber predecessors) and a grand stairway in front for access from the middle terrace. Some of these buildings were replaced or embellished later, and in the third century AD the inevitable set of baths was added east of the lower terrace.

A fair amount of sculpture has turned up both in the city and the sanctuary. The older finds went to ISTANBUL, the later to Rhodes or the museum in Cos town. It is unlikely that there was a markedly local style.

Bollettino d'arte, Rome, XXX, pp. 136–42 and XXXV, pp. 54–73, 219–46, 316–31 (1936 and 1950)
Reports on excavations in the city
Herzog, R., and Schazmann, P., *Kos*, I, Berlin, 1932. A detailed report on the Asclepieum

18 Lindos

Greece

The big island of Rhodes contained three considerable cities till 408 BC, when they combined to form a unified state with the new city of Rhodes as its centre; and though the old cities were not completely deserted, they sank to minor country towns. Of the three Lindos on the east coast had the best harbours and the most famous sanctuary. It was on an important route to the eastern Mediterranean and presumably did well.

The ancient city has largely been obliterated or overbuilt. More remains on the *acropolis*, when one has passed the works of the Knights of St John, but even that is mostly of Hellenistic date, when Rhodes was most prosperous. At the far end, the highest point, was the temple of Athena Lindia; it was about 25 × 70 feet (7.75 × 21.5m) in plan, with a porch of four Doric columns at each end, and was built in the later fourth century BC to make good a sixth-century temple (not necessarily the first) which had burned down. In alignment with it, but not directly in front (since the temple was sited – picturesquely – on the cliff edge) an outsize *propylaea* was constructed around 300 BC, with central stairway some 70 feet (21m) wide. A century later a Doric *stoa* with projecting wings and nearly 300 feet (88m) wide was added symmetrically in front of the stairway. The concept, in the new Hellenistic manner, was grandly and rather ludicrously axial, since at its culmination the temple was very small.

The island could always support craftsmen. Its Protogeometric and Geometric schools of

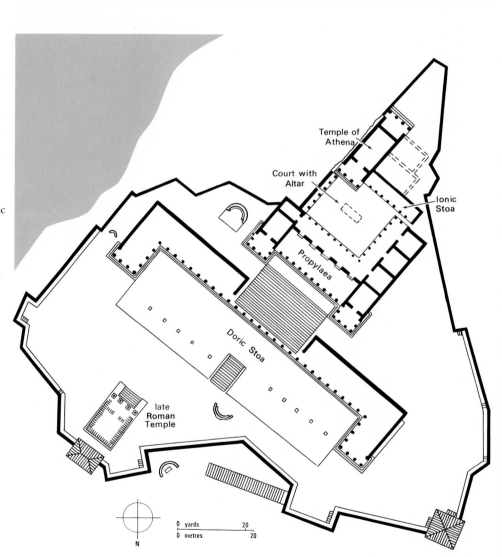

Lindos. Opposite: Plan of the acropolis. *Above: Model of the* acropolis, *as in the third century* A D, *seen from the northeast*

pottery had character; for the next four centuries its arts were usually content to follow the leads of its neighbours; and in the Hellenistic period it had sculptors of distinction and perhaps a special local manner. We do not know what was Lindos's share in this production before 408 B C: afterward, of course, activity was based on the city of Rhodes. Finds at Lindos of sculpture and minor objects were not of general interest: most went to ISTANBUL, but some to the National Museum at Copenhagen. A curious discovery was an inscription of 99 B C, the so-called Temple Chronicle, which lists with uncritical zeal notable dedications (many lost in the fire of 348 B C) and miraculous interventions of the goddess.

Blinkenberg, C., etc., *Lindos*, I–III, Berlin and Copenhagen, 1931–60. Detailed report on excavations of *acropolis* and also in the city

Cyprus

Cyprus is the third largest island in the Mediterranean, considerably smaller than Sicily and Sardinia, slightly larger than Crete. It lies about 40 miles (64km) from the south coast of Anatolia, 70 miles (113km) from Syria, 260 miles (418km) from Egypt and 500 miles (800km) from Athens. Its maximum length is 138 miles (222km), southwest–northeast, and its maximum width 60 miles (96km), north–south. Along the northern coast runs the mountain range of Pentadaktylos, 3,397 feet (1,035m), and along the southwest part of the island the Troödos or Olympus range, 6,407 feet (1,953m). Between them lies a fertile plain, Mesaoria, which extends from Morphou Bay to the Bay of Famagusta. In antiquity this plain was thickly forested and provided wood for shipbuilding as well as for the smelting of the copper ores from the mines which lie principally along the northwestern and southeastern slopes of Troödos. (The word 'copper' derives ultimately from the name Cyprus.) The island has no proper rivers, only streams that cross the central plain, rising mainly in the eastern area of the Troödos mountains.

They flow only in winter, but on the two mountains there are perennial springs, around which important settlements grew up from the prehistoric period onward. The climate is mild and together with the island's fertile soil favoured the development of agriculture.

The earliest settlements, dating back to the Neolithic period (beginning of the sixth millennium B C) were farming villages concentrated mainly in the west and along the lower slopes of the Kyrenia mountains. These early Cypriots, of a mixed Mediterranean race, came probably from Anatolia.

There are two main Neolithic cultural phases, an a-ceramic phase, when stone, bone, and flint were used for containers and tools, and a late period characterized by pottery, the burial of the dead inside or outside their habitations, in graves furnished with gifts, and small human statuettes of stone (andesite) or clay, probably used in religious ceremonies.

The Chalcolithic period, from 3000 to 2300 B C, is marked by the appearance of copper, but it was only during the subsequent period that the copper mines were systematically exploited.

In the Early Bronze Age (2300–1850 B C), the copper trade initiated contacts with the Near East, which brought in material wealth and enriched its culture. This period is so far known only from the tombs (rock-cut chambers), now in separate cemeteries at a distance from the settlements. They contain rich gifts, pottery, bronze tools and weapons, and jewelry, including gold and silver hair ornaments and beads of faïence.

Following the transitional Middle Bronze Age (1850–1600/1550 B C), the Late Bronze Age (1600/1550–1050 B C) is a period of great prosperity but also of serious political changes that affected the future development of the island. With the establishment of peaceful conditions in the eastern Mediterranean after the expulsion of the Hyksos from Egypt, trade flourished, especially with the appearance of Mycenaean Greeks after 1400 B C. The Mycenaeans established small trade colonies in the already flourishing harbour towns along the east and south coasts of Cyprus (Enkomi, Hala Sultan Tekké, CITIUM, Maroni etc.) and from there they traded with the whole of the eastern

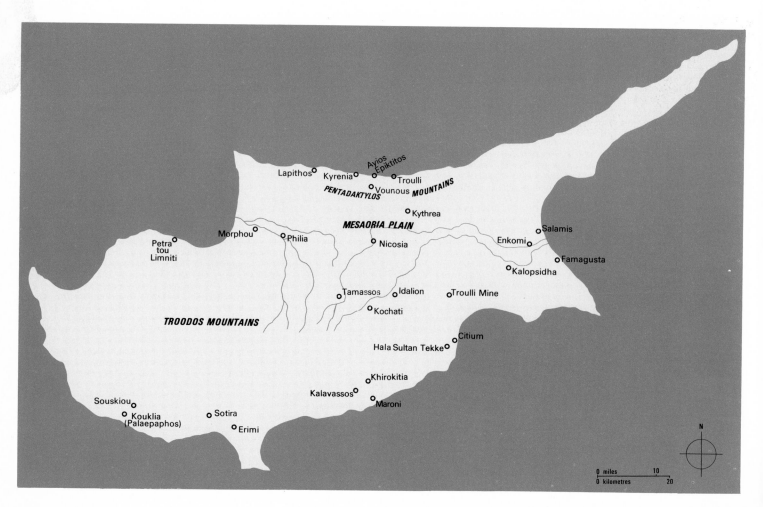

Mediterranean, introducing new tastes (Mycenaean pottery) and borrowing artistic ideas from the Orient. Toward the very end of the thirteenth century, Achaean Greeks arrived as colonists in Cyprus and settled in the existing Late Bronze Age towns, introducing new styles in art, architecture, and religion. They also brought their Greek language (an Aegean linear script had been introduced at the end of the sixteenth century). The island was thus Hellenized by successive arrivals of colonists through the twelfth and eleventh centuries BC. A natural phenomenon, probably an earthquake, put an end to the Late Bronze Age culture of Cyprus, after which new towns were built, including SALAMIS on the east coast, initiating the city-states of Cyprus of the first millennium BC.

The Iron Age was a period of successive invasions and occupations by foreign powers. A 'dark age' that lasted for two centuries was followed by the appearance of the Phoenicians at Citium toward the middle of the ninth century. They not only held political and economic control of this harbour town, but

also extended their influence over a number of other towns. In 709 the island's kings recognized the king of Assyria (Sargon II) but were left to exercise their own independent cultural and political activities as long as they paid tribute to Assyria. This was a period of prosperity and grandeur for Cyprus, as seen in the 'royal tombs' of Salamis. The Egyptians occupied Cyprus in 560 BC, but their stay lasted only for a short period. The Cypriot kings recognized the king of Persia in 545 BC. Persian rule lasted for more than two centuries, during which the Cypriots found themselves fighting for their freedom, often in common with other Greeks under Persian rule. Close contacts with Greece were revived, especially under the leadership of the fourth-century BC Salaminian king Evagoras.

When Alexander the Great was besieging Tyre, the kings of Cyprus sent him one hundred ships. In recognition of their contribution to his victory Alexander granted them autonomy. After his death in 323 BC Cyprus came under the Ptolemies of Egypt. Its independent kingdoms were dissolved and a unified govern-

ment was established under a military governor. The cultural and political institutions of Cyprus were henceforth those of the rest of the Hellenistic world.

By 58 BC Cyprus had passed to the Romans and formed part of the province of Cilicia, with a proconsul as governor. Roman rule was ruthless, though there were benevolent emperors who favoured the cities of Cyprus, particularly Salamis and PAPHOS. The latter became the capital, replacing Salamis. As early as AD 45 Paul and Barnabas preached Christianity, which became predominant by the end of the fourth century.

Finds are housed in the Cyprus Museum, Nicosia, in the local museums and in the British Museum, London.

Gjerstad, E., *The Swedish Cyprus Expedition*, IV, 2, Stockholm, 1948.

Karageorghis, V., *Cyprus*, Geneva, 1968 *(Archaeologia Mundi)*

I Citium

Cyprus

The site of this ancient city lies beneath modern Larnaca, on the southeast coast, at a short distance from the sea. In antiquity it had an inner harbour, linked to the sea by a navigable channel. Citium (the Greek name is Kition) had a rather poor hinterland and its importance derived mainly from its harbour and trade; perhaps the salt from the nearby Salt Lake also favoured its economy. At a short distance to the northeast are the copper mines of Troulli and to the west the mines of Kalavassos; the ore may have been transported to Citium for smelting and subsequent export.

The earliest remains uncovered so far date to the beginning of the thirteenth century BC. After an earthquake, *c.* 1050 BC, Citium was rebuilt and lived on until *c.* 1000 BC, when its inhabitants built another town nearer to the sea. The silting up of its inner harbour may have been one of the causes. Recent excavations reveal Phoenician domination of Citium (known in the Bible as Kittim) by the middle of the ninth century BC. The city was in direct subordination to its 'mother town' Tyre until the Assyrian ascendancy of the eighth century BC. The successive periods of foreign domination of Cyprus favoured the Phoenicians of Citium, who extended their rule or influence to other towns of Cyprus during the classical period. Tamassus and Idalium were already within their sphere. They were particularly favoured by the Persians, who appointed a Phoenician king even at SALAMIS in the fifth century BC. Citium remained Phoenician despite repeated efforts by the Greeks to liberate it.

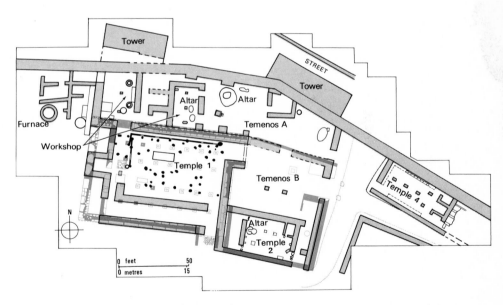

Citium. Temples and other remains in Area II, with the Phoenician temple of Astarte (ninth century BC) in brown

In 312 BC Ptolemy I killed the last king of Citium, Pumiathon, and put an end to the Phoenician dynasty. During the Hellenistic and Roman periods it was a flourishing town, as we know from inscriptions, with temples and public buildings, such as a gymnasium, but none of these has been excavated so far.

Recent excavations have revealed the northern part of the Late Bronze Age and Phoenician towns. The former includes the Cyclopean wall, with monumental rectangular

bastions, sanctuaries (2 and 3 in Area II), and north and west of this an industrial quarter, consisting of three workshops for the smelting of copper and the production of bone ash, used as a flux. The unroofed workshops were built along the city wall so that the south winds might blow away their poisonous fumes.

In the middle of the ninth century the largest of the Late Bronze Age temples was transformed into a Phoenician temple of Astarte, 117 feet (36m) in length and 73 feet (22m) in

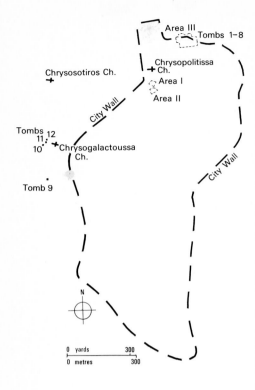

width. It consists of a rectangular courtyard, with two porticoes along the north and south sides, each supported on two rows of seven pillars of wood (their stone bases have been uncovered), and a holy-of-holies along the west side. Destroyed *c.* 800 BC, the temple was rebuilt several times until it was finally demolished in 312 by Ptolemy I. The site was then reserved as a bathing establishment during Hellenistic and Roman times.

Karageorghis, V., *Kition, Mycenaean and Phoenician discoveries in Cyprus*, London, 1975.

Karageorghis, V., *Excavations at Kition, I The Tombs*, Nicosia, 1974.

Citium. Above: Site plan showing city wall and excavated areas. Right: Statue of Artemis found on the site

The site of Salamis is now occupied by a forest of mimosas and eucalyptus, about 5 miles (8km) north of the medieval city of Famagusta. The ancient city was first built, in the mid-eleventh century BC, round a natural harbour, and it was then extended. It had been preceded by an earlier settlement, called Enkomi by archaeologists after the nearby modern village, about a mile inland behind a rocky plateau. Enkomi was presumably connected with the sea by a navigable channel in the estuary of the Pedias or Pedieos river: from a modest start as a small agricultural settlement, it grew into a rich and important centre of copper smelting and export. It was destroyed *c.* 1075 BC by a natural disaster, probably an earthquake. Instead of rebuilding it, the inhabitants moved nearer to the sea and founded Salamis. Much later, in the Hellenistic and Roman periods, the centre of gravity of Salamis shifted to the north, where public buildings were constructed, as well as a new harbour after the old one had silted. Two successive earthquakes destroyed Salamis in AD 332 and 342, after which a new Christian city, Constantia, was built, on a smaller scale and confined within a defensive wall. The new town was itself destroyed in the seventh century during the Arab invasions and was subsequently succeeded by Famagusta, destined to become the most important city of medieval Cyprus.

Of the original city only one tomb and remains of a sanctuary have been found, in the vicinity of the harbour. No remains have yet been brought up of archaic or classical Salamis proper. From Herodotus and Isocrates we know that under kings Onesilos and Evagoras, Salamis became the champion of Greek political and cultural ideas and was constantly at war against the Persians. The wealth of the city from the eighth to the fourth centuries BC is further illustrated by the discoveries in the tombs of its necropolis, which extends to the west between the Salamis forest and the monastery of St Barnabas. Though most of these tombs were looted in the nineteenth century, in their spacious *dromoi* were found remains of chariots, horse burials, furniture of ivory, and other objects that recall Homeric burial customs but at the same time illustrate the pomp and power of the Salaminian kings.

Within the city site, in the south sector, the remains of the large Hellenistic temple of Zeus have recently been brought to light. Its plan follows the models of Greek architecture and was remodelled in the Roman period. To the

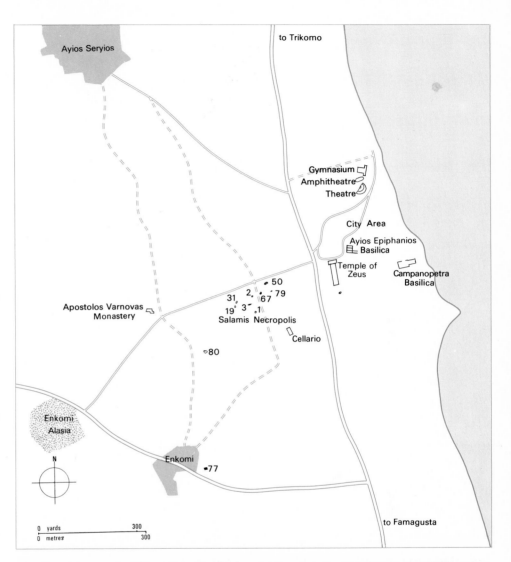

Right: General view of the northern part of Salamis, showing the gymnasium (foreground) and the theatre

Above: The gymnasium of Salamis from the west

north it faces the Roman *forum*, along the north side of which the main water reservoir of the town was built in the early Byzantine period. The north sector also includes the monumental remains of a Hellenistic gymnasium, remodelled and enlarged in Roman imperial times. It was rebuilt as the baths of the Christian city after the fourth-century earthquake. A large theatre has been excavated south of the gymnasium. Its orchestra has a diameter of nearly 92 feet (28m). The *cavea*, however, is poorly preserved, as the theatre provided building material for the reconstruction of the gymnasium baths after the earthquake. Outside the city the remains of an aqueduct are still visible; it brought water to Salamis from Kythrea (near Nicosia) some 30 miles (48km) away.

Karageorghis, V., *Salamis in Cyprus, Homeric, Hellenistic and Roman*, London, 1969.
Dikaios, P., *Enkomi* I–III, Mainz, 1969–71.

3   Old Paphos   **Cyprus**

The remains of Old Paphos (or Palaepaphos) lie beneath the houses of the village of Kouklia, about 10 miles (16km) southeast of New Paphos (its successor in the fourth century B C), on elevated ground approx. 2 miles (3km) from the sea. The surrounding area was already inhabited in the Chalcolithic period, but the town itself flourished mainly from the Late Bronze Age onward. Its mythological king Kinyras was known to Homer, as was the famous temple of Aphrodite, the goddess *par*

excellence of Cyprus. The development of Paphos during the first millennium is centred round this temple, often mentioned in Greek literature. Tombs excavated at the site of 'Evreti', on the southeastern outskirts of Kouklia, have produced an extraordinary wealth of gold and ivory objects of the twelfth century B C, indicative of the wealth and importance of Old Paphos at the end of the Late Bronze Age. Richly furnished tombs of the eleventh century and later periods have also been found along

the eastern side of the village.

The now visible remains of the temple of Aphrodite lie on the southwestern outskirts of the village, on the edge of the plateau overlooking a fertile plain and the sea. They consist of a monumental entrance leading to a courtyard to the west, flanked along the north and south sides by a portico. Large ashlar blocks, recalling the temples of Citium, form part of these walls, but it is only recently that archaeological investigations have brought to light

Below: Old Paphos. Site of the city gate, and the fortified mound. Bottom: Plan of the Kouklia gate

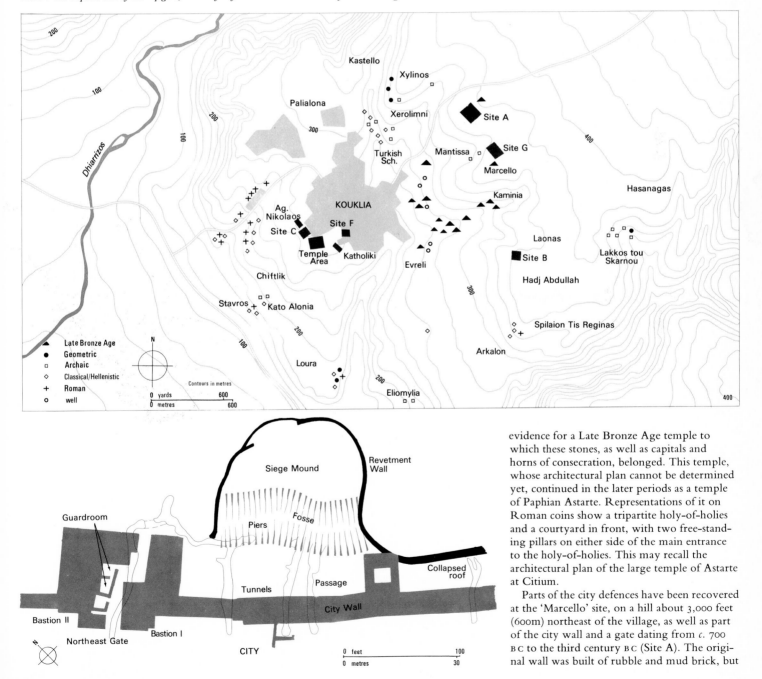

evidence for a Late Bronze Age temple to which these stones, as well as capitals and horns of consecration, belonged. This temple, whose architectural plan cannot be determined yet, continued in the later periods as a temple of Paphian Astarte. Representations of it on Roman coins show a tripartite holy-of-holies and a courtyard in front, with two free-standing pillars on either side of the main entrance to the holy-of-holies. This may recall the architectural plan of the large temple of Astarte at Citium.

Parts of the city defences have been recovered at the 'Marcello' site, on a hill about 3,000 feet (600m) northeast of the village, as well as part of the city wall and a gate dating from *c.* 700 B C to the third century B C (Site A). The original wall was built of rubble and mud brick, but

Part of the temple of Aphrodite, Old Paphos

its sides were revetted with stone blocks in the fourth century. Its thickness was 21 feet (6.4m). The gate has massive bastions on either side and the entrance was a winding one with guardrooms all along. Outside the walls, east of the gate, there is a siege mound erected by the Persian besiegers in 490 BC after the Ionian revolt. Subterranean tunnels were dug by the defenders underneath the mound from inside the city to undermine it. Four of the tunnels have been found, supported by wooden beams, which were set on fire by the defenders to cause the collapse of the mound.

Maier, F. G., *Archäologie und Geschichte. Ausgrabungen in Alt-Paphos*, Konstanz, 1973

Maier, F. G., reports in: *Archäologischer Anzeiger* and *Report of the Department of Antiquities, Cyprus*, since 1967

The Black Sea

Within the framework of the widespread colonization movement carried on by the Greeks throughout the archaic period (eighth to sixth centuries BC), the Black Sea occupied a particular place that has been acknowledged ever since antiquity. For ATHENS, as for other cities of mainland Greece, the western and northern coasts of Pontus Euxinus (as it was known in Greek, or often simply Pontus) were for several centuries the main source of grain supplies. In return, the Pontic region, especially in the earlier period of contact, was a favoured recipient of certain manufactured goods (in the first instance pottery), and of olive oil and wine.

These relations have always been known from the surviving writings of the historians and geographers of antiquity, and from fourth-century BC Athenian orators (notably Demosthenes), who occasionally provide credible figures of the volume of goods exchanged

between Aegean and Pontic Greeks. Further information has accrued since the early nineteenth century, thanks to travellers and dilettanti who described ancient ruins and collected coins, inscriptions and the relatively rare works of art. Archaeological exploration began relatively late, and so far only OLBIA and ISTRUS (Histria under the Romans) have been systematically excavated.

Apart from the few Greek settlements at the Caucasian end, of which not even the ancient names are always known, and of those on the southern shore (northern Asia Minor), which were part of a different cultural complex, with a different history, the main colonies were as follows: on the Thracian coast, from south to north, Apollonia (and its own colony, Anchialus), Mesembria, Odessus, Bizone, Dionysopolis, Callatis (MANGALIA), Tomis, and Istrus; on the Scythian coast, Tyras, Olbia, Chersonesus, Theodosia, Panticapaeum, Phana-

goria, and Gorgippia. Three – Mesembria, Chersonesus, and Callatis – were Megarian in origin; the others, at least according to tradition, Milesian.

The colonies on the west coast were established among Thracians, who were themselves distributed among different tribes, whereas those on the north coast had as their principal neighbours Scythians (until the latter were overrun by migrants from the east, including Sarmatians). Pacific relations were quickly established between the Greeks and these neighbours, based on mutual interests. Thus, in return for the right to farm their lands and trade with the interior, the Greeks paid an annual tribute (*phoros*) to the more powerful of the local chieftains (such as Saïtapharnes in the third century BC); to others, of lower rank, they made payments called gifts (*dora*) in the documents. Formal agreements to this effect are best known from the cities of the Dobruja,

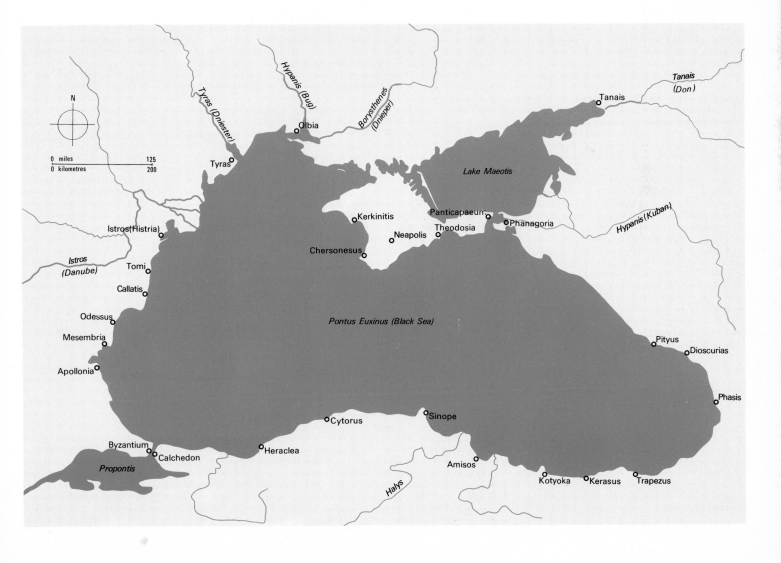

where inscriptions have been found giving the names of kings (*basileis*) of the Getae who 'protected' them: Zalmodegikos, Rhemaxos, Moskon.

One notable consequence of these relations, which were hostile at times as well as peaceful,

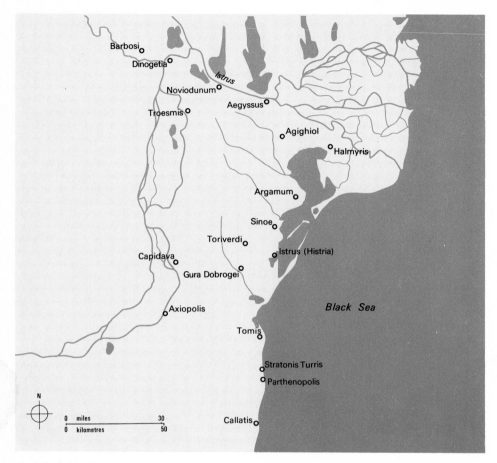

The Dobruja in antiquity

then reversed on the west coast of the Black Sea with the Roman conquest at the beginning of the Christian era. The province of Moesia was created under Tiberius (later divided into Moesia Superior and Moesia Inferior), and in AD 45 or 46 the client-kingdom of Thrace was

was the considerable influence exercised by the Greeks on the economic, social, and cultural development of the native peoples. The most visible and most durable expression was the creation of the 'Scythian' art of the seventh to fourth centuries BC (preserved in the Hermitage in Leningrad), in which Greeks surely played a larger part than is commonly acknowledged; and of the 'Thraco-Getic' art of the fourth century BC (in which the hand of Greek artists is even more obviously discernible) that produced treasures as famous as those of the *kurgans* (barrows) of the Ukraine.

However, as the military strength of the 'barbarians' increased, the freedom and prosperity of the Greek cities became more and more precarious, until, toward the middle of the first century BC, the 'great king' Byrebistas became master of all the colonies along the coast from Olbia to Apollonia. Relations were

converted into a province. From that date the Balkan peninsula was part of the Roman empire; then it passed to the Byzantine sphere until the creation of the Bulgar kingdom around the year 700.

So long as the Romans maintained firm control of the Danube frontier, the old Greek cities on the coast continued their traditional way of life, barely modified by the creation of a federation of cities, at times five and at other times six, presided over by an official called the *pontarchos*. However, a new situation developed in the hinterland. Thanks to the protection afforded by the *limes* and the settlement on the land of many veteran contingents, there grew up not merely villages of mixed Thraco-Roman population but also urban centres that were granted the status of *municipia* or *coloniae*: Oescus, Novae, Durostorum, Tropaeum Traiani, Troesmis. Despite repeated

invasions by migrating peoples (among them Goths, Avars, and later Slavs), the situation remained fairly stable until the breakdown of the Danubian *limes* in the seventh century.

The development on the north coast was very different. That area was never attached to the Roman empire; the Romans in fact made only sporadic appearances, installing garrisons in Tyras and Olbia, and creating a naval base at Charax in the CRIMEA. In consequence, the Greek population was submerged by neighbouring nomads and then by successive waves of migrating peoples. Of the latter, the Goths stayed longest, converting the Crimea into a base for raiding expeditions all along the west coast of the Black Sea, into the Aegean and even into the Mediterranean.

As for the material and spiritual relations between the Greek settlements and their mother cities (as well as with other Greek centres both in Greece proper and in Asia Minor), the essential point is that they continued for centuries. Trading relations were substantially reduced in the Hellenistic age, partly because of the appearance on the grain market of two new producers, Ptolemaic Egypt and Numidia, partly because of the growing insecurity of life in the Black Sea communities and of their difficulties in producing enough for their own subsistence. Yet even then, spiritual ties remained strong and effective. The civic and religious institutions were in all respects similar to those of the mother cities; the language of the inscriptions remained a pure Greek; even the proper names are astonishingly reminiscent of those of the homelands. The outstanding exception was Tanaïs, at the mouth of the Don river, where it would be no exaggeration to speak of 'barbarization'. Everywhere else, not excluding Olbia, the ethnic mixture that was completed in the first centuries AD culminated in the Hellenization (or Romanization) of the natives both within the cities and in the hinterland. Henceforth they were an integral element within the very cities that had long lived a life apart from that of their neighbours. In the final analysis, therefore, the biological, social, political, and cultural race mixture, which meant for the natives a step forward from their traditional 'underdeveloped' state, was a capital development in Greek history.

Bilabel, F., *Die ionische Kolonisation*, Leipzig, 1920
Boardman, John, *The Greeks Overseas*, 2nd ed., Harmondsworth and Magnolia, Mass., 1973, Ch. 6
Minns, E. H., *Scythians and Greeks*, Cambridge, 1913.
Pippidi, D. M., *I Greci nel Basso Danubio dall'età arcaica alla conquista romana*, Milan, 1971
—, *Iranians and Greeks in South Russia*, Oxford, 1922
—, *Scythica Minora, Recherches sur les colonies grecques du littoral roumain de la Mer Noire*, Amsterdam, 1975

Mangalia

Ancient Callatis (modern Mangalia) was the only Dorian settlement on the Romanian coast of the Black Sea. Founded at the end of the sixth century BC by settlers from Heracleia Pontica (modern Ereğli) on the northern shore of Asia Minor, Callatis was an agrarian community from the outset. Throughout its history its prosperity appears to have been based on its extensive rural territory. In the fourth century BC it ranked as the most important Greek city-state on the west coast – hence it was twice besieged by Lysimachus in the struggle for succession after the death of Alexander the Great – and in the next century it was powerful enough to wage war, in alliance with ISTRUS, against Byzantium for control of the market centre of Tomis (modern Constanţa) which was 25 miles (40km) to the north.

In the first half of the first century BC, Callatis was allied with King Mithridates VI Eupator of Pontus and was attacked by the Roman proconsul of Macedonia, M. Terentius Varro Lucullus. Mithridates' garrison was expelled and Callatis changed sides to become allied with Rome: a substantial Latin fragment of the treaty, c. 70 BC, is preserved on an inscription. Once the Romans had established themselves in the area and transformed the kingdom of Thrace into a province (AD 45 or 46), Callatis lost its economic and political primacy to Tomis. In the course of the ensuing centuries, it was subject to numerous attacks by migratory peoples, but the exact date of its disappearance is unknown (possibly in the seventh century).

Modern underwater archaeology has revealed that a portion of the port has disappeared into the sea. Systematic excavation has also been hindered by the existence of the modern town, first established in the Middle Ages. Sporadic work has uncovered a Roman rampart on the northern side (second or third century), and, at the eastern extremity of this wall, the imposing remains of a Christian *basilica* in Syrian style. Several burial grounds outside the city limits, some Hellenistic, others Roman, have been excavated. A papyrus was found in one fine stone tomb of the fourth century BC, but it unfortunately disintegrated before its character had been established. From numerous inscriptions it is clear that the civic institutions were identical with those of Megara in Greece, and that the cult of Demeter and Dionysus was especially popular in the local religious life.

Hanell, K., *Megarische Studien*, Lund, 1934

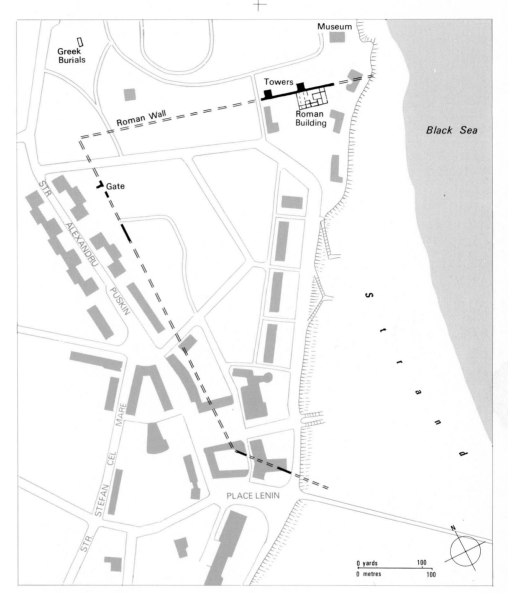

Right: Callatis. Marble bas-relief, first century AD, showing Artemis hunting

A Milesian foundation of the seventh century
BC on the west coast of the Black Sea, between
the mouth of the Danube and the present-day
port of Constanţa, Istrus (Histria, or Histria-
norum civitas, in Roman times) had a continuous history of habitation until the beginning of the seventh century AD. Situated
on a gulf, later transformed into a lagoon, it
was first a market centre for the distribution of
Greek goods to the Getae living along both
banks of the Danube, and a centre for fishing
in the river delta. Eventually the silting up of
the port turned the inhabitants to farming;
under the Romans, Histria was therefore a
farmers' town with a substantial rural hinterland.

    The many centuries of prosperity were
punctuated by grave crises. Istrus was sacked
at the end of the sixth century BC, possibly by
Scythians, and again at the end of the fourth
century BC, perhaps by Lysimachus. Twice it
was totally destroyed, in the first century BC
by the Getae under Byrebistas, and in the third
century AD by the Goths, but both times it
was rebuilt on the same site: an inscription
refers to the earlier of these reconstructions as
'the second foundation of the city'. Under
Augustus, Istrus was incorporated into the
Roman Empire; under Domitian it became
part of the province of Moesia Inferior, under
Diocletian of the new province of Scythia.
An Avar invasion in 595 brought about the
final abandonment of the site.

    Systematic excavations since 1914 have so
far brought to light four distinct precincts, of
different periods. The most imposing one
comes from the time of reconstruction after
the destruction by the Goths in about AD 260.
The wall of this precinct, best preserved on the
western and southern sides, reveals the dramatic
circumstances in which it was built: columns
and other architectural elements as well as
inscribed *stelae* were all employed as building
materials.

    Within the walls, archaeologists first con-
centrated on the surface remains, revealing late
buildings (fourth to sixth centuries AD). They
include several well-proportioned civic *basilicas*, a Christian *basilica* on the town square, a
thermal installation and a business quarter.
A residential quarter of the same late period
has some fine large houses, one of which
contains a private chapel and may have been
the episcopal residence. More recent excavations in the area adjacent to the Sinoe Lagoon
have revealed, at a depth of 10 to 13 feet (3–
4m), an ancient assemblage of sacred buildings,
among them a fifth-century BC temple of Zeus
Polieus, the ruins of unidentified altars, marble
fragments of a Doric temple of the third
century BC dedicated to the Thracian divinity
whom the Greeks called 'The Great God'
(*Theos Megas*), and a temple of Aphrodite

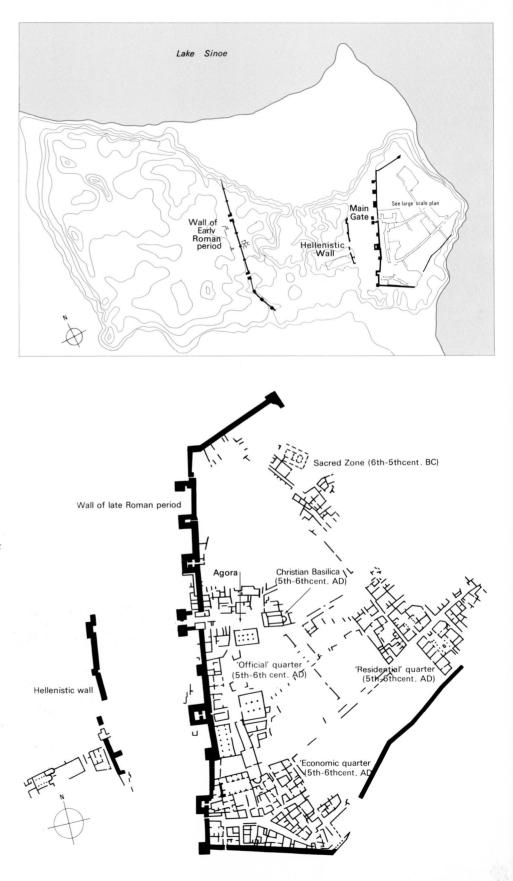

Above: Istrus. The sacred zone, seen from the south, showing the temple of Zeus Polieus. Below, left: Small vase-statuette in the form of a kore (maiden) with dove, found at Istria

erected in the archaic period and reconstructed in the Hellenistic age.

Histria reached its greatest extent in the first two centuries A D, when the expansion of the city to the west culminated in a new rampart built under Hadrian. Between the old and the new walls there have been found a thermal building to be dated in the second or third century, a late Christian *basilica* surrounded by a cemetery, and scattered remains of Hellenistic houses and workshops. Still farther to the west there was an enormous cemetery: more than a thousand mounds have been counted so far. The Greek burials in this necropolis date from the sixth century B C to the third century A D, and there were also a number of tombs of chieftains of the Getae, buried in the midst of both human and animal victims.

Finds, including sculpture, architectural elements, and numerous inscriptions, are housed in Istrus and also in the Archaeological Museum of Constanţa and the Museum of History, Bucharest.

Condurachi, E., and Pippidi, D. M. (eds), *Histria*, Bucharest, vol. 1, 1954, vol. 2, 1964, vol. 3, 1974
Pippidi, D. M., *Epigraphische Beitrage zur Geschichte Histrias*, Berlin, 1962

3   Olbia   U.S.S.R.

This Milesian foundation on the right bank of the Bug estuary (near the present-day Parutino), also known as Borysthenes in the sources, was established in 647 BC according to the ancient tradition. Modern archaeology has shown that, though the first settlers in fact arrived in the seventh century BC, they established themselves on the little island of Berezan (once a promontory) just under a mile (1.5km) off the coast. The finds – remains of cabins and shops, many fragments of imported pottery, even a private letter written on lead – reveal a flourishing market centre by the sixth century BC. Then, with settlement on the mainland, Berezan gave way to Olbia and ceased to be of importance.

Olbia's greatest period of prosperity was in the fifth and fourth centuries BC, when it was a major exporter of Scythian grain to the Greek world. A slow decline then set in, as a result both of internal difficulties and of hostile attacks from the nomads of the steppes and from more distant raiders. Of the former, the Scythians from time to time exercised a considerable hold over the city, requiring the payment of tribute as a condition of peaceful coexistence. Of the latter, the most damaging was a severe sack by the Getae under Byrebistas, between about 55 and 50 BC, when the finest monuments were destroyed. Other raids are known, from the late fourth century BC into Roman imperial times, until Olbia finally received assistance from the Romans. Antoninus Pius established a garrison there; when it withdrew with the arrival of the Goths, in the reign of Philip the Arab (AD 244–9), Olbia disappeared from the record until its rediscovery, and identification by finds of coins and inscriptions, in the early nineteenth century.

Archaeology has established that in its earliest period Olbia was not laid out according to any master plan, and covered more ground than in the classical period. The later city centred round the *agora* and a sacred zone (*temenos*) in which the temple ruins of several

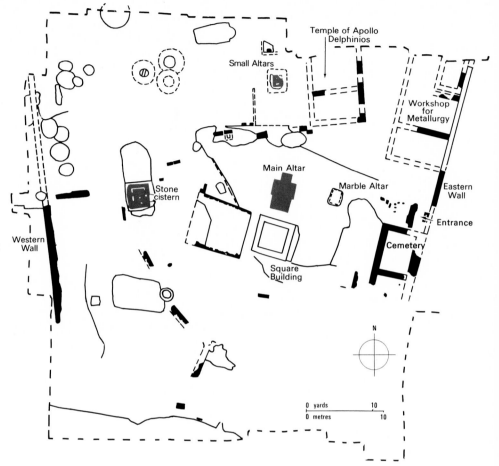

major divinities have been identified, including Zeus, Athena, and Apollo Delphinios. Substantial foundations of the city walls have also been uncovered: from literary sources it is known that they had been destroyed and rebuilt on several occasions.

Outside the walls, classical, Hellenistic, and Roman cemeteries have been excavated to the south, north, and west. The varied tombs include trench graves, alcoves, and underground vaults, at first merely cut into the loess but later lined to form genuine chambers.

Diehl, E., 'Olbia', in *Paulys Realencyclopädie,* vol. 17, Stuttgart, 1937, Cols 2405–23

Gajdukevič, V. F. (ed.), *Olbia: Temenos i Agora,* Moscow and Leningrad, 1964

Wasowicz, A., *Olbia pontique et son territoire,* Paris, 1975

4   Crimea   U.S.S.R.

According to the Greek geographer Strabo, the Crimean peninsula, known to the Greeks as the Taurikē (or Scythikē) Chersonesus, was first inhabited by Cimmerians, who were expelled by the Scythians. Then Greek colonists arrived and established themselves all along the coasts: Chersonesus in the west (a Megarian settlement), and, in the east, Theodosia (founded,

like Callatis, by Heracleia Pontica), Nymphaeum (supposedly established by the Athenians under Pericles in the 430s), and Panticapaeum (of unknown origin) were the most important.

Chersonesus was an independent city-state from its foundation to the end of the second century BC, exploiting a rich agricultural hinterland which included substantial vine-

yards just outisde the city proper. It maintained its independence despite the permanent menace of the Scythians of the interior, but then fell to Mithridates VI Eupator, king of Pontus in Asia Minor, who took control of the north coast of the Black Sea from about 110 BC. The city's civil and religious institutions were much like those of the other Megarian settlements; the

one notable exception was the adoption of a
native female goddess, whom they called
Parthenos, probably borrowed from the neighbouring Tauroi.

The eastern side of the peninsula was unified
from the early fifth century BC into a Graeco-
barbarian state known as the Kingdom of the
Bosporus, at first under the Archeanactid
dynasty, then under the Spartocids. A number
of smaller Greek settlements on the east bank
of the Straits of Kerch and Tanaïs at the mouth
of the Don river were also incorporated.
Structurally this kingdom was a forerunner
of the Hellenistic states of Asia, with a highly
centralized government and a minority of
Greek citizens dominating and exploiting a
mixed population of 'barbarians' in the rural
districts. For some centuries the rich harvests
of the Bosporus helped feed the Aegean world,
and in particular ATHENS, which maintained
the closest relationship with the Spartocid
dynasty. A union with the kings of Pontus,
Mithridates VI and then his son, Pharnaces II,
embroiled the Bosporus in their war with
Rome. Although the victorious Romans made
no effort to annex the Bosporus, they reduced
it to a client-kingdom and converted the Black
Sea into a Roman lake.

Little remains of the architecture of the
Greek cities of the Crimea, apart from the
imposing walls and some Byzantine churches
in Chersonesus. The underground tombs of
Theodosia, Nymphaeum, and Panticapaeum,
some with painted decorations, have a certain
grandeur and were stocked with imported
vases and sumptuous jewelry. But the greatest
of the finds are the 'Scythian' metalwork from
the settlements on the Straits of Kerch, made
by Greek artisans of the cities of the Black Sea
area, and now housed in the Hermitage,
Leningrad.

Gajdukevič, V. F., *Das bosporanische Reich*, Berlin,
1971

*Right: Gold 'Scythian' earring, fourth century BC, from a
tomb in Theodosia, Crimea*

Asia Minor

Asia Minor, a modern historian's term for roughly the area covered by Turkey in Asia, experienced the emergence early in the first millenium B C of a number of small kingdoms in the territory once controlled by the empire of the Hittites. The kingdom of Phrygia, of a legendary wealth associated with the name of Midas, was little more than a memory to classical antiquity; the kingdom of Lydia, however, established a stable dominion over the west of Asia Minor from its capital at Sardis and its last and most famous king, Croesus, had considerable dealings with the Greek world. He succumbed to the expanding Persian empire during the sixth century B C, and the Greeks settled in the west of Asia Minor joined Lydia as part of the empire of Cyrus. An unsuccessful attempt at rebellion by the Greek cities, principally of that part of the west of Asia Minor known as Ionia (the so-called Ionian revolt), provoked two Persian invasions of Greece, in 490 and 480 B C, in order to punish Athenian and Eretrian help sent to the rebels.

The resounding defeat of Persia was followed by the creation of a league of Greek cities against Persia under the leadership of Athens; in effect an Athenian empire, it kept Persia at bay until the last years of the fifth century B C. Then Sparta, in order to get Persian help in her quarrel with Athens, surrendered the Greeks of Asia Minor once more to Persia. Persian control of Asia Minor was never again effectively challenged until the invasion of Asia by Alexander the Great of Macedon in 334 B C. Successive Persian armies were defeated in three great battles, at Granicus in the west of Asia Minor, at Issus in northern Syria, and at Gaugamela in Mesopotamia, and Alexander inherited their empire. His premature death in 323 B C led to the division of his empire among a number of successor kingdoms, notably that of the Ptolemaic dynasty in Egypt, the Seleucid dynasty in Mesopotamia, Syria, and eventually much of Asia Minor, and the Antigonid dynasty in Macedon.

Roman expansion from 200 B C onward overwhelmed one successor kingdom after another; the Seleucid, Antiochus III, was defeated at the battle of Magnesia-ad-Sipylum in 190 B C; a period of informal control over the Greek East was followed by the progressive extension of direct rule. Roman rule in Asia Minor began with the bequest to Rome in 133 B C by its last king of the kingdom of Pergamum, which had been carved out of Seleucid territory during the third and second centuries B C, not least as a result of a prudent decision to support Rome.

The king of Pontus, Mithridates, in the

course of three wars in the early first century BC, attempted to block Roman expansion, but was finally defeated by Pompey. Exploited by Roman governors and hence ready to ally with Mithridates, maltreated in the course of the civil wars that marked the end of the Roman Republic, Asia Minor entered a period of peace and prosperity under the autocracy established by Augustus. Eventually the progressive occupation of the western half of the Roman empire by barbarian tribes in the course of the third, fourth, and fifth centuries AD, and the crises of government that accompanied this process, left Asia Minor largely unharmed, to form the core of the Byzantine empire. Despite a number of vicissitudes, it was only after the battle of Manzikert in AD 1071 that most of Asia Minor passed finally out of Byzantine control.

Visited and perhaps occasionally settled by Greeks in the Bronze Age, Asia Minor in the first millennium BC saw the foundation of many hundreds of Greek cities. Much of the west coast was settled by men from Greece in the tenth and ninth centuries BC, creating cities that were in turn responsible for other foundations even farther afield, a venture in which cities in Greece also shared. In the Hellenistic period cities were founded or developed as garrison towns or royal capitals; finally, a few Roman colonies came to join the Greek cities. Throughout, communities of native peoples often became Hellenized and acquired the institutions of a Greek city. By the mid-first century AD the Roman province of Asia, comprising the west alone, was popularly supposed to contain 500 cities.

As elsewhere, most of the early Greek settlements in Asia Minor were round the coast. Penetration was slow, except in the west, in large measure for geographical reasons. The mountain chains parallel to and close beside the north and south coasts (merging in the east into a single range) leave on the whole only small coastal plains and inhibit movement inland. There are the plains of Pamphylia and Cilicia in the south; in the north there is an extensive low-lying area round the Sea of Marmara and two great rivers, the Sangarius and the Halys, break through from the central plateau to the sea. The central plateau itself is uninviting – very high and therefore cold in winter, much of it infertile, in part watered by rivers with no exit to the sea and terminating in salt lakes. It is in the west that the plateau breaks down into a series of parallel ranges of mountains, separated by river valleys that provide both fertile land in quantity for settlement and ready access to the interior, the Caicus, Hermus, Cayster, and Maeander (the modern Bakir, Gediz, Küçük Menderes, and Büyük Menderes).

Apart from its agricultural resources and the timber on its mountains, Asia Minor possesses a variety of forms of mineral wealth; iron and silver were mined in the far northeast in antiquity, silver in Cappadocia; electrum, a naturally occurring mixture of gold and silver, was washed in the rivers of the west and provided the metal for the earliest coinage of classical antiquity, that of Lydia. Apart from the great marble quarries of Docimium and Proconnesus, whose products were widely exported in the Roman period, few areas were without marble of some sort. Architectural innovation was a feature of the early civilization of Ionia, as the area in the centre of the west coast of Asia Minor was called, an area that provided the name for one of the three chief orders of Greek architecture, the Ionic. In the later Hellenistic period, Asia Minor not only gave a name to a highly ornate rhetorical style, but also went in for buildings on a vast scale and richly decorated. The baroque splendour of the north gateway of the South Agora at MILETUS is an outstanding example in an almost perfect state of preservation.

The earliest Greek cities of Asia Minor were in theory independent and self-governing communities; the status of later foundations ranged from a wholly free one to a largely subservient one, exemplified for instance by the position of a royal garrison city. But almost all of the cities of Asia Minor had for almost the whole of their history to live in the shadow of a ruling power, whether Lydia, Persia, a Hellenistic kingdom or Rome. Even a power that paid lip service to the concept of city autonomy was apt to ignore it in practice.

Within the framework provided by its immediate territory and by the wider world of the rest of the Mediterranean basin, and within the constraints imposed by the great powers, the cities of Asia Minor organized their political life and set out to provide the amenities that made civilized life possible. Sharing a common ideal, established by the fifth century BC, they created a physical and institutional environment that, allowing for differences in the wealth of one city and of another, was remarkably uniform.

The cities of Asia Minor provided fertile ground for the early Christian missionaries. According to an early legend, Mary came to EPHESUS and died there (her house is still shown to tourists); much of the exploration of the classical sites of Asia Minor in modern times was an incidental accompaniment of voyages to visit the 'Seven Churches of Asia'.

Akurgal, E., *Ancient Civilisations and Ruins of Turkey*, Istanbul, 1973 (Guidebook)

Bean, G. E., *Aegean Turkey*, London, 1966. (Guidebook)

—, *Turkey Beyond the Maeander*, London, 1971 (Guidebook)

Cook, J. M., *The Greeks in Ionia and the East*, London, 1962

Hanfmann, G. M. A., *From Croesus to Constantine: The Cities of Western Asia Minor and Their Arts in Greek and Roman Times*, Ann Arbor, Mich., 1974

Jones, A. H. M., *The Greek City: From Alexander to Justinian*, London, 1940 (reprinted 1966)

Magie, D., *Roman Rule in Asia Minor*, 2 vols., Princeton and London, 1950 (reprinted 1966)

Brief reports of excavations in Asia Minor appear from time to time in *Archaeological Reports*, a suppl. to *Journal of Hellenic Studies* (London); annual reports by M. Mellink published in *American Journal of Archaeology* (Baltimore).

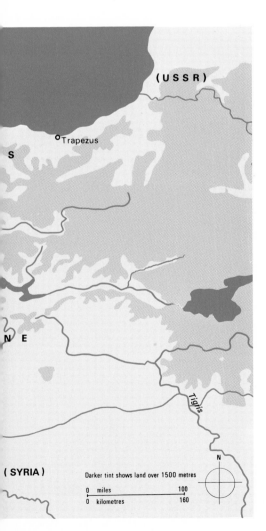

(USSR)

Trapezus

S

N   E

(SYRIA)

Tigris

N

Darker tint shows land over 1500 metres

0 miles 100
0 kilometres 160

I   Smyrna

First settled by Greeks on an already inhabited site early in the first millennium BC, Smyrna originally lay on a small hill at the head of the long bay into which the Hermus flows. Seized from its original Aeolian inhabitants (Aeolian is the name given to the Greek settlers in north-western Asia Minor) by Ionians from Colophon, the city was destroyed by the Lydian king Alyattes about 600 BC; it subsisted in some form until refounded by Alexander the Great on the slopes of Mount Pagus about 5 miles (8km) away round the bay to the south.

New Smyrna became a prosperous city in the Hellenistic period and remained so under Roman rule; its superb harbour, relatively unaffected by silting (the course of the Hermus was diverted as a precautionary measure in AD 1886), has ensured that, unlike many of the Greek cities of Asia Minor, Smyrna (now Izmir) is still a great city.

A typical early colonial site, Old Smyrna has been excavated from 1948 onward. The excavations have revealed the plan of the early city and the foundations of a seventh-century BC temple, also the enormous siege mound raised by Alyattes. It is remarkable that such a tiny community as Old Smyrna, with a total population of perhaps 5,000, was clearly prepared to offer considerable resistance to Alyattes.

Most of the material from Old Smyrna is in one of the two museums of Izmir.

Cadoux, C. J., *Ancient Smyrna*, Oxford, 1938
Cook, J. M., *Annual of the British School of Athens* (London), LIII–LIV, 1958–9, pp. 1–34, Old Smyrna

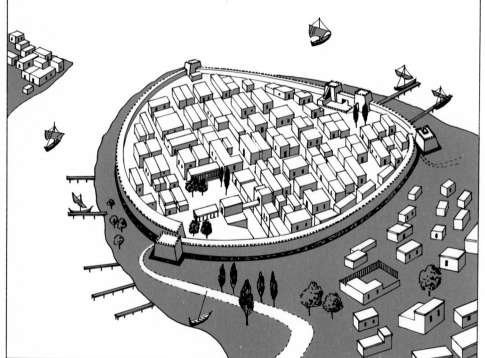

Old Smyrna from the northeast in the late seventh century
BC: *an imaginative reconstruction*

2 Miletus and Didyma

Miletus was founded at about the same time as SMYRNA, on a site earlier occupied by Greeks in the Bronze Age, but unlike Smyrna survived the pressure from Lydia and became in the sixth century B C the greatest Greek city of Asia Minor. Already in the seventh century B C the population had been large enough to provide for the founding of numerous colonies, mostly on the Sea of Marmara and the Black Sea, notably ISTRUS and OLBIA. Archaeological evidence shows the archaic settlement of the seventh and sixth centuries already around the northernmost of the harbours on the west of the promontory (Bay of the Lions), in the area of the theatre and the temple of Athena, and on Kalabak Tepe to the south. During the same period Miletus came to control an extensive territory on the mainland and a number of offshore islands such as Leros and Patmos. The consequent wealth of Miletus supported an ambitious élite – Miletus saw two tyrannies in the archaic period and *stasis* between rich and poor – and men of culture such as the philosophers Thales, Anaximander, and Anaximenes; the same wealth supported extensive building activity and the cult centre of Didyma.

The strength of Miletus no doubt encouraged King Cyrus of Persia to accept her overtures and leave her 'free' as under Lydia; her strength no doubt induced her to lead the Greek revolt against Persia in 499–494 B C, which ended in the capture and sack of the city. The population before the sack was perhaps about 60,000.

Miletus survived the sack; a building that is perhaps the *prytaneum* was in continuous use before and after 494, and the whole city was rebuilt on the grid pattern devised by Hippodamus of Miletus (perhaps following the principles implicit in the earlier lay-out to their logical conclusion). The first phases of many of the commercial buildings round the Bay of the Lions and the North Agora and the Delphinium, dedicated to Apollo, belong to the classical period; the temple of Athena is on the same alignment as this area and was built in the fifth century B C. Miletus was also still powerful enough to be a distinctly unruly subject of the Athenian empire, developed after the defeat of Persia. The fourth century saw the construction of the first version of the theatre; it underwent modification in the Hellenistic and Roman periods and survives as the most spectacular monument of the site and perhaps the finest theatre in Asia Minor.

Didyma, some 9 miles (15km) south of Miletus, was a pre-Greek cult centre that belonged to Miletus throughout her known history. The site of an oracle, cultivated like that of Delphi by King Croesus of Lydia, Didyma possessed by about 700 a sanctuary building, perhaps already with a *naiskos* (little shrine) for the god Apollo in the centre. A

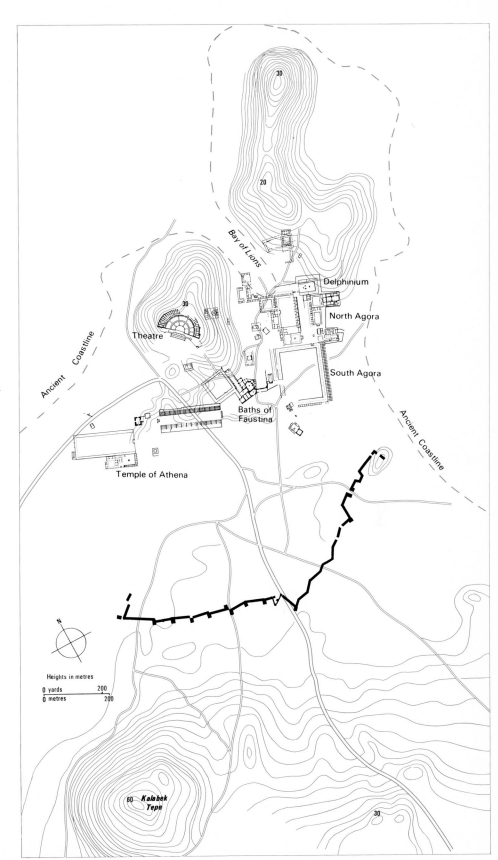

Plan of Miletus

Opposite, above: The theatre, Miletus. Opposite, below left: Fragment of frieze, Miletus. Opposite, below right: Fragment of frieze, with a head of Medusa, from Didyma.

Below: The temple of Apollo, Didyma. Bottom left: Plan of Didyma

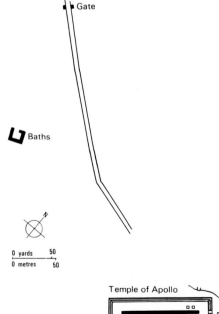

colonnade was added in the seventh century and the sanctuary rebuilt; the *naiskos* built, or rebuilt, in the sixth.

The sanctuary was devastated in 494 and the priestly family of the Branchidae exiled; unlike Miletus itself, the sanctuary did not revive until the Hellenistic period. Largely at the instance of King Seleucus I, the sanctuary that is visible now was begun; a combination of patronage by other Hellenistic monarchs and civic effort finally completed it in Roman times. Games in competition with the great games of Greece, the Didymeia, were held from about 200 BC onward.

Meanwhile, the main city of Miletus, like countless other Greek cities in the Hellenistic period, also benefited from royal patronage; the *stoa* in the South Agora is probably due to Antiochus I, the son of Seleucus I. The patronage of Hellenistic monarchs was succeeded by that of Roman emperors and wealthy Romans; the great north gateway of the South Agora, now reconstructed in the Staatliche Museen, Berlin, belongs to the second century A D.

Many of the most spectacular finds from Miletus and Didyma, even apart from the north gateway of the South Agora of Miletus, are in the Staatliche Museen, Berlin; there is also a museum at Miletus.

Kleiner, G., *Die Ruinen von Milet*, Berlin, 1968
Knackfuss, H., *Didyma* I, Berlin, 1941
Rehm, A., *Didyma* II, Berlin, 1958
Tuchelt, K., *Vorarbeiten zu einer Topographie von Didyma*, Tübingen, 1973

Around the coast of southwest Asia Minor from Telmessus to Limyra and up the Xanthus and Kasaba valleys there lived at least from the sixth century BC onward a non-Greek people, the Lycians (perhaps of Hittite origin), with their own language and script and with distinctive styles of grave monuments, and presumably also a distinctive architecture. Their art, however, was substantially Greek and their dynasts issued coinage on the Greek model.

The most important Lycian city was Xanthus (modern Günük), with the federal sanctuary of the Letoön, sacred to Apollo, about

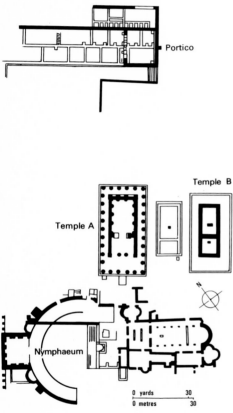

Left: Plan of the Letoön. Right: Plan of Xanthus

6 miles (10km) away across the river Xanthus. Its sanctity saved it from Mithridates during his invasion of the Roman province of Asia in 88 BC. The city owed homage, albeit notional, to Persia in the sixth century BC and remained independent from Athens in the fifth century BC; it no doubt owed its wealth and strength to the rich plain above which it was situated. After Alexander the Great, the Lycian language was progressively abandoned and the history of Xanthus resembles that of other cities in Hellenistic Asia Minor. Sacked by Brutus and Cassius in 42 BC to raise money, the city recovered and enjoyed a modest prosperity under the Roman Empire, owing some

of its buildings to imperial patronage.

On the way up to the Lycian acropolis from the north, beside the later *agora* and theatre, stands the so-called Inscribed Pillar, a dynastic monument of the period of the Peloponnesian War with an abbreviated Greek version of the Lycian inscription. There also is the so-called Harpy Monument, a dynastic tomb of the early sixth century BC, using Greek artistic skills in the interest of the Lycian ruling house, just as Lycian coinage does later. The sculptures of the Harpy Monument, apart from a fragment of a head in Istanbul, are in the British Museum, London: on three sides are male members of the dynasty, on the fourth side a

woman, with on either side Sirens (not Harpies), bearing off the souls of the dead. Beyond the Lycian acropolis stands the Nereid Monument, the sculptures from which are also in the British Museum; it belongs to the end of the fifth century BC and is in a more perfect Greek style than the Harpy Monument.

At the Letoön, besides a theatre, there were two temples: Temple B, a Doric temple of the second century BC, perhaps dedicated to Apollo and Artemis; Temple A, an Ionic temple, perhaps older, perhaps dedicated to Leto. Between lay a fourth-century BC building of uncertain function. To the south lay a *nymphaeum*, built under the reign of Hadrian, to the north a

Above: The Harpy Monument, now in the British Museum

portico with Hellenistic and Roman phases, built, it is now becoming clear, above substantial structures of the Lycian period. A recent dramatic discovery is a trilingual *stele* in Lycian, Aramaic, and Greek, of 341–334 BC, relating to the Persian satrap Pixodarus.

Demargne, P., and Metzger, H., 'Xanthus' in *Paulys Realencylopädie der klassischen Altertumswissenschaft,* vol. IXA, Stuttgart, 1967, cols 1375–1408

Kjeldsen, K., and Zahle, J., in *Archäoligischer Anzeiger* (Berlin), 1975, pp. 312–50. For the boundaries of Lycia

Marcadé, J., in *Revue des études anciennes,* Bordeaux, 1964, pl. iii, 1. For the fragment of a head in Istanbul

Metzger, H., in *Revue archéologique,* Paris, 1974, pp. 313–40. Excavation report of the Letoön with earlier bibliography

4   Pergamum   **Turkey**

Alexander the Great, by his victorious campaigns between 334 and his death in 323 BC, subjected Asia Minor, the Levant, Egypt, and areas farther east to Graeco-Macedonian rule, a rule perpetuated even if in a fragmented state by the successor kings Ptolemy I in Egypt, Seleucus I in the Levant, and their successors. Western Asia Minor, fought for initially by the Ptolemies and the Seleucids and other less durable dynasties, fell eventually to a new dynasty based on Pergamum.

The most perfectly preserved dynastic capital is that of Pergamum, a place of no consequence before the Hellenistic period. Originally held for Lysimachus when he controlled western Asia Minor, it became the independent base of its commander Philetaerus when Lysimachus was killed in battle in 281 BC and the treasure of Lysimachus passed also to Philetaerus. The latter passed on his rule to his adopted son Eumenes in 263, Eumenes to his adopted son Attalus in 241. The dynasty achieved its greatest success in 230 BC with the defeat of the aggressive Celtic tribes settled

Right: Pergamum. Part of the main frieze of the altar of Zeus, showing Artemis attacking Giants

in central Asia Minor from 279 BC onward.
Allied to Rome from the late third century,
the Attalids eventually left their kingdom to
Rome in 133. They had meanwhile used the
treasure of Lysimachus and the wealth accruing
from booty and from the rich territory under
their control to beautify the city of Pergamum,
to attract men of culture to the court, and to
endow numerous Greek cities with new public
buildings.

The city of Pergamum occupies a high rocky
hill. At the top are the palace, temples, library,
and theatre, also the altar of Zeus, built to
commemorate the victory over the Celtic
tribes and decorated with a sculptured representation of the battle of the Gods and the
Giants, symbolizing the Attalid victory over
the barbarians. The altar is now reconstructed
in the Staatliche Museen, Berlin.

*Above: Detail of the Pergamum altar frieze, showing
Athena attacking Giants. Opposite, above: The whole
altar. Right: Plan of Pergamum*

Lower down the hill lies the largest *gymnasium* in the Greek world, originally built in
the second century BC and several times altered
and extended in the succeeding centuries; in it
the youth of Pergamum, like the youth of
other Greek cities in their *gymnasia*, trained for
war, practised athletics, and listened to lectures
on philosophy and rhetoric. The *gymnasium*
at Pergamum is some 655 feet (200m) across
as its widest point and extends for about 490
feet (150m) down the hillside on three distinct
levels.

On the plain below lies the Asclepieum, in
its present form largely of imperial date, a
combined sanctuary to Asclepius, centre for
miracle cures, and consulting rooms for doctors
such as Galen. Beginning his career as a doctor
for gladiators in Pergamum, his native town,
Galen became court physician in the Rome
of Marcus Aurelius, where he spent the last
years of his life.

Apart from the material in the Staatliche
Museen, Berlin, there is an increasingly rich
collection of finds from Pergamum in the
museum in the modern town of Bergama.

Hansen, E. V., *The Attalids of Pergamum*, 2nd ed.
Ithaca and London, 1971 (with earlier
bibliography)

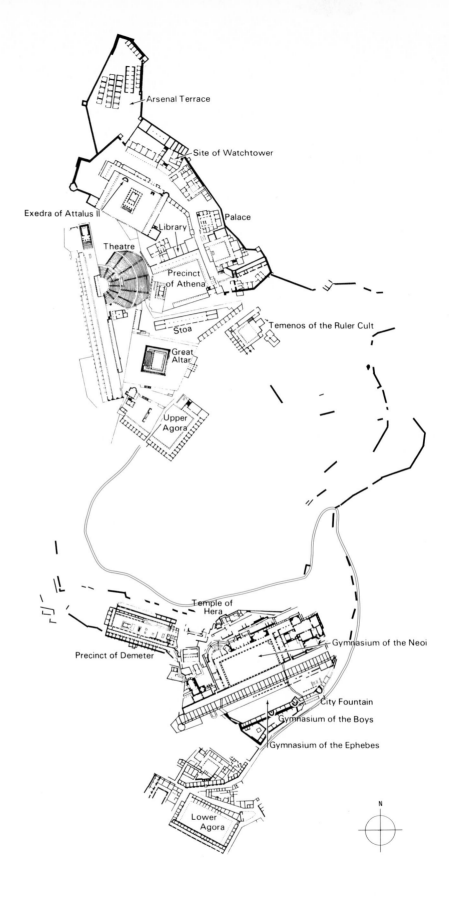

5   Priene   **Turkey**

Priene originally lay farther up the Maeander (now called Büyük Menderes) from its present site, though it is not known exactly where; the Maeander delta advanced and left the original city isolated from the sea and so during the fourth century BC the city was moved. The coastline continued to advance, however, and already by Roman times the new city was in its turn isolated from the sea. It declined and was for the most part unable to erect new buildings itself or attract benefactions – its earlier wealth clearly depended not only on agricultural territory, but also on its ability to export its own products and those transported down to the sea from central Asia Minor. The city remains as a perfect example of a middle-range Hellenistic city, its building almost all of a single period.

Right: Model of Priene showing the centre of the city from the southeast

All the characteristic buildings of a Greek city are there, laid out with great skill on a site where the highest point is 330 feet (100m) above the lowest point: a temple of the city's principal deity, Athena, and a theatre; between the theatre and the temple lies the *bouleuterion*, to the south the *agora*, and to the south again the *gymnasium* and *stadium*. Around lie the houses and streets of the city on a grid pattern like that of Hippodamus of MILETUS.

Schede, M., *Die Ruinen von Priene*, 2nd ed. by G. Kleiner and W. Kleiss, Berlin, 1964

Below: Plan of Priene. Opposite: Priene. The bouleuterion

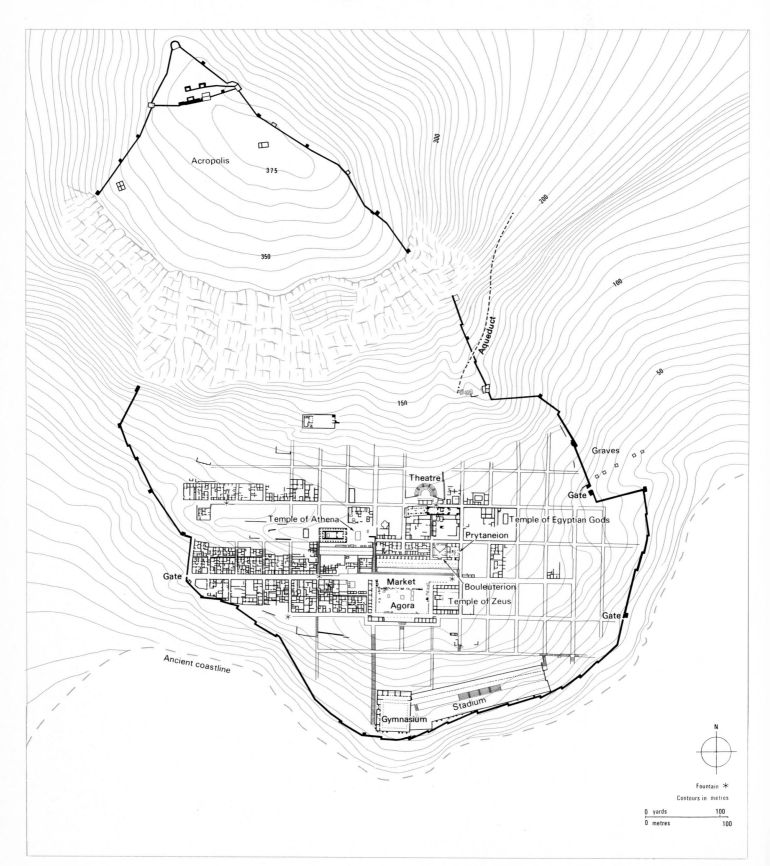

Acropolis

375

350

300

200

100

50

Aqueduct

150

Graves

Gate

Theatre

Temple of Athena

Temple of Egyptian Gods

Prytaneion

Bouleuterion

Gate

Market

Agora

Temple of Zeus

Gate

Ancient coastline

Stadium

Gymnasium

N

Fountain ✳

Contours in metres

0 yards 100

0 metres 100

6   Nemrut Dağ

The kingdom of Commagene achieved independence from the Seleucids in 163 B C, under a ruling house of mixed Greek and Iranian origin. This independence was maintained with occasional interruptions until the area was incorporated in the Roman Empire in A D 72. A grandson of the last king, C. Iulius Antiochus Epiphanes Philopappus, became a civic benefactor at ATHENS, building the monument on the Museum Hill still named after him. The chief monument of the dynasty itself is the astonishing dynastic sanctuary on top of Nemrut Dağ (ancient name unknown). Built by Antiochus I, a contemporary of Mark Antony, it consists of a tumulus, with courtyards to west, north and east; the east courtyard contains reliefs depicting Antiochus' Iranian and Greek ancestors and Antiochus welcomed by the gods. The deities that look

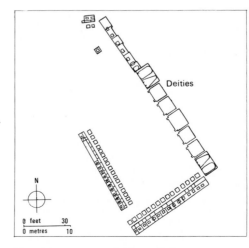

Plan of the west courtyard, Nemrut Dağ

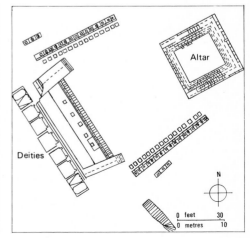

Plan of the east courtyard, Nemrut Dağ

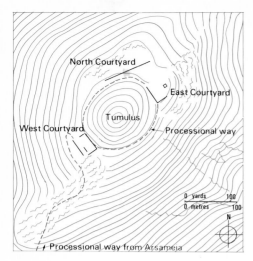

down on the courtyard are bizarre syncretions of Greek and Iranian gods; all the sculpture is in a style deriving from that of the Hellenistic sculpture of the chief centres of the Greek world. Similar statues and reliefs decorate the west courtyard; the site also sports a stone lion sculpted with the horoscope of Antiochus.

Antike Welt (Zürich), 1975, special no.

Above: Head of Fortuna, on the west terrace, Nemrut Dağ

Above: Heads of Zeus-Oromasdes and Apollo-Mithra (background) on the west terrace

---

7   Aphrodisias   **Turkey**

Aphrodisias was the city of Asia Minor that profited earliest and most effectively from the interest of Roman aristocrats of the late Republic and that of the dynasty of Augustus. Possessed of a shrine of a deity who could be assimilated to Aphrodite-Venus, the city succeeded in attracting the attention of Sulla, who regarded himself as under the special protection of Venus, then of Caesar, who claimed descent from Venus, and of his adopted son, who became the emperor Augustus. The result was a highly privileged status within the framework of Roman rule and spectacular benefactions. Possessed of great wealth and good marble quarries, Aphrodisias rapidly became a city of marble and the home of a flourishing school of sculpture. A large temple of Aphrodite, a theatre, a *stadium* and an *odeum* survive in a remarkable state of preservation, also

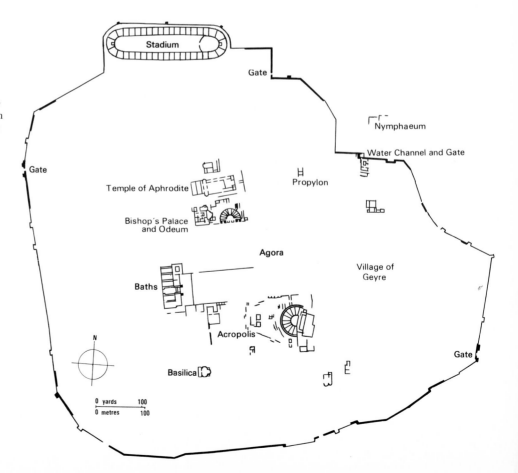

numerous pieces of sculpture and inscribed monuments; a wall within the theatre complex bears an archive of documents relating to the status of the city inscribed in the third century A D.

The city continued to flourish in the early Byzantine period, declining as a result of the wars of the seventh century A D. The main centre of the valley in which Aphrodisias lies developed under the Turks at Karacasu;

Aphrodisias was largely abandoned and its site is now occupied by the tiny village of Geyre (probably a corruption of Caria, the name for southwestern Asia Minor in antiquity).

Most of the finds from Aphrodisias are housed in a new museum on the site.

The current excavations are reported by the excavator, Professor K. T. Erim, in *Türk Arkeoloji Dergisi* (Ankara) (in English).

Aphrodisias. Top: Fragment of frieze now in the museum at Izmir. Above: The stadium

8   Ephesus

An early Greek settlement in Asia Minor, Ephesus shared the fate of most of the other Greek cities, passing from Lydia to Persia, then to Athenian hegemony, then back to Persia. After a series of vicissitudes under Alexander the Great and his successors, Ephesus passed to Rome in 133 BC and became the place of residence of the Roman governor of the province of Asia (central western Asia Minor). Originally standing on Mount Pion, Ephesus was moved by King Croesus to the flat land to the east, then by Lysimachus to the site where the Roman city developed. The expenditure generated by the Roman presence largely explains the evident size and opulence of the city.

The Artemisium or temple of 'Diana of the Ephesians', like other cult centres of Asia Minor, lay outside the city, to the northeast; the site has been excavated, but nothing survives to be seen. In the city itself, the most remarkable building is the library of Celsus, built in memory of C. Iulius Celsus Polemaeanus, governor of Asia in AD 106–7, endowed by his son. Along the street to the northeast is a temple of Hadrian, a fountain built in honour of Trajan and a temple of Domitian; the theatre lies in the other direction.

Much of the material from early explorations at Ephesus is in the British Museum, London, and in the Kunsthistorisches Museum, Vienna; there is a museum near the site.

Keil, J., *Führer durch Ephesos*, Vienna, 1964

Bammer, A., *Die Architektur der jüngeren Artemision von Ephesos*, Wiesbaden, 1972

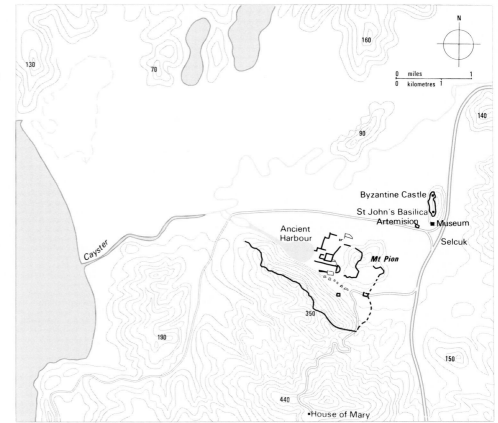

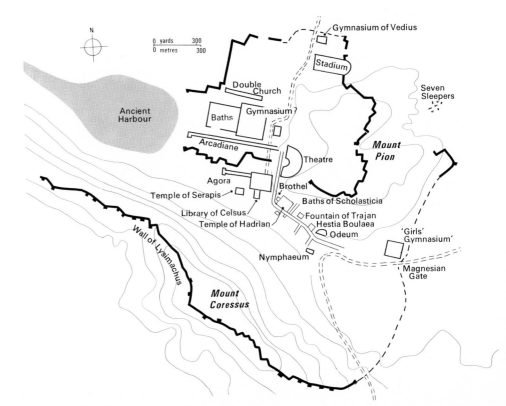

Ephesus. Above, right: Location map. Right: Site plan. Opposite: The library of Celsus, during restoration in 1976

Ephesus. The temple of Hadrian

PLATEAU

Theatre

Stadium

Graves

Baths

Graves

Baths

Courtyard

Acropolis

Aqueduct

Gate

Graves   Graves

Agora

Graves

Temple

N

0   yards   300
0   metres   300

Ancient Coastline

Ancient Coastline

The remains of Perge, Aspendus, and Side are the most prominent today in the plain of Pamphylia; unlike the Attalid foundation of Attaleia (Antalya), they were largely uninhabited from the end of antiquity and substantial ruins survived to be excavated in modern times.

All three cities are presumably originally native settlements, gradually Hellenized in the pre-Roman period. Little is known of any of the cities before Alexander the Great and the visible remains belong for the most part to the Roman period. There is a fine theatre at Aspendus, also a well-preserved aqueduct, a theatre at Perge, and a theatre at Side, among other buildings. Salt production is attested for Aspendus, otherwise the wealth of the cities is likely to have been largely agricultural in origin, with a few great landowning families as the intermediaries; it is interesting that the great family of Perge, the Plancii, is Roman in origin, no doubt descended from the Roman men of business who flocked to the east in the last century of the Republic in order to exploit the newly opened-up areas.

Top: Plan of Perge. Right: The theatre, Perge

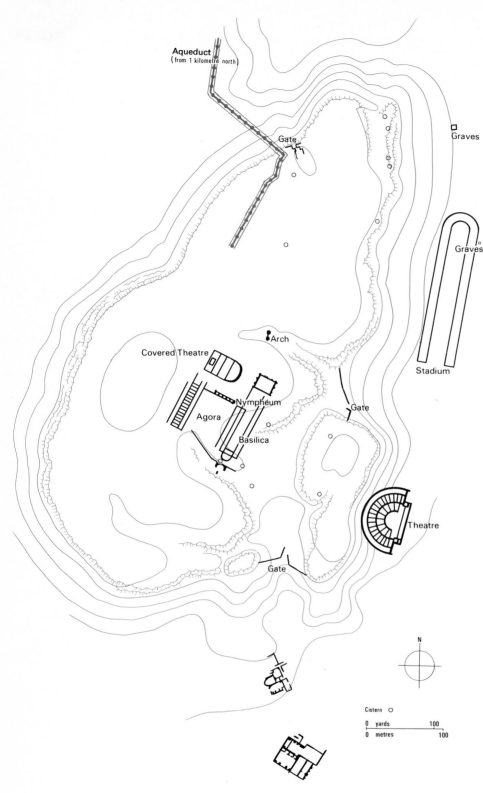

Aqueduct
(from 1 kilometre north)

Gate

Graves

Graves

Stadium

Arch

Covered Theatre

Nympheum

Agora

Basilica

Gate

Theatre

Gate

N

Cistern ○

0 yards 100

0 metres 100

Bean, G. E., Turkey's Southern Shore: An
    Archaeological Guide, London and New York, 1968
Mansel, A. M., and Akarca, A., Excavations and
    Researches at Perge, Ankara, 1949
Mansel, A. M., Die Ruinen von Side, Berlin, 1963

Above, left: Plan of Aspendus. Top right: Fragment of
frieze with head of Medusa, at Side. Right: Mask from
the theatre frieze, at Side. Opposite, above: General view
of Side. Opposite, below: Plan of Side

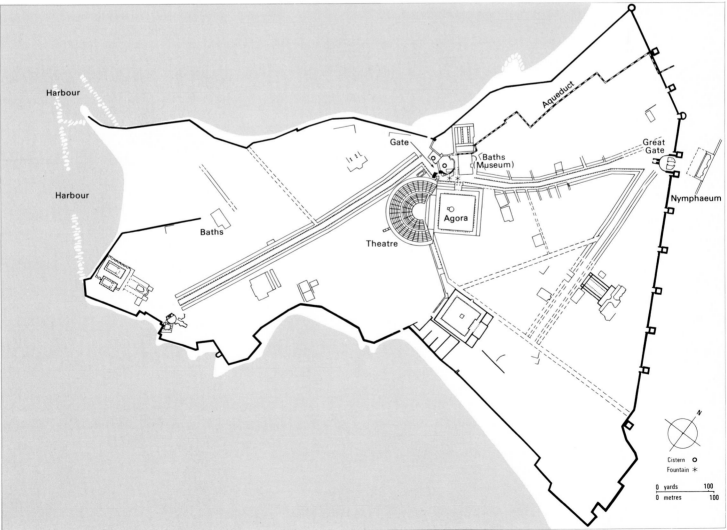

Harbour

Harbour

Baths

Gate

Theatre

Agora

Baths
(Museum)

Aqueduct

Great
Gate

Nymphaeum

Cistern ○
Fountain ✳

N

0 yards   100
0 metres   100

10   Istanbul

Byzantium was a foundation of Megara, of the seventh century BC. To the surprise of ancient as well as modern scholars, Byzantium was founded later than Chalcedon across the Bosporus, despite its natural harbour which was ideal as a base for a city anxious to control the Bosporus and impose tolls. Rarely independent in the period before Alexander the Great, Byzantium suffered in the third century BC from barbarian pressure in the hinterland. Under Roman overlordship Byzantium made the mistake of supporting Pescennius Niger against the emperor Septimius Severus in AD 193. Sacked and for a time reduced to the

status of a village, Byzantium remained relatively unimportant.

Meanwhile, the area of the Bosporus had grown in importance as a centre of communications in a Roman empire increasingly under attack in the third century AD. Heracleia Thracica, Cyzicus, and Nicomedia were all imperial mints by the reign of Diocletian, who spent much of his time at Nicomedia (Izmit).

When Constantine had defeated his last rival Licinius in AD 324 at Adrianople and Chrysopolis (the latter across the Bosporus from Byzantium), he determined to refound Byzantium as Constantinople (i.e. Constantine's City), a

new Christian capital of his empire, a new Rome. The situation and harbour of Byzantium had come into their own: Constantinople became one of the greatest cities of medieval Europe and a capital city for some 1,600 years, first of the Byzantine empire (until 1453), then, as Istanbul, of the Turkish empire; Ankara only became the capital of Turkey in 1923.

Beck, H.-G. (ed.), *Studien zur Frühgeschichte Konstantinopels*, Munich, 1973

Dagron, G., *Naissance d'une capitale*, Paris, 1974

Sumner-Boyd, J., and Freely, J., *Strolling Through Istanbul*, Istanbul, 1975

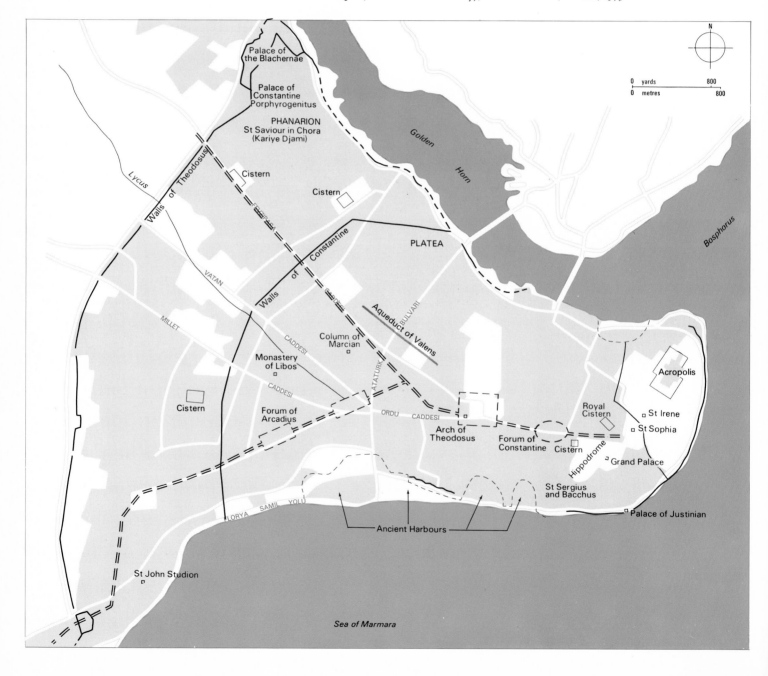

Alexander's Route. Early in 334 BC Alexander and his main force crossed the Aegean Sea to Asia Minor. He died in Babylon on 10 or 11 July, 323. The following dates indicate the tempo of the eleven-year expedition: battle of Issus, late 333; fall of Tyre after siege, July 332; visit to the oracle of Ammon at Siwah, early 331; sack of Persepolis, 330; crossing of the Hindukush, early 329; expedition to India, 327–325.

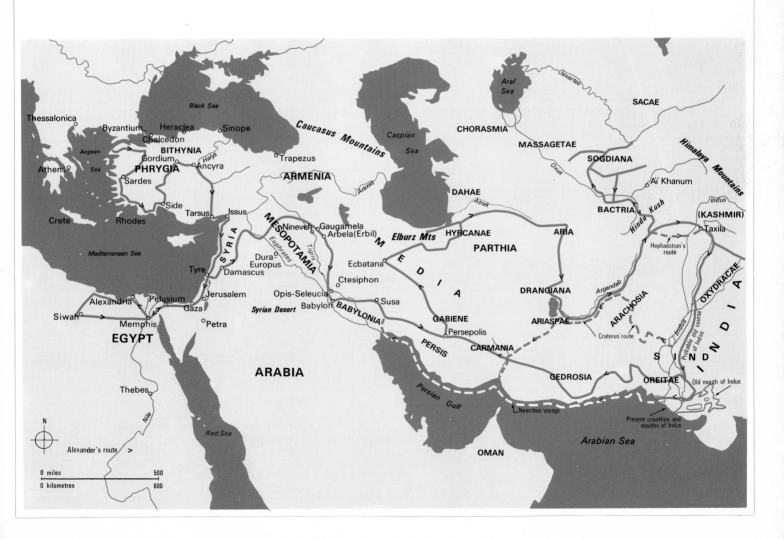

Syria-Palestine

The eastern coastline of the Mediterranean Sea is paralleled not far inland by a great north–south depression through which flow the Orontes river in the north and the Jordan river farther south. Most of this depression is bounded on either side by mountainous ridges that form a protection for the fertile valley between them and a natural barrier for those who wish to travel eastward toward the desert or – more important – westward from the desert to the sea. South of the Dead Sea, into which the Jordan flows, the broad Wadi 'Araba constitutes a continuation of the inland depression to its termination in ancient Aela at the head of the Gulf of 'Aqaba. To the west of the 'Araba is the forbidding wilderness of the Negev desert, which is linked to the Sinai peninsula and the

North African desert; to the east is the dramatically bleak landscape of the Jordanian Hisma, which, with its mudflats and sandstone peaks, merges with northwest Saudi Arabia.

Outside the well-watered valleys of the Orontes and the Jordan, land use depends upon springs and the winter rains. The coastal strip north of the Negev desert has always been the most desirable since it catches more of the rain and has immediate access to the sea, and that is why it is now divided among no fewer than four nations (Turkey, Syria, Lebanon, Israel). In the interior, on the other side of the mountains, there is a narrow strip of sown land. On the vast plateau that rises north of the Hisma four great river beds, the wadis of the Yarmuk, Zerqa, Mujib, and Hesa, stretch eastward from

the inland depression and always carry water. But the sown land quickly gives way to steppe and desert, the realm of nomads and their flocks of sheep and goats. The settled peoples alongside the desert, with their cities and agriculture, had and still have an uneasy relationship with the nomads. In antiquity, as today, this relationship was complicated by the fact that the desert territory lies not only to the east of the town but also to the south as it extends into the Sinai. It is no wonder that the sedentary peoples of Palestine found it expedient for communication and security to found cities in the Negev and to develop for this purpose some remarkably sophisticated irrigation systems.

The area of Syria and Palestine was vital in

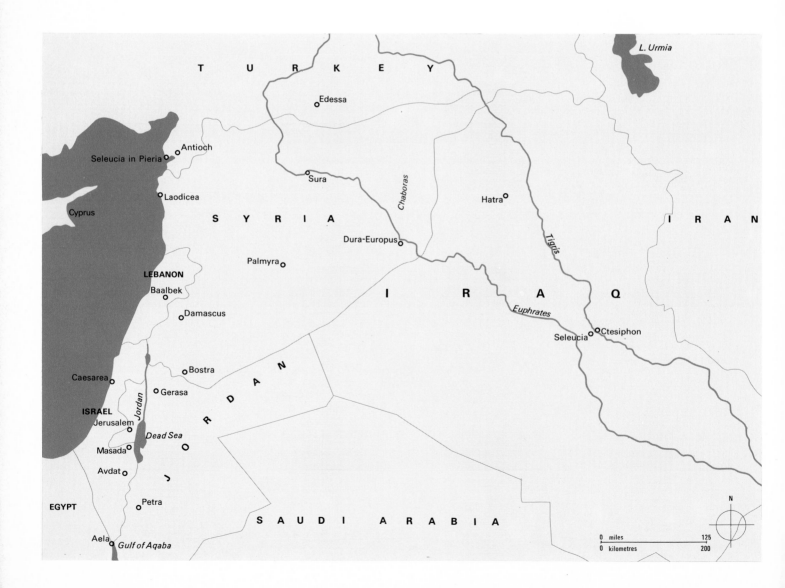

classical times for the trade in spices from India, silk from China, and perfumes from southern Arabia. These goods were destined for emporia on the Mediterranean coast and, to a large extent, depended for their transport upon the caravans and entrepreneurs of the desert. One major trade route extended from southwest Arabia north to PETRA, where it veered westward to the Mediterranean outlets. From Petra the traveller could also go north on the so-called Royal Road up to Damascus. Another trade route passed northwest from the Euphrates, along which came merchandise from the Persian Gulf, over the Syrian desert by way of the great oasis of PALMYRA. Still other routes farther north served to carry the Chinese silk, which had come overland from Asia, on to the Mediterranean. The discovery that regular monsoon winds could be exploited for sea trade and the consequent development of sea transport to the coast of Egypt in the first century AD seriously undermined the land traffic through Petra and thereby provided opportunities for expansion on the part of the desert merchants in the north (at Palmyra and elsewhere).

To understand the classical sites in Syria-Palestine, it is necessary to recognize the significance of the invasion of Alexander the Great in the late fourth century BC. Although Greek civilization was not unknown in the Near East before Alexander, the kingdoms carved out of his empire by his successors proved to be the decisive Hellenizing force. Two of Alexander's generals, Seleucus and Ptolemy, acquired the territories of Syria and Egypt respectively. In the third century BC the dynasty of Ptolemy also controlled western Palestine; but early in the following century this was taken over by the Seleucids, who became the sole Greek authority in Syria-Palestine until they were displaced by the Romans under the command of Pompey the Great. The Seleucids were, from the start, keen on cities and founded many throughout their huge kingdom, which stretched originally as far as modern Afghanistan. The site of the new city of ANTIOCH, named after the first Seleucid king, was carefully chosen; it was connected to the port cities of Seleuceia and Laodicea. GERASA across the Jordan was another Seleucid foundation. While the kings were organizing and enlarging their kingdom, a tribe of Arab merchants was gradually settling the east side of the Jordan and the Negev. These were the Nabataeans, who had already established themselves in Petra by the end of the fourth century and successfully resisted the aggression of the Greeks. They prospered from their complete monopoly of the overland trade from southern Arabia to the Mediterranean. The Nabataeans built up a rich culture, which

included desert farming by irrigation and a highly distinctive style of art. In the early first century BC their control extended to the north as far as Damascus.

The Seleucid kingdom was already weak when Pompey annihilated it and created the Roman province of Syria in 64 BC. At that time the Nabataeans, still strong and useful as clients of Rome, were left untouched whereas western Palestine under the rule of the quarrelling Hasmonaeans was subjected to the Syrian governor. The arrival of the Romans added a new ingredient to the mixture of Semitic and Greek in the Near East. Herod, the king of Judaea who emerged triumphant from the dynastic squabbles in western Palestine, symbolized the convergence of traditions. Himself an Idumaean Jew, he favoured the Greek style of city life and commemorated his political alliance with Rome by naming rebuilt cities after Caesar Augustus. Thence came the name of CAESAREA. On Herod's death his kingdom too became a Roman province. The Jewish population there suffered a grievous loss when Roman soldiers destroyed the Second Temple at JERUSALEM in the course of suppressing the revolt that broke out in AD 66 and lasted until the capture of Masada in 73. In the early second century the Jews once more stood against Rome, first in the last years of Trajan and then under Hadrian, who crushed the rebellion of Bar Kochba in 135 and turned Jerusalem into a Roman colony.

Across the Jordan the Arab kings ruled throughout the first century AD. They created a new centre of government at Bostra, in the north of the kingdom, when the overland trade by way of Petra began to lose its importance. Bostra stood at the head of a desert passage from central Arabia, the Wadi Sirhan, which the Nabataeans cleverly exploited. However, in 106 their kingdom was transformed into the Roman province of Arabia. Henceforth the merchants of Palmyra monopolized the commerce of the desert, and the ruins of their city testify to their affluence. By the mid-third century they had dominated Syria-Palestine, nominally as representatives of the enfeebled Roman government, which had proved unable to cope with the menace of the new Sassanian dynasty in Persia. In the revolt of Palmyra's queen Zenobia against Rome the city's power and self-confidence were revealed. It required a strenuous campaign of the emperor Aurelian to put an end to Palmyrene pride in 273.

Byzantine Syria-Palestine suffered the same fragmentation of the Roman territory into smaller administrative units as the rest of the empire. Christianity, which became the state religion under Constantine, took a firm hold; churches, basilicas, and bishoprics proliferated.

The cities of the Negev were conspicuously revived in an age that also saw fresh vigour at ANTIOCH, Gerasa, Bostra, and other provincial centres. The Persians posed a constant threat to these cities, but it was not until the advent of Islam in the seventh century that a new civilization overwhelmed that remarkable blend of older traditions – Arab, Jewish, Greek, Roman, and Christian.

Dussaud, R., *Topographie historique de la Syrie antique et médiévale*, Paris, 1927

Abel, F.-M., *Histoire de la Palestine*, 2 vols., Paris, 1952

Avi-Yonah, M., *The Holy Land from the Persian to the Arab Conquests: A Historical Geography*, Ann Arbor, Michigan, 1966

I Antioch

Seleucus I Nicator founded the city of Antioch (modern Antakya) in 300 B C at a location admirably suited to the control of the Syrian Near East. The site is at the southwest corner of the fertile Amik plain, at the point where the Orontes river (modern Nahr el 'Asi) cuts through the mountains to the sea. Antioch stands at the focal point for communications with Palestine to the south by way of the Orontes and Jordan rivers and with the Euphrates to the east by way of Aleppo. A road led southwest through the suburb of Daphne to the Seleucid seaport of Laodicea, and another road to Antioch's own harbour town, Seleuceia. Antioch became naturally a commercial and administrative centre with a population that reached perhaps a half million by the late fourth century A D. When Pompey established the Roman province of Syria in 64 B C, Antioch was included within it as a nominally free city. It grew in importance as a centre of literature, philosophy, and theology; and it had substantial Jewish and Christian communities. In the fourth century A D it became one of the leading cities of Christendom while being at the same time a capital of pagan culture. From the fourth to the sixth centuries Antioch was notorious for its factional disturbances, provoked by chariot racing and theatrical spectacles. The city suffered repeatedly from earthquakes, of which one in 526 levelled it. After a brief period of Persian control, Justinian recovered Antioch and helped to rebuilt it.

The ancient city, on the east bank of the Orontes, is largely covered by the modern Antakya. However, selective excavation and aerial photography have made possible an authoritative reconstruction of the plan of the ancient city. Many of the modern streets follow the ancient ones. Most important of these is the straight main road that runs from north to south for some 2 miles (3km) over the course of one of the second century A D. Soundings have shown that the old road was 30 feet (9m) wide, paved with limestone blocks, and lined on both sides with colonnaded porticoes (many in grey or pink granite). Along the slopes of Mount Silpius east of the city the remains of Justinian's city wall are clearly visible, and the hippodrome can be seen in the northwest corner of the city on what had been an island in antiquity. The Antioch excavations uncovered many superb mosaics, of which some are in the Antakya Archaeological Museum and others in the Museum of Princeton University.

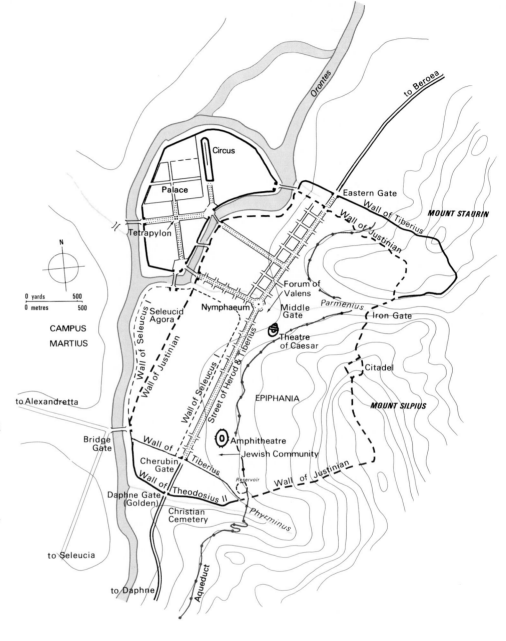

Downey, G., *A History of Antioch in Syria*, Princeton, 1961

Lassus, J., *Les Portiques d' Antioche*, Princeton, 1972 (vol. 5 in the Princeton publication of the excavation)

Liebeschuetz, J. H. W. G., *Antioch: City and Imperial Administration in the Later Roman Empire*, Oxford, 1972

The ruins of Gerasa (modern Jerash) lie in a fertile region, once forested, on the road from Amman to Irbid in northwest Jordan. A route from PETRA in the south passed this way to Bostra and Damascus. The city's water came from the Wadi Jerash, through which flowed the Golden River (Chrysorrhoas) in antiquity. Although excavations have shown that Gerasa was occupied in Neolithic and Early Bronze Age times, little is known before the foundation of a Hellenistic city here under the name of Antioch-on-the-Chrysorrhoas. The name Antioch identifies the founder as a Seleucid king. After the weakening of the Seleucid

dynasty, Alexander Jannaeus captured the city; and it remained a Hasmonaean possession until detached by Pompey in 63 BC. Gerasa was then incorporated in the Roman province of Syria. It subsequently became one of the ten cities of the Decapolis, a loose confederation of cities near the Jordan valley, and in the first century AD it enjoyed considerable prosperity. When the province of Arabia was formed in AD 106 Gerasa and the environs became a part of it. Hadrian visited the city in 130. From the middle of the third century the city suffered a decline that lasted about two centuries. In the later fourth century a great Christian metro-

Above: The oval forum and main street, Gerasa. To the left of centre are the remains of the temple of Zeus, and the south theatre. At the top, just to the right of centre, is the temple of Artemis.

polis grew up with over a dozen churches.

Most of the visible remains at Gerasa date from the time of the Roman Empire. On the road from Amman the triple triumphal arch in honour of Hadrian is the first sign of the ancient site; behind it lies the hippodrome. The city itself is enclosed by a vast wall of 4,000 yards (3,660m) built in the second half of the first century A D. It presupposes the axial city plan which is clearly delineated by the main street at right angles with the others and with tetrapylons at the crossroads. At variance with this plan and presumably representing an earlier layout is the *forum*, of an unusual oval shape, above which stand the Zeus temple and the south theatre. Along the main street to the west between the two tetrapylons are the splendid second-century *propylaea* leading toward the podium of the Artemis temple 130 × 72 feet (40 × 22m). Near this are the remains of a fourth-century cathedral and several later churches.

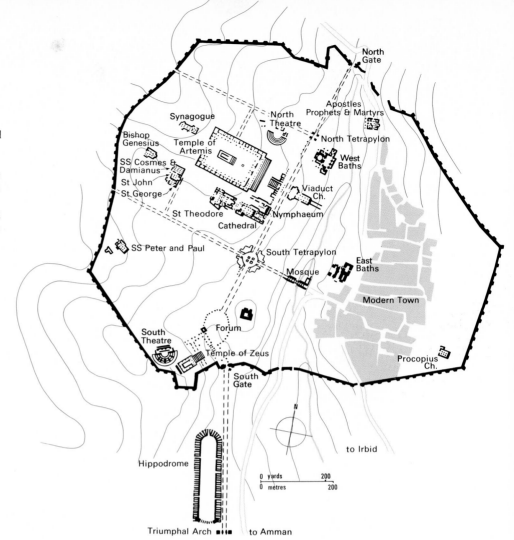

Kraeling, C. H., *Gerasa: City of the Decapolis*, New Haven, Conn., 1938. The standard account

3 Caesarea

Israel

The ancient port city of Caesarea (modern Qisarya) lies on the Israeli coast midway between Tel Aviv and Haifa. Although it has been excavated in part, much still remains beneath the sand. The original name for the site was Turris Stratonis (Strato's Tower), of which the earliest mention occurs in a papyrus of the third century B C. The city belonged first to the Ptolemies, then to the Seleucids; at an unknown date in the second century one Zoilus, called a tyrant, ruled there. In 104 B C the city fell to the militant king of the Jews, Alexander Jannaeus, who incorporated it in the realm of the Hasmonaeans. Pompey the Great liberated it in 64 B C, and his legate Gabinius launched building projects in the following year. In the thirties B C Strato's Tower came briefly into Cleopatra's possession, after whose death it passed to Herod the Great. As a friend of the emperor Augustus and as an enthusiastic philhellene, Herod vastly enlarged the city in

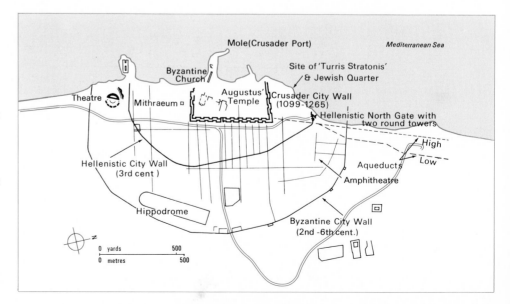

Caesarea. Above: Theatre and remains of the Byzantine fortress. Below: Corinthian capital (with acanthus)

the Greek style and renamed it Caesarea in honour of Caesar Augustus. The Greek theatre, built by Herod at the southern end of the city, has been excavated and is now one of Caesarea's most striking remains. The remains of a hippodrome, possibly but not necessarily Herodian, have been excavated to the northeast of the theatre. Two aqueducts brought the city its water from Mount Carmel. Remains of the Herodian harbour are visible, as well as the foundation of a temple of Augustus.

Caesarea soon became the capital of Judaea. Its mixed population of Jews and Gentiles was important in starting disturbances that led to the Jewish rebellion of AD 66. The emperor Vespasian elevated Caesarea to the rank of a colony at the close of the revolt. In the second century it became the capital of Palestine. It was a major centre of Jewish and Christian scholarship. The city is today enclosed by three walls, the innermost from a Crusader

occupation, the middle from the days of Strato's Tower, and the outer from the late Roman and Byzantine age. In the early 1960s the site of Caesarea yielded the first inscribed stone with the name of Pontius Pilate as *praefectus* of Judaea. Very recently an American excavation uncovered a Mithraeum (a shrine for the worship of the oriental god Mithras) in part of a large granary complex south of the Crusader wall.

Reifenberg, A., in *Israel Exploration Journal* I, 1950, pp. 20–32

Frova, A., *Scavi di Caesarea Marittima,* Milan, 1965. Excavation report

Levine, Lee I., *Caesarea under Roman Rule,* Leiden, 1975. History of the city

The history of Jerusalem stretches back at least as far as the early second millennium BC. It is mentioned in texts of the nineteenth–eighteenth centuries BC as well as in the later Amarna letters from Egypt. Situated on slopes near the Gihon spring to the west of the northern end of the Dead Sea, it became an important Canaanite city, of which walls, foundations, and water channels have been unearthed. Captured by David, Jerusalem was made the capital of his kingdom. Under Solomon the first temple was built, to be destroyed in the Persian invasion of 587 BC. After the Babylonian exile of the Jews (587–536 BC) the second temple was gradually constructed. Alexander the Great allowed the city to enjoy its privileges, although, contrary to legend, he probably never visited it. Following a period of Ptolemaic rule, Jerusalem passed to the Seleucids. King Antiochus Epiphanes caused a major uprising in 167 BC by his repressive measures, enacted perhaps in response to internal struggles in Jerusalem between devout and philhellenic Jews. The successful efforts of Judas Maccabaeus on behalf of the devout led to the establishment of the Hasmonaean dynasty.

Over the course of a century the Hasmonaeans themselves became the victims of fierce internal struggles and finally gave way in 37 BC to the philhellenic rule of Herod the Idumaean, known as the Great. Herod was responsible for extensive building in the city, including a magnificent reconstruction of the Temple. To the north of the Temple precinct was Herod's fortress, the Antonia, named after his patron Antony. To the west Herod built himself a luxurious palace in marble and gold (of which a tower is still visible). He also built the city's second wall; not much later Herod Agrippa I built the third to enlarge the city area, and this is the wall of today's 'old city'.

After the death of Herod the Great, Jerusalem became part of the Roman province of Judaea which counted a population of two and a half million souls. In the suppression of the Jewish revolt of AD 66–73 several of the chief monuments of Herodian Jerusalem were destroyed. Both the Temple and the Antonia lay in ruins. Obliteration was carried a stage further when Hadrian in AD 135 turned the city into the Roman colony of Aelia Capitolina as a consequence of the revolt of Bar Kochba. An arch from Hadrian's city still crosses the Via Dolorosa at the site of the Antonia. In the temple precinct the Dome of the Rock now stands in the centre, and south of it is the Al Aqsa mosque. In the time of Constantine, the first Christian emperor, several new buildings were raised at Jerusalem in recognition of its importance for the new state religion. The most significant was at the site of the Holy Sepulchre on the hill of Golgotha, where parts of the Constantinian edifice can still be seen.

Because Jerusalem is a city with a present no less rich than its past, the visitor in search of classical remains is likely to be overwhelmed by the interlacing of antiquities from many different periods in areas where there is a busy modern community as well. A map of the city in the time of the second temple does not, as with some classical sites, plot extant remains in a territory now deserted, but rather the layout of a territory that is now very changed. The Dome of the Rock and the beginning of the Via Dolorosa to the north of it (on the site of the Antonia) provide the best points of

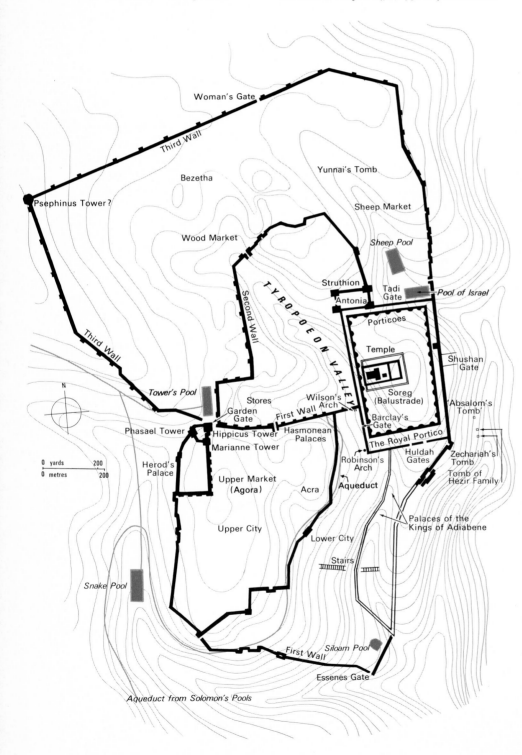

orientation. To the west just below the platform of the 30-acre (12ha) temple precinct is
the Herodian 'wailing wall', where Jews pray
and bewail the destruction of the second
temple. Archaeological finds are displayed in
parts of the Israel Museum, notably the Shrine
of the Book and the Bronfman Bibilical and
Archaeological Museum, in Jerusalem.

Kenyon, K. M., *Jerusalem: Excavating 3000 Years of
    History*, London, 1967
Jeremias, J., *Jerusalem in the Time of Jesus*, London,
    1969

Jerusalem. Excavations of the Herodian south wall

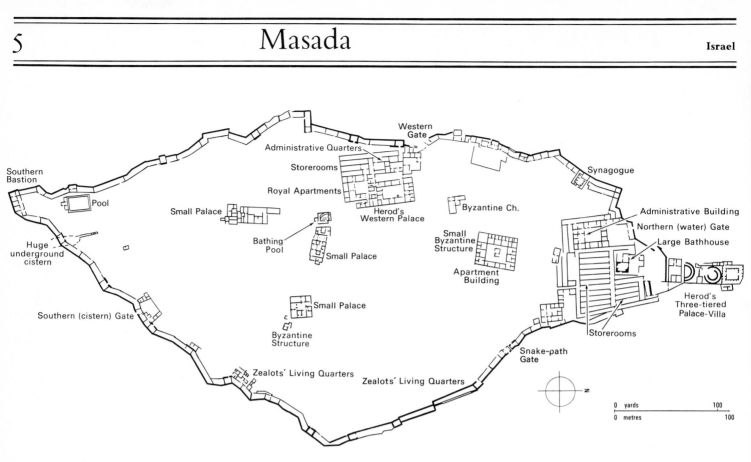

The impressive rock of Masada rises above the western shore of the Dead Sea south of En Gedi. Its flat and inaccessible top was well suited to withstand a siege, and it must have been envisaged as a place of retrenchment from its first occupation by the Hasmonaeans. In 40 BC Herod, later 'the Great', took over Masada and, in the following decade, equipped it as a fortress. To deal with problems of water supply he constructed a group of twelve cisterns, each holding 140,000 cubic feet (4,000 m^3), fed by neighbouring wadis which were dammed to deflect their rainwater. Herod also built a strong double wall, with rooms in the space between, around the whole of Masada's summit except for the northern end. There he constructed a fantastic palace in three terraces that appear to hang down from the top, where the first terrace is located. The second is 66 feet (20m) below it, and the third 50 feet (15m) below the second. The terraces were elegantly decorated with frescoes, remains of which can still be seen; and the views are breathtaking. For administration Herod built another palace, 43,000 square feet (4,000m^2) in size, on the west side of the summit.

During the great Jewish revolt of AD 66–73 a band of Zealots took possession of Masada,

Opposite: Frescoes on the walls of the bottom terrace of the northern palace, Masada. Above: Masada from the north

where they were ruled by a certain Eleazar. Their resistance to the Romans, eloquently told by Josephus, has become legendary. To take Masada the Romans built eight siege camps, the outlines of which are clearly visible today when looked down on from the top of the site. The Zealots ultimately entered into a suicide pact as the end drew near. Excavation has uncovered 25 skeletons of men, women, and children, as well as coins and scrolls. Ritual baths and the probable living quarters of the Zealots have been identified. After the fall of Masada in spring 73 (or 74, according to

some), the Roman soldiers occupied the site until at least 111, which is the date of the garrison's latest coins.

The ascent to the summit can be made comfortably on foot from the west by a modern path in about 20 minutes. The ancient 'snake path', as Josephus called it, lies on the east and is very strenuous.

Richmond, I. A., in *Journal of Roman Studies* 52, 1962, pp. 142–55
Yadin, Y., *Masada: Herod's Fortress and the Zealots' Last Stand*, London, 1966

6

Petra

Locked within the sandstone mountains that rise at the western edge of the Jordanian steppe north of the Hisma depression lies the fabled city of Petra. Although known from literature it had not been seen by any European in modern times until John Lewis Burckhardt went there, at considerable risk, in 1812. Still a dangerous place in the early years of this century, Petra is now easy to reach by the north–south highway and well equipped to welcome tourists. The rich colours (especially pink and yellow) that weathering has brought out in the sandstone give the city a unique beauty. The Wadi Musa, which enters Petra through a narrow defile, called the Siq, is the source of water and gives its name to the modern settlement. To avoid flooding of the Siq in the rainy season the ancient inhabitants diverted the waters of the wadi by a dam, and recently the modern inhabitants have done the same. For it is through the Siq, from the east, that visitors enter the city.

The virtually impregnable site of Petra appears to have been occupied from prehistoric times, but archaeologists now reject the once traditional identification of Biblical Sela, meaning 'rock', with Petra, also meaning 'rock'. It is not until 312 BC that the history of Petra becomes clear, and all the major monuments date from the centuries after this. In 312 one of Alexander the Great's successors attempted unsuccessfully to capture Petra, which was then the home of the Nabataean Arabs. The Nabataeans, formerly a nomadic people, gradually settled in the area of modern Jordan and the Negev as they became the prosperous traders who brought spices and perfumes from India and southern Arabia overland by way of Petra to the ports of Gaza and El 'Arîsh (ancient Rhinocolura) on the Mediterranean. Petra was their capital, and their commerce soon brought them into contact with Hellenistic culture. The art and architecture of Petra is a blend of native and Greek elements which no one has yet been able to disentangle. The Nabataean culture of Petra reached its height in the early

days of the Roman Empire. By the end of the first century AD the trade through Petra had declined as an inevitable result of the discovery of the monsoons in the Indian Ocean and the use of sea routes to ports on the Egyptian coast. Yet Petra continued to be an important intellectual and religious centre even after the

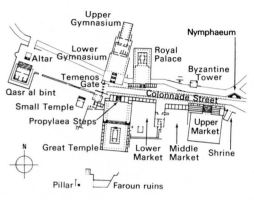

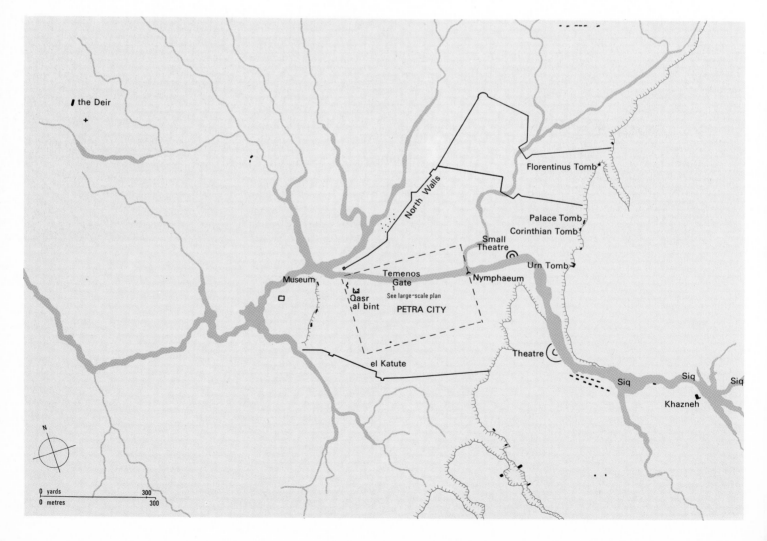

Nabataean kingdom was annexed by Rome in AD 106 as the province of Arabia.

Toward the end of the Siq gorge appears the façade of the Khazneh ('Treasury'), first glimpsed through a slit in the towering rocks. It is a structure of uncertain date with a strongly Hellenized character, carved in the living rock like most of the Petra buildings. The Khazneh (92 × 130 feet; 28 × 40m) is thought to be a temple or temple-tomb. Farther on, as the Siq widens, a theatre emerges on the left, and high up to the right are several more façades in the rock face. Proceeding along the Wadi Musa the visitor eventually enters a colonnaded street, running from east to west, and terminating in a triple-arch gate. Beyond the gate is a sacred precinct at the end of which, on the south side, is the free-standing temple known as Qasr al bint on a podium with an altar-platform opposite. The Qasr was once thought to be of Roman date but now seems, in the light of recent excavation, to be a Nabataean construction of the late first century BC. Nearby is a tourist hotel and a local museum. Farther west on a plateau stands another imposing rock-cut façade, the Deir ('Monastery').

Starcky, J., 'Pétra et la Nabatène', *Supplément au Dictionnaire de la Bible*, Paris, 1964. The best scholarly survey

Browning, I., *Petra*, London, 1973. A lively account in English with excellent illustrations

Petra. Opposite, above: The central area of the city. Opposite, below: Location map. Below: Deir ('The Monastery')

Above: The theatre, Petra

7   Ba'albek   **Lebanon**

The imposing temples of Ba'albek lie at the eastern edge of the fertile plain of the Beqa'a, across which the mountain ranges of the Lebanon and Anti-Lebanon confront each other. The site was a holy place, evidently sacred to the Semitic Ba'al. In the Seleucid period Greek settlers identified the indigenous deity with their own Helios (sun) and named the town Heliopolis, city of the sun. In time Ba'albek became the centre of a cult of the so-called Heliopolitan triad, Jupiter-Zeus, Venus-Aphrodite, and Mercury-Hermes. Syncretistic theology amalgamated Jupiter and Ba'al, Venus and Atargatis; the Semitic equivalent of Mer-

Right: Coffered ceiling of the peristyle, temple of Bacchus, Ba'albek

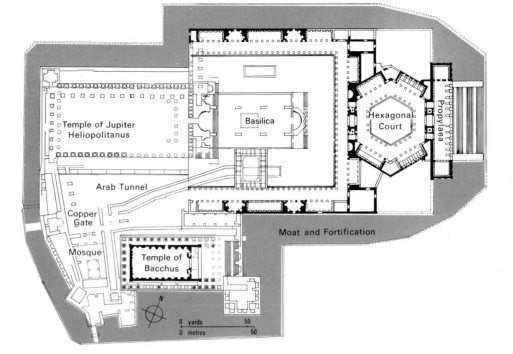

cury remains a problem. During the second and early third centuries AD the great Jupiter temple now standing on the Baʿalbek *acropolis* was built. Baʿalbek reached the height of its prosperity during the ascendency of the Roman emperors of Syrian origin in the early third century. After the establishment of Christianity as the religion of the empire, the pagan cults were suppressed. A Christian *basilica* was built, probably toward the end of the fourth century, in the courtyard of the temple of Jupiter.

The site is entered by way of a large staircase to the *propylaea* on the eastern side. After passing through a hexagonal courtyard the visitor comes into a vast area some 440 × 370 feet (135 × 113m) which was covered in antiquity by a wooden ceiling. To the north and south of the later *basilica* built there lie pools that were once on either side of the central pagan altar. Beyond the courtyard to the west is the Jupiter temple, resting on a huge substructure that elevates it on a rectangle of about 290 × 146 feet (88 × 44m) above the surrounding buildings. Six columns on the south side were reinforced in modern times and evoke the original colonnade around the temple. To the south below this platform is an independent temple in a good state of preservation. It is known as the Temple of Bacchus, although it may in fact have been sacred to Venus-Atargatis. The monumental doorway, 42 feet (13m) high, to the *cella* is superbly decorated with intricate carvings. Not far from the Baʿalbek *acropolis* is a quarry containing a single finished block of stone, lying where it was dug out, once intended for the temple complex. It measures some 70 × 14 × 16 feet (21 × 4 × 5m) and has been judged to weigh 2,000 tons.

Wiegand, T., *Baalbek, Ergebnisse und Untersuchungen in den Jahren 1898 bis 1905*, 3 vols. Berlin, 1921–5
Robinson, D. M., *Baalbek-Palmyra*, New York, 1946

Right: Baʿalbek. The temple of Jupiter Heliopolitanus, with Mount Hermon and the Anti-Lebanon in the distance

8   Palmyra   Syria

At the oasis generated by the waters of the Efqa spring in the Syrian desert rise the magnificent remains of the city of Palmyra. The Semitic name for the site has always been Tadmor, which – whatever its true etymology – sounded like the word for date palm (*tamar*) and thus gave rise to the classical name, Palmyra. Both documents and excavations have shown that there was a settlement here no later than the early second millennium BC. The oasis constituted the most important stop on the desert journey from the Euphrates to the Mediterranean. Little is known of the Palmyrene community before 41 BC, when Antony attacked it. The centre of early Palmyra was probably the broad esplanade on which the Temple of Bel now stands. Archaeological investigation has established that this elevation is artificial and of great antiquity.

Most of what is now visible at Palmyra dates from the first three centuries AD, the period of the city's greatest power and splendour. During the first century AD, the present temple of Bel, the temple of Ba'alshamin, the *agora*, and some of the colonnades were built. Inscriptions reveal the commercial activity of Palmyrene traders and their caravans, which went as far as the Persian Gulf. One relief in the Palmyra Museum depicts a Palmyrene merchant with his ship. At some point in the first century Palmyra was incorporated in the Roman province of Syria, and in AD 129/130 the emperor Hadrian made a state visit there. The city continued its spectacular growth in the second and third centuries as a result of the decline of the old overland trade route in the south by way of PETRA. When the Roman emperor Valerian was captured by the Persians in 259, the Palmyrenes were able to fill the vacuum created by the removal of Roman authority in the Near East. Odaenathus and his wife Zenobia dominated the entire area of Syria-Palestine, nominally on behalf of Rome. When Odaenathus died, Zenobia set herself up as an independent ruler and launched campaigns of conquest as far as Egypt. She was finally defeated by the emperor Aurelian, who destroyed Palmyra in 273. After that time the city was no more than a military post in the Byzantine network of desert fortifications. Estimates of Palmyra's population in Odaenathus' day have run as high as 150,000.

Although the orientation of the esplanade (690×675 feet; 210×205m) of the Bel Temple is noticeably not aligned with the rest of the city, the present temple was actually built in the first century AD. It stands in the midst of a courtyard with porticoes on all four sides and is entered through a richly ornamented gate on the western side. In the interior can be seen the characteristically Syrian niches for images of the Palmyrene gods. To the northwest of the Bel esplanade is a monumen-

tal arch at the head of a long colonnaded street, off which, on the south, lie the city's theatre and *agora*. To the north is the little temple of Ba'alshamin. At the western end is a transverse colonnade beyond which are the recently uncovered temple of the goddess Allat and the so-called Camp of Diocletian. This end of Palmyra was formerly thought to be a late-third-century development but is now considered part of the original urban design. Outside a sixth-century enclosure wall rebuilt by Justinian are numerous ancient tower tombs and an Arab castle. Sculptures, reliefs, and inscriptions of Palmyra can be seen in the Palmyra Museum and in the National Archaeo-

logical Museum in Damascus (where a reconstructed *hypogaeum* admirably illustrates Palmyrene funerary art).

Starcky, J., *Palmyre*, Paris, 1952

Crouch, D. P., *Mélanges de l'Université Saint Joseph* 47, 1972, pp. 241–50. A study of the population of ancient Palmyra

Gawlikowski, M., *Le Temple palmyrénien*, Warsaw, 1973

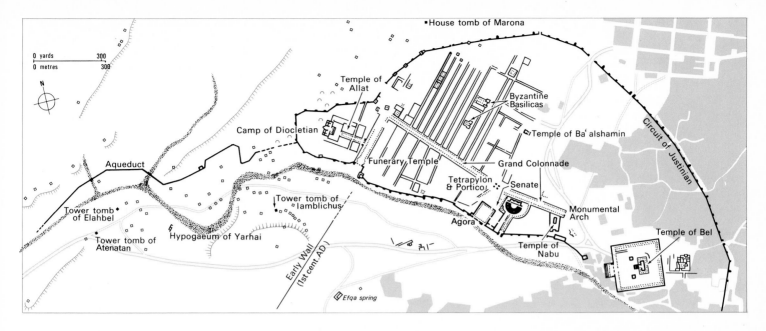

*Palmyra. Opposite: Interior of the temple of Bel. Above:
View to the northwest from the esplanade of the temple
of Bel*

ʿAvdat was a settlement of the Nabataean Arabs on a mountain ridge in the Negev desert. It lay on the route northwest from PETRA to the Mediterranean and was therefore also on the way for travellers coming north from Aela (ʿAqaba) after they turned west onto the road from Petra. The place was called Oboda in antiquity, undoubtedly in commemoration of one of the Nabataean kings named Obodas. Evidence for a third-century AD temple to Zeus-Obodas has been discovered on the site; and since there is reason to believe from literary texts that Obodas I (c. 96–85 BC) was deified, he is probably the king after whom the city is named.

Recent Israeli excavations have revealed that the site was first occupied in the third century BC and then temporarily abandoned in the early first century BC. A half century later the *acropolis* was fortified; substantial remains of the walls and towers can be seen. The Nabataean population inhabited the northern part of the mountain ridge, and they farmed with the aid of dams built to hold the desert rainfall. A potter's workshop from the first century AD has been discovered on the *acropolis* north of the buildings. The Romans incorporated ʿAvdat into their province of Arabia in AD 106. An army camp near the potter's workshop may reflect the Roman presence. A layer of ash found by the excavators implies a time of destruction in the first or second centuries AD, but the date and nature of the event are alike obscure. Inscriptions show that the site was occupied as late as AD 126, and again in the third century after AD 242. The destruction may have occurred between those dates.

From the early sixth century ʿAvdat flourished as a Christian city of the Byzantine world. The *acropolis* is dominated by buildings from this late phase: the rectangular citadel (180×160 feet; 55×50m) with towers and the two churches that lie to the west of it. The citizens developed an extensive irrigation system for agriculture, and remains of dams and canals are visible. Winepresses and equipment for drying fruit have been discovered. This late prosperity ended with the Persian sack of 614.

Negev, A., *Archaeology* 14, 1961, pp. 122–36. A preliminary general account by the excavator
Negev, A., *Israel Exploration Journal* 13, 1963, pp. 113-24
Evenari, M., and others, *The Negev*, Cambridge, Mass., 1971. Includes a fascinating reconstruction of ʿAvdat irrigation

Right: Columns in the Byzantine north church, ʿAvdat

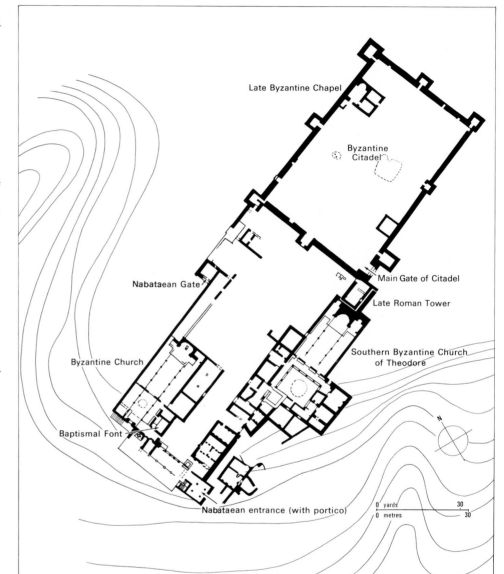

Late Byzantine Chapel

Byzantine Citadel

Nabataean Gate

Main Gate of Citadel

Late Roman Tower

Byzantine Church

Southern Byzantine Church of Theodore

Baptismal Font

Nabataean entrance (with portico)

0 yards 30
0 metres 30

Above: Aerial view of 'Avdat from the west

East of Palmyra

The Syrian desert stretches eastward from the PALMYRA oasis to meet the Euphrates as it arches from northwest to southeast. The range of the Jebel Bishri, running from east to west, provides a barrier against the north. The Euphrates flows into the Persian Gulf and thereby forms the vital link between the Gulf and the desert merchants. On the east side of the Euphrates and extending to the Tigris is the alluvial land of Mesopotamia. This valuable territory was a buffer zone in classical antiquity between the Iranian empires to the east and the Roman Empire to the west. The city of DURA-EUROPUS, on the western bank of the Euphrates, was well situated for overlooking and controlling the opposite shore, and the struggle for power in Mesopotamia is illustrated by the changing fortunes of that city as it passed from the Seleucids, to the Parthians, to the Romans, and ultimately to the Persians.

Beyond Mesopotamia is the great Iranian plateau, enclosed by the Zagros mountains in the west, the Elburz mountains in the north, the Hindu Kush in the east, and the Persian Gulf in the south. This was the heartland of the Iranian empires. It stood astride the overland traffic from the Far East, and it dominated

the Gulf. Alexander the Great passed this way and went on over the Hindu Kush mountains. Here, just as in the Mediterranean countries farther west, his passage marks a turning point in the history and culture of the area. The recent discovery of a city, strongly Greek in character, at AÏ KHANUM in Bactria above the Hindu Kush furnishes a striking example of the spread of Hellenism. Alexander himself may well have founded the city. But in so remote a world, vulnerable to invaders from inner Asia, it was bound not to last.

When Alexander destroyed the empire of the Achaemenid Persians and marched over into Bactria, he absorbed into his own empire the entire territory included in this part of the Atlas. After his death the Seleucid kings succeeded Alexander as the nominal rulers. But, despite the cities they founded (like Dura or Seleuceia farther down the Euphrates), their satrapies in Iran and Afghanistan could scarcely be managed and soon fell away in the third century BC. An independent kingdom had emerged in Bactria by the 270s, and a few decades later the Arsacid Parthians took over Iran. The Parthians henceforth proved a constant threat to Rome's empire in the East

and, where they did not actually rule, were sometimes supported by small local dynasties such as that in control of Hatra in northern Mesopotamia. Both the emperor Trajan (in AD 115-17) and Septimius Severus (in AD 197-8) attempted to resolve the uncertainties of the Euphrates frontier by the conquest of Mesopotamia, but to no avail. In the period between their invasions, Lucius Verus had waged war against the Parthians (in AD 162-5) and at least succeeded in recovering Dura, which had been captured several centuries before.

The end of the Parthian dynasty at the hands of the aggressive Sassanian line of Persian kings in about 226 meant much greater danger for Rome. The Sassanians soon overwhelmed Hatra and Dura, and captured a Roman emperor. Palmyra, which held out against them, was useful to Rome and knew it. The revolt of Palmyra, crushed by Aurelian in AD 273, put an end to a valuable protector of the eastern flank of the Graeco-Roman East and prepared the way for the Persian Wars of subsequent centuries.

Schlumberger, D., *L'Orient hellénisé*, Paris, 1970

I   Dura-Europus   Syria

On a commanding height above the Euphrates, at Salihiya, 57 miles (92km) southeast of Deir ez-Zor, lies the 180-acre (69ha) site of the city of Dura-Europus on the Roman-Parthian frontier. With a steep cliff facing the river to the east and two very deep wadis at the north and south sides, Dura is accessible only from the west where the plateau of the Syrian desert is on the same level as the city. The rocky eminence of Dura was ideal for controlling the Euphrates at this point as well as the low fertile land of Mesopotamia opposite. The city has to be entered through the main ('Palmyra') gate in the west wall.

Although Dura may have originally been settled by Assyrians, its history is unknown until the city, now excavated in part, was founded by Seleucus I Nicator about 300 BC. In 114 BC this Seleucid foundation fell into the hands of the Parthians, and its original Greek culture was gradually fused with that of its

conquerors. In AD 165 Dura passed into the empire of Rome as one of the conquests of the emperor Lucius Verus. The city survived as a Roman military outpost until it was besieged and captured c. 257 by the Sassanian king of Persia, Shapur I. The Persians entered the city from the west. The desperate efforts of the inhabitants to pile up earth against the inside of the wall served to preserve over the centuries the buildings they buried.

Less than half of Dura has been uncovered, but the finds have revealed a remarkable mixture of Greek, Parthian, Semitic, and Roman civilizations. There were evidently commercial and religious ties with Palmyra, as can be inferred from the temple of the Palmyrene gods in the northwest corner and the Palmyrene inscriptions discovered at Dura. There were both Jewish and Christian communities. A synagogue with paintings in exceptionally good condition was discovered under the earth thrown up against the west wall during the

siege. The palace of the governor occupied a splendid location overlooking the river. On a level below this and separated by a ravine stands a well-preserved citadel 315 yards (288m) long guarding the river bank with three towers and three gates.

Much Dura material, including sculpture, inscriptions, and the entire interior of the synagogue, is preserved in the National Archaeological Museum in Damascus. Other remains, including parchments and papyri, are at Yale University.

Rostovtzeff, M., *Dura-Europus and its Art*, Oxford, 1938
Perkins, A., *The Art of Dura-Europus*, Oxford, 1973
Welles, C. B., 'The Population of Roman Dura', *Studies in Roman Economic and Social History in Honor of A. C. Johnson*, Princeton, 1951. pp. 251-74

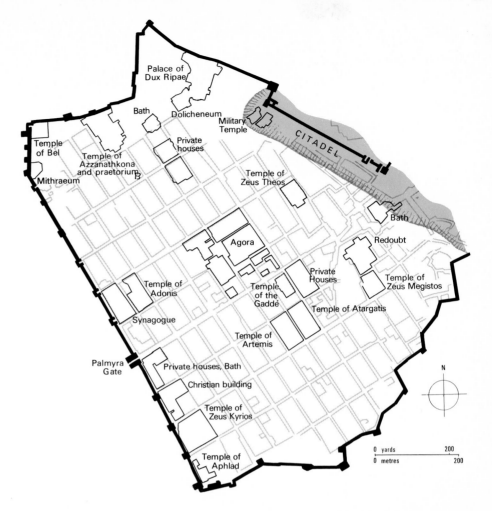

Temple of Bel
Temple of Azzanathkona and praetorium
Mithraeum
B
Bath
Palace of Dux Ripae
Dolicheneum
Private houses
Military Temple
CITADEL
Temple of Zeus Theos
Bath
Agora
Redoubt
Temple of Adonis
Temple of the Gaddé
Private Houses
Temple of Zeus Megistos
Synagogue
Temple of Atargatis
Temple of Artemis
Palmyra Gate
Private houses, Bath
Christian building
Temple of Zeus Kyrios
Temple of Aphlad
N

0 yards 200
0 metres 200

*Below: Dura–Europus, seen from the south. The Palmyra
Gate is at the left of centre*

Hatra

Hatra was the site of the Arab dynasty of Sanatruq, which flourished in the first and second centuries A D. The city lies 62 miles (100km) south-southwest of Mosul at the modern Al Hadhr on the western side of the Wadi Tharthar. Arab tribes appear to have settled here in the later Hellenistic age, and the dynasty of kings which emerged by the end of the first century A D presided over a rich Graeco-Iranian culture. A large number of recently discovered Aramaic inscriptions, found by the Iraq Department of Antiquities, has considerably enlarged our knowledge of the personalities and religious life of Hatra. The location of the city and the dynasty's Parthian sympathies made it an effective buffer against Roman aggression in Mesopotamia. It was besieged unsuccessfully by Trajan in A D 116 and by the emperor Septimius Severus in 197 and 198. After the collapse of Parthian power in 226, Hatra became a client city of Rome, serving then as part of an outlying defence system against the new Persian kingdom of the Sassanians. Hatra was garrisoned by the Romans, as Latin inscriptions prove, and resisted the Sassanian force until Shapur I captured it about 257.

The ruins of Hatra are approached through the opening in the eastern part of the vast circuit of city walls, over 2 miles (3km) around. In the centre of the walled territory is an imposing temple precinct, also entered from the east. At the opposite end of the large courtyard is a complex of temples, walled off from the courtyard and entered through two gates. The inner section is itself divided by an east–west wall into two sections, in each of which is a great *iwan* (an open-ended, vaulted hall characteristic of Iranian architecture), as well as smaller *iwans*. To the left, in the southern section, is a square temple dedicated to the sun god Shamash with two small *iwans* and a large one beside it. The Iranian *iwans* contrast strikingly with a double-colonnaded temple on a podium in the courtyard near the gates to the temple complex. This represents the earlier Hellenistic style. Outside the temple precinct are tower tombs, smaller temples, and dwellings. Finds from the recent excavations at Hatra can be seen in the Mosul and Baghdad museums.

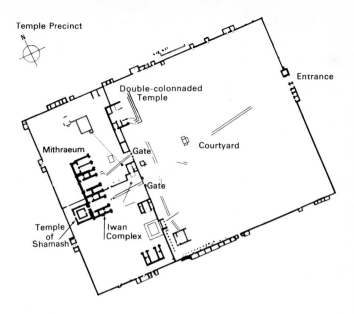

Temple Precinct

Double-colonnaded Temple

Entrance

Mithraeum

Gate

Courtyard

Gate

Temple of Shamash

Iwan Complex

Andrae, W., *Hatra*, I, Leipzig, 1908; II, 1912
Maricq, A., in *Syria* 34, 1957, pp. 288–96. On the last
    years of Hatra
Homès-Fredericq, D., *Hatra et ses sculptures parthes*,
    Istanbul, 1963.
    Much new material is being published in Arabic
    in the journal *Sumer*.

Opposite: The great iwan *and smaller* iwans *at the
western end of the temple precinct, Hatra. Below: Aerial
view of Hatra from the south*

3   Aï Khanum

In 1961 King Zahir of Afghanistan was hunting in the north of his kingdom near the Soviet border when he came upon a Corinthian capital and a small stone pillar near the confluence of the Amu Darya (ancient Oxus) and Kokcha rivers. This was the discovery of a lost Greek city, which is now known by the name of the adjacent modern village, Aï Khanum ('Lady Moon'). The site, north of Kabul over the Hindu Kush mountains, is the first and only Greek city so far discovered in Hellenized Bactria of the period before the influence of Kushan culture. A French excavation has now uncovered several important parts of the site.

Aï Khanum's location was well suited to controlling the approach into Bactria from the north. The city was set beneath an *acropolis* on a low plain along the eastern bank of the Oxus and opposite the mountainous western bank (now part of the Soviet Union). It appears to have been founded in the late fourth or early third century BC. It may even have been a foundation of Alexander the Great as he passed that way. The Hellenic inheritance is manifest in the city's gymnasium, its large peristyle courtyard, about 445 × 355 feet (136 × 108m), which may be an *agora* or a palace, and its Greek inscriptions. One inscribed text records how a certain Clearchus went personally to Delphi to copy its moral maxims and bring them to this city on the Oxus. As at Dura, there are also conspicuous oriental influences, including a temple in Mesopotamian style. Particularly striking are a group of six coins of

the Bactrian ruler Agathocles (*c.* 275 BC): they are square-shaped, with a text in Greek on one side and in Brahmi on the other. Aï Khanum was destroyed by fire toward the end of the second century BC and never recovered – possibly because of the spread of malaria.

In the central area of the city is the peristyle courtyard which is joined at the southern end to an administrative quarter by means of a vestibule with eighteen Corinthian columns. To the north near the river is a *heroön*, where the Clearchus inscription was found; the gymnasium appears to have been not far away. In the northeastern part of the city, against the mountains and near the straight north–south road, is the oriental temple with a vestibule

approximately 45 × 20 feet (14 × 6m) and *cella* about 20 × 18 feet (6 × 5.5m), flanked by two sacristies. At the southwest corner of the city a residential quarter has been uncovered. The city was enclosed by walls on the three low sides as well as over the southeast part of the acropolis. Outside the north wall a manor house, a building on a podium, and a mausoleum (in a necropolis area) have come to light.

Bernard, P., *Comptes-rendus de l'Académie des Inscriptions et Belles-Lettres*, 1966–72; 1974–5. This is the year-by-year account of the excavation

Bernard, P., *Fouilles d'Aï Khanoum* I, 1965–8, *Mémoires de la Délégation archéologique française en Afghanistan* XXI, Paris, 1973

General area map of Aï Khanum

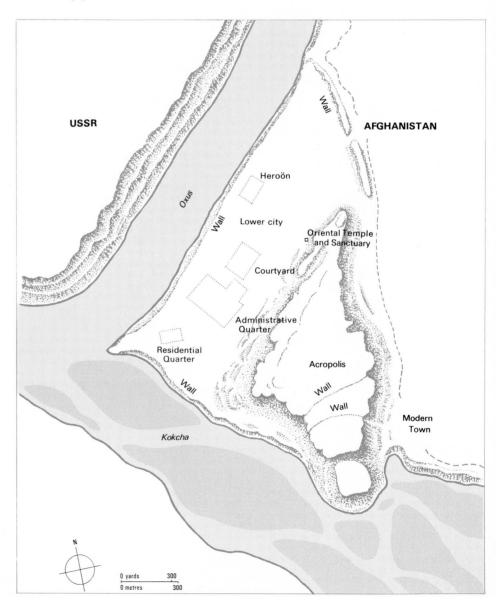

Enlarged scale plan of peristyle courtyard area

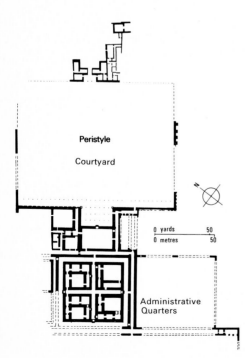

Appendices

Chronological Table

BC	Italy and the West	BC	Greece and the East
		c1000	OLD SMYRNA FOUNDED
c850	Beginning of 'Villanovan culture' in Italy	776	First Olympic Games (traditional date)
c753	FOUNDATION OF ROME (traditional date)		
c750	First Greek 'colonists' in Sicily		
	Phoenicians arrive in Carthage	709	Cyprus acknowledges Assyrian suzerainty
c700	Appearance of Etruscan culture in central Italy – Phoenician settlers at Motya (Sicily)		
c630	Greek settlers at Cyrene	c650	Greek settlement on Bug Estuary (Olbia)
c600	MASSALIA (MARSEILLE) FOUNDED	c600	Temple of Hera built at Argos
580	FOUNDATION OF ACRAGAS (AGRIGENTO)		
c560	Temple of Olympian Zeus begun at Syracuse	c560–546	Croesus king of Lydia
		c545–510	Pisistratid tyranny in Athens
509	Rome becomes a Republic (traditional date)	490–479	Persian Wars
		490	Battle of Marathon
480	Battle of Himera	480	Battle of Salamis
476	Hiero I of Syracuse defeats Etruscans at Cumae		
c460–450	'Temple of Concord' built at Acragas	c460	Temple of Zeus built at Olympia
		447–432	Construction of the Parthenon
		431–404	Peloponnesian War
415–413	Athenian expedition against Syracuse		
450–367	Dionysus I tyrant of Syracuse		
396	Rome captures Veii		
c390	Sack of Rome by Gauls		
		c375–370	Temple of Asclepius built at Epidaurus
		c360	Theatre of Epidaurus begun
		338	Victory of Philip II of Macedon at Chaeronea
		336–323	Alexander the Great
		331	FOUNDATION OF ALEXANDRIA
310–306	Invasion of North Africa by Agathocles of Syracuse	300	ANTIOCH FOUNDED BY SELEUCUS I
264–241	First Punic War		
250	Destruction of Selinus by Carthage		
218–201	Second Punic War		
215	Dedication of temple of Venus Erucina on the Capitol at Rome		
212	Rome captures Syracuse		
		190	Rome defeats Antiochus III at Magnesia
181	Latin colony founded at Aquileia	c180	Great Altar of Pergamum constructed
146	Rome destroys Carthage	146	Rome destroys Corinth
		133	Kingdom of Pergamum bequeathed to Rome
		120–63	Mithradates VI Eupator (King of Pontus)
118	ROMAN PROVINCE OF NARBONENSIS CREATED		
102	Romans defeat Teutones at Aix-en-Provence	64	ROMAN PROVINCE OF SYRIA CREATED
55–54	Julius Caesar invades Britain		
44	Julius Caesar assassinated	44	CORINTH RE-FOUNDED BY ROME
		31	Battle of Actium
27	Pantheon built in Rome		
16	Maison Carrée built in Nîmes		

AD	Italy and the West		Greece and the East
9	Defeat of Roman army by Arminius		
49	ROMAN COLONIA FOUNDED AT COLCHESTER		
60	Revolt of Boudicca in Britain		
64	*Great fire in Rome*		
		66–70	Jewish revolt
c70	*Colosseum built at Rome*		
79	Destruction of Pompeii and Herculaneum		
100	TIMGAD FOUNDED AS VETERANS' TOWN		
105	Conquest of Dacia completed		
115	Jewish revolt in Cyrene		
c121–127	*Hadrian's 'villa' constructed at Tivoli*		
		132–35	Second Jewish revolt (under Bar Kochba)
140	*Antonine Wall built in Britain*		
211–217	*Baths of Caracalla built in Rome*		
		267	Sack of Athens by the Herulians
298–306	*Baths of Diocletian built in Rome*		
313	Constantine's 'Edict of Toleration'		
		324–330	FOUNDATION OF CONSTANTINOPLE
391	Edict of Theodosius I closing pagan shrines		
410	Sack of Rome by Alaric		
411	Council of Carthage outlaws Donatist heresy		
429	Vandals occupy Carthage		
442–443	Beginning of Anglo-Saxon domination of Britain		
533	Byzantine defeat of Vandals in Tunisia		
540	Byzantine 'exarchate' of Ravenna established		

Roman Emperors

Some short reigns in periods of anarchy are omitted.
Co-rulers are not included.

JULIO-CLAUDIANS	31 BC–AD 14	Augustus
	14–37	Tiberius
	37–41	Caligula
	54–68	Nero
	68–69	Galba, Otho, Vitellius in succession
FLAVIANS	69–79	Vespasian
	79–81	Titus
	81–96	Domitian
	96–98	Nerva
ANTONINES	98–117	Trajan
	117–138	Hadrian
	138–161	Antoninus Pius
	161–180	Marcus Aurelius
	180–192	Commodus
	193	Pertinax
SEVERI	193–211	Septimius Severus
	211–217	Caracalla
	218–222	Heliogabalus
	222–235	Severus Alexander
	235–238	Maximinus Thrax
	238–244	Gordian III
	244–249	Philip the Arab
	253–268	Gallienus
	268–270	Claudius Gothicus
	270–275	Aurelian
	275–276	Tacitus
	276–282	Probus
	284–305	Diocletian
	305–306	Constantius I
	306–337	Constantine I
	337–361	Constantius II
	361–363	Julian
	363–364	Jovian
	364–375	Valentinian I
	375–392	Valentinian II
	379–395	Theodosius I

WESTERN EMPERORS

393–423	Honorius
424–455	Valentinian III
457–461	Majorian
461–465	Libius Severus
467–472	Anthemius
475–476	Romulus Augustulus

EASTERN EMPERORS

383–408	Arcadius
408–450	Theodosius II
450–457	Marcian
457–474	Leo I
476–491	Zenon
491–518	Anastasius I
518–527	Justin I
527–565	Justinian I

Glossary

acropolis: the elevated part, or citadel, of a Greek city

agora: the civic centre of a Greek city

amphitheatre: an arena, literally a double (usually oval) theatre

amphora: jar for storing and transporting provisions, especially oil (see p. 249)

anaktoron: a sacred building (or part of building), used chiefly in connection with 'mystery' religions

Anatolia: the older name for Asia Minor (q.v.)

antefix: covering tile, often decorated, along the ridge of the roof

apodyterium: changing room in a *palaestra* or bath house

archaic: conventional term, originally in art history, for the earliest period of Greek history, roughly 800–500 BC; also used, though less frequently, for early Rome

architrave: the main beam of the entablature, running from column to column

aryballos: flask for toilet oil and perfume (see p. 249)

ashlar: masonry of rectangular blocks laid on horizontal courses

Asia Minor: conventional modern name for roughly the area now covered by Turkey in Asia

atrium: the first main room (reception room) of a Roman house, with the centre open to the sky

basilica: a large oblong hall, usually with rows of internal columns and one or more apses; then the early form of the Christian church

bouleuterion: the council house in a Greek city

cadaster: a land register

caldarium: the hot plunge in a bath house

Capitolium: The Capitoline Hill in Rome, its most important religious centre; later 'reproduced' in many cities in Italy and the Roman west

cardo: the north-south base line in centuriation (q.v.)

castrum: the Latin for fortified post or army camp (hence -cester, -chester in English place names)

cavea: the auditorium of a Greek theatre

cella: the walled room for the cult statue and temple treasure in the centre of a normal Greek temple

centuriation: Roman land surveying on a grid system, used especially for land allocation in such important foundations as *coloniae* (q.v.)

Cimbri: a Germanic tribe who, together with the Teutones, posed a serious military threat to the Romans at the end of the second century BC

circus: a place where Roman games were held, especially chariot races

civitas: originally an organized community or state, in the Roman Empire the word meant self-governing municipal unit

classical: a conventional term with various meanings; one, originating in art history, is used to mark off the fifth and fourth centuries BC in Greek history

colonia: originally a military colony of Roman citizens; then, in the later Republic a broader range of Roman colonies; finally, in the Empire, the most privileged rank among the municipalities

colonus: originally 'cultivator', the word also came to mean both 'tenant farmer' and 'citizen of a *colonia*'

Corinthian: the third of the Greek architectural orders, growing out of Ionic, relatively uncommon until Roman times (see p. 251)

cryptoporticus: a vaulted subterranean corridor or sunken portico

curia: the meeting place of the senate in Rome, then of local senates in other cities

Cyclopaean: an ancient Greek name for masonry of huge stone blocks (from the Cyclops in the *Odyssey*)

decumanus: the east-west base line in centuriation (q.v.)

decurion: a local councillor in the fully developed Roman municipal system

deinos: bowl for mixing wine and water (see p. 249)

diocese: a group of provinces in Diocletian's reorganized provincial system; in ecclesiastical use, the territorial unit of church administration

diolkos: slipway for the passage of ships across a strip of land

Doric: a proper adjective variously applied, e.g. to one of the Greek dialects, but in archaeology chiefly used to label one of the two main orders of Greek architecture (see p. 250)

dromos: a race or race course; also various metaphoric uses, e.g. the formal entrance to a large tomb or a colonnade

entablature: in one of the classical orders, all the parts of a building above the capitals of the columns, except the roof

exarch: the highest Byzantine official in Italy and Africa

fascia: in architecture, a flat continuous band of plank width

fibula: a clasp or brooch

forum: the civic centre of a Roman city

frieze: the middle member of the entablature (q.v.) which normally contained the carved reliefs, if any; hence any band of continuous carved reliefs

Geometric: conventional name for the period c. 900–700 BC in the history of Greek pottery

gymnasium: a public building or complex of buildings in a Greek city, predominantly for training and practice in sport but increasingly also the social centre for the leisured classes

Hellenistic: conventional term for the period of Greek history following the conquests of Alexander the Great; also used to refer to post-Alexandrian Greek culture

herm: a pillar surmounted by a bust, originally restricted to gods but in Hellenistic and Roman times common for private portraits

heroön: shrine of a hero, in the form of a temple

hieron: Greek for a shrine or temple

hydria: water jar (see p. 249)

Hyksos: foreign, probably Palestinian, invaders who ruled northern Egypt for some 250 years between the Middle and New Kingdoms

hypogaeum: an underground chamber

impluvium: a basin to receive rainwater from the roof, in the *atrium* (q.v.), for example

insula: a block of flats or tenement house

Ionic: a proper adjective variously applied, e.g. to one of the Greek dialects, but in archaeology chiefly used to label one of the two main orders of Greek architecture, originating in Asia Minor (see p. 250)

kotyle: two-handled cup (see p. 249)

krater: large bowl for mixing wine and water (see p. 249)

kylix: two-handled cup (see p. 249)

latifundia: Latin for 'large estates'

Latin colony: a Roman *colonia* (q.v.) in which the settlers were granted a status somewhat below that of Roman citizen

lebes: bowl for mixing wine and water (see p. 249)

lekythos: flask for unguents or perfume (see p. 249)

lesche: a public building or meeting hall

Ligurians: the pre-Roman population of the Mediterranean coastal area and hinterland from the Rhône to the Arno

limes: in the Roman Empire, the fortified and garrisoned frontier line

macellum: a provision market

Magna Graecia: the ancient name for southern Italy, heavily settled by Greeks in the archaic period

megaron: modern name for a rectangular hall entered from an open porch by a single door, sometimes with an ante-room

metope: one of the elements of a frieze (see pp. 250–1)

Mithraeum: a temple of the god Mithras
municipium: originally an Italian community allied to Rome; in the Roman Empire, a municipal status below that of *colonia* (q.v.)
mysteries: a mystical cult, often with secret rites

naïskos: Greek for shrine
nymphaeum: literally a sanctuary of the Nymphs, then used for a fountain or water-supply system with an architectural background

odeum: a building, usually roofed, for music and recitations
oinochoe: wine jug (see p. 249)
oppidum: a town, commonly applied by the Romans to native settlements in conquered territories in the west
opus incertum: an early style of Roman concrete, in which the facing stones were of irregular shape
orchestra: the dance floor in a theatre, where the choruses performed

palaestra: a colonnaded space and accompanying rooms, for training in wrestling and other sports
pelike: a variety of amphora (see p. 249)
peristyle: a colonnade or the space between a colonnade and parallel wall
Pontus: 'sea' in Greek, commonly used for the Black Sea; also a kingdom, later a Roman province, in Asia Minor
porta praetoria: main gate of a fort or camp
praefectus: in the Roman Empire, a high official of second (equestrian) rank, e.g. the governor of Judaea
praetentura: legionary barracks
praetorium: tent or house of a military commander; later also the house of a provincial governor
Principate: modern name for the period of Roman history beginning with Augustus and ending with the accession of Diocletian
principia: headquarters (military)
proconsul: in the Roman Republic, a high official of senatorial rank, normally an ex-consul, in charge of a province or in command of an army
propylaea (or **-on**): monumental entrance gateway
Protogeometric: the style of Greek pottery

immediately preceding Geometric (q.v.)
prytaneum: town hall
Punic: Carthaginian (from the Latin noun, *Poeni*)
pyxis: cosmetic box (see p. 249)

scaenae frons: front of the stage in a Roman theatre
skyphos: two-handled cup (see p. 249)
stamnos: wine jar (see p. 249)
stele: a narrow slab of stone set upright, usually with an inscribed text and/or decoration
stoa: a long covered portico

tablinum: room behind the *atrium* (q.v.) in a Roman house
temenos: Greek for a sacred area or precinct
terramare: archaeologist's label for the Po Valley civilization of the late second millennium BC
terra sigillata: Roman moulded pottery with a red gloss
Teutones: see Cimbri
thesaurus: Greek for a strongroom or treasure house
tholos: a round building (Greek)
tophet: Carthaginian sacrificial burial ground
triumvirs: in Roman public law, a board of three; commonly used with the direct article to refer to Caesar, Pompey and Crassus 60–53 BC (First Triumvirate) and to Octavian, Antony and Lepidus from 43 BC (Second Triumvirate)
tropaeum: a victory monument
trophy: see *tropaeum*
tyrant: Greek term for a man who seized power, as distinct from a hereditary monarch
tumulus: a burial mound or barrow

vallum: an earthen wall or rampart; through a misunderstanding in early modern times, the word is used for the flat-bottomed ditch flanked by earthen mounds along Hadrian's Wall in Britain
vicarius: a word with a varied history in Roman legal and administrative usage; in Diocletian's provincial reorganization, the governor of a *diocese* (q.v.)

Zealots: a popular Jewish sect who spearheaded the revolt against Rome in AD 66–70

Right: A selection of the most commonly found types of Greek vases. Within each type there is considerable variation, both in size and precise shape. The vases selected here are 'average' examples. The names, though Greek, are conventional modern labels.

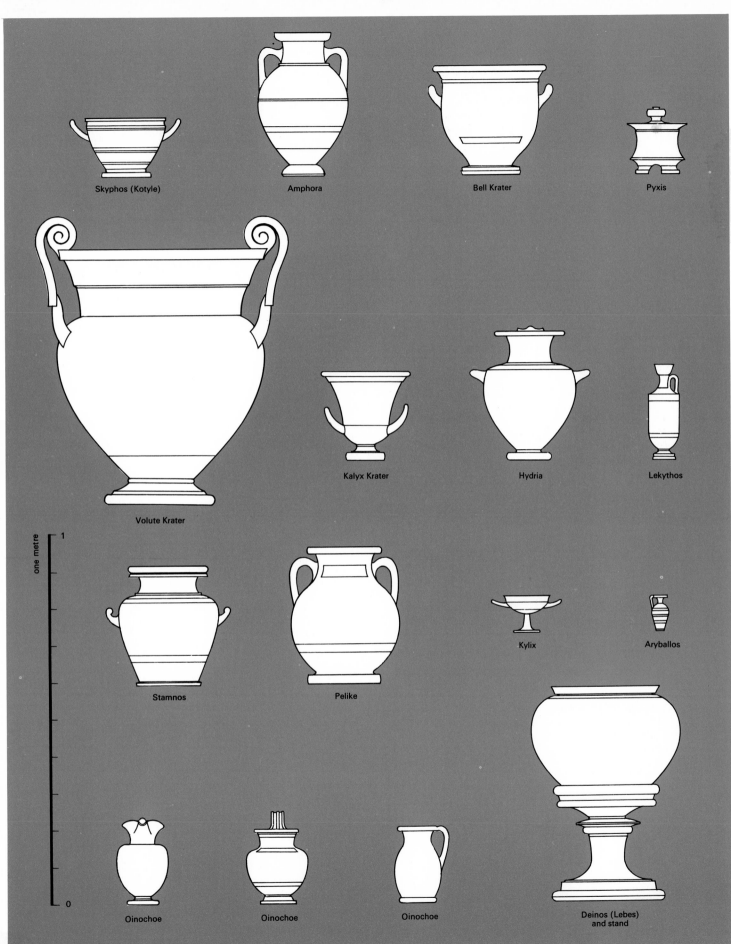

Skyphos (Kotyle)

Amphora

Bell Krater

Pyxis

Volute Krater

Kalyx Krater

Hydria

Lekythos

one metre

1

0

Stamnos

Pelike

Kylix

Aryballos

Oinochoe

Oinochoe

Oinochoe

Deinos (Lebes)
and stand

The Greek Architectural Orders

Showing entablature, capital and base

DORIC

IONIC

CORINTHIAN

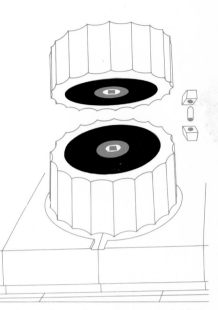

Construction of columns, showing centring pins holding column drums firmly in place

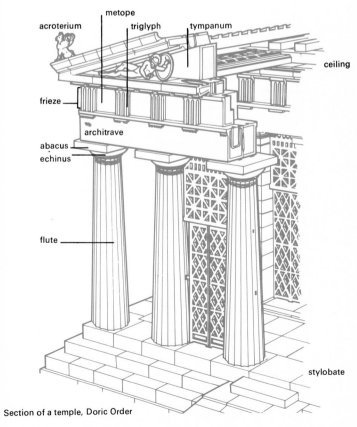

acroterium
metope
triglyph
tympanum
ceiling
frieze
architrave
abacus
echinus
flute
stylobate

Section of a temple, Doric Order

Index

Italic figures denote pages on which illustrations occur